The Corner of the Living

MIGUEL LA SERNA

The Corner of the Living
Ayacucho on the Eve of the
Shining Path Insurgency

FIRST PEOPLES
New Directions in Indigenous Studies

The University of North Carolina Press | Chapel Hill

Publication of this book was made possible, in part, by a grant from the Andrew W. Mellon Foundation.

Set in Arno and The Serif by Rebecca Evans
Manufactured in the United States of America

The paper in this book meets the guidelines for permanence and durability of the Committee on Production Guidelines for Book Longevity of the Council on Library Resources.

The University of North Carolina Press has been a member of the Green Press Initiative since 2003.

Library of Congress Cataloging-in-Publication Data
La Serna, Miguel.
The corner of the living : Ayacucho on the eve of the Shining Path insurgency / Miguel La Serna.
p. cm. — (First peoples : new directions in indigenous studies)
Includes bibliographical references and index.
ISBN 978-0-8078-3547-0 (cloth : alk. paper)
ISBN 978-0-8078-7219-2 (pbk : alk. paper)
1. Sendero Luminoso (Guerrilla group) — History. 2. Peru — Politics and government — 1980– 3. Chuschi (Peru) — Social conditions. 4. Chuschi (Peru) — Politics and government. 5. Ayacucho (Peru) — Social conditions. 6. Ayacucho (Peru) — Politics and government. I. Title.
F3448.2.L36 2012   985.06′4 — dc23   2011033283

Part of this book has been reprinted with permission in revised form from "To Cross the River of Blood: How an Inter-community Conflict Is Linked to the Peruvian Civil War, 1940–1983," in *Power, Culture, and Violence in the Andes*, edited by Christine Hünefeldt and Milos Kokotovic, 110–44 (Brighton, U.K.: Sussex Academic Press, 2009).

cloth   16 15 14 13 12   5 4 3 2 1
paper   16 15 14 13 12   5 4 3 2 1

For Joy

CONTENTS

xi Acknowledgments

 1 Introduction

ONE
19 To Trace the Tracks: Internal Conflict and Resolution

TWO
62 To Venture Out: Intercommunity Relations and Conflict

THREE
101 To Walk in Shoes: Race and Class

FOUR
136 To Cross the River: Initial Peasant Support for Shining Path

FIVE
167 To Defend the Mountaintop:
     Initial Peasant Resistance to Shining Path

SIX
197 To Turn the Corner: After Shining Path

215 Conclusion

221 Notes

255 Bibliography

269 Index

Illustrations

The main square in Chuschi 3

The main square in Huaychao with *juez rumi* 5

Varayoqs of Huaychao with authority staffs 44

River separating Chuschi and Quispillaccta 66

Administrative center destroyed by Shining Path rebels 137

Shining Path guerrilla 144

The original *ronderos* of Huaychao surrounding grave of
Senderistas killed during *linchamiento* 177

Lacking formal arms, many *ronderos* went into battle with
improvised weapons such as wooden guns 199

Maps

1 Peru and the Department of Ayacucho, circa 1990 xvi

2 District of Chuschi, circa 2000 xvii

3 Community of Huaychao, circa 1990 xviii

ACKNOWLEDGMENTS

Latin American history was pretty low on my list of priorities during my youth—I was much more concerned with getting Jillian Joy Brogdon to laugh at my jokes. I can still remember getting hand cramps in high school while taking notes in Liz Guyer's World History class, or struggling to make sense of Latin American literature in Juan Amezcua's Advanced Spanish. I was unaware at the time that Ms. Guyer and Sr. Amezcua were introducing me to the themes around which I would build my career. The same goes for my undergraduate professors at the University of California, Davis. Without even knowing it, professors Alan Taylor and Charles Walker set my career in motion with their inspirational lectures. But it was Arnold Bauer, Clarence Walker, and Stefano Varese who recognized my potential and encouraged me to pursue a career as a historian of Latin America. I thank each of these teachers and mentors for sparking the initial fire that led to the writing of this book.

I consider myself most fortunate to have counted on not one but several dedicated mentors every step of the way. First and foremost is Christine Hünefeldt, an outstanding mentor in every sense of the word, and one whose intellectual depth is matched only by her kind spirit. Michael Monteón exhibited tremendous patience and offered essential guidance during the early stages of this project, and whatever I have achieved through my research and writing is a direct reflection of his initial involvement. The same goes for Everard Meade, who instructed me in the craft of writing. My friend and colleague Kathryn Burns graciously advised me during my latter stages of writing and continues to be a source of intellectual support. And although our studies vary drastically in terms of time and place, my work has benefited tremendously from Eric Van Young's vast scholarship, expertise, and gracious tutelage with respect to indigenous peasant mobilization and culture. As my own work began to take an ethnographic turn, it was Nancy Postero who, in addition to overseeing my research and writing, exposed me to a whole new world of methodologies, theories, studies, and contacts in the field of anthropology. Simply put, Professor Postero is a talented teacher, innovative researcher, and dedicated mentor. Finally, I can say with confidence that this book would not be half of what it is were it not for the selfless mentorship of Orin Starn. In addition to being involved in literally every stage of this project, Professor Starn offered the most thought-provoking, constructive manuscript critiques that I have ever read.

Other colleagues offered varying degrees of assistance, for which I am most grateful. I would be remiss not to thank Latin Americanist bibliographers Karen Lindvall-Larson and Teresa Chapa, who in addition to helping me locate important sources in the United States, acquired microfilm of the Gustavo Gorriti Collection on the Peruvian Insurrection (aka "Documenting the Peruvian Insurrection") from Princeton University so that I and others could have access to a rich archival source on the Shining Path years. I am also indebted to María Elena García, Billie Jean Isbell, Kimberly Theidon, and Caroline Yezer for tolerating my early queries about Ayacucho and Shining Path. I particularly would like to thank Ponciano Del Pino, Jaymie Heilman, Cecilia Méndez, and Charles Walker for their advice and critiques at various stages of this project. Many of them, in addition to Susan E. Ramírez and Brandon Williams, commented on portions of the text. Finally, I am grateful to my friends and colleagues Zach Brittsan, John Chasteen, Lloyd Kramer, Stephanie Moore, Jesús Perez, Cynthia Radding, Adam Warren, Todd Welker, Chris Wisniewski, and especially Louis Pérez Jr. and Joe Glatthaar, for enriching this project with their continued dialogue, support, and encouragement.

But it was my Peruvian contacts who most directly impacted my research. I benefited from conversations with Iván Caro, Carlos Contreras, Alejandro "Chan" Coronado, José Luis Igue, Rodrigo Montoya, Rosario Narváez, Raquel Palomino, and Marté Sánchez Villagómez at various stages of my research. I especially thank Oscar Medrano for graciously furnishing me his iconic photography, which has enriched this book beyond description. Additionally, I am grateful to Nilda Guillén, Freddy Taboada, and Luis Uriategui for their hands-on orientation to Ayacucho's people, culture, and language, and especially to Ponciano Del Pino, who had a hand in virtually every stage of my research and writing. Likewise, Julián Berrocal and Alberto Tucno of the Centro de Investigación Social de Ayacucho (CEISA) not only oriented me in Ayacucho's political landscape but also charitably served as my research assistants for my ethnographic work in my two field sites of Huaychao (Julián) and Chuschi (Julián and Alberto). Any richness in my ethnographic fieldwork or oral history is a direct reflection of Alberto and Julián's cultural sensitivity, academic intuition, and industrious work ethic. Thanks also to Adela and Cipriano López, Freddy and Abel Cisneros, Delia Martínez, and Abel Maygua, who went out of their way to make me and my family comfortable in Ayacucho City. Most of all, I thank the authorities and villagers of Chuschi and Huaychao, who welcomed me into their communities and homes and shared their life histories. I especially would like to thank Leandro Huamán (Huaychao) and Marcelino Carhuapoma (Chuschi) for inviting Julián, Alberto, and me to stay in their homes during our visits.

Individuals aside, I owe a tremendous debt of gratitude to the numerous Peruvian institutions that granted me access to their resources. I thank Martín Tanaka and Marisa Remy for allowing me to affiliate with the Instituto de Estudios Peruanos during my research year in 2005–6. I also thank the directors and archivists of the Archivo General de la Nación, the Archivo Regional de Ayacucho, the Biblioteca Nacional, *Caretas* magazine, the Corte Superior de Justicia de Ayacucho, the Defensoría del Pueblo, the Ministerio de Agricultura de Ayacucho, the Pontificia Universidad Católica del Perú, the Proyecto Especial de Titulación de Tierras, the Universidad Nacional Mayor San Marcos, the Universidad Nacional San Cristóbal de Huamanga, and the Subprefecto de Huanta for allowing me to peruse their collections. For facilitating my work with these sources, archivists Teófilo Cuba, Juan Gutiérrez, Virgilio Gutiérrez, and Constantino Pariona deserve special mention.

Nor would this project have been completed without generous financial and editorial support. Fellowships by the University of California at San Diego, the UCSD Center for Iberian and Latin American Studies, the Fulbright Foundation, the Ford Foundation, the Guggenheim Foundation, and the Carolina Postdoctoral Program for Faculty Diversity facilitated each stage of my academic career culminating in the writing of this book, for which I am truly grateful. I am equally indebted to the University of North Carolina Press for taking on this project and turning out a quality product. Elaine Maisner, my editor, offered amazing guidance, patience, and vision throughout the whole publication process. I thank her, as well as my two anonymous reviewers, whose insights and recommendations were exactly what I needed to produce a book of which I could be proud.

On a personal note, I would like to thank my family for sticking with me through thick and thin. My parents, Sabad and Susan La Serna, always supported my aspirations as an academic and writer even when my high school counselors and teachers suggested otherwise. I thank my children,

Mateo Gael and Micaela Renee, for giving me inspiration to get my work done each day so that I could come home and enjoy watching them grow up. My sister and brother, Korah and Matías, were a rock of emotional support during the most difficult times. My La Serna relatives living in Peru—Carlos, Karlos, María, Olenka, Piotr, Ricardo, Teresa, and especially *abuelita* Yola and *abuelito* Jorge—made my time abroad pleasant, productive, and memorable. My in-laws in the United States, Lawrence and Rosalie Kaiser, supported my family and our decisions in every way possible, for which I cannot thank them enough.

But it is their granddaughter, Jillian Joy Brogdon (now La Serna), for whom I save my most heartfelt thanks. Of the two of us, Joy, you were always the one with the most potential. Yet, for whatever reason, let's call it love, you were willing to pack your bags and come to San Diego for six years and give my career a try. As if that were not enough, you then left behind a dream job in San Diego to live for a year and several summers in Lima and Ayacucho. You spent a good deal of my research year living in these places by yourself while pregnant, undergoing a major operation in a foreign clinic to give birth to our first child. To top it all off, you then walked away from a life in your hometown so that I could pursue my academic dreams in North Carolina, where our second child was born. Throughout it all, you never stopped believing in, encouraging, and supporting me. Thank you for all this, but mostly for laughing at my jokes.

The Corner of the Living

Map 1. Peru and the Department of Ayacucho, circa 1990

Map 2. District of Chuschi, circa 2000

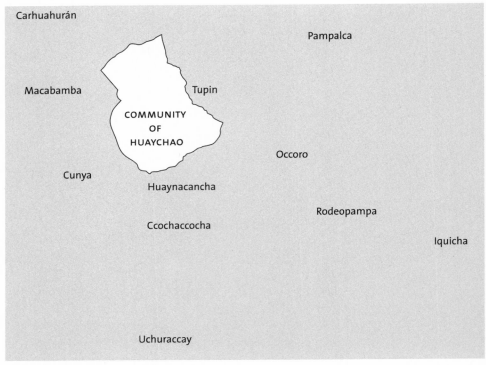

Map 3. Community of Huaychao, circa 1990

Introduction

ON 17 MAY 1980—the eve of the first democratic elections in Peru after twelve years of military rule—five hooded Shining Path guerrillas entered the voter registration office in Chuschi, a village of mostly Quechua-speaking peasants in the Andean department of Ayacucho. Once inside, the Senderistas tied up the registrar on duty and set the registry and ballot boxes ablaze. The event, known thereafter as the Inicio de la Lucha Armada (Initiation of the Armed Struggle—ILA), symbolically ignited the Shining Path guerrilla insurrection. In the coming years Chuschi would serve as an early rebel stronghold and the location of numerous insurgent acts.

Three years later, on 21 January 1983, a column of eight Senderistas descended on Huaychao, another Ayacuchan village, chanting revolutionary slogans and waving the red Communist flag. Just as villagers from Chuschi had greeted the militants with loud cheers of support in years past, so did the indigenous peasants of Huaychao, who shouted: "Long live the armed struggle!" The Huaychainos escorted the Senderistas into their *despacho*, a small assembly room with a thatched roof and dirt floor located at the edge of the village square. After a lengthy debate, the Huaychainos attacked the guerrillas in a swift, coordinated assault. The villagers then dragged their captives outside and tied them to the large *juez rumi* (rock of justice) in the village square before torturing and killing them. The *counter*rebellion in Huaychao led to the proliferation of peasant counterinsurgency militias known as the *rondas campesinas*.

WHY DID INDIGENOUS PEASANTS in Ayacucho have such disparate reactions to Shining Path? More important, why did these reactions involve heavy doses of violence? Perhaps it had something to do with the name *Ayacucho*, which in Quechua means "the corner of the dead." Given its history as the epicenter of a civil war that between 1980 and 2000 claimed the lives of 69,000 people—most of them Quechua-speaking highlanders—this seems a disturbingly appropriate name for the department occupying Peru's south-central sierra.[1] Yet, while on the surface this designation appears to characterize late twentieth-century Ayacucho, this book, *The Corner of the Living*, renders the violence comprehensible by situating it within a deeper, more complex history of indigenous peasant struggle and survival. This comparative study uses the long-term experiences of the two historically significant communities introduced above—Chuschi, the symbolic birthplace of the insurgency, and Huaychao, the birthplace of the counterinsurgency—as a lens for understanding the divergent yet violent responses that indigenous peasants across Peru had to Shining Path. Before getting into this, however, an introduction of these two communities is in order.

A Tale of Two Villages

Chuschi is the capital of a district that bears the same name in the region of Cangallo Province known as the Pampas River Valley. Today, visitors enter the community by way of a dirt highway surrounded by rolling golden hills. Nearing the community, one encounters a handful of small neighborhoods of adobe huts and cobblestone corrals with pigs and other livestock. The closer one gets to the village center, the more sophisticated the buildings become, some of them with concrete walls and arched columns. Surrounding the main plaza, one encounters a municipal center, a Catholic church, a police station, a corner store, and even a small hotel. Only the street immediately surrounding the plaza is paved, occupied by local women in multicolored blouses and petticoats carrying small children and other loads in their woven back-sacks, or *qepis*. Men wear pants, jackets, and baseball caps. The baseball caps are for the sun, which shines bright most days. The jackets are for the high-Andes air, which is generally crisp and sometimes a bit chilly, particularly in the shade. The main plaza is roughly the size of a football field, paved, and with steps, benches, a few trees, and a decorative arch. This scene is set before a backdrop of golden hills peppered with green eucalyptus trees and adobe huts.

Before the 1980 ILA, the community consisted of about 1,100 inhabitants (219 families), most of them Quechua-speaking peasants.[2] The village was ideal for agriculture, encompassing a variable ecological climate with fertile valleys and rivers at an altitude of 9,500 feet and high grazing lands peaking at 15,000 feet. Following the "vertical archipelago" agricul-

The main square in Chuschi. Photograph by author.

tural model, Chuschino farmers took advantage of the diverse climate and landscape to produce a wide range of crops in different ecological niches.[3] In the high-mountain *punas*, the highest habitable ecological niche, Chuschino peasants grew potatoes and other tubers. In the foothills directly above the valley, peasants cultivated corn as well as a number of fruits such as peaches, apples, and *tuna* (prickly pear). In the valley farmlands surrounding the village center, visitors could find such vegetables as onion, cilantro, parsley, and lettuce.[4]

Most peasant households in Chuschi were self-sufficient, growing the above crops on small individual plots known as *minifundios*, whose size averaged about 1.58 hectares per family. In addition to these foodstuffs, each household possessed its own livestock, which its members grazed in the *punas*. The most common animals were sheep (2.5 per household), chickens (0.8 per household), pigs (0.6 per household), and cows (0.05 per household). In addition to these animals, peasants raised guinea pigs, llamas, and alpacas; a few owned horses and mules. While some of these animals and their byproducts were consumed by the peasants, most were sold and traded in local markets.[5]

Since Chuschi was a regional trade center, most of this commercial activity took place around the village square. Peasants and nonpeasants from across the region gathered in the village square every Thursday evening to participate in an open-air market that continued on through the following evening. In 1962 the completion of a main road connecting the village to the departmental capital of Ayacucho City, some 125 kilometers to the northeast, facilitated this market exchange.[6] This commercial activity produced a fair degree of social stratification within the community, with a small portion of villagers taking up full-or part-time occupations as merchants. As of 1967, there were eight stores in the village, with eighty-one villagers supplementing their income through a specialized trade.[7] Another means through which Chuschinos could rise socially was through education. The village had both girls and boys elementary schools, with a total enrollment of about 200 students from throughout the district. Although very few of these students went on to high school or college, peasants did value education as a means of achieving upward social mobility.[8]

Neighboring Chuschi is Quispillaccta, a more populated but less developed indigenous peasant village. Quispillaccta's ecological, geographical, and social landscape is similar to that of Chuschi, with the added presence of some salt, silver, and lead mines. Other villages in the district included Uchuirre, Canchacancha, and Chacolla. For the purposes of this study, I will focus primarily on the village of Chuschi and secondarily on the neighboring hamlet of Quispillaccta.[9]

Like Chuschi, Huaychao on the eve of the Peruvian insurrection was a village of mostly Quechua-speaking farmers. Huaychao is located about twenty-five kilometers from Huanta City, in the Huanta Province zone commonly known as the Iquichano highlands, after the ethnic label that outsiders have imposed on the zone's indigenous inhabitants.[10] To get to the hamlet, visitors may now take a winding dirt road that narrowly hugs the sides of cliffs and mountain slopes—a road that did not exist before the political violence. Descending into the village, one is usually

The main square in Huaychao with *juez rumi*. Photograph by author.

greeted by a sea of cloud cover that dampens the already icy air. Instead of visible neighborhoods, isolated huts with thatched roofs and dirt floors occupy the surrounding hills. A handful more of these huts surround the "main square," a flat slab of grass less than half the size of a football field. The only things occupying this square, other than the occasional pig or chicken, are two soccer goal posts and the rather imposing rock of justice. The surrounding buildings are equally derisory: the dirt-floored *despacho*, a tin-roofed school building, and the cobblestone steeple that is all that remains of a church. Unlike the inhabitants of Chuschi, where village life emanates from the main plaza, Huaychainos are more dispersed. Venturing out into the surrounding hills, one encounters the occasional peasant woman grazing her cows while clutching her faded shawl for protection against the cold. There, in the hills, one may also come across a poncho- or jacket-wearing peasant man returning from a long day of work on his potato farm.

Huaychao had existed as a hacienda until 1975–76, at which point it and several neighboring haciendas were broken up and the *grupo campesino* (peasant collectivity) of Huaychao was formed, in accordance with the national Agrarian Reform Law. At the time of the land reform, about fifty-five peasant households (with a total of roughly 250 occupants) lived within the appropriated territory. Several more lived in the surrounding annexes and estates of Macabamba, Ccochaccocha, Tupín, Patacorral, Mallau, and Llalli. Most of these territories have since been recognized as independent peasant communities and cooperatives, but for the purposes of this study we will consider them part of the community of Huaychao. All told, we can estimate the total population of Huaychao at around 500 inhabitants in 1980.[11]

Huaychao's ecology and landscape are far less varied than those of Chuschi. Although officially recognized as an annex of Huanta District, Huaychao in 1980 had no major roads connecting it to the provincial capital. Instead, villagers traveled to the city on foot with the assistance of llamas and other beasts of burden. The closest accessible town was Tambo, in La Mar Province. To get there, peasants had to walk for twenty kilometers before reaching a road that took them the remaining forty kilometers. Huaychao's geographical isolation was due in large part to the surrounding landscape, which was every bit as unforgiving as the climate. At an altitude of 12,591 feet in the valley and 13,674 feet in the surrounding mountains, Huaychao's harsh, damp climate renders the soil unfavorable for most types of crop cultivation other than tubers. In fact, only 130 of the hacienda's 700 hectares were considered cultivable at the time of the land reform. Of those, the average household rented a plot of 0.85 hectares. Tenants cultivated the remaining cultivable plots in rotation for the hacienda owner, grazing livestock on the remaining 570 hectares of uncultivable land. This explains why the average household possessed sixty-seven animals—mostly sheep, cattle, swine, poultry, and guinea pigs—at the time of the 1975 land reform.[12]

After the Agrarian Reform, Huaychainos lived primarily as subsistence farmers, with virtually no villagers producing for the commercial market, specializing in trades, or becoming full-time merchants. The absence of a school within the community further restricted social mobility. This is not to say that Huaychao was a closed corporate community. On the contrary, the community's stagnant climate and ecology impelled villagers to rely on regional trade networks as a means of diversifying their diet and maintaining subsistence levels. These networks extended throughout the Iquichano highlands.[13]

Due in large part to the role they played during the civil war, Chuschi and Huaychao received considerable scholarly and media attention during the insurgency. The narratives and debates about these two villages that emerged during this period is emblematic of broader discourses about the political violence, and about the Ayacuchan peasantry, that developed at the time. Despite some very good intentions, scholars, journalists, and activists offered surprisingly static views of Andean peasants.

Chuschi was one of the few Ayacuchan communities to have been the subject of academic and government research in the years leading up to the Shining Path insurgency.[14] Yet, no one outside of the village or Shining Path itself saw the ILA coming. Even after the insurgency got under way, the connection between Shining Path and Chuschi remained unclear. Why, people wondered, did Shining Path choose to launch its insurgency in Chuschi, of all places?[15] Never did it occur to intellectuals in Lima or elsewhere that the reverse was also true: that the Chuschinos *chose* to allow Shining Path to launch its insurgency in their village. In his controversial 1991 article, "Missing the Revolution," North American anthropologist Orin Starn argued that his colleagues in the field had been spending too much time looking for examples of "authentic" Andean identity and practice, oblivious to the very fluid identities and relationships that led some Chuschinos to support Shining Path in the first place.[16] While not everyone agreed with Starn's critique, his larger point about the tendencies of intellectuals to overlook the complexities of Andean peoples during this period is well taken.

The events surrounding the January 1983 counterrebellion in Huaychao provide a fitting example. The incident generated a good deal of skepticism in Peru and elsewhere. Journalists and scholars alike had trouble believing that indigenous peasants were capable of committing such acts of counterinsurgent violence on their own. Some of Lima's most respected scholars, journalists, and activists immediately began speculating that the Peruvian military had either compelled the Iquichanos to take up arms against Shining Path or carried out the massacre itself. This skepticism led a group of eight Peruvian journalists to investigate what "really happened" in Huaychao. The journalists headed to the community the only way they could: on foot. Before reaching the village, the journalists were killed by the Quechua-speaking peasants in the nearby hamlet of Uchuraccay.

In the interest of getting to the bottom of the events in the Iquichano highlands, the Peruvian state commissioned none other than Peruvian novelist and future Nobel laureate Mario Vargas Llosa to determine what had transpired there. His team, which included prominent anthropologist Luis Millones, offered a set of conclusions about the indigenous peasantry that buttressed the static portrait of Andean peoples so prominent at the time. First, it suggested that the region's indigenous inhabitants were a people embedded in a culture of violence. The commission reported that the notion of "fighting bravely and ferociously" was "a constant in Iquichano tradition," making Iquichanos a people with a "bellicose and indomitable disposition."[17] Second, the commission stated that the Iquichanos lived—as they always had—in utter isolation from the outside world, be it the state, modernity, or civilization: "Isolated and removed from all [state] authority[,] . . . the communities of the *punas* of Huanta make up one of the most miserable and unappreciated human specimens. Lacking water, electricity, medical attention, roads to connect them to the rest of the country, or any type of technical or social services, they have lived isolated and forgotten since pre-Hispanic times in the highest and most uninhabitable lands of the mountain range."[18] Third, the commission found that, because of this supposed isolation, the Iquichanos had a long, deep history of hostility toward "outsiders."[19] Given the Iquichano highlanders' culture of violence, isolation, and hostility toward outsiders, the commission concluded with "absolute conviction" that the region's residents had acted of their own volition, having mistaken the journalists for Senderistas, and without the instigation or intervention of the counterinsurgency police, the *sinchis*.[20]

Despite its shortcomings, the Vargas Llosa Commission did get a major part of the story right: the Iquichanos had taken up arms against Shining Path, and the peasants of Uchuraccay had mistaken the journalists for guerrillas. As with the Huaychao event, however, critics refused to believe that the massacre of the journalists had been carried out by the indigenous peasantry alone; the military must have had a hand in it.[21] This attitude reflected a broader misunderstanding among leftist intellectual circles in Lima and abroad not just about Peru's indigenous peasantry, but about how violent the insurgency really was. It was not until much later that scholars on the left began to challenge this hypothesis, arguing that it stripped Andean actors of their historical agency.[22] In making this argument, though, some of these scholars engaged in what historian Eric Van

Young calls the "apotheosis of agency," portraying peasant militiamen as heroic actors who were calling all the shots.[23]

Moving beyond these conventional debates, narratives, and visions, this book seeks a more nuanced analysis of why some Ayacuchan peasants initially supported or resisted Shining Path. Specifically, I intend to identify the conditions under which ordinary, flawed Andeans in places like Chuschi would embrace Shining Path's radical violence, while those living in places like Huaychao would engage in violence against the rebels. In short, I hope to contribute a deeper understanding of the long-term internal dynamics that shaped the civil war histories of Chuschi and Huaychao.

But this book is about more than two faraway villages in the Andes, or even Shining Path. Simply put, this is a work about the late twentieth century. The third and final aim of my study is therefore to offer a narrative of this turbulent period as experienced by indigenous peasants in the most seemingly remote corner of the Andes. In illustrating how national and global events particular to the latter half of the twentieth century directly impacted the histories of these two communities—and how in turn these communities impacted national and global histories—this book renders an ostensibly remote "corner" of the world a "living" one in a historical sense, thus making a case for a greater inclusion of the indigenous Andes in historiographical conversations about the period.

This was a period in which violence itself became normalized and politicized, and in which the boundaries between peace and war became increasingly blurred. These realities were ever present in Ayacucho, where conflict and violence long predated Shining Path. This is to say nothing of the violence that manifested itself each day through things like poverty, migration, and power relations. Nor did Ayacucho escape other phenomena that affected the world since the middle of the twentieth century: the advent of global capitalism, urban migration, peasant mobilization, agrarian reform, military dictatorships, struggles for citizenship, and the Cold War. Nevertheless, Andean peasants experienced and interpreted these historical developments through a *localized, cultural* prism, which is why it is so important to explore them microlocally. It is in this sense that this book attempts to go beyond existing analyses of the Peruvian insurrection in an effort to understand the more complex, modern, multilayered nature of experience in these two locales in the middle of the Cold War century, before, during, and after Shining Path.

Indigenous Peasants and Shining Path

The issue of whether or not the Peruvian insurgency and counterinsurgency should be considered indigenous peasant movements is a complicated one. The first problem arises with the identity of Peruvian Andeans. Whereas Andean people elsewhere in Latin America have embraced their indigeneity in recent years, those living in Peru have been far more selective in their adoption of an indigenous identity.[24] In any event, it is worth mentioning that indigenous identity in Peru is complex, fluid, and ever changing.[25] The same holds true for the term *peasant*, a label that is also evolving. For the purposes of this study, however, I will describe Quechua-speaking Andeans who live and farm in the countryside and observe customary practices as indigenous peasants.

Even if we agree on our definition of an indigenous peasant, the fact remains that only a small portion of indigenous peasants actually joined Shining Path or the counterinsurgency. The majority of Shining Path's leaders and combatants were not Quechua-speaking peasants but rather mestizo intellectuals who lived in urban centers and spoke Spanish. That being said, there were many ways to support the insurgency indirectly: carrying the communist flag, serving as runners to report incoming military incursions, cooking food for and housing the rebels, informing on one's neighbors, and simply showing up to and participating in Shining Path's popular trials. The same goes for the counterinsurgency. Once again, it is impossible to deny the presence of state security forces—made up mostly of urban mestizos—in organizing and carrying out the national counterinsurgency effort. Nevertheless, indigenous peasants did play a vital role in combating the guerrillas through more informal means: informing, organizing civilian militias, cooperating with state security forces, and rejecting the guerrillas' requests for food and lodging. When it comes to indigenous peasant support for both the insurgency and counterinsurgency, we therefore find that many forms of action lay, as Richard G. Fox and Orin Starn appropriately put it, "between resistance and revolution."[26] This sphere of *support* of political violence, more so than direct participation in it, is what concerns us here.

But was this support voluntary? It is well known that both insurgent and state forces used violence and the threat of violence to obtain the cooperation of the Quechua-speaking peasantry.[27] Some have suggested that Andean peasants were essentially caught "between two fires," forced by the competing armies of Shining Path and the Peruvian state to fight against their will, their only alternative being to flee their rural homes and risk being discovered and killed by either side.[28] This concern with state and insurgent atrocities continued after the violence had dissipated, culminating in the creation of the government-sponsored Truth and Reconciliation Commission in 2001. Comprised of Peruvian and international scholars, lawyers, religious and civil leaders, and human rights advocates, the Truth Commission collected 17,000 testimonies from victims of the violence and in 2003 presented its findings in a nine-volume, 8,000-page *Final Report.*

The human atrocities notwithstanding, I will argue that, particularly during the initial phase of armed conflict (1980–83), Andean actors *voluntarily* supported the political violence; some even *welcomed* it.[29] What occurred in these communities supports Stathis N. Kalyvas's thesis that civil war violence "privatizes politics" inasmuch as civilians "use" guerrilla actors to settle local scores.[30] This approach allows us to move beyond descriptions of the Peruvian insurrection as a case of opposing armies victimizing or manipulating indigenous peasants and to recognize that the reverse was also true. To clarify, I do not deny that state and insurgent forces sometimes used and abused indigenous peasants. Particularly after 1983, sporadic raids, massacres, and rape became part and parcel of the opposing armies' war tactics. Yet, as this study argues, indigenous peasants also took advantage of the civil war to bring about violent solutions to local matters that were often only tangentially related to the macropolitics of the armed conflict itself.

Theoretical and Methodological Framework

Why would indigenous peasants willingly support an insurgency that they knew to be so violent and that they knew would target other Andeans? In answering this question, I pay special attention to the historical conditions that shaped indigenous peasants' responses to the Shining Path insurgency. Most studies of the Peruvian civil war have focused on the period of immediate conflict and its aftermath.[31] Historians have only recently begun to weigh in on the historical precursors to the political violence. These recent studies explain the civil war as the most recent and radical manifestation of a broader historical struggle for indigenous peasant citizenship.[32] This book draws from and expands each of these frameworks by illustrating how local experiences and cultural understandings also conditioned indigenous peasants' responses to the armed conflict.

I find the work of Charles Tilly and Stathis N. Kalyvas particularly insightful. Tilly explores the points of intersection between social relations and mass violence, pointing out the necessity of examining the dynamics of interpersonal interactions in order to understand the multiple causes and manifestations of collective violence.[33] Whereas Tilly examines various manifestations of collective violence, Kalyvas focuses specifically on civil wars. Emphasizing systematic, localized research, Kalyvas explains violence not as a mere *product* of civil wars, but also as a larger process of local conflict and tension that *produces* them.[34] Following these authors, I contend that in order to make sense of the different manifestations of collective violence during the Shining Path civil war, we must first understand the dynamics of local relationships and conflicts during times of peace. Both Tilly and Kalyvas leave out an all-important cultural factor, however. After all, it was precisely in the villages where indigenous peasants perceived that a subversion of their cultural mores had taken place that Shining Path received the most enthusiastic support. Much like the indigenous supporters of the Mexican independence movement described by Van Young, Ayacuchan peasants on both sides of the conflict "stayed pretty close to home, seemingly preoccupied with reequilibrating local social relationships, settling old scores, and protecting community integrity."[35]

Of course, this is not the first historical study to examine culture. Historians began taking the cultural turn in the 1980s and have been writing cultural history ever since.[36] I seek to build on this tradition by offering insights into the ways in which we can arrive at culture. As we will see, Andean peoples did share some core principles and values. At the same time, local events, power relationships, and practices played an equally crucial role in shaping indigenous peasant consciousness. Given this incredible variation across time and place, we must pay attention to the local, sometimes unexpected contours of communal experience. This requires a long-term exploration of peasant communities from within. In the pages that follow, I offer an analysis of Ayacuchan communities that explores the complexities of community life and the historically specific, shifting nature of cultural understanding.

I arrive at this analysis through a fusion of historical and anthropological methods.[37] As anthropologist Nicholas Dirks illustrates from his own experience, the archive itself can be an intimidating terrain for the nonhistorian.[38] Truth be told, I had a similar experience the first time I entered an archive. Yet as a trained historian, I knew that this was to be expected, that I would have to suppress these anxieties and plug forward—I had to; my research depended on it. The reason for this was that I shared the conventional wisdom within my discipline that, as Dirks so aptly summarizes, "historians can only really become historians or write history once they have been to the archive."[39] Conversely, I found my introduction to ethnographic fieldwork every bit as chaotic, unfamiliar, and intimidating as Dirks's first visit to the archive.

I came to this realization during my first visit to Chuschi with my research assistants Julián and Alberto. Julián and I got to the shuttle station at 3:55 A.M. to catch the 4:00 A.M. shuttle from Ayacucho City to Chuschi. It was dark, the shuttle was overcrowded, and we were tired, but it did not take long for us to realize that Alberto, our main Chuschi contact, was not there. Julián jumped into a taxi to swing by Alberto's place, suspecting that the Chuschino researcher had slept in. As I sat there on the shuttle guarding my friends' seats with gusto, I thought, *Great. Now this shuttle is going to take off and I'll be arriving in Chuschi for the first time alone.* A few moments later, Alberto arrived. I told him Julián had just left to get him. He frowned, "Why? Didn't we agree to meet at four o'clock?" Luckily, Julián arrived within ten minutes, although he could have arrived in thirty and still had time to spare, because our driver did not leave until almost 5:00 A.M.

Once on the road, I went over our oral history questions with Alberto, reviewing key names, dates, and events about Chuschino history that I had pulled from the archive. I told him about Humberto Azcarza, a mestizo power holder who had abused the local indigenous population nonstop between 1935 and 1975.[40] Later on, Alberto showed me an obscure text that he had come across that was a brief history of Quispillaccta, written by Quispillacctinos. I leafed through the pages and began reading aloud a passage about a 1960 conflict between Chuschi and Quispillaccta. The Chuschinos, the authors claimed, were led by the likes of Azcarza and other "foreigners" who had settled in Chuschi. "That's not true," interrupted the woman sitting directly across from me and with whom I had been grinding knees for the past two hours. "What makes you say that?" I asked, to which she replied, "Humberto Azcarza was my grandfather."

My heart sank and I could feel my face turning flush red. Less than an hour earlier I had been talking about Humberto Azcarza as though he was a literary villain and his granddaughter had been sitting next to me all along! Rather than apologize, I decided to let her know about my research. She was very friendly and actually seemed curious to know more: "What other names have you come across in your research? I bet I know them." We spent the next hour exchanging what we knew of certain people and episodes in Chuschino history. Humberto, her mother's father, had told my fellow passenger about some of them when she was a young girl living in Chuschi. Others, her father had told her about. "What's your dad's name? Maybe I've come across him in the record," I asked. "My dad is Blanco." *This just can't be,* I thought, asking, "Vicente?" She smiled. "That's him. You've heard of him?" I had not just "heard of" Vicente Blanco.[41] I knew that the mestizo power holder had gotten his fair share of complaints from *comuneros* (indigenous commoners) during his rise to local political power in the 1970s. I knew that he had been charged with a number of serious crimes against the indigenous peasantry. I knew that he had once gotten North American anthropologist Billie Jean Isbell expelled from the community for political reasons. I also knew that during the Shining Path insurgency, the rebels submitted Blanco to fifty lashes before chasing him out of town. "Yeah, I've heard of him," was all I could muster. She said that he was in town for the Independence Day festivities, and I told her that it would be fabulous to interview him sometime. She assured us that her father would be happy to participate. When we got off the bus around 8:00 A.M., I gave her my card and she invited us to come to her father's house later that morning. "Can I borrow that book?" she asked Alberto, referring to the one about Quispillaccta. He agreed, and Alberto, the son of *comuneros*, never saw the book again.[42]

In many ways, my initial trip to Chuschi reflects the challenges of doing historical anthropology about the late twentieth century. The historical component of most historical anthropology focuses on periods whose human subjects have long since passed away.[43] If living subjects are consulted at all, they are separated from the written record by one or more generations. In my case, however, the very people about whom I had been reading—and forming opinions—in the archives were still living. Even in cases where the historical actors had passed away, their children and neighbors still lived. As such, I had to deal with something I never anticipated: the feelings of my archival subjects. Given the intimate familiarity that villagers had with the people and events that I had read about, these feelings were quite strong. How I interpreted my data suddenly mattered in that it could affect my standing with my informants. Moreover, mine and my research assistants' relative power vis-à-vis my research subjects was more obvious, as was my subjects' relative power within the community.

While this interdisciplinary methodology created tensions, it also enabled me to conduct my research with greater sensitivity and precision. For one, the perspective I gained in the field enabled me to return to the archive with a better understanding about the authority and judgment that I imposed on the documentary record. At the same time, the written texts that I collected in local, regional, and national archives and libraries enabled me to conduct much more informed ethnography and oral history in my field sites. I found this useful first in simply helping my informants to remember. For instance, whenever informants told me they could not recall having seen or heard of a given situation, I could readily counter with a historically specific case to jog their memory.

This approach also enabled me to draw important conclusions about the ways that my subjects construct and employ historical memory. In applying this approach, anthropologist Thomas Abercrombie discovered what he has called "structured forgetting," a phenomenon in which informants choose to erase a particular memory from their collective consciousness in order to better shape the community's historical narrative.[44] More often than not, though, I was impressed with the degree of historical accuracy that my informants exhibited, or at least the extent to which their recollections matched my findings from the written historical record. To this effect, my findings support Joanne Rappaport's observation about the primacy of historical memory in Andean community identity.[45] Thus, while engagement with written material can be a useful strategy, it is not the be-all and end-all of historical research. As Florencia Mallon argues, such privileging of written sources overlooks "a whole series of dimensions within human history."[46] Interdisciplinary analysis thus allows us to appreciate the degree to which local histories of domination and conflict shape macropolitical developments.

My study thus draws on detailed archival research, ethnographic fieldwork, and interviews conducted in Lima and Ayacucho over the course of one year and two summers. Due in large part to the availability of sources, my discussion of Chuschi is much more heavily based on the written archival record, while that of Huaychao draws mostly from my interviews and ethnographic fieldwork. I frame the civil war within a deeper history of local power relationships for a full generation before the emergence

of Shining Path. This chronology enabled me to contextualize local responses to the insurgency rather than treating it as an ephemeral political
struggle. The main question I attempt to answer in my study, then, is not
why indigenous peasants rebelled but rather why they advocated the type
of violence that siding with the insurgency or counterinsurgency entailed.

In answering this question, I make frequent reference to a phenomenon that I have termed a *power pact*. Emphasizing the cultural component
of peasant moral economy, a power pact refers to the tacit, collectively
and morally established expectations that subjugated peoples have of
the individuals who subjugate them.[47] Dominated peoples are willing to
submit to and legitimize the dominion of local power holders provided
that the latter live up to these implicit cultural expectations. Thinking of
interpersonal relations of domination in terms of a power pact helps us to
understand why subjugated peoples will accept, tolerate, and even *repro-
duce* their own subjugation in given geohistorical settings while in others
they are more apt to question, challenge, and resist it. As only a localized
approach such as this one can show, it was precisely in the villages where
a significant portion of the population felt that power holders had broken their end of this power pact that subversive groups such as Shining
Path received the earliest and staunchest support. By contrast, in regions
where customary authority and justice had largely preserved this power
pact, Shining Path cadres met fervent and even violent resistance. In es-
sence, then, it was long-developing power relationships, social conflicts,
and cultural understandings at the local level that conditioned indigenous
peasants' responses to the Maoist rebellion.

The analysis that follows is divided into six chapters. The first three
examine locally meaningful power relationships, social conflicts, and
events in Chuschi and Huaychao before the Shining Path rebellion. Having established the particular dynamics of communal experiences on the
eve of the armed conflict, I follow in the final three chapters the historical trajectory of these two villages through the political violence of the
1980s and 1990s. Here, I argue that the reactions of *comuneros* in Chuschi
and Huaychao were entirely consistent with their unique local histories,
thereby rendering comprehensible their collective behavior during the
armed conflict. At issue here were indigenous peasants' notions of power,
justice, and public order. I argue that Shining Path received the most enthusiastic support in communities, like Chuschi, where manifold power
pacts had been breached beyond repair despite the interventions of cus-

tomary authorities. Conversely, Shining Path received the staunchest opposition in locations, such as Huaychao, where peasants believed that customary authority and justice had successfully preserved historically and culturally established power pacts, collective values, and codes of conduct. Shining Path guerrillas' proposal to replace what peasants viewed as an effective and just correctional system with their own radical one met violent resistance in these communities.

I hope that the comparative analysis that follows, in emphasizing the lived experiences and cultural perceptions of indigenous peasants in Ayacucho, will contribute to our understanding of why some indigenous peasants initially supported the Shining Path insurgency while others violently rejected it. This approach can be useful not only in deepening our comprehension of collective action in the Andes but also in exploring the historical linkages between culture, power, and violence.

CHAPTER ONE

To Trace the Tracks

Internal Conflict and Resolution

Two INDIGENOUS PEASANTS — one from Peru and the other from Bolivia — are talking one day about the similarities and differences between their two countries. At some point in the conversation, the Peruvian turns to the Bolivian and asks, "Why is it that you have a navy when in Bolivia there is no sea?" The Bolivian scratches his head for a moment and replies, "Why is that you have a Ministry of Justice when in Peru there is no justice?"

I heard different iterations of this joke throughout my stay in Ayacucho. The punch line invariably caused everyone present to chuckle heartily, then sigh, then fade into awkward silence. The joke hit home for me as a historian, for I had spent countless hours reviewing written records on Ayacuchan indigenous peasants who had invested all their time, money, and energy into seeking justice from a state juridical system that rarely worked in their favor. But the worst of it was that I had consulted many of these records in Lima's National Archive, which, by some cruel twist of fate, was located in the basement of the Palace of Justice.

BY THE MID-TWENTIETH CENTURY, many peasant communities had already turned to grassroots or customary justice to counteract what they perceived as an incompetent state juridical system. Some of these localized systems were more effective than others. Nowhere is this disparity more apparent than in the cases of Chuschi and Huaychao. As we will see, indigenous peasants from both communities held similar views when it came to condemning social trespasses such as *abigeato* (livestock theft), domestic impropriety (incest, adultery, spousal abuse, and the abandonment of one's paternal duties), and "free-riding" (neglecting one's duties toward the collective).[1] Indigenous peasants seemed willing to tolerate their neighbors' occasional slippages with respect to these moral trans-

gressions provided that they made a concerted effort to correct these behaviors, for these deviants threatened the public order of the community.

Where Chuschi's and Huaychao's histories diverge is in the extent to
which local systems of justice curbed this degenerate behavior. In Chuschi
and neighboring Quispillaccta, we find the same individuals committing
one or more of these social infractions throughout most of their adult
life — some even before that. This was a direct consequence of a breakdown in the local administration of justice in the district. Not only did the
customary law of the *varayoqs*, the indigenous authorities of the traditional
civil-religious prestige hierarchy, fail to correct these individuals' behavior,
but so did the penal system of the Peruvian state.[2] By contrast, customary
justice in Huaychao, which was administered by local authorities, had succeeded in dissuading individuals from habitually subverting local values.
Thus, even though these authorities were sometimes at odds with their
subalterns, Huaychainos saw their power as legitimate and necessary because of their actual and symbolic role in safeguarding communal mores.

Chuschi's and Huaychao's local experiences speak to a greater incapac-
ity of the Peruvian state to administer justice in the countryside. This is
not to say that the state was absent in the rural highlands. Peasants in the
most remote communities had access to at least one channel of the state's
judicial apparatus — be it appointed officials, judges, or policemen. The
problem for Quechua-speaking peasants was not one of accessibility but
one of reliability.

Community, Justice, and the State

Peru was not the only Latin American country with an ineffective judicial apparatus during the mid-twentieth century. In El Salvador, judges
often deflected their responsibilities onto their untrained staff. Nor was
it uncommon for justices of the lower courts to solicit bribes or confiscate valuable evidence such as vehicles for personal use. One reason for
this was that Salvadoran judges received miserable salaries and often only
worked part time. Equally troublesome was the inability of the Salvadoran
system to convict prisoners. Before the 1980s, 90 percent of all Salvadoran
prisoners remained unsentenced.[3] Faced with similar crises, some Latin
Americans, particularly those living in impoverished areas where crime
was rampant and justice scarce, turned to extralegal measures to restore
a sense of order in their communities. The political violence in 1940s and

1950s Colombia offers a fitting example. During that period, Colombia's political parties held considerable sway over both the judicial and policing systems, effectively turning them into partisan machines. As a result, many of the armed civilian groups (guerrillas and paramilitaries) that emerged at this time began targeting individuals who had eluded justice at the local level.[4] Nor was this strictly a rural problem. Brazil, a country where the urban poor complained that the justice system did not work in their favor, experienced a rise in mob lynching during the 1970s and 1980s.[5] Indeed, state-administered justice was so unreliable during the middle of the century that most Latin American countries overhauled their entire judicial and policing systems during the 1980s and 1990s.[6] Peru was among those countries.

The judicial official with whom Andean peasants had the most direct contact was (and remains) the *juez de paz*, the justice of the peace. While some peasant notables received these titles, justices of the peace were usually men from powerful mestizo families who, despite possessing minimal education, received virtually no judicial oversight from the superior courts that appointed them. They alone decided how to resolve local disputes. A justice might imprison one suspected *abigeo* (livestock rustler) in the village holding cell while setting another free under similar charges and with similar evidence. Justices used the same discretion when determining which cases to send to higher authorities and courts in the provincial, departmental, and national capitals. Indeed, many peasants believed that the most effective way to get a justice of the peace to send a case to the upper courts was to bribe the justice with money, goods, or services.[7]

Even if a justice of the peace did advance a peasant's case to the higher courts, there were no guarantees that it would ever be resolved. For starters, litigants had to contend with the tremendous financial burden that bringing a case before the Peruvian courts entailed. In addition to paying fees for just about every transaction and procedure, litigants had to pay for the services of scribes, clerks, and attorneys, who themselves were known for their price gauging, foot-dragging, professional ineptitude, and general alignment with the landowning class.[8] Add to this the costs plaintiffs accrued traveling to district, provincial, and departmental capitals to have their cases heard, and one can appreciate why peasants sometimes elected to drop their original charges.[9] In many cases, however, the courts were the ones to abandon the case. The very language highlanders used to describe the judicial process illustrates their awareness of this reality. Using

the Spanish term *derivar* (to drift) to refer to the act of submitting litigation through judicial channels, Quechua speakers voiced their uncertainty
as to whether their cases would be heard at all.[10]

Outside of the courts, peasants could turn to the political hierarchy of
the state. At the communal level, the central political authority was the
lieutenant governor. In district capitals such as Chuschi, the lieutenant
governor was outranked by the governor, who in turn was outranked by
the mayor. The extent of these officials' authority and duties varied widely
from community to community, as did their social, racial, and educational
backgrounds. In most cases, however, these leaders settled local disputes
between villagers and reported serious cases to the provincial subprefects,
who responded directly to the departmental prefects. Some villages also
had officials who represented the community in disputes with external
communities and landowners. This job was originally reserved for the
personero, a popularly elected communal representative. After 1969, however, the position of *personero* was replaced with that of the communal
president (also known as the president of administration) as part of the reform measures adopted by the Revolutionary Government of the Armed
Forces (GRFA).[11]

The problems with this political hierarchy mirrored those of the judicial system. The men who held these posts were typically mestizos with
considerable power at the local level. They usually came from the same
social strata as the justices of the peace, and many had even served as justices at one point. Local authorities received virtually no oversight from
the provincial subprefects and departmental prefects, leaving disciplinary
measures up to their own discretion. Personal authority aside, peasants
were subject to the same financial burdens they endured when dealing
with the Peruvian courts. In many instances, peasants had to travel to district, provincial, and departmental capitals to have their cases heard, and
once they got there they were often showered with clerical fees. Nor was it
uncommon for peasants' petitions to go unanswered or unresolved. Thus,
while the state political hierarchy offered peasants some recourse when it
came to voicing complaints, it did little to establish a sense of justice in the
countryside.

The final state institution to which Andean peasants turned for the
resolution of local conflicts was the Civil Guard, created in 1922 as a sort
of police force. As with many justices, police guards tended to be uneducated mestizos. Few, if any, were from the districts under their jurisdiction.

Civil Guard posts were seriously understaffed, manned by only an officer or two. Moreover, they were responsible for a vast geographic jurisdiction. This forced peasants to travel long distances to report crimes and then wait several days for a response. Peasants found this particularly frustrating when it came to crimes such as livestock theft, as the thieves usually fled or disposed of the stolen animals long before the police showed up to investigate.[12] Besides, many peasants believed that police did more harm than good whenever they visited rural towns. During their visits, officers sometimes confiscated goods, issued random arrests under trumped-up charges, and sequestered youths for their obligatory military service. All this led peasants to believe that the police were in bed with the landed elite.[13] Others felt that the officers were in cahoots with the thieves, doing everything from ignoring theft to aiding and abetting livestock rustlers.[14] Still others accused the police of compelling illiterate peasants to endorse documents of whose contents they were unaware, only to find out later that they had unwittingly confessed to crimes they did not commit.[15]

Considering the systemic unreliability of the state's judicial, political, and policing systems, it should come as no surprise that petty crime — particularly livestock theft — ran rampant in certain parts of the highlands at various historical junctures.[16] Some believed that this broken system would improve when the Peruvian armed forces, led by General Juan Velasco Alvarado, seized executive power in 1968, promising an array of sweeping reforms designed to address peasant grievances. Among the measures enacted under Velasco was an overhaul of the judicial system, including the replacement of Supreme Court justices and the creation of a special body, the Consejo Nacional de Justicia (National Council of Justice), to appoint justices at various levels. Additionally, the GRFA created the Juzgado de Tierras (Agrarian Tribunal, or Land Court), to deal exclusively with agrarian disputes.[17] Unfortunately for many peasants, the judicial reforms did little to address the structural problems outlined above. This is not to say that the Peruvian countryside was a criminal cesspool. On the contrary, communities developed a wide range of strategies to combat delinquency and preserve internal order.

A noteworthy example is the *rondas campesinas* (peasant patrols) of northern Peru.[18] Even after the implementation of Velasco's reforms, communities in Cajamarca and Piura continued to experience rampant theft. In the absence of a strong police force, peasants organized vigilante patrols to capture, interrogate, and punish suspected vandals. In time, the disciplinary function of the *rondas campesinas* went beyond repressing cattle rustling, as *ronderos* (patrollers) began working with their communities to discipline everyone from corrupt authorities to quarrelling spouses. The movement for rural justice caught on quickly, and by the 1980s the *rondas campesinas* patrolled virtually every community in northern Peru.[19]

Although the *rondas campesinas* remained concentrated in the north, peasants in the southern Andes developed their own grassroots mechanisms of communal justice. Between 1975 and 1977, Aymara peasants in the community of Calahuyo (Puno Department) stopped using the state judicial apparatus altogether, opting to resolve all local conflicts internally via the communal assembly. The punishments meted out by the Calahuyo assembly included the imposition of fines, public censorship, flogging, forced labor, loss of access to communal resources, demotion (in cases involving communal authorities), or even expulsion from the community.[20] Other communities relied on the civil-religious hierarchy of the *varayoqs*. Typically, these customary indigenous authorities ensured that *comuneros* fulfill their communal obligations, such as the payment of communal taxes and participation in public works projects and religious festivities. These authorities also served as a sort of informal police force, investigating *comunero* disputes and punishing alleged wrongdoers. While perhaps arbitrary, this authority structure offered a form of customary justice for cultural trespasses that did not necessarily constitute crimes in the eyes of the state. The disciplinary power and reach of the *varayoqs* varied from community to community. In some villages, the hierarchy served as a sort of indigenous parallel to the district-level state bureaucracy, responsible for preserving social and cosmological order in the village. In others, the indigenous authorities acted alongside state officials, ostensibly working together to preserve internal public order.[21]

Ayacucho was also home to its share of grassroots justice. In 1975, villagers from Carhuahurán, an Iquichano community near Huaychao, executed nine members of the Huamán Curo and Díaz Curo families. Members of the two families had been associated with numerous conflicts and robberies throughout the zone since the 1950s. When it became clear that the state penal system would not bring them to justice, local authorities and villagers took the law into their own hands.[22] At around the same time, the peasants of Iruro (Lucanamarca Province) strangled four suspected *abigeos* to death after repeated attempts to denounce their theft before state officials.[23]

As we have seen, the strategies that Andean communities developed to compensate for an inadequate state system varied widely from community to community. Given the general unreliability of the Peruvian state when it came to maintaining public order in the countryside, a community's success in maintaining that order hinged almost entirely on its localized, grassroots system of justice. However, not all systems of communal justice were as effective as the ones described here. Just as the practices of justice varied from community to community, so did the efficacy of those practices. As we will see, although communal justice in Huaychao was as unique as that in any of the jurisdictions mentioned above, it did have one thing in common with them: villagers believed their justice system was effective. By contrast, villagers in Chuschi increasingly viewed both state and communal justice as inadequate and unreliable. We now turn to the Chuschi case.

Local Deviants in Chuschi and Quispillaccta

This section will focus on several key personalities who over the years established a reputation as moral backsliders in Chuschi. We can think of these individuals as a type of local power holder. Yet their power stemmed not from class, race, or political authority but from their freedom to disregard social mores with impunity. The justice they eluded was not only that of the state but also that of the indigenous peasant community. The authority they wielded was not moral and admirable but illegitimate and detestable because it stemmed from their disregard for *comuneros'* shared assumptions, beliefs, and practices. These men, in the eyes of their contemporaries, were social degenerates, misfits, and troublemakers. They were, in a word, thugs. But they were no ordinary cattle rustlers. As we will learn in chapter 4, each of the men described here would become a key figure in the civil war violence of the 1980s.

The Men with the Scarred Faces: Adult Misfits

Teobaldo Achallma had some explaining to do. The year was 1976, and police interrogators had just discovered that the scar-faced Quispillacctino was concealing tags from stolen mules under his crotch. During the investigation that followed, authorities found among Achallma's household possessions three stolen documents: a permit to transport four bulls and a pair of stolen certificates of good conduct.[24] Achallma understood that this all seemed suspicious, particularly given his admission that he had stolen livestock on two separate occasions over the past three years. But this time was different, Achallma insisted: "I want to add that those were the only two times that I've committed these acts and that I did them under the initiative of other people and not on my own initiative." Besides, he was desperate back then, motivated by "the poverty in which I live with my wife and my four children."[25] Achallma's unconvincing alibi aside, the prosecutor dropped the charges, and the court closed the case indefinitely.[26]

What led Teobaldo Achallma to his life of petty crime? To understand this, we might go back to June 1961, when Achallma walked into the office of the subprefect in Cangallo City to dispel a nasty rumor that he was sleeping with his own mother. Quispillaccta authorities had already called Achallma's mother into a village chapel to reproach her, before God and the patron saints. The officials at the chapel claimed that Achallma had upset the cosmos, precipitating a recent wave of hailstorms that had destroyed local harvests. Teobaldo Achallma was aware of the social repercussions of these allegations: "Accusations of such a grave . . . and reprehensible conduct have caused profound alarm and repudiation against me within the village psyche. . . . Most of the villagers have believed these allegations and are constantly threatening our lives, considering us to be a rare, strange, and offensive species."[27] Such accusations "have gravely injured our honor and dignity," Achallma continued, "and on the other hand our personal safety is also in grave danger, given the fury [felt] by the majority of our neighbors on receiving word that the hailstorm was our fault, that it came as a punishment to ruin the crops."[28] Achallma had been married and divorced twice, and he suspected his second wife of spreading the rumor.[29] Did Achallma's ex fabricate the rumor to settle a score? Or was it Achallma's Oedipus complex that caused her to leave him in the first place? We simply do not know.

What we do know is that Achallma had his share of marital problems. The scar-faced peasant married another Quispillacctina, Teresa Ccallocunto, in February 1965. By March, Ccallocunto had filed a complaint against one of Achallma's former lovers. Ccallocunto contended that the woman in question had forced herself into the newlyweds' home and refused to leave, proclaiming that *she* was Achallma's rightful partner since he had fathered her child.[30] This may have been what led Ccallocunto to move back in with her parents seven months later. After a futile attempt to demand his wife's return—Ccallocunto's family chased him away from their home—a frustrated Achallma demanded that local authorities force Ccallocunto to return. When this failed, he took his complaint to the provincial subprefect.[31] Whether she did so under her own initiative or because the provincial authority ordered her to, Teresa Ccallocunto eventually moved back in with her husband. Unfortunately, she now had to contend with Achallma's first wife, not the one who accused him of incest or the one who said he had fathered her child but a local named Martina Núñez from whom Achallma had been separated for eighteen years. Achallma complained to the subprefect that Núñez had been "bad mouthing" him and his wife. While he elected not to repeat Núñez's words, they seemed to have had an effect on Ccallocunto, who was now considering leaving him again. To discredit his ex-wife, Achallma suggested that she was "a loose woman [*una mujer de vida alegre*] who engages in dishonest acts [and] who has borne six children from different people."[32] Núñez responded with an equally gendered charge, reminding the subprefect that one of those six children was Achallma's and that he had long since abandoned his paternal duties as the boy's father: "[Achallma] has neither taken care of nor clothed nor protected [his] son in any way." Núñez maintained that all she had done was remind Achallma of his obligation to feed his son.[33] In short, Achallma's reputation as a partner and father left something to be desired. Twice divorced and having failed at numerous additional relationships, Achallma was a prototypical *mujeriégo* (womanizer) who scoffed at his patriarchal duties toward his lovers and children.

The women in Achallma's life were not the only Quispillacctinos who felt that he had abandoned his responsibilities. In August 1975, twenty-four peasant leaders and villagers from his neighborhood of Catalinayoq notified the subprefect that Teobaldo Achallma had ignored his communal duties in at least three ways. First, he neglected to pay the seventy soles per year that each *comunero* was expected to contribute to Quispillaccta's communal fund. Second, he chose not to participate in village *faenas*, the collective public works projects that included the maintenance of irrigation ditches and communal pasture lands as well as the construction of buildings. Finally, Achallma had illicitly appropriated eighteen hectares of communal lands in addition to several of his neighbors' private plots.[34] Increasingly, then, Achallma's neighbors came to regard him as a free-rider who put personal profit and security over that of the collective. Whether the scar-faced Quispillacctino turned to a life of petty crime and delinquency in the 1970s in spite of his neighbors' attitudes or because of them remains a mystery.

Simply put, Teobaldo Achallma's neighbors viewed him as a degenerate. His long history of livestock theft was only the beginning of his problems. If his court and police testimonies are any indication, he was also a chronic liar. This, together with the stolen and forged certificates of conduct found in his home, paints the picture of a man willing to lie, cheat, and steal at the expense of his fellow villagers for his own benefit. Moreover, his unwillingness to participate in communal works projects and pay *comunero* fees signaled to some that he was also a free-rider, a man who willingly shunned the implicit duties of a *comunero* yet was happy to reap the benefits of communal citizenship. This behavior posed as much a threat to the cosmological order of the village as it did to the social and public order.[35] This was to say nothing of Achallma's sexual misconduct and unwillingness to fulfill his inherent paternalistic duties toward his lovers and children. As far as his neighbors were concerned, Teobaldo Achallma was beyond saving.

Another Quispillacctino with a similar reputation was Amancio Rejas Pacotaipe. By 1959, the nineteen-year-old peasant had been implicated in at least three robberies. Rejas even looked the part, his profile marked by a stubby beard and scarred forehead. He was also unusually light skinned for an indigenous person, so much that he passed for a mestizo the first time he was the subject of a criminal investigation. The fact that Rejas passed for mestizo before he had a criminal record and then was considered an indigenous person in each of the subsequent cases—after he had established himself as a local troublemaker—is suggestive of the way state officials racialized rural crime.[36] To his Quispillaccta neighbors, though, Rejas was just another *comunero*, albeit not a very good one. Time and again, Rejas's neighbors complained about his poor social conduct.

Antonio Galindo was one of the first Quispillacctinos to press charges against Rejas. In August 1958, Galindo had made the mistake of selling a young bull in the presence of Rejas. Not long after the transaction, Galindo locked up his home in the hills and went into the village to attend to some trivial matters. Galindo returned only to find the lock on his door jimmied and the 900 soles from the transaction missing. "Given that [Rejas] is a person with a [criminal] past who is accustomed to committing robberies of the nature of the one I'm reporting," Galindo explained to the judge, "my suspicions fell squarely on him."[37] Rejas confirmed Galindo's suspicions shortly after the robbery when he began spending large sums of money on aguardiente around the village. At one point, Rejas paid for a bottle of the cane liquor with a bill of 100 soles. This was curious enough, considering that Rejas made a daily income of about one sol. Even more peculiar was the nonchalant manner in which Rejas told the store clerk that he would return for his change at a later date. All this may have convinced Galindo of Rejas's guilt, but it did not convince the presiding judge, who acquitted Rejas of all charges.[38]

Amancio Rejas Pacotaipe managed to keep his name out of the Cangallo court record for the next decade. Perhaps his early brush with the law taught him the value of earning an honest living. Maybe he continued to negotiate his way out of trouble without involving the authorities, as Galindo suggested he had done in the past. In any event, Rejas's name reappeared with a flurry of cases in the 1970s.[39]

One of these cases involved fellow Quispillacctina Cayetana Casavilca. Casavilca lost six heads of cattle from her corral on 13 February 1975. The next day, she organized a search party of "a number of people," who traced the footprints toward the town of Niñobamba. At around 5:00 P.M., the patrollers spotted three men, two on horseback and another afoot, steering her cattle. The members of the search party gave chase and the suspects scattered, setting the cattle free. The pursuers caught up to the man, whom they quickly identified as Amancio Rejas. Casavilca told the judge that this was not the first time that Rejas had stolen livestock from her. She had elected to ignore his four previous robberies since the value of the individual llamas was not worth the hassle of reporting each case. This time, however, things were different. "I cannot allow, Your Honor, [Rejas] to get away with taking my animals," she explained, for it was clear to her that the man had become one of Quispillaccta's most "vindictive thieves," like so many others who were "committed to a life of robbery."[40]

Casavilca was not alone. She was joined by two more villagers, each claiming to have been a victim of Rejas's thievery. Casavilca and her neighbors expressed the urgency of the situation to the judge: "Given that the defendant Amancio Rejas Pacotaype [sic] is a delinquent [hombre acostumbrado] . . . with a heavy [criminal] record and an ex-convict [who has been accused of] various crimes, we implore you to punish him in the most exemplary manner."[41] Casavilca and company must have felt that they had the case locked up when they reported to a judge in late 1975 that a policeman of the Civil Guard had found twenty-six stolen llamas and five cattle at the house of Rejas's sister.[42] Imagine their surprise when the verdict came back the following year acquitting Rejas of all charges.[43]

Quispillaccta's authorities fared no better than the Peruvian courts when it came to correcting Rejas's behavior. In May 1975 village leaders held a special assembly to address the Rejas problem. Three separate villagers maintained that Rejas had stolen a bull from Basilio Galindo in the Chuschi annex of Uchuirre two months prior, only to reach an agreement with the local justice of the peace that the charges be dropped. Another Quispillacctino went as far as to suggest that Rejas had threatened to kill him. Still another came forward and said that Rejas had sold his coworker stolen cattle. The assembly participants resolved to solicit both the provincial prosecutor and the president of the National Council of Justice in Lima, "so that [they] take drastic measures and [make an] example of this deviant [*maleante*], for the crimes he's committed are multiple, not to mention that he doesn't fulfill his duties as a *comunero*." Unfortunately for the village authorities, their pleas fell on deaf ears.[44]

During that same 1975 assembly, Quispillacctino Bernabé Núñez stood up and charged: "Amancio Rejas declares that all the women in [the neighborhood of] Tuco are his. Moreover, all the inhabitants of Tuco know that this Subject is an adulterer."[45] Apparently, this boastful womanizing was only one of many gendered transgressions that Rejas had committed. As sixty-eight-year-old Quispillacctino Víctor Núñez told Alberto, Julián, and me, Rejas was also a known wife-beater and rapist.[46] I found no documentary evidence to substantiate these charges. However, it is worth mentioning that *tayta* (Mr., Sir) Víctor had no trouble coming up with names and details in support of the rape allegation.[47] And while I found no written evidence that Rejas habitually beat his wife, I did find an accusation by one of Rejas's neighbors that he had beat a peasant woman named Melchora Núñez.[48] Whether he was guilty of this gendered misconduct or not, though, Rejas's neighbors clearly saw him as someone who mistreated women.

Amancio Rejas was accused of many of the same social and moral infractions as his neighbor Teobaldo Achallma. In addition to his reputation as a womanizer, rapist, and wife-beater, Rejas's taste for alcohol probably did not help his image. As we have seen, some of his social transgressions were precipitated by heavy bouts of drinking. We also saw in the special assembly an accusation that he was a free-rider who neglected his communal duties. Most important, though, Rejas was a well-known thief. To be sure, other peasants had resorted to robbery on occasion. The descriptions that Rejas's neighbors gave of him, however, suggested that he was not just someone who had been in the wrong place at the wrong time. On the contrary, Rejas had *professionalized* the crime; he was a sort of career criminal.

The testimonies that *comuneros* gave Alberto, Julián, and me during our visit to Chuschi confirmed these observations. When we asked Víctor Núñez which locals had the biggest reputation as cattle rustlers, he replied without hesitation: "Ah, Rejas." Asked to elaborate, he added,

> That guy would steal from his own brother, and from his wife's sister, too. . . . He drank a lot, too. He'd go around the streets [drunk] acting all tough, saying, "Who's going to stop me? Not anyone from this town." . . . He was always picking fights, getting into arguments, because when the *comuneros* would drink they would challenge him, saying, "You're an *abigeo*!" And he would act like a tough guy [*se ponía macho*], and people were scared of him. . . . Everyone was afraid of him because everyone had a few animals [that he could potentially steal]. If someone was out in the fields, [Rejas] would say, "Alright, where are all his livestock? How many cows does he have, how many sheep?" And then he'd go and steal them.

Yet for all Rejas's infractions, *tayta* Víctor could not recall a single instance in which he was brought to justice for his local misconduct.[49] Thus, Rejas's power derived not only from his monopoly over theft, but also from his monopoly over justice. In fact, the only documented case in which the Peruvian courts found Rejas guilty of any wrongdoing occurred outside of the district. In that case, the judge ruled that Rejas had teamed up with a Chuschino butcher to steal cattle from the nearby community of Totos.[50]

The name of that butcher was Felipe Aycha.[51] Although he was fifteen years Rejas's elder and from Chuschi, Felipe Aycha had a good deal in common with the misfit from the other side of the river. Like Rejas, Aycha could pass for mestizo due to his "copper" skin tone. Like Rejas, Aycha had a scar on his face, but Aycha's covered his left cheekbone. Like Rejas, Aycha drank alcohol and chewed coca leaf regularly, and like Rejas, Aycha had a checkered past.[52]

Vidal Chuchón's run-in with Aycha took place on 8 October 1968. That evening, Aycha had contracted Chuchón and a friend to steal and slaughter a bull from a Quispillaccta neighbor. Chuchón did not care to cast moral judgment on the theft itself, focusing instead on how Aycha had treated him and his partner. After the job had been completed, Chuchón lamented, Aycha had sent him home "without having paid [me] any money or treating me to a single slab of meat for the job."[53] Chuchón's testimony paints an image of Felipe Aycha as a villager who did not appreciate the behavioral norms for reciprocal exchanges between indigenous peasants.

A case involving *abigeato* earlier that year provides another example of how Aycha breached *comuneros'* tacit codes of conduct. Emilio Quichca was grazing the cattle of his *patrón* (lord, employer), mestizo Ernesto Jaime, in the hills above Chuschi in late August when he noticed that three of the animals were missing. As Jaime later articulated to the judge, the mystery was solved when brothers Marino and Juvencio Ochoa later attempted to trade the cattle with "the well-known *abigeo*" Aycha.[54] When authorities brought Marino Ochoa in to testify in court, he once again focused on Aycha's inappropriate social conduct. Marino contended that even though Aycha was his brother-in-law, the two were not on friendly terms. The reason for this, he explained, was that Felipe "constantly abused" his wife. Marino's staunch defense of his sister had created "an irreconcilable enmity" between him and Aycha. Given their turbulent history as in-laws, then, Marino rejected the notion that he would have had any dealings with Aycha.[55] After denying the charges of cattle rustling, Aycha confirmed Marino's story. He told the judge that he had indeed "exchanged words" with the Ochoa brothers with respect to his treatment of their sister. He did not care to go into detail about the altercation, saying only that it was severe enough to preclude further socialization between him and his in-laws.[56] This alibi was sufficient to exculpate Aycha, and the court ruled in his favor.[57]

How long would the Chuschino butcher stay out of trouble? For Ernesto Jaime, the answer to this question must have been nine years, for that was how long it took Jaime, a *vecino* (non-*comunero* resident), to reintroduce *abigeato* charges against Aycha. This time, Jaime alleged, Aycha had teamed up with Bernardo Chipana, a migrant who had spent a good deal of time living outside the village, and two locals with the surname Allcca.[58] Jaime asserted that during the first week of 1979 the men in question stole a pig from one of his corrals. Maybe Jaime felt that the rustlers were picking on him, for he complained that a week later they were at it again, this time stealing a pair of horses from his other corral. Jaime gave five reasons to suspect that Aycha, Chipana, and the two Allccas had committed the crimes. First, the foursome made up "a gang [*cuadrilla*] of Chuschi *abigeos*" who all lived in Aycha's residence and had criminal records. Second, Jaime said that he had personally overheard a drunken Aycha strutting around the streets of Chuschi during Carnival boasting about how he and his mates had put the horses and pig to good use. Third, the *comuneros* of nearby Chaqueccocha had informed Jaime that during another drunken holiday rant, Aycha had reproached his partners-in-crime for double-crossing him, demanding to know "how it was possible that they would steal from him after having split [Jaime's pig] between [the four of] them." Fourth, Felipe Aycha was a thief, and everyone in the village knew it: "I know that this Felipe Aycha has committed various robberies against various people who don't press charges because he threatens to make all their cattle and horses disappear." Finally, Jaime claimed that Aycha and Chipana had both made verbal promises to repay him for his damages.[59] At first, Aycha and Chipana denied the *vecino's* allegations. But when it became clear that Jaime was prepared to go through with this accusation, the two men quickly offered signed statements in which they took full responsibility for the robberies and offered to repay Jaime for his losses.[60]

With Aycha, we can now detect a pattern. This was a man whose neighbors and relatives had accused of undermining local mores. In the domestic sphere, he had been suspected of beating his wife. Even his fellow thieves complained that he had not respected the implicit code of reciprocity that structured Andean patron-client exchanges. Indeed, these *peones* (laborers, serfs) seemed more concerned with this social breach than with the fact that the job for which they had been contracted involved livestock theft. This brings us to another of Aycha's character flaws. Like his Quispillacctino counterparts, Aycha's neighbors considered him a "well-known" cattle rustler who was tied to an organized "gang" of *abigeos*. His official title of butcher did not fool anybody, serving as a convenient cover for his theft of livestock. But Aycha was no ordinary cattle rustler. When Alberto, Julián, and I asked villagers what they remembered most about Aycha's dealings, they described him as a sort of *abigeo* "boss," claiming that all Chuschino cattle rustlers responded directly to him. "He was an *abigeo*," Víctor Núñez insisted. "They say that all the thieves would go to his house, [he'd] make *mondongo* [a regional soup] and *chala* [jerkey] [with the stolen meat] right there in his house with the thieves. The thieves would just walk right in like it was nothing, but they had to take an oath [of allegiance] first. . . . He was Aycha, after all, the father of all *abigeos*." As *tayta* Víctor explained, it was not so much Aycha's cattle rustling that bothered people but the fact that he did not *need* to do it: "People said that he was a 'bad' *abigeo* because he stole in spite of having livestock, not because he lacked it."[61]

The manner in which *tayta* Víctor described Aycha indicates how intimidating a figure he was: "He was short and stocky with a commanding voice, handsome, manly." According to *tayta* Víctor, Aycha used his intimidating presence in the village to his advantage, bullying other *comuneros* and subverting the authority of local leaders. *Tayta* Víctor witnessed this intimidation firsthand when he was about nineteen. He had recently been appointed village authority when he learned that Aycha had stolen a horse from his community. Together with two other *varayoqs*, *tayta* Víctor went to Aycha's house to detain him. *Tayta* Víctor suspected that Aycha might be difficult to bring down, but as he said, "I was a young guy, and I wasn't afraid of anything." *Tayta* Víctor had the two *varayoqs* wait for Aycha outside with ropes while he entered alone through the front door to confront the suspect. When *tayta* Víctor got inside, he was greeted by Aycha's wife. He informed the peasant woman that he had orders from Quispillaccta to capture her husband, but she said that he was out of town. "Don't you lie to me," he warned, but the woman was not impressed. Looking the scrawny teenager up and down, she asked mockingly, "What, do you think *you* are going to take down my husband?" *Tayta* Víctor ignored her insinuation and headed to the back of the house, where Aycha was waiting for him. "I beg your pardon, Señor Felipe, but you have to come back with me to Quispillaccta," the youngster informed him. "What, *you* are going to take *me* away?" Aycha chuckled. "I don't think so, son." Aycha assumed a fighting stance, prompting *tayta* Víctor to take out his *chicote* (a short Andean whip) and remark, "You're coming with me one way or another." *Tayta* Víctor then grabbed Aycha by the neck while the other two *varayoqs* came in with the ropes and tied his hands behind his back. After subduing Aycha, the three men escorted him back to Quispillaccta and turned him over to state authorities for trial. According to *tayta* Víctor, Aycha never did end up paying for the crime.[62]

Aycha also used his local power to intimidate anyone who opposed his lifestyle. Ernesto Jaime's claim that Aycha often threatened to "disappear" the cattle of anyone who reported his crimes is supported by *tayta* Víctor's oral account:

> [His crimes] were frowned on, but no one could touch him, hurt him, nothing. On the contrary, people would have to buy him drinks—buying him a drink was their way of saying, "Please don't steal *my* livestock." . . . No one ever crossed him because everyone was scared of him and respected [his power] even though he wasn't even an authority or anything. . . . They only called him a thief behind his back. . . . [But if word got back to Aycha that someone was complaining about him], they'd have to apologize to him the very next day . . . [or else] he'd go and steal an animal from the person who had offended him.[63]

It was much better to get on Felipe Aycha's good side. *Tayta* Víctor told us that the *abigeo* boss once attempted to bribe him as well, saying, "If you need any livestock just let me know, tell me which ones and they're yours."[64] In this way, Felipe Aycha sat at the top of a power hierarchy that ran parallel to that of the indigenous authorities. Yet while *comuneros* such as *tayta* Víctor felt compelled to tolerate Aycha's local power, they recognized that it was illegitimate.

Felipe Aycha was not the only member of his family with a reputation for disregarding local mores. Aycha's sixteen-year-old son, Ignacio,[65] also got into his share of trouble with local authorities. A student at the National University of San Cristóbal de Huamanga (UNSCH), Ignacio Aycha had spent a good deal of time living and studying in Ayacucho City. Yet it was during his return visits to Chuschi that Ignacio got into the most trouble. In many ways, Ignacio Aycha embodied a generation of troubled youth who afflicted Chuschi at the time.

Like Father, Like Son: Troubled Youth

Before the 1970s, most cases of delinquency involved adults. Indeed, the youngest *abigeo* mentioned in this chapter was Amancio Rejas, who first appeared in the criminal record at the age of nineteen. In the 1970s, the number of criminal proceedings involving adolescent boys increased.[66] This change in youth behavior represented a generational conflict in which an increasing proportion of local youths were engaging in criminal activity, shunning traditional values and practices, and challenging local leaders. Elders and *varayoqs* were aware of this generational shift, and they often complained that local youths no longer respected their authority.[67]

Perhaps no single youth better represents this generational conflict than Ignacio Aycha. Just before midnight on 20 October 1977, *varayoq* Teófilo Achallma—not to be confused with the deviant Teobaldo Achallma—spotted Ignacio and two friends walking suspiciously in the direction of the communal stable. Achallma caught up with the boys and asked them where they were headed. They replied that they were "just going up there" into the hills and assured him that their intentions were pure. Achallma reluctantly let them run along. This decision would eat at the *varayoq* for the next several hours until he finally returned to the hills to check on the status of the livestock. By the time he got there it was almost four o'clock in the morning and the young men were gone. Also gone were eight horses, including two for which Achallma had been held responsible.[68]

Provincial authorities arrested Ignacio and recorded his testimony on 28 October. "As a matter of fact I did commit the robbery under my own initiative," the Chuschino student confessed. "I did it because I didn't have the economic resources to subsist *and still* meet my school's [financial] requisites." Ignacio said that it was under these circumstances that he struck a deal with Fernando Tapahuasco, a janitor at UNSCH: Ignacio would steal some horses from his home village and sell them to the janitor for 1,500 soles a head. To make the transaction appear legitimate, Ignacio stole some papers bearing his father's seal from his days as Chuschi's lieutenant governor and forged an official transaction.[69]

Ignacio Aycha's victims were not content with his confession, much less with his explanation. Over the course of the trial that ensued, the plaintiffs attempted to convince the judge that this was a professional job spearheaded by a juvenile delinquent. "Without a doubt," they contended, "this smacks of a well-organized, well-protected *abigeo* gang, and . . . given that it is a gang, they [sic] forge fake sales receipts [and] fake certificates for one another, most likely subverting authorities and falsifying documents so that together they can conceal the crime and give it some vestige of legality."[70] Heading this gang was the Chuschino Ignacio Aycha. "This is clearly the act of a GANG, headed by the minor Aycha, a professional in this crime, who in this way mocks the law," one of the victims asserted.[71] Achallma agreed: "Ignacio Aycha has been in the habit of robbing livestock from a very tender age. Why, many times he has done so alongside his father."[72] To cement their claims about Ignacio, the plaintiffs secured a rather uncharitable character assessment of the teenager from village authorities:

> The Pledged Authorities of the Peasant Community of Chuschi . . . *certify*: That, don Ignacio Aycha, native and resident of this locality, has, as far as we are concerned since childhood, maintained a very poor conduct within our Chuschino society and habitually resorted to delinquency. On numerous occasions complaints against the aforementioned Ignacio Aycha have appeared before our offices for crimes involving the robbery of livestock and other materials and, as far as we are concerned, every member of that family, starting with the father don Felipe Aycha, and [including] mother and children, is dedicated exclusively to this aforementioned poor conduct.[73]

Only on rare occasions did the authorities from Chuschi and Quispillaccta find something on which they could agree; this was one of those occasions. Quispillacctino authorities issued a similar statement: "*Jóven* [young man] Ignacio Aycha and his parents . . . are dedicated exclusively to the theft of livestock, materials, and other things, which have appeared before our Offices."[74]

As the plaintiffs explained, the crime of *abigeato*, when committed in such an organized, premeditated manner by repeat offenders, disrupted a balance within the community: "We reject this act because the crime of *abigeato* is not something that can be forgiven. Only the monetary losses can be forgiven, but not the crime itself. . . . The robbery committed against the community, and against *comuneros*, goes well beyond the [physical act] of stealing livestock. . . . Therefore, we request an exemplary punishment."[75] Here, one gets a sense of the severity of the crime of *abigeato*. When it represented a lifestyle rather than an isolated act of desperation, cattle rustling was an unforgivable crime that disrupted public order and therefore required swift and exemplary justice. If the Peruvian court made an example of anyone, however, it was neither Ignacio nor his buddies. Instead, the court found the janitor Fernando Tapahuasco solely responsible for the crime and sentenced him to a year in prison. Court records leave no indication that any of the accused youths served any jail time.[76]

This must have been particularly unsettling for the Chuschino plaintiffs and authorities, for it convinced them that Ignacio no longer cherished the common good. The numerous references to Ignacio's delinquent background and character were intended to paint an image of him as a youngster who had gone astray from the Chuschino pack. Although the plaintiffs never suggested it, they may have seen Ignacio as a geographical and intellectual deviant as well as a moral one, for the boy now lived and studied in Ayacucho City. Moreover, in stealing horses owned by the village council as well as those owned by individual Chuschinos, Ignacio demonstrated his prioritization of personal livelihood and enrichment (i.e., getting an education) over that of the community and his fellow *comuneros*.

The Men with the Staffs: Customary Authority and Justice in Chuschi

The recalcitrance of the men and youths described above speaks to a deeper crisis in Chuschi's system of customary authority and justice. Chuschi's system, like that of many Andean communities, was run by the *varayoqs*.[77] The *varayoqs* operated as a sort of moral authority, charged with reinforcing villagers' collective values by ensuring that they practiced reciprocity, participated in communal works projects, observed important religious rituals and festivities, and looked out for the communal good. Since they had virtually no legal power in the eyes of the state, Chuschi's *varayoqs* held largely symbolic authority. Status within the prestige hierarchy was directly related to the amount of public service that male *varayoqs* provided to the community. The higher the rank of the *varayoq*, the more respect he commanded from the *comuneros*.[78] Wooden staffs known as *varas* symbolically reinforced the authority of the *varayoqs*. The higher the rank of the *varayoq*, the more ornate was his staff.[79] Although single adolescents could enter at the lowest end of the prestige hierarchy as *alguacil* (constable), most of the power was in the hands of married men.[80]

This customary authority structure began to lose legitimacy during the latter half of the twentieth century. One *varayoq* articulated this concern to anthropologist Billie Jean Isbell, complaining that "everyone used to tremble at the sight of the staff, but no more. We have lost our authority and no one pays us proper respect as they should."[81] Apparently, the peasant who made this statement was not the only one who felt this way, for in January 1970 *comuneros* decided to abolish the entire high-authority structure, reasoning that the *varayoqs* "were no longer necessary and cost too much, and that the prestige and respect previously accorded the *hatun* [high] authorities had all but disappeared."[82] Why did customary authorities lose legitimacy during this period?

This breakdown in Chuschi's traditional authority structure was due in large part to changing demographics. Beginning in the 1940s Peru experienced a population boom unlike any other in the nation's history.[83] A number of factors contributed to this boom, such as the development and dissemination of new vaccinations, a sinking infant mortality rate, and the construction of new irrigation and drainage systems. As a result, Peru's population rose from 6.5 million in 1940 to 9 million in 1961; a decade later, that number had jumped to 13.5 million.[84] This population boom was widespread, affecting the highlands and lowlands alike. In Ayacucho, it was coupled with an untimely ecological crisis. In the 1940s, severe hailstorms and frosts devastated crops throughout the department, precipitating an economic recession that would last for decades. In response to this rural crisis, the Peruvian government in the 1940s began controlling agricultural prices, making it extremely difficult for peasants to profit from farming. Many began looking for new ways to make a living.[85]

From the 1940s onward, waves of Andean peasants began flooding Peru's coastal capital in search of employment and better wages.[86] Scores of highland peasants occupied vacant lots on the outskirts of Lima and converted them into squatter settlements known as *barriadas*. Later, under the first Belaúnde government of the 1960s, populist politicians began referring to these communities as *pueblos jóvenes*, or young towns, a politically correct term connoting development and modernization. Although the inhabitants came from all across the highlands, two departments produced more settlers than any others in Peru. One was Ancash; the other was Ayacucho.[87]

One of the consequences of this demographic shift was a breakdown in local authority and justice in the countryside. No longer inhibited by the moral pressures traditionally imposed on them by village elders, authorities, and kinship networks, Andean men began to challenge traditionally established behavioral norms. Moreover, if someone as physically powerful as Felipe Aycha were to refuse a *varayoq*'s order, the latter had very little recourse, particularly since the Peruvian juridical system would not back him up. By the 1960s and 1970s, it was clear to most Chuschinos that local authorities were no more reliable than the state judiciary when it came to administering justice.

These structural factors also contributed to the rise in youth delinquency. Young people, particularly men, made up the majority of migrants who left their rural communities for cities such as Ayacucho and Lima. These young men often returned to their communities questioning long-established notions regarding local authority and searching beyond traditional avenues to upward social mobility.

One way young men and women sought to improve their status was through education. As Ignacio Aycha claimed, crime could be a means to pay for university education. Increased access to education—both at the university and high school levels—may also have led some rural youth to question and challenge the status quo.[88] Because they could theoretically achieve upward social mobility and prestige via education, some educated youths felt less obliged to respect customary authority and practices. For others, public education opened their eyes to the many injustices that existed in the Peruvian countryside, therefore prompting them to challenge and resist the status quo.

THE VILLAGERS I HAVE DESCRIBED were a type of local power holder. Their power stemmed not from class, race, or political authority but from their ability to disregard local mores without consequence. Because of this, *comuneros* considered their power illegitimate and were on the lookout for alternative means of bringing them to justice. This search for an alternative justice was all the more important given the structural changes that the community was undergoing during the middle of the twentieth century.

But these structural changes affected different communities at different rates. Not all villages experienced emigration at the same rate as Chuschi, or with the same consequences. Huaychao, which operated as a hacienda until the mid-1970s, did not experience rapid emigration. The Huaychaino *comuneros* who left the Huanta highlands to live in Lima could be counted on one hand, and there is no record that any villagers ever obtained more than a high school education. Because their livelihood was based in Huaychao, Huaychaino peasants felt less inclined to challenge local forms of authority and justice. This is not to say that Huaychao was free of the kinds of social infractions that existed in Chuschi. What differed between the villages, though, was the effectiveness of customary authority and justice in settling these conflicts and, by extension, preserving internal order.

Conflict and Resolution in Huaychao

As we sat discussing how men from different communities challenged one another's masculinity during fiestas, I was struck by a comment made by Esteban Huamán, a Huaychaino in his fifties: "If someone who you think has stolen your livestock starts acting macho, then you put him in his place by saying, 'Oh, you must be so macho from eating all my livestock!'"[89] This statement suggests that Huaychaino men distinguished between the type of bravado displayed by "honorable" men and that of cattle rustlers, whose masculinity they saw as illegitimate because it was earned through dishonorable means. The social stigma associated with cattle rustling served as a sort of moral check against the practice, which is just one reason livestock theft was not a major source of conflict in Huaychao as it was in Chuschi. Whereas several Chuschinos and Quispillacctinos appeared poised to professionalize *abigeato*, no single Huaychaino stands out in the archival record or in collective memory as a career rustler. This is not to say that livestock theft did not occur in Huaychao; it was as commonplace in the Iquichano highlands as it was anywhere else at the time. What distinguishes Huaychao from Chuschi is that when peasants did engage in the act, they typically targeted livestock from *other* villages.[90] I discuss this intervillage theft in greater detail in the next chapter. For now, let us turn to the exceptional instances in which intravillage livestock theft made it to trial. It is in their exceptional nature that these recorded cases of intravillage cattle rustling in Huaychao explain why the practice there never reached the scale that it did elsewhere in Ayacucho.

Footprints: Cattle Rustling

In 1967 Víctor Guillén, a peasant in his late twenties, testified to having stolen a cow from one of his Huaychaino neighbors. It all began one February evening, Guillén claimed, when Víctor Quispe, a friend from the village of Pucaraccay, passed through Huaychao and suggested that the two of them go looking for cattle to steal. Guillén had hoped to steal the cattle from another community, but it was late and they could easily see that his neighbor Francisco Cayetano had left his cattle unattended. The two Víctors untied one of the cows and took it with them back to Quispe's home in Pucaraccay, where they slaughtered it together. They had planned on selling the meat the next day and splitting the profit, so Guillén stayed the night at Quispe's home. The next morning, Guillén awoke to the warning calls of Quispe's teenage sons, who announced the arrival of Cayetano's search committee. The committee had traced the footprints of the stolen heifer through the mud and into the village. Panicked, Guillén shoved the meat into the hollow trunk of a peppertree and hid inside Quispe's home; Quispe had already fled the scene. When Cayetano's committee found Guillén in the home, he had little choice but to come clean.[91]

Here, we find that the theft involved not only Huaychainos. Guillén's partner in crime was a peasant from a distant village who offered him an external and seemingly safe refuge in the aftermath of the theft. Rare were the instances in which Huaychainos stole one another's animals without involving third parties from outside villages. The obvious explanation for this is that it would have been difficult for a local peasant to steal from his neighbor without the entire village learning of it. Yet this only gives us part of the explanation. Chuschi was also a small village, albeit not nearly as small as Huaychao, and yet the prospect of public scrutiny, gossip, and scandal was not sufficient to keep Chuschinos from living a life of robbery. Why, then, were Huaychainos more reluctant than Chuschinos to steal from their neighbors?

The exceptional 1979 conflict between Cesário Pacheco and Lucas Ccente, both from the annex of Macabamba, provides us with some clues. Ccente's was one of two criminal cases between the years 1940 and 1983 for which a Huaychaino stood accused of stealing another Huaychaino's animals. Pacheco lost five rams during Carnival. While drinking with his neighbors one night, Pacheco learned that his fifty-five-year-old neighbor Lucas Ccente, together with his twenty-three-year-old son, Elías, had stolen the sheep. Enraged, Pacheco beat Elías, giving him a black eye. But Pacheco was not finished. Later that night, he and two of his relatives—one of them a woman—barged into the house where Lucas was sleeping and began hitting him over the head with rocks. According to Lucas, his attackers literally took the shirt off his back, leaving him half naked and half dead. Lucas immediately reported the incident to Huaychao's communal authorities, but the local leaders declined to take action.[92]

Lucas Ccente vowed to take the law into his own hands: "If I don't get justice in my village of Huaychao for what [the Pachecos] have done to me, then [my son and I] will have no choice but to fight our enemies to the death."[93] When Cesário Pacheco learned that Lucas was seeking revenge, he brought criminal charges against him for conspiracy to murder. In the ensuing criminal case, Lieutenant Governor Santos Quispe, one of the authorities who had earlier declined to intervene on Lucas's behalf, penned a letter to the judge in support of Pacheco. In it, the communal authority juxtaposed Pacheco, a man of "honor," with Lucas Ccente, a "common criminal and thief" who had stolen from Pacheco and others. Moreover, Quispe said that Lucas had lost all his neighbors' respect since it was well known that he would often hit local women "as if they were animals."[94]

The judge threw out the case, ruling that Lucas Ccente's verbal threats alone were not enough to convict him of conspiracy to murder.[95] The verdict does illustrate a major philosophical difference between state and local authority with respect to justice, however. By taking no action against Lucas Ccente's aggressors, village authorities such as Santos Quispe were tacitly approving Pacheco's vigilante justice. The reason for this was that, as Quispe later articulated, Lucas Ccente's neighbors saw him as a local cattle rustler and woman abuser who had it coming. This was the sort of judgment that only local indigenous authorities who were attuned to the nuances of each individual case could provide, and it was the main reason that their authority was so valued in the village.

The Throne of Gold: Customary Authority and Justice

Communal President Fortunato Huamán pulled a whistle from his pocket and stepped out of the *despacho*. Fortunato, a Huaychaino in his midsixties, climbed atop a soggy hill and gave three long, loud blows on the whistle before returning to the dusty assembly room. Within moments, dozens of men, women, and children had gathered in the room, taking seats along the stone stumps that lined its walls. The villagers had convened that morning to participate in Tiyarikuy (the Seating or Enthroning), an annual fiesta in honor of the *teniente gobernador* (lieutenant governor) and the *varayoqs*. The guests of honor sat behind a table opposite the *comuneros*. Once everyone had been seated, President Fortunato addressed the villagers in Quechua, inviting them to bring any matters of local concern to the attention of the communal authorities. After several men and women had stood up and done this, a teenage boy poured a small portion of soda into a single cup and handed it to the lieutenant governor. The latter then lifted the cup in a toast, took a sip, poured the remainder onto the dirt floor, and passed the cup to his chief *varayoq*. This ritual was repeated until the cup had gone around the entire assembly room several times and all the soda had been consumed.[96]

Varayoqs of Huaychao with authority staffs. Photograph by Oscar Medrano, *Caretas*; reprinted with permission.

At one point, President Fortunato invited me to take a picture and video footage of the entire room for their *recuerdos* (memories). When I got around to the *varayoqs* and the lieutenant governor, the authorities insisted on posing with their *varas*. When I asked President Fortunato what the staffs represented, he explained that they were symbols of respect and power. "Like stripes on a military officer," chimed in Leandro, Fortunato's nephew and a former soldier in the Peruvian military. Leandro and his uncle told me that before the period of political violence, a *varayoq* would never have been seen in public without his *vara*. "That way, people could know from a distance who was in charge in this community," Leandro boasted. "Were *varayoqs* around even during the days of the hacienda?" I asked. President Fortunato nodded: "Even before, *hermano*. And back then, the *varayoqs* were even *more* respected than today. . . . [They were] even *feared*, because they had so much power!"[97]

As President Fortunato said this, Clemencia Quispe and Serafina Rimachi stood up and announced that they were going to perform a Qarawiy, a song of reverence for the *varayoqs*. Singing a high-pitched tone, the women cried as they cited the Quechua verse that had been passed on to them by their mothers and grandmothers:

Señor Authority
How well enthroned you are
Oh how enthroned you are
Aww [reverence]

On a throne of gold
On a golden seat
Aww

You have no idea what
Life has in store for me
Aww

How hard you work to serve the people
[???]
Aww

You are like the *jilguero* [a species of wild bird]
That gives food
Aww

Soon you will know, Señor Authority
Señor Governor
Aww

How to talk with the people
Live with the people
Aww

Talk, Converse
Señor Authority
Señor Governor
Aww, Aww, Aww, Aww[98]

One of the main reasons why Huaychainos had respected their authorities so much then and in years past was because of the authorities' role in administering justice and upholding public order within the community. In what follows, I will articulate this argument by discussing the role of Huaychao's principle authorities during the period leading up to, and following, the Agrarian Reform. Before the land reform, which reached Huaychao in 1975–76, the main indigenous authorities in the region were the customary *varayoqs* (also known as *envarados*), the lieutenant governor, and the foremen of the region's haciendas, known as *caporales* or *administradores*. As part of Velasco's reforms, the positions of president and vigilance councilman were also created.

Of these authorities, the only ones with no official ties to outside institutions (e.g., the state, the hacienda) were the customary *varayoqs*. Unofficially, however, the *varayoqs* became co-opted by the state bureaucracy, serving as political underlings of the lieutenant governor. The oldest Huaychainos, people in their late nineties, remember this civil-religious prestige hierarchy being around long before the state bureaucracy was in place. As in other Andean villages such as Chuschi, the chief function of Huaychao's *varayoqs* was to preserve the community's core social, economic, and political structures and uphold public order. The prestige hierarchy was inclusive and participatory only to the extent that (1) village heads of household collectively determined who would serve each year, and (2) it was a rotational post, meaning that all qualified villagers could, and indeed were expected to, participate. Yet, since only married men could enter the prestige hierarchy—and by extension participate in local political life—village politics were actually quite exclusive.

Consequently, the traditional authority structure in Huaychao, as in Chuschi, was rigidly patriarchal. Huaychainos even conceived of this authority system through a gendered prism. Take Ciprián Quispe, who entered the prestige hierarchy in the early 1980s as an *albacea*, a sort of apprentice or personal servant to the *varayoqs*. When asked to describe his duties, *tayta* Ciprián, now in his fifties, told us, "I was like the *varayoq*'s wife, because I knew what the *varayoq* drank, what he ate. . . . I even had to wait around while he slept." The gendered aspect of this relationship was not lost on the other *varayoqs*, either. According to *tayta* Ciprián, the customary authorities would tease young Huaychaino men who had not yet ascended to the position. Authorities treated these newcomers "as if they were young women," aiming their authority staffs at them and mocking, "bend over and take this *vara*!" All this changed as soon as *tayta* Ciprián became authority: "After I became *varayoq*, everything was fine. . . . After you become *varayoq*, no one teases you anymore."[99]

As was the case in Chuschi, Huaychao's authority structure was age-based. Younger newlyweds entered at the bottom rungs of the hierarchy, while men who were older and had been married longer held higher-ranking positions, enjoying more social prestige and respect. Newly anointed *varayoqs* also depended on village elders for tutelage. As *tayta*

Ciprián explained, the elders expected younger *varayoqs* to heed their advice in order to ensure that the authorities ran the community properly from one generation to the next: "As soon as you got married the [elders] would say, 'You have to serve [as *varayoq*] now. . . . And you have to do it while we are still alive, because if you wait until we have passed away there will be no one around to teach you and help you.'" This help came not only in the form of mentorship, but also in a very tangible form, for it was the elder men and women in the community who typically prepared food and drink for the authorities during their tenure in office.[100] In short, elders had a practical, valuable social function within the community's patriarchal structure.

One of the main points that elder men and women tried to get across to young *varayoqs* concerned their social life. *Tayta* Ciprián remembered that Huaychaino elders had made him promise to "cut off his tail" before becoming a *varayoq* in the early 1980s. Asked to expand on this, the erstwhile *varayoq* explained, "When you become an authority, you can only drink at home with your family, and you can no longer parade around the mountains during Carnival. And if you don't stop your old ways then folks will hit you and shun you, and you will bring dishonor and disrespect [to your post]. And that's why they would say: 'You must cut off your tail.'"[101] As was the case elsewhere in the Andes, young singles in Huaychao typically used the occasion of Carnival to engage in carnal relations outside of the village center. The message against drinking outside of the home and frolicking about in the mountains was thus a clear warning for young *varayoqs* to practice sexual fidelity. They were now not only married but also the political face of the community. As such, they needed to exhibit moral authority.

Another reason why Huaychainos required their customary authorities to exhibit sound moral judgment was because they turned to these same authorities to administer justice. "Sure there were some [abusive] authorities," Alejandra Ccente, a villager in her sixties, told us one day, "but they resolved conflicts." *Mama* Alejandra explained that when neighbors quarreled over livestock theft, land boundaries, or domestic issues, the *varayoqs* were the ones who went to the location of the conflict to settle the matter: "The [other] authorities [the lieutenant governor and later the communal president] didn't go to the homes [of the people involved in the dispute]; they stayed in their *despacho*. Only the *varayoqs* were dispatched to resolve the issue. When there was a problem, they would show up on the scene and announce: 'We've been sent by the [lieutenant governor] to resolve this problem.'"[102] Only if they failed to resolve the issue on their own would the *varayoqs* then bring the afflicted parties before the lieutenant governor, who served as the ultimate arbiter of justice at the community level. In this sense, *varayoqs* served as unofficial policemen, responsible for helping the lieutenant governor maintain internal security. Now in his mid-sixties, former *varayoq* Isidro Huamán explained: "[The *varayoq*] was like the lieutenant governor's right-hand man. There were six in all . . . and they helped the lieutenant governor resolve every type of dispute, and they took turns bringing those who were involved in disputes [to the *despacho*]."[103]

As more than one Huaychaino intimated to me, *varayoqs* were respected, even feared by their fellow villagers because of their capacity to administer justice. In addition to carrying their authority staffs, *varayoqs* used their *chicotes* (whips) against people they deemed guilty of moral transgressions such as excessive domestic violence, theft, and sexual deviance. This last category had less to do with rape than with adultery and incest, as *tayta* Fortunato's experience as *varayoq* elucidates: "There was a rape case from [the annex of] Tupín when I was *secretario*. The rapist had raped his blood sister, so we took him back here [to central Huaychao] and detained him and interrogated him until he confessed: 'How many times did you rape her? Where, in the mountains?' . . . Of course, we [flogged him with a *chicote* three times:] Father, Son, Holy Ghost."[104] As *tayta* Ciprián told us, villagers associated strong leadership with the ability to administer justice: "[An authority was considered good] if he cared for his neighbors while at the same time knowing how to resolve conflicts [between villagers]. If he did those things we would say, 'Now that guy is doing a good job and is within his rights.'" When asked if any authorities ever overstepped their boundaries, *tayta* Ciprián shook his head: "Only the *abigeos* [were out of line], not the authorities. The authorities only whipped people with the *chicote* if they had it coming, like if they hit or left their wife."[105]

These authorities also settled violent altercations between fellow villagers. *Mama* Alejandra discussed the nature of these fights: "Back in those days men would fight hard, especially during Carnival. They'd hit each other with *esquilas* [a bronze musical instrument typically played during the festivities], and with *látigos* [leather whips, longer than *chicotes*]." After these clashes, communal authorities would intervene to effect reconciliation between the opposing sides. Seventy-six-year-old Brígida Cayetana described this process: "[The authorities] might whip [the fighters] with a *chicote* and then have them face each other and ask each other forgiveness right there in front of the authorities and the [religious] effigies. [The fighters] would then hug each other and say, 'Forgive me.'"[106] *Mama* Alejandra made a similar observation, adding that after reconciling, the two sides, together with the authorities, would partake in a libation ceremony in the presence of the communal patron saints. "After that," she said, "the two sides would forget about everything [they were fighting about] and go about their business as if nothing had ever happened."[107] To be sure, this highly ritualized act of reconciliation did not always do the trick, and sometimes the two neighbors would walk away vowing to revisit the conflict "whenever, wherever," as *mama* Brígida put it.[108] Yet the ritualized display of physical humiliation followed by reconciliation served as a public reminder of why one ought to avoid such confrontation in the first place.

And if physical and moral retribution did not do the trick, the civil one often did. "The authorities would make people pay each other for blood spilled during a fight," *mama* Brígida explained. "They would pay [the aggrieved party] money or, if it was a lot of blood, they might have to give [the other party] a goat."[109] *Tayta* Ciprián made a similar observation involving a case that he resolved during his tenure as *varayoq*: "One time I brought an *abigeo* before the lieutenant governor and together we settled the matter. [The *abigeo*] was from right here in Huaychao, and he had robbed two sheep. So we told him he had to repay the owner, which he did, because he admitted to it, saying, 'I'm guilty.'" Asked if he had physically punished the guilty party, *tayta* Ciprián shook his head: "*Manam* [No]. We never physically punished them when they admitted it. We only did that when [the suspect] started acting macho, saying 'I didn't do it and I assume no responsibility.'"[110]

This last statement led me to the distressing conclusion that authorities probably flogged innocent people. After discussing the issue further with *tayta* Ciprián and other former *varayoqs*, however, I realized that it was not so much the *denial* of guilt that got people into trouble as the *way* the suspect pleaded his case. The emphasis in *tayta* Ciprián's statement, for instance, was on the fact that the suspect "*se puso macho* [started acting macho]," rather than on the denial per se.[111] *Tayta* Isidro explained this to Julián and me one afternoon: "[*Varayoqs* whipped people] for not respecting their authority. People knew they had the authority to do that, which is why they tried their best to behave themselves and to give them due respect."[112]

Another way for *varayoqs* to administer justice was through the use of the *juez rumi*, the rock of justice. The *juez rumi* is a five-foot-tall, three-foot-wide boulder occupying the center of Huaychao's village square. Huaychainos claim the rock has been there since their "grandparents' time," and it remains there to this day. Whenever authorities wanted to make an example of someone for a social breach they considered too minor for economic sanctions or a flogging, they would tie the guilty party's hands behind his back with a rope, press his back to the *juez rumi*, and tie him to the rock with a longer rope.

Tayta Ciprián, who was born in the mid-1950s, admitted that communal authorities never resorted to this form of punishment during his lifetime, but he said that his father and grandfather mentioned having used it on the hacienda. They told him that one type of infraction deserving of this punishment had to do with communal work projects, the *faenas*: "Back then when they constructed the fence surrounding the village square some people would neglect to bring their own rock to the *faena* [to contribute to the construction] . . . and whoever came without their rock was tied to the [*juez*] *rumi*. . . . They would tie them upright to that [*juez*] *rumi* instead of punishing them with a *chicote*. Afterward [the authorities] would let them go and they would return carrying their own rock [for the fence construction]."[113] Mariano Quispe, who was at least twenty years Ciprián's elder, could not remember a specific incident in which authorities had used this technique, either. Nevertheless, he confirmed *tayta* Ciprián's story, claiming that people had been tied to the rock for not helping to build the local church. *Tayta* Mariano added that authorities also submitted more serious offenders, such as thieves and adulterers, to the rock of justice. Yet after tying villagers to the boulder for these more serious offenses, authorities would also have them publicly flogged.[114] *Tayta* Isidro's parents told him the same thing, saying that, more than any other offenders, it was the *abigeos* who received this treatment.[115]

Perhaps the most remarkable thing about the *juez rumi* is that there is no definitive evidence that it was ever actually used as a method of justice. Whenever elders mentioned the rock, they did so with the caveat that they never actually saw it used as a form of punishment. All they could say was that the rock was in place as long as they could remember and that their parents spoke of using it to administer justice on the hacienda. It is entirely possible, then, that the *juez rumi* was an "invented tradition," a sort of local fable that served as a constant public reminder to Huaychainos of the fate that *could* await them if they ever placed self-interest ahead of the community.[116] Notice, for example, that the first people supposedly brought to justice by the rock were those believed to have fallen short of their collective labor obligations at the very moment when the key symbols of the community—the local church, the village square—were being constructed. Likewise, those who ostensibly experienced the more severe punishment of being tied to the rock *and* flogged were villagers whose material and sexual avarice had jeopardized communal solidarity: people like the adulterers and the socially denigrated *abigeos*. In the final analysis, the issue of whether the *juez rumi* was actually used to enforce moral conduct on the hacienda or whether it was a narrative fabrication is irrelevant. Either way, it served as a discursive symbol that had shaped local historical memory and reinforced social mores about village justice. Whether or not Huaychainos had actually used the technique themselves mattered little, for they knew exactly how they *could* use it should circumstances so require—something to keep in mind when we discuss Huaychainos' initial responses to Shining Path.

Although a good deal of the *varayoqs'* authority derived from their ability to administer justice, this alone was not enough to legitimize their power. Equally important was the extent to which they honored villagers' expectations of paternalism. We need look no further than the Tiyarikuy ceremony for evidence of this. The lyrics of the Qarawiy emphasized the service aspect of the job, reminding incoming authorities of their duty to "feed" their constituents, as a mother bird would her chicks. This notion was reinforced when each villager drank from the *varayoqs'* cup before consuming food that the latter had prepared for the occasion.[117] Both the lyrics and the ritual consumption reminded the new patriarchs that they would ultimately be held responsible for the well-being of a village susceptible to famine and drought. But villagers held their leaders responsible for more than their material livelihood. As *mama* Alejandra told us, women who participated in the ceremony—her mother included—spoke for the collective when they reminded the new authorities: "We are in your hands now, *señores autoridades*. This year we are with you. We are *all* your children now."[118]

Huaychainos believed that the best way for *varayoqs* to achieve this paternalistic leadership was through an open dialogue with their constituents. The notion of "talking" and "conversing" with the villagers appears in the lyrics of the Qarawiy and is reinforced at the outset of the ceremony when villagers bring local matters to the attention of the new leaders. Another tradition that preceded the Tiyarikuy was the *vara visita* (*vara* visit). During this occasion, which took place at the beginning of each year, when the new *varayoqs* were named, the incoming leaders would visit each household in Huaychao and its annexes. The six *varayoqs* and their assistants would approach each peasant household explaining that they were the new *varayoqs* and they would serve at the pleasure of the community. The authorities would take the occasion to cordially invite the heads of household to attend the upcoming Tiyarikuy ceremony in their honor. In turn, the heads of household would then treat their guests to drinks of *trago* (liquor), raising their cups and toasting, "*Michiykuwankiku, difindiykuwankiku* [You will be our shepherds, you will defend us]."[119]

The main authority to whom the *varayoqs* answered was the lieutenant governor. It is unclear when the position of the lieutenant governor was created in Huaychao, but it appears to have already been in place when hacendado Enrique Juscamaita purchased the estate in 1962. Lieutenant governors were technically state officials, intended to serve as bureaucratic mediators between the regional government and the local populace. Huaychao's lieutenant governors responded directly to the governor in Huanta City. Unlike in Chuschi, where most bureaucratic officials were appointed mestizos, lieutenant governors in Huaychao were drawn from and elected by the indigenous peasantry.[120] Huaychainos thus held these local political leaders to the same cultural standard to which they held their *varayoqs*. At the same time, villagers recognized that a lieutenant governor's uniqueness lay in the fact that his authority had been legitimized by the state. This could be potentially advantageous, for the officials could serve as the community's political ambassadors to the Peruvian government. For this reason, Huaychainos exalted the position of lieutenant governor to the top of the local hierarchy, conferring on these leaders more administrative power than the *varayoqs* themselves. Understandably, this power sometimes fomented tensions between these indigenous bureaucrats and their fellow villagers or *varayoqs*. For the most part, however, Huaychainos increasingly legitimized the lieutenant governor's political rule because of his symbolic and actual role in enforcing moral conduct and upholding collective interests, values, and public order through a customary administration of justice.

Jesús Ccente was one of these authorities during the hacienda period. In 1963 Subprefect Vidal Alcántara Cárdenas issued a letter to the governor of Huanta District reprimanding him for failing to control Ccente. Describing the lieutenant governor as "a leading agitator of the Indians of the Huaychao estate," Alcántara ordered the governor to fire Ccente immediately and bring him into custody. Three days later a frustrated Alcántara reported to the departmental prefect that his efforts to capture the recalcitrant Huaychaino had been unsuccessful.[121] While the written record left no indication of the specifics of the case, Ccente's contemporaries told Julián and me that Ccente had been leading an effort to dismantle the hacienda at the time. This is very likely, given that a broader, grassroots struggle for land reform had been developing in the Huanta highlands that same year. Today, Huaychainos credit Ccente for having brought land reform to Huaychao.[122]

Another lieutenant governor on Juscamaita's hacienda was Zenobio Quispe, who assumed the post in August 1972. State authorities seemed happier with Quispe's comportment as a local leader than with Ccente's. When census taker Marcial Huamán visited the hacienda in September 1972, he reported to his superior in Huanta City that Quispe was a man "of great humanist character" who extended him the utmost respect and hospitality during his visit. The same could not be said of the *varayoqs*, he lamented. During Huamán's entire visit to Huaychao, the customary authorities had wanted nothing to do with him, remaining, he speculated, "hidden or lost or something." Locals told the census taker that the chief *varayoq* was ill and could not meet with him, while second-in-command Marcelo Yaranqa "failed to recognize the authority of the lieutenant governor" and disappeared after a brief meeting with the state official.[123]

What the census taker might not have known was that the lieutenant governor's political legitimacy was being challenged at the time. Following the official's visit to the hacienda, Quispe penned a note to the census bureau's provincial engineer complaining that Yaranqa and the other *varayoqs* had no respect for his authority. In addition to the customary authorities' failing to participate in the census, Quispe explained, Yaranqa had begun a local campaign against him and the Peruvian state.[124] The *varayoq* Yaranqa joined with three other *comuneros* in explaining villagers' opposition to the local leader. As far as they were concerned, Quispe had been appointed lieutenant governor "to uphold moral [conduct] and good customs" on the hacienda. In this regard, they informed the subprefect, the lieutenant governor "left much to be desired." Quispe, a married man, had been living with another woman. At the same time, he had "given away" his twenty-two-year-old daughter to another married man. Quispe had done all this, they complained, "with no respect for social mores." The petitioners explained that these actions were particularly offensive coming from a communal authority: "Given that an immoral authority loses the respect of his neighbors, it is necessary to have him removed."[125] Records do not specify whether the subprefect granted the Huaychainos' request, but they do reveal that Quispe was no longer lieutenant governor as of 1975.[126]

What was behind this insubordination on the part of the *varayoqs* and *comuneros*? It is important to contextualize this rift historically. The census being taken at the time was known as a *censo agropecuario*, pertaining to agriculture and livestock. It was undertaken by the Revolutionary Government of the Armed Forces in accordance with the Agrarian Reform Law, enacted in 1968. The land reform first reached the Iquichano highlands around the time this census was taken, between 1972 and 1975. The *varayoqs* may have sensed that they would lose their local hegemony to the lieutenant governor if the hacienda were dismantled. Along the same lines, they may have sided with the hacendado and therefore saw no practical reason to replace him as the principal arbiter of justice in the community.[127] These structural changes do not entirely explain the conflict, however, for there was also an important cultural component. The complaint about Quispe's sexual deviance is consistent with the descriptions that Huaychainos gave us about the standard of conduct to which they held their *varayoqs*. Even though he was under no moral contract in the eyes of the Peruvian government, indigenous Huaychainos felt strongly that, as a local leader, Quispe needed to exhibit sound moral judgment when it came to his gendered conduct.

Other ways for a lieutenant governor to lose his moral authority were to associate with cattle rustlers or administer justice improperly. To Anselmo Quispe, an indigenous man from the annex of Ccochaccocha, Lieutenant Governor Vicente Quispe was guilty of both. It all started, Anselmo told the judge, in July 1980, just seven months after Vicente had been nominated lieutenant governor. Three locals had recently stolen a pair of horses and a mule during a trip to the neighboring province of La Mar. When they returned to Huaychao, the lieutenant governor forged a certificate of ownership for the three animals so that they could sell them. But rather than endorse the certificate himself, Vicente signed Anselmo's name on it. Sure enough, the owner of the stolen animals found them along with the forged certificate and sent police to arrest Anselmo. Anselmo claimed that the lieutenant governor had later apologized to him for his actions, but when Anselmo made it clear that he would press charges, Vicente detained him in the village holding cell and submitted him to physical abuse. "This authority," Anselmo added, "is involved in a conspiracy and coverup and has abandoned his duty as administrator of justice."[128] Once again, the criminal proceedings do not indicate how the case was resolved, but we do know that the following year Huaychaino Pedro Huamán had replaced Vicente Quispe as lieutenant governor.[129] As numerous Huaychaino elders told Julián and me, Pedro Huamán was a man of honor and integrity. For this reason, villagers elected him as the community's first president around 1980.

Anselmo Quispe's accusation demonstrates a shared assumption among Huaychainos that the lieutenant governor's most important duty was to administer justice—and to do so fairly. Huaychainos only brought the most serious offenses to the attention of the lieutenant governor, cases involving repeat offenders who had failed to correct behavior that violated social norms. These included *abigeos*, fathers who had abandoned their families, and cheating spouses.[130] These were also cases that the *varayoqs* alone could not resolve. *Mama* Alejandra reminisced about the effectiveness of this system one morning: "In those days [of the hacienda and immediately afterward], the authorities were honorable. The lieutenant governor would tell [his *varayoqs*], 'Find those [wrongdoers] wherever they may be and bring them to me to solve the problem.'"[131] The lieutenant governor, *mama* Alejandra added, also had the power to discipline people who had failed to recognize the authority of the *varayoqs*: "People used to obey the [*varayoqs*' orders] without question, because if someone talked back, saying, 'Get lost, I've got livestock to graze!' then the *varayoqs* would report this to the lieutenant governor and without hesitation he'd lock the person who disrespected the authority in the holding cell . . . for a really long time."[132]

Once an internal conflict had been brought to the attention of the lieutenant governor, he could draw from a number of customary techniques to resolve it. Like the *varayoqs*, a lieutenant governor carried a whip. Yet whereas the *varayoqs* used the smaller *chicote*, the lieutenant governors carried the *látigo*, which was longer and with a nastier bite. Only the lieutenant governors are said to have had the authority to tie suspected wrongdoers to the *juez rumi* or demand civil retribution; the *varayoqs* merely aided in the process. Lieutenant governors also had the sole authority to lock deviants in the holding cell for as long as they saw fit. Finally, the *despacho* itself had the psychological impact of a police station, for it was the location where the lieutenant governor carried out his interrogations and hearings. Thus, unlike the *varayoqs*, who went out to investigate local disputes, the lieutenant governor had the psychological advantage of administering justice on his own turf. Seventy-year-old Santos Huaylla told us about an occasion when he had reported a cattle rustler to the lieutenant governor. Once the suspect had entered the *despacho*, the lieutenant governor had the man's hands tied behind his back with a rope and began flogging him. Between lashes, the authority interrogated the suspect: "Why did you steal? [I won't stop whipping] until you talk or confess!"[133] The best lieutenant governors, however, only employed these tactics as a last resort. *Tayta* Ciprián remembered with satisfaction a time when he had reported a fellow villager to the lieutenant governor for stealing one of his sheep. Rather than castigate the suspect, the authority simply shamed him into confession: "He said, 'Why did you steal from this person? If you're going to steal, you should steal from somewhere far away.' And so the guy answered: 'I admit I was wrong to do it and I'll pay him back.'"[134] Thus, even though there were plenty of cases of conflict between authorities and their subordinates, this alone was not enough to undermine their political legitimacy. In the final analysis, Huaychainos recognized that the lieutenant governors, like the *varayoqs*, served an important function with respect to the local administration of justice and communal security.

The only local authority not to survive the 1975 land reform was the *caporal*, whose official duty was to ensure that his fellow peasants worked diligently for his boss, the hacienda lord. On the one hand, *caporales* served as mediators between the indigenous tenants and the hacendado. On the other hand, *caporales* had a rather tenuous relationship with the indigenous peasantry because their power was not necessarily consensual. *Varayoqs* were always chosen by indigenous heads of household. Even lieutenant governors were nominated by their indigenous constituencies, although final approval of the provincial subprefect had to be obtained for all such appointments.[135] In contrast, hacendados handpicked their indigenous foremen based on their personal loyalty and capacity to delegate. Nevertheless, Huaychainos still held these local power holders to the same moral standards to which they held their popularly elected leaders.

The story of Huaychaino Luis Huamán, *caporal* of the neighboring hacienda of Tupín, is exemplary.[136] Huamán began working on the estate around 1950, where over the next five years he rented a modest plot of about six *yugadas*.[137] Huamán considered himself a good tenant who paid his rent "punctually" and labored "enthusiastically."[138] Hacendado Julio Ruiz Pozo must have agreed, for he appointed Huamán *caporal* sometime around 1955. Huamán did not last long in his new post, however. In June of that year, Huaychao's lieutenant governor, Basilio Huaylla, penned a letter to the hacendado in which he called Huamán's behavior into question. Speaking on behalf of the other Huaychaino tenants, the local authority charged that Huamán was "a habitual and insolent thief who robs potatoes from the hacienda." Huaylla went on to cite three separate instances in which Huamán had stolen llamas from his fellow tenants. He closed with the following reminder: "Señor Ruis [*sic*], you have the right to correct this matter of criminality and robbery."[139] The hacendado took immediate action, evicting Huamán from the estate and naming Ramón Bautista—Huamán's brother-in-law, no less—as the new *caporal*. Huamán refused to budge, however, remaining on the hacienda through the new year. Then, on 17 February 1956, the mestizo land baron penned his new *caporal* an urgent note:

> Dear Ramón:
> First thing after you arrive [at the estate] tomorrow you all [*sic*] are going to collect all the potatoes that have been harvested on the hacienda and later those with [cargo] animals can bring them to me. Without further [adieu],
> Your sincere *patrón* and yours truly,
> Julio Ruiz Pozo.[140]

Reading between the lines, Bautista took the note as an order to confiscate Huamán's harvest. The next day Bautista appeared before his brother-in-law's home with a small army of about eighteen indigenous serfs and ordered him to turn over his entire potato harvest—roughly twenty-five sacks—to the hacendado.[141]

Although Huamán felt that the mestizo landlord bore some of the blame, he held his brother-in-law primarily responsible for the incident. Lamenting that Bautista's record as *caporal* was "nothing to brag about [*nada recomendable*]," Huamán informed the prefect that Bautista "has taken out all his wrath against me and my family, out of jealousy that all my hard work has paid off in getting me a couple of animals and some economic progress."[142] Bautista maintained that he was merely following the hacendado's orders.[143] The hacendado initially denied this, claiming that his *caporal* had simply misunderstood the spirit of his letter.[144] However, when it became clear that Huamán could not control his behavior, this excuse was no longer necessary. On the morning of 1 February 1957, Bautista accused Huamán of stealing potatoes from his fields in retaliation for his actions of the previous year. At first the two men exchanged words; then they exchanged blows.[145] This was all the proof Ruiz needed to admit that he had indeed intended to evict Huamán. The hacendado explained that his indigenous tenants had denounced Huamán as "a bad seed [*un mal elemento*] and an *abigeo*" and that they had demanded his eviction from the hacienda. Given this situation, he continued, "I had no choice but to have him vacate my estate, and as a consequence he no longer had any right to harvest [his crops], and that's why my new *Caporal* wouldn't even let Huamán near my hacienda." The judge agreed, ruling in favor of hacienda justice.[146] What is interesting about this case is that even though Huamán was not elected by his fellow tenants, they still held him to the same moral standard to which they held other local authorities. Once it was clear that he had failed to adhere to his end of the power pact, the indigenous tenants pressured the hacendado to have him replaced and evicted from the estate. In this way, communal justice prevailed over the avarice of an individual power holder.

Most Huaychainos believed that their *caporales* had done a fair job in living up to their end of the power pact. When asked to talk about their *caporales*, men tended to focus on their overseers' patriarchal qualifications. President Fortunato and *tayta* Esteban, for instance, said that most of their *caporales* "commanded well" and were "most respected" by the hacienda serfs. Similarly, *tayta* Mariano told us that *caporales* "took care of" their workers.[147] Women, on the other hand, tended to focus more on the *caporales*' empathy. Ernestina Ccente, a peasant in her seventies, talked about how the hacienda administrators would explain why they were so bossy: "The *caporal* would order us around in Quechua . . . saying, 'If you don't work faster, the landlord is going to reprimand me.' And so the [serfs] would go ahead and fetch firewood, work the cornfields, etc."[148] *Mama* Alejandra made a similar observation: "[The *caporal*] would make us work, yelling at us occasionally, 'Work hard so that you don't get in trouble with the landlord.'"[149]

More than anything, Huaychainos valued their *caporales'* role in upholding public order and instilling peasants with a solid work ethic on the hacienda. Just as the *varayoqs* of years past were fabled to have tied lazy workers to the *juez rumi*, so the *caporales* patrolled the perimeter of the hacienda to ensure that the serfs labored industriously. The difference, however, was that *caporales* threatened slackers and malingerers with the *chicote*. *Mama* Alejandra remembered that as a child, the adult tenants would alert one another whenever the *caporal* came around: "The *caporal* is coming! Work faster so he doesn't hit us!" After making this statement, *mama* Alejandra reflected, "The *caporal* used to be respected—out of fear."[150] *Tayta* Mariano recalled that *caporales* helped settle disputes that erupted between tenants during work shifts: "The *caporal* alone would reprimand [quarreling tenants] and they would apologize to each other, recognizing that they had simply gotten caught up in the heat of work."[151] Sometimes, sheer reasoning was not enough to resolve these disputes. This was when the threat of the *caporal*'s whip came into play. As *mama* Ernestina recalled, *caporales* sometimes cracked their *chicotes* on the backs of male tenants—women were never punished physically—if deemed necessary to keep workers in line.[152] The fact that *caporales* respected cultural norms with respect to gender and violence may have granted them legitimacy in the eyes of the Huaychainos.

Another way for villagers to validate their *caporales'* authority was to elect them to other leadership positions once their tenure as *caporales* had expired. In this way, the position of the *caporal* and its role in administering local justice was essentially incorporated into the post-hacienda political structure, for it coincided with the creation of two additional political posts, the communal president and the vigilance councilman, and the expansion of the power of the lieutenant governor. Such was the career of Santos Quispe, a former *caporal* who was elected both president and lieutenant governor following the dismantling of the Huaychao hacienda.[153]

THE HIGH ESTEEM in which Huaychainos' held their indigenous authorities cannot be explained as a case of childlike natives blindly adoring their patriarchal leaders. As we have seen, villagers recognized and legitimized the power of these local leaders because of the latter's crucial role in preserving and reproducing the social, political, and cultural fabric of the community. In the absence of a strong state structure in the Iquichano highlands, Huaychainos relied heavily on their indigenous leaders to maintain internal order through a flawed but, in their view, effective system of local justice. Nor was this the first time in their history that peasants from the zone turned to the grassroots to maintain public order. Iquichano peasants created their own extralegal administrative government during the nineteenth century, following Peru's political independence from Spain. From their headquarters at the nearby Uchuraccay hacienda, peasant leaders did everything from collecting tithes, to organizing communal works projects, to administering justice. This parallel justice system settled local disputes involving land, authority, theft, and sexual conduct, offering local peasants a viable alternative to the Peruvian courts.[154] Although Huaychainos today have very little to say of the system that prevailed in the years after independence, its striking resemblance to the current system of authority leads one to surmise that elements of the nineteenth-century system may have remained in place in twentieth-century Huaychao.

Covering the Tracks

Internal conflict was as common in Andean communities as anywhere else. Even when they were equals in terms of race, class, and geographic origin, indigenous peasants still created hierarchies of power. In Huaychao, the hegemony of local authorities prevailed over that of moral backsliders. There, villagers legitimized the rule of the former largely because local authorities could repress violators of social order through a locally, customarily established system of justice. To be sure, the power of Huaychaino authorities was at times a source of conflict. For the most part, however, the moral majority in Huaychao succeeded in displacing abusive, unjust, or immoral leaders from public office.

By contrast, deviants in Chuschi held the upper hand in the internal power struggle precisely because of their ability to disregard morally and culturally established codes of conduct with respect to age, authority, gender, and communal citizenship. One might ask how, given the crisis of justice that developed during this period, Chuschino society remained intact without any major social or political ruptures. As other scholars have pointed out, the perception of external threats can often have a unifying effect within Andean peasant communities, prompting villagers to put long-term antagonisms on hold temporarily, or at least to hold off on radically redressing them until either the threat is extinguished or political opportunities change.[155] As we will see in the next chapter, this is precisely what took place in Chuschi.

CHAPTER 2

To Venture Out

Intercommunity Relations and Conflict

I WAS RESEARCHING in the Regional Archive of Ayacucho when I got an urgent call from Julián. He said that he had checked on seating for the Chuschi *combi* (shuttle), which we were supposed to take the next morning. Since Fiestas Patrias (Independence Day celebrations) were around the corner, the seats were filling up fast; we needed to get our tickets right then and there. I dropped everything and caught a cab to pick up Julián at his CEISA (Center for Social Research of Ayacucho) office. When we arrived at the station—a small garage big enough to fit one van, Julián nudged me and nodded toward the lone graffiti on the wall: "Ojecuna." It took me a moment to register that the writing on the wall was an alternative spelling of the Quechua word *Occekuna*, meaning "darkies." *Occe* was the word that kept coming up in the written historical record whenever the Chuschinos wanted to insult the Quispillacctinos. The word has a double meaning. The salt that is native to Quispillaccta is known for its murky tint. But as many a Chuschino would tell us with a wry smile, the Quispillacctinos were simply more dark-skinned than they, an observation that my own eyes could never quite confirm. For the Chuschinos, then, the Quispillacctinos were a people as darkly complected as the salt that crystallized in their own mountains.[1]

THIS CHAPTER EXPLORES the sources of intercommunity conflict in mid-twentieth-century Ayacucho. The first section overviews the historical context in which these conflicts took place. The second section reconstructs the historic rivalry between Chuschi and Quispillaccta, a conflict understood by indigenous villagers to be an interethnic struggle for control over land, livestock, women, and religious symbols. Turning from Chuschi to Huaychao, the final section shows that the Iquichano village did not have such a clear-cut rival. Instead, Huaychainos were involved in ephemeral conflicts with inhabitants of several nearby communities, never focusing their aggression on a single foe. When conflicts did emerge between Huaychainos and other Iquichanos, they often occurred within the culturally legitimate space of the village fiesta. This, combined with the strong kinship and social networks that tied Huaychainos to other Iquichano villages, mitigated the kind of intercommunity conflict that took shape in Chuschi. But peasant communities mobilized not only against one another during this period. Indeed, these village rivalries can only be understood in the larger context of peasant mobilizations that took place in Peru and elsewhere.

Peasant Mobilization and the Land Movement

The mid-twentieth century was a period of drastic change for peasants around the world. In response to mounting population pressures and capitalist penetration in the countryside, the rural poor in many agricultural nations began mobilizing at an unprecedented rate.[2] While these mobilizations varied in their goals and tactics, a common motivation was the issue of land. One of the earliest and most profound peasant mobilizations during this period took place in Bolivia in 1946 and 1947. There, peasant organization took two forms. The first involved conflicts between serfs and their landowners; the second involved highland communities' massive land invasions of neighboring haciendas.[3] Bolivia's peasant movement took on new force in the wake of the 1952 revolution. By the end of the year, peasants across the countryside had attacked virtually every aspect of the traditional land-tenure system and were posing a serious threat to the stability of the new regime.[4] Over the next thirty years, movements of this kind materialized throughout Latin America. In 1958, for example, 3,000 Mexican peasants invaded 20,000 hectares of irrigated land in the state of Sinaloa.[5] The following decade, some 500 peasant land invasions took place in Venezuela as the nation attempted agrarian reform.[6] In Chile during the late 1960s and early 1970s, Mapuche Indians allied with nonindigenous peasants to carry out massive land grabs throughout the countryside.[7] Nor were these peasant land movements unique to Latin America. In 1959 and 1960, Hutu tenants revolted against their Tutsi overlords in an effort to transform Rwanda's land-tenure system.[8] A similar development occurred in India, where a land invasion in the village of Naxalbari sparked a peasant movement throughout Bengal, with peasants throughout the region carrying out violent attacks against local landlords.[9]

Peruvian peasants also began turning to land invasions during this period. The first major peasant mobilization occurred in late 1959, when villagers from the Pasco communities of Yanacocha and Rancas invaded the hacienda San Juan de Paría, claiming that the lands had belonged to them in the first place.[10] The successful occupation convinced many activists that the forceful takeover of hacienda lands was a viable strategy. Eventually, even hacienda tenants began exploring this option. The most notable case occurred in 1962 in La Convención, a valley in Cuzco Department. Led by Hugo Blanco, a middle-class Trotskyist fluent in Quechua, armed tenants refused to pay rent for their individual plots and eventually invaded those of their landlords as well. Concerned with quelling the budding social unrest in Cuzco, the Peruvian military assumed executive power through a military junta in late 1962 and immediately issued an agrarian reform of La Convención.[11] This served as a watershed moment for peasants across the sierra. Over the next year, peasants across the region began organizing similar occupations. Nor did these mobilizations cease when civilian Fernando Belaúnde Terry claimed the presidency on 28 July 1963. During Belaúnde's first 100 days in office, the newly unionized tenants of Cuzco's Paucartambo valley haciendas organized a massive strike that precipitated an act of reconciliation between the landlords and tenants.[12] By the end of the year, a wave of invasions had swept the department. Most of the occupations pitted peasant communities against hacienda lords, but in some instances it was the hacienda tenants who mobilized against their landlords.[13] Nor were these actions limited to Cuzco. On the day Belaúnde was sworn in, 3,000 villagers from San Pedro de Jajas (Junín Department) invaded 8,000 hectares of Hacienda Chinchausuri.[14] Later that year the peasants of Huasicancha, a community near the Junín, Huancavelica, and Lima borders, invaded 3,000 hectares of the neighboring Hacienda Tucle after a failed attempt to recover their lands through legal channels.[15] By the end of the year, peasant land invasions had spread throughout the Peruvian countryside.

Another type of mobilization also took place during this time, one that pitted peasant villages against one another. Generally speaking, intercommunity conflict has received far less academic attention than the class conflicts mentioned above.[16] Yet, as we will see below, intervillage conflict could be a primary mobilizing force for Andean peasants. And while land disputes were a major stimulus for village-on-village conflict, they were by no means the only one. In many cases, cultural factors conditioned the intensity and prevalence of these disputes. Our two case studies offer a fitting example. While both Chuschi and Huaychao experienced contentious relationships with neighboring communities over questions of territoriality, these tensions boiled over in Chuschi and not in Huaychao. Cultural factors of identity, kinship, religion, gender, and power served to ameliorate intercommunity conflict in Huaychao; the opposite was the case in Chuschi.

Intercommunity Conflict in Chuschi and Quispillaccta

The Chuschi River trickles down Mount Condorccacca, flowing northward from Piedra Redonda through the village of Chuschi. On the other side of this river, just a stone's throw away, is the hamlet of Quispillaccta. Although Quispillaccta president Emilio Núñez Conde told the *juez de tierras* (land court judge) in 1981 that Chuschi and Quispillaccta were separated by "an insignificant stream,"[17] the historically rooted rift between the two villages was quite significant.

In late 1940 Quispillaccta authorities discovered that *comuneros* and authorities from Chuschi had petitioned Indigenous Affairs for legal recognition as a *comunidad indígena* (indigenous community), a recognition that afforded the village certain economic and political rights vis-à-vis the Peruvian government.[18] This would not have been a problem, the Quispillacctinos assured the prefect, were it not for the fact that the boundaries the Chuschinos had drawn up for federal approval included territories that had belonged to Quispillaccta "since time immemorial."[19] In a letter penned to the General Director of Indigenous Affairs, the Quispillacctinos argued that, if anything, *they* were the ones in need of state protection: "[The Chuschinos] are taking advantage of *our* ignorance and humble condition, they being from the district capital and having many citizens with a certain level of education who use [their education] to extort the indigenous masses."[20] The petitioners added that the Chuschinos had recently invaded Quispillaccta territory under the cover of darkness, remaining there until the next morning, when Quispillaccta residents "repelled the attack and forced them off our invaded lands." Such behavior was intolerable, the petitioners insisted, warning that they had "resolved

River separating Chuschi and Quispillaccta. Photograph by author.

to defend—even if it costs us our lives—our only patrimony, which will be for our children [to inherit]."[21]

It took a special hearing between village *personeros* at the Indigenous Affairs headquarters in Lima the following 19 May to resolve the dispute. The chief of the administrative section decided to send a divisional inspector to the disputed territories to settle the matter.[22] The villagers waited and waited, but the inspector never came. Finally, after more than two months of waiting, Quispillaccta's indigenous heads of household penned another letter to the director of indigenous affairs requesting the inspector's immediate presence.[23] Inspector Luis F. Aguilar finally arrived at the scene two months later to evaluate the situation. Chief among Aguilar's proposals was to draw an imaginary line down the middle of the disputed territory—a total area of ten by four kilometers—and divide it equally between the two villages.[24] Community representatives agreed to the terms of the resolution, signing an Act of Conciliation on 21 October 1941. The bureau applauded its own efforts at reaching a "transactional [*sic*] and amicable solution to the conflict," a resolution that reflected the "indigenist politics of the Government."[25] With the stroke of a pen, the bureau closed the case in 1941, claiming to have reached a "definitive end" to the heated intercommunity conflict.[26]

Or had it? In April 1953, eighty Quispillacctinos issued a letter to the Provincial Council, the Cangallo subprefect, and the Ayacucho prefect demanding their village's full political and economic autonomy from the district capital. Claiming that the Chuschinos had failed to cooperate with various public works projects that would have benefited Quispillaccta, the solicitors argued that they would need the legal authority to allocate public funds where they saw fit. After hearing their request, provincial authorities granted the village economic and administrative autonomy.[27]

Struggles over material possessions—namely, land and livestock—remained at the forefront of the legal battle between Chuschi and Quispillaccta for the next forty years. Of course, Chuschi was not the only Ayacuchan district afflicted by intercommunity boundary disputes during this period.[28] What is unique about the Chuschi-Quispillaccta rivalry, however, is how deep it went. Records of boundary disputes between the two communities date as far back as the sixteenth century.[29] Given the historical tensions between the two villages, it was perhaps naive of Indigenous Affairs to believe that it could eradicate intervillage strife through imaginary lines and legal decrees.

Fording the Waters: Early Altercations

Records of major territorial discrepancies between the two villages did in fact subside following the peace accord. Litigation resurfaced less than twenty years later, however, with representatives from both villages charging that their adversaries had never really respected the truce. On 29 November 1959, Quispillaccta *personero* Mamerto Pariona issued a letter to the Cangallo subprefect alleging that earlier that morning a group of Chuschinos, riding on horseback and using work tools as weapons, had stormed past the imaginary line into the territory of Accopampa. Pariona requested that the subprefect take legal action against the invaders, warning that his clients had already armed a "communal mass" to force the Chuschinos off their land.[30] Apparently, this was not the first time that the 1941 accord had been breached. On 6 May 1960, more than thirty *comuneros* and officials from Quispillaccta signed a letter addressed to the general director of indigenous affairs alleging that in addition to "committing a series of offenses such as the violation of our women," the Chuschinos had infringed on several parcels of their land in recent years. In 1957, for example, they had invaded the territory of Loreta.[31] The following year they added Suyoccacca, Amacuyo, Natillapuquio, and Ticlautapuquio to the list of usurped lands; they even laid claim to the Quispillacctinos' irrigation water. The letter went on to allege that in 1959 the Chuschinos began planting crops, constructing houses, and grazing plots of land with the Quispillacctinos' own livestock.[32]

The Chuschinos had their own grievances to report. On 29 November 1959 indigenous *comunero* Gonzalo Rocha Huamaní solicited the subprefect for guarantees against Pariona. Rocha claimed that it was the Quispillacctinos, through the counsel of Pariona, who were in the wrong: "They want to strip me of my terrain called Huacctacancha, which rests within the boundaries of Chuschi, and these *comuneros* want to appropriate the fraction that belongs to Chuschi." This had been going on for some time, Rocha maintained: "Every year they take my potato, broad bean, and barley crops, they even directly threaten to take my life. . . . Why, as recently as the month of August, they mistreated me, declaring that they would cut my life short if I didn't kindly vacate the aforementioned terrain."[33]

Not knowing whose version of events to believe, and no doubt hoping to buy enough time to assess the situation, the office of the Cangallo subprefect in December 1959 ordered the authorities and *personeros* from both communities to have their constituents "abstain from exacting damages and invasions" in the disputed territories until the completion of a formal investigation.[34] Villagers grew impatient waiting for an official response. According to the legal accusation of Nilo Hinojosa, prosecutor of the Superior Court of Ayacucho, the Chuschinos cemented their claim over the disputed territory by erecting a chapel at Lachocc on 27 March 1960. The Quispillacctinos responded by attempting to erect their own chapel in the same location.[35] When their nemeses prevented them from doing this, the Quispillacctinos responded with what Chuschi *personero* Braulio Pacotaipe deemed "punishable and shameful acts."[36] On 30 and 31 March, he explained, villagers from Quispillaccta, led by their communal authorities, invaded the sites of Accoccasa, Lachocc, Yuracc-coral, Pallcca, and Ingahuasi, forcing off the small number of Chuschinos residing there. When the evicted Chuschinos informed their communal leaders of the incident, the latter set out to confront the squatters. On 1 April, Chuschi leaders found the Quispillaccta authorities waiting for them, along with a mob of 700 *comuneros*. After a brief verbal exchange, the Quispillacctinos began hurling sticks and stones at the Chuschino leaders, forcing them to run for their lives.[37]

The crowd made its way to the newly erected chapel in Lachocc, forced open the door, and stormed in. They robbed the chapel of its gold and silver riches, to be sure, but what they had really come for was something that money could not buy: the patron saint of the church of Chuschi, the Virgin Saint Rose of Lima. The Quispillacctinos found the relic inside a wooden case.[38] She was only sixty-five centimeters tall and forty-five centimeters wide, but her beauty undoubtedly overshadowed her stature. Her body was draped in fine, white silk; a black cape cloaked her delicate shoulders. Her front side was laced with golden thread, and her rosary was adorned with white pearls.[39] Relic in hand, the looters vacated the premises—one wonders if they ever stopped to admire their prize's beauty before setting the roof on fire. When all was said and done, Pacotaipe lamented, the chapel had been destroyed quite literally "from the ground up [*desde los cimientos*]." The Quispillacctinos then took the saint back to their community before delivering it to the bishop in Ayacucho City.[40] Meanwhile, the Quispillacctinos set up camp in Lachocc, sacking the homes of thirty Chuschino residents and robbing household goods and work tools. On 3 April, the invaders finally left Lachocc for Yuracc-coral. There, they rustled cattle, raided the homes of the ten Chuschino families

who lived there, and destroyed another chapel. The Quispillacctinos occupied Lachocc and Yuracc-coral for several days without resistance.[41]

The attacks did not end there. According to the Chuschinos, a throng
of some 6,000 Quispillacctino men and women went about ransacking
Chuschi territory on 5 April. They first seized the lands of Suyuccacca,
whose residents had already fled. One of the residents whose hut was
attacked was the indigenous *comunero* Miguel Pacotaipe.[42] As I discuss
below, Pacotaipe would become a central figure in the upcoming conflicts
between the two communities. The horde obliterated yet another small
chapel, along with the humble dwellings of four Chuschino residents. The
Quispillacctinos then made their way to Qenhua, once again finding the
site abandoned. After destroying the homes of three more locals, the mob
headed toward Tapaccocha, where the Chuschinos were in full retreat.
After looting and pillaging the site and destroying the homes of six more
comuneros, the crowd turned to Quimsacruz, where it easily routed a small
Chuschino defense. The Quispillacctinos encountered stiffer resistance
in Pachanca in a high-noon battle that left more than half a dozen Chuschinos injured. Meanwhile, back in Lachocc, where the dust had barely
settled from the eruption of five days prior, another battle was under way.
This time, a horde of some 2,000 Quispillacctinos faced off against 80
Chuschinos. Participants from both villages used their *huaracas* (slings)
to fling rocks at each other, wounding at least three Chuschinos and an
undetermined number of Quispillacctinos. The battle raged on for several hours before the Quispillacctinos finally retired to their side of the
disputed territory. Two days later the raiders returned, this time targeting
Cconchalla, where they and their cattle feasted on their neighbors' potato
crops.[43] Once the dust had settled, several villagers on both sides of the
conflict reported injuries, and thirty-three Chuschinos reported "an infin-
ity of stolen animals."[44]

The Chuschinos were not to be outdone. As Quispillacctino elders
Luis Núñez Ccallocunto and Martín Vega Tomaylla later dictated to an
official scribe, during these weeks Chuschino authorities were rumored to
have gone into Quispillaccta to purchase multiple cases of bullets suitable
for a .22 caliber handgun. Did they intend to shoot Quispillacctinos with
their own bullets? The answer to this question would come the following
month, as Chuschinos embarked on what the old men called a "march of
death" into Quispillaccta territory.[45]

Before describing the March of Death, I would like to discuss three

themes that emerge from the above accounts. The first has to do with
the numbers that the Chuschinos attributed to the mobilization of their
neighbors. Take, for example, the claim that the Quispillacctino attackers numbered as many as 6,000. It is difficult to get 6,000 people to do
anything, much less engage in collective violence. Add to this the fact that
Quispillaccta's total population at the time numbered only between 3,000
and 4,000 and we are faced with what appears to be a clear-cut case of
narrative hyperbole. That alleged victims of collective violence sometimes
embellish the details of their victimization in order to gain judicial sympa-
thy should come as no surprise, but it is worth exploring why these particular plaintiffs elected not to cite more credible numbers. The explanation
has little to do with Andean peasants' level of education (or lack thereof).
Andean highlanders have historically excelled in numeracy, relying on
mathematics in nearly all aspects of daily life.[46] If Quechua-speaking peasants are so adept at mathematics, why did the Chuschinos assign such incredible numbers to the mobilization of their neighbors? In all likelihood,
the Chuschinos consciously engaged in numerical hyperbole in order to
assign moral authority to their own position vis-à-vis others. To be sure,
the relationship between morality and alterity is by no means unique to
the Andes. Chuschinos grossly overestimated the number of Quispillacctino attackers so that there could be no doubt as to which side was in the
wrong. The Quispillacctinos did not fight fair, bringing far more people
into battle than was necessary and perhaps even including people from
other communities. More important, framing the narrative in this way
gave moral justification to any retaliation by the Chuschinos.

   This was not the only case I found in which Andean peasants exaggerated numbers as a means of establishing moral authority. Shortly after
I arrived in Huaychao for the first time with Julián and fellow historians
Ponciano Del Pino and Freddy Taboada, villagers informed us that one
person worth talking to about the hacienda period was Inocencio Urbano, Huaychao's oldest villager. When we went to talk to the elder, one
of the first things he did was tell us how old he was. Ponciano and I communicated how impressed we were that the man had lived to be 104, at
which point Julián and Freddy, both native Quechua speakers, clarified
in Spanish that the number *pachaq tawa chunka*, which *tayta* Inocencio
had given us, is not 104; it is 140! Ponciano and I exchanged a fleeting
look of concern, convinced that the old man was delirious. However,
the more we conversed, the more *tayta* Inocencio impressed us with his

keen recollection of specific names, events, and moments in Huaychao's distant history. Although blind and frail, *tayta* Inocencio was remarkably lucid. Why, then, would he have so shamelessly exaggerated his age?[47] In reality, *tayta* Inocencio may not even have had a legitimate claim to the 104 years that Ponciano and I mistakenly attributed to him. According to the community's *libros de actas* (books of acts), *tayta* Inocencio was 100 at the time of our interview; noteworthy, to be sure, but a far cry from 140.[48] As far as *tayta* Inocencio was concerned, though, he was 140, at least on that particular day. On another he might be 180. To him, it did not really matter one way or another. The point was that he was old—very old—and that his age was far beyond our reach or that of anyone else in the community, for that matter. As such, his fellow villagers had an ethical obligation to respect his unique status in the community. As with the case of the Chuschino narrative described above, numerical hyperbole fueled *tayta* Inocencio's being with a sense of moral purpose and authority.

Another theme that emerges from the above discussion is the role of gender in intervillage disputes. Florencia Mallon discusses the paternalistic logic behind Andean peasant mobilizations, arguing that "the defense of women, and especially of virgins, emerged as the culminating motive for confrontation. The virgins are the gendered symbol of unity, among ethnically and spatially defined factions, the discursive marker that designates a moral frontier beyond which resistance was inevitable."[49] If we compare this description to Quispillacctinos' charge that the Chuschinos had "violated" their women, we get a sense of what was at stake for the villagers. If the Quispillacctinos' charges were substantiated, they would have had, in their view, a paternalistic obligation to respond with force. Even if the accusation was fabricated, it served as a rhetorical justification for the Quispillacctinos to mobilize against their neighbors.

Even though this was the only case in which I found an explicit mention of the rape of indigenous peasant women, stories, however vague in detail, about the defense of women against aggressions from the other side of the river remained strong in villagers' collective memory. One such account involved a Quispillacctino teenager who sneaked into the home of his Chuschina girlfriend for a midnight rendezvous sometime around 1968. In those days, unmarried girls slept in the kitchen, near the center of the house, where they would be best protected against such threats. It so happens that the young woman's father came calling on her in the midst of her carnal pleasure: "*Hija* [daughter]!" When the young man heard this, he did as most teenagers would do and dashed out of the home. The Quispillacctino youngster is said to have stumbled and fallen while running across the family lot, allowing the father to catch him and beat him to death with a stone. The story ends with the father turning himself in to provincial police.[50]

I found no archival record of this incident. Yet regardless of whether or not it actually took place, the persistence of the story in Chuschinos' collective consciousness speaks to their paternalistic sensibilities. The Chuschino father appears as the story's hero, a man who took the necessary steps to safeguard his daughter's virtue by lodging her in the kitchen and coming in to check on her in the middle of the night. He further cemented his patriarchal authority by killing the Quispillacctino who had deflowered his daughter. Finally, his willingness to turn himself in and face the legal consequences of his actions demonstrates that, but for this "understandable" act of aggression, he was an upstanding and law-abiding citizen. This anecdote of *individual* paternalism may have served as a discursive reminder to Chuschino men of their *collective* responsibility to defend the virtue of their community's women. This also explains the significance of stealing Chuschi's *virgin* patron saint. In doing so, Quispillacctinos were exposing in a symbolic way Chuschinos' paternalistic impotence. If Chuschinos' could not keep their rivals' hands off their most sacred virgin, what did this say about their communal integrity?

Of course, the events surrounding the stealing of the patron saint tell us as much about villagers' religious sensibilities as they do about gender. In Chuschi, as elsewhere, religious icons served as important symbols of communal identity and solidarity.[51] Indigenous Chuschinos attempted to validate their own claims to territorial autonomy by erecting chapels equipped with patron saints. Similarly, in capturing the patron saint "totem" and burning the chapel to the ground, the Quispillacctinos were symbolically conquering the neighboring village, rendering its "sacred" symbols of religious power "profane."[52] Such a culturally offensive action had the potential of escalating intervillage hostilities and provoking violent reactions—reactions such as the March of Death that followed.

The River Runs Red: Intervillage Violence

The march took place on 5–6 May 1960.[53] According to elders Núñez and Vega, it began when 80 foot soldiers and 100 horsemen from Chuschi breached the invisible border. The mob, comprised of both men and women, appeared poised to "sweep the entire Community." The Chuschinos had their sights on the Cceullahuaycco ranch, the site of the local chapel and *cofradía* (religious brotherhood) houses. After completing a "total destruction" of the chapel, the invaders took twenty goats and several religious ornaments owned by the *cofradía* and looted the homes of two Quispillacctinos.[54] The raiders even took with them a Quispillacctino hostage, sixty-eight-year-old farmer Asunción Ccallocunto Núñez. After taking random household items and upward of 440 soles in cash from his home, the Chuschinos denounced Ccallocunto as a thief and led him to the hills of Arapa, where they tied him to a large rock and assailed him with punches, kicks, and whiplashes. The Chuschinos then dragged the Quispillacctino elder back to Chuschi and locked him in the jailhouse for three days without food before finally releasing him.[55]

The following morning, 6 May 1960, Núñez and Vega were helping their fellow Quispillacctinos comb the area to assess the damage when they learned that their adversaries had "continued with this disastrous and criminal task" by invading Quimsacruz, one of the zones along the Chuschi-Quispillaccta border.[56] As many as 500 Quispillacctino men, women, children, and elders hurried to the site, armed with sticks, stones, and slings.[57] Two of the elders were Núñez and Vega, who, according to their testimony, went along "to see just what the Chuschinos were up to."[58] When the Quispillacctinos arrived at Quimsacruz, they found 300 Chuschinos waiting for them behind large boulders atop the nearby hills.[59] Chuschino men and women waited for their adversaries with clubs; at least a dozen had their slings poised for an air assault. Suddenly, Núñez and Vega reported, a swarm of Chuschinos "came running down, assailing us with *hondazos* [sling shots] and *cocobolos* [a metal-tipped whip]." Before the Quispillacctinos could shake themselves loose, the loud cracks of Winchester rifles pierced the air. Núñez and Vega recalled that they and their neighbors had no choice but to drop to the ground amid this "painful surprise."[60] Martín Mendieta, a *comunero* in his mid-twenties, was the first to get shot, dropping right where he stood. His wife, Cristina Huamaní Ccallocunto, had been holding down the rear of the Quispillacctino defense. When someone informed her of what had happened to her husband, she pushed her way through to the front line, only to find Martín lying dead, his blue jacket and striped green shirt stained with his own blood.[61]

More shooting ensued. One of the bullets struck nineteen-year-old

Justiniano Mendoza Conde in the right rib, a projectile that would still be there when he reported the incident to the judge more than a month later.[62] Another bullet, fired from behind a stack of *ichu* (an Andean thatch) just five meters away, ripped through thirty-five-year-old Pascual Conde Huamán's left shin, leaving him hospitalized for two weeks.[63] At least nine other Quispillacctinos also took hits.[64] With bullets, stones, and pebbles whizzing past them, Núñez and Vega said, they and the remaining Quispillacctinos scurried into retreat, forced to leave behind their fallen compatriots. Finally, the shooting ceased. But just when the besieged Quispillacctinos thought it was safe to emerge from their cover behind the rocks, a swarm of Chuschino horsemen and foot soldiers assailed them with slings and *cocobolos* to add "a dramatic epilogue to our situation." Fortunately, the two elders managed to escape with only minor injuries.[65]

The attack left three Quispillacctinos dead and dozens wounded. Court prosecutors estimated the value of damaged and stolen possessions at over 18,500 soles.[66] After the assault, the Chuschinos left their neighbors to lick their wounds. Pascuala Huamaní de Mejía testified that she had remained in her Quispillaccta home during the attack. Earlier that day, her husband, Sebastián Mendieta Tucno, joined the search party for Asunción Ccallocunto. When she learned of the attack at Quimsacruz, Pascuala feared that Sebastián was one of the Quispillacctino victims. She hurried to the battlefield and found her husband lying on the ground, still alive but bleeding from a gunshot wound and in desperate need of medical attention. Just then, another figure caught her eye. It was that of her dead brother-in-law, Martín Mendieta. Four days later, her husband would die of his injury.[67] Unlike Pascuala, Marcela Mejía Huamaní had not heard news about her husband, a middle-aged indigenous man named Antonio Galindo Espinoza. It was not until nightfall that she finally saw him, severely wounded by a gunshot, carried off on a stretcher. He managed to tell her the name of his assailant before being rushed off to the hospital in Ayacucho City, where he died days later.[68]

The man he identified was the mestizo mayor, Ernesto Jaime. After the incident, the Quispillacctinos brought criminal charges against Jaime and other Chuschi authorities, alleging that they had spearheaded the assault. One of the men implicated in the attack was Felipe Aycha, the indigenous butcher and cattle rustler introduced in chapter 1. Both Jaime and Aycha vehemently denied these allegations, claiming to have been out of town at the time of the incident.[69] These were convenient alibis that Quispillacctino witnesses eagerly contradicted. The elders Núñez and Vega had seen Chuschi's mayor at the battlefield, disguised in "*comunero* clothing and a black hat." According to their deposition, when Jaime ran out of bullets in his carbine rifle, he pulled out a small revolver and fired it on the Quispillacctino crowd.[70] Aycha's accusers denounced him with equal fervor. At a court hearing on 13 August 1963, Quispillacctino Leonardo Conde stood before the accused Aycha and testified to having watched from eighty meters away as he dismounted his golden horse to embrace the gunman who shot Martín Mendieta.[71] Two other witnesses, Daniel and Bernabé Núñez, also appeared in court that day to accuse Aycha of riding around on his golden horse during the Quimsacruz battle; Daniel saw him shoot the Quispillacctinos Marcelino Tomaylla and Justiniano Mendoza.[72] According to the elders Núñez and Vega, rumors had been circulating in the district before the assault that Jaime, Aycha, and other Chuschino authorities were holding secret meetings to plot the attack. The Quispillacctino elders were convinced that these men enjoyed "absolute dominion and control over Chuschi's indigenous mass," which made it easy for them to get *comuneros* to join their cause. When sheer persuasion did not work, they said, Jaime and Aycha obliged their constituents "under threat of a fine, and punishment as a traitor."[73]

None of the Quispillacctino plaintiffs suggested that the reverse may have been the case—that it was the *comuneros* who demanded that their political authorities lead them into battle against their rivals. However, as I argue in chapter 3, indigenous Chuschinos expected their mestizo leaders to defend and protect them materially, politically, and if need be, militarily. Jaime's military leadership during the pitched battles against the Quispillacctinos convinced many *comuneros* that he possessed this paternalistic quality and it cemented popular opinion about his legitimacy as a nonindigenous authority. Indeed, Chuschinos would remember Jaime's role in the communal defense for years to come. *Profe* (Professor) Ignacio Huaycha did not need for me to bring up the battle to start talking about Jaime's role in it: "He led the Chuschino cavalry," he said fondly. When I asked *profe* Ignacio if Jaime had enjoyed the *comuneros'* support, he nodded: "That's why he did it. Because we needed his military expertise. Because you can't just cede your [communal] lands to other people."[74] The same may have been the case for the Felipe Aycha. Aycha was nothing if not a thug, and who better than to lead the community into battle than a man who had time and time again used physical intimidation and violence to get his way? In this particular instance, villagers were willing to overlook Aycha's moral trespasses provided that he exhibit sound leadership on the field of battle.

Village council records from the period support this assessment. Early on 16 April 1960, community members held an emergency assembly and unanimously elected Jaime, the indigenous Aycha, and several other mestizo notables to top administrative positions. The results of the ad hoc election were met with applause and a "lively voice of satisfaction," for they signaled that the "the integrity of our town" had been placed in good hands. More than 100 heads of household signed or made their mark on the corresponding minutes.[75] Later that afternoon, Chuschi residents held yet another assembly, this time to discuss "the defense of territorial integrity." According to the official transcript, "The whole community spontaneously offered to cooperate in creating funds [to support litigation], in accordance with the state of each *comunero*'s means." In addition to this economic assistance, *comuneros* pledged to defend their village's lands "materially or personally until the end of the litigation," adding, "this is about the integrity of our territory, as proven by the title that we've kept since [the time of] our ancestors." One hundred and thirty-two heads of household signed or made their mark on the pledge sheet.[76] While we cannot rule out the possibility of coercion, these records indicate that indigenous *comuneros* expected their mestizo and indigenous power holders to lead in the communal defense effort, putting aside any differences for the time being. As we will see in chapter 4, Jaime's enthusiasm and competence in leading in this effort would pay dividends during the Shining Path insurgency. This might also have been the case for Felipe Aycha, were it not for his reputation as a local deviant. Was Aycha's military leadership during the intercommunity conflict enough to override the popular view that he was an unrepentant bully? We will find out the answer to this question in chapter 4. For now, it is enough to appreciate the impact that the March of Death had on the local historical consciousness.

Events can have a history of their own, radically breaking from and altering the status quo.[77] The episode that took place on 5–6 May 1960 had this effect on Chuschi and Quispillaccta. Up until that point, the intercommunity struggle had been defined by legal petitions, land invasions, and petty vandalism. The rules of the game changed in May 1960. Blood had been shed; there was no going back. From that point forward, lethal violence became a viable means of settling scores between Chuschinos and Quispillacctinos.

Indigenous peasants Miguel Pacotaipe and Dámaso Allcca found this out the hard way. Pacotaipe and Allcca were two of the Chuschinos whom Quispillacctinos held responsible for the March of Death. Although Pacotaipe and Allcca's names appeared on the prosecutor's list of suspects for the May 1960 attacks,[78] their accusers failed to produce enough evidence to convict either one. The court's ruling did little to convince Quispillacctinos of their innocence, however. Some believed that Pacotaipe was among the Chuschinos who fired on the Quispillacctinos during the 6 May battle; others held him responsible for the kidnapping of Asunción Ccallocunto the day before.[79] While we cannot know for sure whether Pacotaipe was involved in these attacks, we do know that he was one of the Chuschinos whose Suyuccacca dwelling was allegedly destroyed by the Quispillacctinos a month prior. This may have motivated him to participate in the May counteroffensive.

Guilty or not, Miguel Pacotaipe and Dámaso Allcca were still free men in 1962. When cattle merchants Ignacio and Juan Pomahuallcca offered them money to herd six heads of cattle to Ayacucho City's San Juan Bautista fair on the morning of 15 March, the indigenous peasants obliged. By the time they rounded up the cattle for the trip, it was already around three in the afternoon. On horseback and with cattle in tow, the four men decided to stop at the corner store owned by Teodoro Mejía in Quispillaccta, no doubt to enjoy a refreshing drink before their long journey. The detour proved to be fatal, for one of them would not make it out of Quispillaccta alive.[80]

Several Quispillacctinos had been drinking aguardiente at Mejía's store when the cattlemen rode by that afternoon. According to Allcca's police deposition, roughly twenty of Mejía's patrons immediately filed out of the store to confront the Chuschinos. *Varayoq* Manuel "Ccoriñahui" (Golden Eyes) Núñez Conde was the most vocal of the Quispillacctinos. Emboldened by the liquor he had been consuming, Golden Eyes accused the Chuschinos of herding cattle that belonged to him.[81] He also claimed to have been given orders to capture them for their role in the March of Death. When the Quispillacctinos closed in on the Chuschinos, Pacotaipe made haste on horseback toward the nearby hills of Chicllaraso.[82]

Lieutenant Governor Teófilo Machaca had just stopped by Mejía's store to purchase some coca leaves when he overheard the commotion outside and shouts about an escaping thief. When he got to the front door, Ignacio Pomahuallcca explained to him that the cattle in question belonged to him, and that he had employed the Chuschinos to steer them to Ayacucho. On hearing this, the lieutenant governor ordered his constituents not to harm the Chuschinos; he would detain the merchants until he could verify their story.[83] But, as Allcca recalled, the *varayoq* refused to back down. He immediately began calling on his fellow *comuneros* to catch the "cattle rustlers" anyway. Before long, a band of mounted Quispillacctinos took off in pursuit of Pacotaipe.[84]

A second group of villagers closed in on Allcca, who also managed to escape on horseback. Allcca did not make it far before his pursuers caught up to him. Quispillacctino Sabino Ccallocunto was on his way home from a long day of work in the fields when he overheard some of his fellow villagers yell: "Get that thief!" Ccallocunto hurried over to find out what all the fuss was about and saw that his neighbors had already snagged Allcca. Ccallocunto later admitted that he could not resist giving the defenseless Chuschino "just one punch in the head" before returning home.[85]

Meanwhile, other Quispillacctinos were in full pursuit of Miguel Pacotaipe. Allcca and *personero* Agripino Aronés informed the judge of what happened next based on the accounts they received from witnesses in neighboring Chacolla. Pacotaipe, they said, drove his horse straight into the Chicllarazo River in a desperate attempt to elude his pursuers. Apparently, the current was stronger than he had expected, carrying both horse and rider downstream for the distance of about half a village block before Pacotaipe finally broke with the animal and swam to the opposite bank, into Chacolla territory. This did not deter his aggressors, who rode their horses into the water after him.[86] Quispillacctino Dionisio Núñez testified that he and his neighbors chased Pacotaipe to the water's edge amid shouts of "The thief is getting away!" After crossing the bridge into Chacolla, they found the Chuschino hiding behind a stack of quinoa inside a corral at the point called Patahuasi. Dionisio and two of his neighbors, Valentín Núñez and Francisco Espinosa, grabbed Pacotaipe and began what proved to be a fruitless interrogation. Pacotaipe was too rattled, too stubborn, or too terrified to comply, for he answered their queries with incoherent statements such as "I don't know"; "Who knows what my name is?"; and "I don't know where I am." His noncompliance apparently struck a nerve with his interrogators, who began kicking and punching his head, face, and body. The Quispillacctinos then dragged Pacotaipe by his own poncho out to the bridge, where the other vigilantes greeted him with additional punches and kicks. The three captors requested a rope to restrain and haul their captive, but the mob could only produce a small rope no longer than a meter in length. They tied the short rope together with fabric from their own belts and fastened it around Pacotaipe's waist. After they crossed the bridge, another group of Quispillacctinos—plenty drunk, by Dionisio's account—caught up with them and began to "barbarously mistreat" Pacotaipe even more.[87]

Then came the war of words. Witnesses claim that around this time Luciano Galindo rode up on his horse and called Pacotaipe a *ladrón* (thief). Perhaps this was all Pacotaipe needed to become responsive again, for he shouted back at his accusers, calling them *occes*. Even the prosecutor in the ensuing case agreed that Pacotaipe's words seemed to have "mortally offended his opponents."[88] This may explain why Pacotaipe wound up at the bottom of a ravine—a straight drop of about ten meters. Some witnesses admitted that Pacotaipe's captors knocked him down into the gorge.[89] Others claimed that Pacotaipe threw himself into the ravine in a desperate attempt to end his suffering.[90] Whatever the case, the fall did not kill him. Realizing that Pacotaipe was still alive, the Quispillacctinos went in after him, forced him to his feet, and made him walk into town. Pacotaipe only made it about three blocks before collapsing. On seeing this, Valentín Núñez retied the rope around Pacotaipe's neck and hauled him by the throat another eighty meters. When it appeared that Pacotaipe was losing consciousness, his captors carried him in his poncho the rest of the way.[91]

It was now nightfall. Allcca, who had remained prisoner in Quispillaccta the whole time, was brought out to watch as his foes dragged Pacotaipe's limp body into view. The Quispillacctinos ordered Allcca to carry his neighbor away from the scene. Suffering, no doubt, from mental and physical exhaustion, Allcca could only muster enough strength to carry Pacotaipe about one block before having to set him back down and rest. After requesting some water, Pacotaipe perished by his neighbor's side.[92] Pacotaipe never got the drink that had brought him to Quispillaccta in the first place. The Quispillacctinos decided to hold both Allcca and the corpse in the nearby house of Ramón Galindo until daylight. That night, Allcca suffered more abuse at the hands of his Quispillacctino captors, who at one point struck him in the face with a whip, wounding his left eye.

The following morning, Allcca and his captors took Pacotaipe's body to Ayacucho City, depositing it at the local cemetery.[93]

Pacotaipe's death represented the culmination of intervillage hostilities in preinsurgency Chuschi and Quispillaccta. Through the bloodshed of 1960 and 1962, we can grasp some of the racial and gendered undertones of the intercommunity feud. With respect to gender, we see that even during the pitched battles, women were either left at home or relegated to the rear, which supports my earlier observation about the paternalistic logic behind the violence. Still, the fact that women participated in the battles at all demonstrates that it was not simply a man's issue. On the contrary, women shared the overarching communitarian identity vis-à-vis the local "others." Indigenous peasant women have carved out a spot for themselves in collective memory about the years of conflict. Vicente Blanco, a mestizo authority and schoolteacher who had had his own share of troubles in the community, told Alberto, Julián, and me about the active role that women played in the intervillage struggle: "The *mujercitas* [little ladies] from Quispillaccta would bathe in the [Chuschi] River and yell at the women from Chuschi, *les mentaban la madre* [they'd curse them out]: '*Ladronas!*' '*Rateras!*' [Thieves! Burglars!] and what have you. In response, the Chuschinas would yell back: '*Occes!*'"[94]

Where did this racialized conception of the local "other" come from? Some of this alterity can be traced back to the preconquest. Chuschi, it seems, was originally settled before the Spanish conquest by two distinct ethnic groups, the Aymaraes and the Canas. The Aymaraes, a group of Incan transplants, settled on the side of the stream that corresponds to modern-day Chuschi, the Canas in Quispillaccta.[95] While this historical narrative has since been contested,[96] its importance may lie in the perception of ethnic superiority held by indigenous Chuschinos. At the same time, Quispillacctinos took pride in their non-Incan origins and identity, using it to fuel their political consciousness in the twentieth century.[97]

These identity politics were certainly expressed in the intervillage conflict described above. The battered Miguel Pacotaipe managed to sting his Quispillacctino aggressors with the racial slur *occe*—an offense that left him lying at the bottom of a ditch. Even Chuschina women resorted to this racial slur during verbal bouts with their Quispillacctina neighbors. This underscores the extent to which indigenous highlanders created their own racial and ethnic categories that went beyond conventional mestizo-indigenous dichotomies. Of course, the creation of color hierarchies among a particular racial group is by no means a phenomenon limited to the Andes. Still, it is worth noting the particular cultural framework through which hierarchization manifested itself in midcentury Ayacucho. On one level, Chuschinos' claim to a distant Incan past gave them a sense of ethnic entitlement over their Cana neighbors. On another level, Chuschino men and women combined phenotypical and geological markers to assert their racial superiority over the indigenous population that inhabited the other side of the river.

Crimson Wakes:
Memory and Conflict after Bloodshed

The bloodshed of the early 1960s marked the height of intercommunity violence in Chuschi. The conflict did not go away, however. For the next twenty years, both communities continued to engage in legal, extralegal, and sometimes violent confrontations to gain the upper hand in the intercommunity struggle and recover disputed territories.[98] While many of these altercations resembled those discussed above, some new strategies did emerge.

One way in which villagers settled scores during this period was through intervillage theft. As we learned in chapter 1, it was difficult to talk about theft in Quispillaccta without mentioning the likes of Teobaldo Achallma. As we have seen, Achallma's Quispillacctino neighbors had problems with his social conduct. Now, he was about to give Chuschinos a reason to object to his behavior as well. When Chuschi authorities came knocking on Achallma's door in October 1975 to accuse him of stealing five bulls from their community, the scar-faced Quispillacctino did not even bother denying the charges. Once caught, Achallma went right into the headquarters of the Civil Guard in Pampa Cangallo and stamped his fingerprint on a written confession. He admitted having stayed the night at the house of his friend Candelario in Hualchancca one Thursday evening in October—he could not remember the exact date. The following morning, the pair went riding toward the district of Chuschi on two horses owned by Candelario. At around midnight, they reached Totora, a site in the hills above Chuschi, where a herd of cattle had been grazing. They rounded up five of the animals and herded them back into Quispillaccta. When they reached the point of Quimsahuasi, they sold two of the bulls to a drifter for 2,500 soles a piece. They took the three remaining bulls to an abandoned house, slit their throats, divvied up the meat, and went their separate ways. Before pressing his finger to the deposition, Achallma added for the record that even after he had confessed to the crime and agreed to pay a fine, the Chuschino authorities had mistreated him badly; he did not go into detail about the nature of the abuse.[99] Candelario endorsed a similar affidavit, explaining that Achallma had gotten himself into a legal dispute that he needed to straighten out by traveling to Ayacucho City. Such a trip required money that the indigenous Quispillacctino simply did not have, so he solicited his friend's assistance in robbing and selling cattle from the rival village.[100] By all appearances, this was an open and shut case.

But it did not end there. The following morning, Achallma and Candelario rescinded their sworn testimonies. Candelario clarified that he not only was innocent of the crime for which he had been charged but also had never even been to Chuschi. Sure, he knew Achallma and even let the man stay in his home from time to time; but he had no idea that his friend "was an element dedicated to cattle rustling." But what of his sworn confession? Candelario remembered having placed his mark on a statement, but only later did he learn of its content. He attributed the miscommunication to the fact that he gave his statement in his native tongue. Since the police did not speak Quechua, they had either misunderstood or altered his statement.[101] Teobaldo Achallma's complaint contained a similar accusation. He had indeed stayed at his dear friend's house in Huallchancca, as his affidavit indicated. However, he went straight home to Quispillaccta the next day, remaining there until the aggrieved Chuschinos came knocking on his door accusing him of stealing their animals. Like his illiterate friend Candelario, Achallma swore to have naively fingerprinted a testimony that he had not understood.[102]

Chuschi authorities could not speak for the outsider Candelario, but they were certain that they had fingered the right man in Achallma. They even signed a written statement, dated 24 November 1975, in which they called the Quispillacctino's credibility into question. The statement certified that Achallma had "a Judicial, Political, and Police record [in] the Province of Cangallo and Ayacucho for the crime of *abigeato*" and that he had now stolen five bulls from the hills of Chuschi.[103]

Which side was to be believed? The Superior Court found the two men guilty and sentenced each to six months in prison.[104] If the court's decision was correct, then it is worth noting that rather than steal from his own village as he had done in the past, Achallma chose to travel all the way to the hills of Chuschi to commit the crime. This suggests that he deliberately targeted cattle from the rival village in the wake of the bloodshed of the previous decade. If, however, Achallma was falsely accused, then it seems that the Chuschinos went out of their way to pin the crime on a Quispillacctino. After all, the aggrieved peasants never went into detail about how they reached the conclusion that Achallma had stolen their bulls. Alejandro Allcca, one of the victims of the crime, only allowed that "after asking around, he learned that one of the perpetrators was Teobaldo Achallma."[105] Achallma's accusers would then have had to fabricate a false confession and later go on record denouncing Achallma's character. Both scenarios illustrate that the intercommunity rivalry was still strong in 1975, and that Teobaldo Achallma was right in the middle of it.

The intervillage conflict continued in various forms into the early 1980s. For example, in March 1980—two months before Shining Path launched its guerrilla struggle—Quispillaccta representative Gregorio Núñez Pacotaipe delivered a series of letters to the departmental prefect alleging that the Chuschinos had violently invaded the same lands that they had invaded back in 1961.[106] This proved to be the first in a series of violent confrontations over the disputed territory.[107] In March 1981 brothers Martín and Faustino Mendieta joined a handful of their Quispillacctino neighbors in stealing several horses and bulls from Chuschi and then feasting on their spoils. The brothers' participation in the intercommunity theft appears to have been an act of retaliation. After all, their father was the late Martín Mendieta, the first Quispillacctino slain by the Chuschinos during the March of Death. When captured, some of the Quispillacctino suspects admitted that the crime had been a deliberate effort to target the Chuschinos and that the Quispillaccta authorities had sanctioned it.[108] Apparently, the twenty-one years that had elapsed since the Quimsacruz battle that claimed Martín Mendieta's life were not enough to keep the Mendieta boys from exacting vengeance against the Chuschinos. But the Mendieta brothers were not the only ones involved in this act of retribution. Another Quispillacctino who participated in the intervillage theft was an indigenous peasant named Asunción Llalli. As we will see in chapter 4, Llalli's participation in the intervillage theft would come back to haunt him during the ensuing years of political violence.

Even Chuschino youths harbored ill will toward their neighbors. Later that year, President Núñez complained that the students of Chuschi's public high school and their parents treated the Quispillacctino students poorly, barraging them with "insults and offenses of a personal character" and defaming them as *occes*. Such behavior convinced the Quispillaccta leader that the Chuschinos had a "superiority complex" and believed his people to consist of a "failed, mentally and economically deficient social stratum."[109] This evidence suggests that local youths in the early 1980s were attuned to their parents' racial animosity toward their rivals—a telling observation, since it was the high school children of the district who would become Shining Path's local foot soldiers.

This was the political climate in Chuschi during the initial months of the Shining Path insurgency. As we have seen, collective memories of the bloodshed of 1960–62 resurfaced time and again over the next twenty years. Joanne Rappaport discusses how Andean peasants in twentieth-century Colombia have used memories of violence to shape their contemporary political agendas and collective consciousness.[110] This certainly seems to have been the case in Chuschi and Quispillaccta, where the bloodshed of the early 1960s was still on peasants' minds when Shining Path began its guerrilla insurgency in 1980. A very different historical trajectory developed in Huaychao, to which we now turn.

Intervillage Relations and Conflicts in Huaychao

In the early morning hours of 1 April 1975, Huaynacancha peasant Víctor Gamboa discovered that nine of his thirty-one llamas were missing from his corral. Gamboa knew from past experience that his livestock sometimes wandered about at night, but this time he found no sign of them in his sheepfold. Once day broke he organized a search commission made up of village authorities and family members to trace the tracks of the missing animals. The footprints led straight to Huaychao. As Gamboa later explained to the judge, Huaychao and Huaynacancha were "barely separated by a hill."[111]

Disputes between peasants of Huaychao and neighboring communities such as Huaynacancha were not uncommon before the Shining Path insurgency. These clashes did not foment the kind of community-level mobilizations and violence that occurred between Chuschi and Quispillaccta, however. An analysis of the types of intervillage networks and cultural practices that were in place in the Iquichano highlands before the rebellion will help explain this difference.

Crossing the Mountains:
Community, Gender, and Violence

Since the hacienda period, Huaychainos maintained ties to other Iquichano populations through a series of communication and kinship networks. In some ways, the hacienda system facilitated this process, drawing peasants from different estates and villages to work as temporary field
hands on the same hacienda. Thus, communication among Iquichano
peasants was both common and multifaceted.

The same went for kinship networks. Julián and I conversed with President Fortunato and *tayta* Esteban about this one afternoon over several
helpings of a flat highland bread called *pan chapla*. Although they were
born on the Huaychao hacienda, both men had family dispersed throughout the Huanta highlands. They recalled making frequent visits to their
relatives' communities during religious festivals and rituals. During these
trips, young men and women would sometimes fall in love, or, as *tayta* Esteban put it, "The woman [would] trick the man," prompting one partner
to settle in the other's community. When this was not possible, nuclear
families remained dispersed, with the father usually working on the hacienda and his wife and children living in another location.[112] After the
dismantling of the Huaychao hacienda in 1975–76, many Iquichano peasants who had previously married into Huaychaino families settled in the
community.[113]

Religious festivals also provided members from extended kinship networks with an opportunity to come together and solidify social bonds. At
the same time, this provided a social channel through which nonrelatives
from different communities could fraternize. Huaychainos usually hosted
Carnival and Easter festivities as well as the August Festival. During these
occasions, peasants from throughout the region would come to Huaychao
and celebrate. A successful celebration would have included as many as
300 visitors from Huaynacancha, Uchuraccay, Llalli, and other nearby villages.[114] As *tayta* Mariano explained, many of the guests were not tenants
of the Huaychao hacienda but simply people "who would come just for
the *chicha de molle* [peppercorn beer]."[115]

These gatherings were not without conflict. As was the case in Chuschi and other parts of the Andes, physical confrontations occasionally
erupted over the defense of local women against external sexual aggression.[116] Perhaps no case better affirms this than that of Eulogio Ramos.

Ramos was an indigenous peasant from Putaja, an annex of the village of Iquicha. Ramos was one of many Iquichano guests in attendance when Huaychao hosted a local Santa Cruz festival on May Day 1975. The fiesta appeared to be a success, with peasants mingling, dancing, and consuming large amounts of *chicha* and aguardiente in sponsor Pablo Quispe's Ccochaccocha residence. By early evening, many of Quispe's guests were good and drunk; some had already passed out. It was around this time when Ramos cornered a sixteen-year-old Huaychaina, Emilia Huaylla. According to Huaylla, Ramos began dancing up on her and suggesting that she "take a walk around the corner" with him. Emilia knew good and well what that meant: Ramos wanted to have intercourse. When the young woman made it clear to Eulogio that she was in no mood to accept his offer, Ramos grew violent, grabbing, punching, and kicking her and attempting to rape her on the spot. Bleeding from the mouth, Emilia screamed for help. Within moments several Huaychainos had come to her defense. One of these "saviors," as Emilia put it, was the eighty-year-old host Pablo Quispe, who happened to be her uncle. According to Emilia, Eulogio rather facetiously asked the Huaychainos if they were defending the young woman because they wanted her all for themselves, a comment that drove the Huaychainos to pounce on him. Not even Emilia could resist retribution, hitting Eulogio in the head with a stick while her male neighbors beat him against the wall.[117] During the assault, Huaychaino Alejandro Quispe—Eulogio's brother-in-law—struck Eulogio over the head with a club, inflicting a wound so penetrating that it killed him later that night. Alejandro later told officials that he been on friendly terms with Ramos before that incident, so much that the two were "like brothers." As far as Alejandro was concerned, there was nothing personal about his actions; he had acted strictly to defend the honor of his neighbor Emilia. Consequently, Alejandro accepted his eighteen-month prison sentence without contest.[118]

Alejandro Quispe's case reveals several important characteristics of Huaychaino attitudes about gender. The physical defense of virgin women against the threat of rape by nonvillagers was so powerful a cultural value that it trumped any protections that extended kinship may have offered: Quispe's relationship with Ramos was not enough to dissuade him from beating him to death. What mattered more was that the outsider Eulogio Ramos had attempted to rape a Huaychaina virgin. Given that virgin women epitomized communal identity and integrity, Huaychainos felt

obliged to violently defend them.[119] This provocation was heightened
by Eulogio's insinuation that the men were really just defending Emilia
because they "wanted her for themselves." Such an accusation, if actually
made, challenged the men's honor by charging them with incest—Pablo,
after all, was Emilia's uncle. Now they not only needed to defend a local
virgin from external rape but also felt compelled to defend their reputation as honorable men.

Men were not the only ones who shared this paternalistic ethos. After
all, it was *Emilia* who testified that Eulogio had made the incest charge.
Thus, even if the verbal exchange never took place, the fact that she in-
serted it into her testimony indicates that she believed such an accusation
merited the violent retaliation that followed. Recall, too, that Emilia described Ramos's attackers as her "saviors." This choice of words implicitly
likened the murderers to Jesus Christ. In using this language, then, Emilia
assigned a sort of moral responsibility to Ramos's killers, placing them in
the role of laudable men who risked incarceration to defend her and the
community's honor. Nor were they alone in the assault. Recall that Emilia,
too, admitted to having beaten Eulogio with a stick, an act that demonstrates her active approval of—and participation in—the violent defense
of local women against external sexual threats. Still, it is worth noting that
her male neighbors took full responsibility for Eulogio's death, since the
ultimate responsibility for communal defense rested with peasant men.

I became aware of this cultural attitude within moments of my first arrival in Huaychao. After escorting me, Julián, and fellow historians Ponciano Del Pino and Freddy Taboada to the *despacho*, twenty-seven-year-old
Leandro Huamán, president of Huaychao's Civil Defense Committee, assembled as many villagers as he could find. After all had arrived, Leandro
gestured toward the large boulder in the main square and announced in
Spanish, presumably so that we visitors would understand: "See that large
rock out there? That's our *juez rumi*, the rock of justice. That's where we
punish sinners, and that's why we have no adulterers in our community."
Later that day Leandro invited Julián and me to stay with him and his wife,
Petronila, during our field research.[120]

This initial encounter reveals a good deal about Huaychainos' paternalistic sensibilities. In making this statement so early on in my field research,
Leandro was drawing a very clear boundary between us, the researchers,
and them, the Huaychainos. *We* were outsiders, and as long as we were
in *their* community, we were to abide by *their* rules. Most important, this

meant that *their* women were off limits. Leandro's none-too-subtle reference to the intimidating rock of justice clarified that if we ignored their social codes or slept with their women, we would be subject to their customary justice. It was only after making this point abundantly clear that Leandro invited us to sleep under the same roof as his wife and children.

This cultural attitude is best represented in a fictional tale that circulates in Huaychao about a *forastero* (outsider) who passes through the outskirts of the village on his way home from a seasonal job. Although married with children, it has been a while since the *forastero* has been with a woman, and he scales the surrounding hills desiring nothing more than the company of a beautiful young peasant. Actually, beauty and age are only secondary concerns for the traveler, who has spent so much time working as a serf on distant haciendas that any woman will do. "I'm going to mount the first woman I see whether she wants it or not—I don't care if she's an old widow!" he assures himself, growing more and more impatient by the minute. No sooner does the *forastero* finish his soliloquy than a breathtaking young virgin passes by grazing her goats. "*Pucha mamacita* [Ooh, mama]!" the *forastero* exclaims, licking his lips carnivorously.[121]

"Careful," the girl warns, calmly turning her back to the stranger and going about her business. But the *forastero* persists, forcefully having his way with her right there on the mountain. When he is finished, he declares his undying love for the girl. "Careful," she warns again, but the *forastero* tells her that he means it: he wants to marry her. "You'll need to get my father's blessing first," she reminds him. "But be careful, he's a very intimidating figure." Gazing down onto the valley of plentiful livestock, hardworking *comuneros*, and playful children, the *forastero* shrugs—*How bad could it be?*—and accepts the invitation.[122]

When he arrives with his new fiancée in the valley, the *forastero* is surprised to find that the quaint, lively village he had identified in the mountain has vanished, replaced by a cryptic cemetery. The girl leads him to an old abandoned house covered in flames and asks him to wait while she goes inside to get her father. A tingle creeps down the young man's spine as the girl's father emerges from the flames. He is no man but rather a demon, with fiery eyes, horns, and hooves. From behind the man-beast emerges a host of smaller demons who quickly surround the *forastero*, subdue him, and tie him to a stake that they set on fire. As he sits there burning, the girl morphs into a demon and addresses the man: "I warned you to be careful, but you didn't listen. I gave you three opportunities to turn and walk away, but you couldn't resist. And you slept with me and offered to marry me knowing full well that you had a wife and children waiting for you back in your hometown. Now you must suffer the consequences for your actions, burning here in hell for all eternity."[123]

The *forastero* remains tied to the stake under the care of the little demons, whose sole responsibility is to ensure that his suffering is uninterrupted, never once stopping to feed, clothe, or nurture him. During his time of suffering, the *forastero* has plenty of opportunity to think about his actions until one day twenty years later he looks up to the heavens and in all sincerity begs God for forgiveness: forgiveness for being unfaithful to his wife, who has since presumed him dead and married another man; forgiveness for abandoning his children and leaving them fatherless; forgiveness for raping a young Huaychaina and deceiving her with empty promises of marriage. At that moment, night turns to day and the *forastero* finds himself unshackled and dressed in fine white clothing inside the village, which once again has transformed into the spirited little hamlet into which he had gazed so many years prior. He is now free to continue along his journey.[124]

This tale offers an appropriate metaphorical prism through which to view Huaychaino culture.[125] Let us begin with the story's protagonist. Labeling the character a *forastero* immediately plays to the Huaychaino listener's sense of self. He is an "outsider," which means that he is likely unfamiliar with local norms and practices. The listeners' suspicions are confirmed when the traveler announces his intent to rape the first woman he sees, even if she is "an old widow." For the listener, this simple confession quickly marks the *forastero* as the story's *an*tagonist, for his gendered transgressions are threefold. First, as a husband and father, he is prohibited from engaging in any extramarital affairs. Second, his willingness to sleep with an elderly widow compromises the collective imagination of these women as asexual creatures. Third, he has vowed to take a local woman by force with no sincere commitment of marriage, an act that would challenge the patriarchal integrity of the community.

Having successfully identified the story's "other," the next step in the tale is to identify the collective self—that is, Huaychao and the Huaychainos. This is first represented in the figure of the young woman. Innocent, beautiful, and, most important, virginal, the young woman symbolizes the moral fortitude of the community and its people. Yet she is not naive. Wise to the *forastero*'s intentions and, evidently, to the fact that he is already married, she warns him over and over to be "careful." Of course, the traveler pays her no mind, charmed, it seems, by her beauty and innocence, and goes about raping her. The rape is both literal and metaphorical—literal in that outsiders do sometimes attempt to rape and seduce *comuneras* and metaphorical in that villagers interpret this or any other act of aggression toward the community as a violation of the collective. The final allusion to Huaychao is accomplished through the physical description of the village. Just like the virgin, the hamlet is beautiful, pleasant, and full of life. Also like the virgin, though, the village can become a veritable hellhole for any outsider who violates or deceives it. The message is as clear to the listener as Leandro's was to me and Julián: Do not sleep with Huaychaina women unless you intend to marry them.

Nor is the allegory without metaphors of power. The girl's father is clearly Satan, and some villagers label him as such when they tell the tale. Paradoxically, this story turns conventional biblical scripture on its head, making the devil appear as the unlikely hero and ultimate moral authority. This figure is the allegorical epitome of the household patriarch, a man who unflinchingly embraces his paternalistic duty to defend the women in his household against external sexual attacks. The smaller demons, by extension, represent the male villagers, who will likewise do their worst to any outsider who threatens the community or its women. It is in this sense that the fictional tale assigns moral purpose to sexual hierarchy and patriarchy.

The men and women we interviewed recalled with candor the altercations that erupted between Huaychaino and non-Huaychaino men over the defense of local women. Intervillage romances were sure to develop during fiestas, in which indigenous peasants from throughout the Iquichano highlands partook. During Carnival, groups of single men and women would parade around the village drinking, singing songs, and ringing bells. Typically, young men and women carried talcum powder and paper streamers to fling flirtatiously at members of the opposite sex. When they could not afford this, they used mud and the native *rayan* plant. When this happened, Huaychaino men became possessive of local women. When we asked President Fortunato and *tayta* Esteban if fights ever erupted between villagers from different communities during the fiestas, the former exclaimed: "Uff! Tons!" The two men told us that when they were adolescents living on the hacienda in the early 1970s, they would get into fistfights with young men from neighboring Uchuraccay, Huaynacancha, and Cunya. Showing us the scar on his forehead from getting hit by a rock during one of these altercations, President Fortunato explained the paternalistic logic behind the confrontations: "For example, let's say someone is dancing with a *señorita* and her boyfriend tries to cut in— people would fight over things like that."[126] According to Juana Cabezas, a *comunera* in her mid-fifties, men had good reason to strike preemptively. Asked if people from different villages fell in love during these occasions, she shook her head: "*Manam*, the [women] were kidnapped." Asked to elaborate, she clarified: "Because during the games, [boys and girls] would just be playing, playing [*sic*] and then [the boy] would treacherously take one of the girls [to the mountains and rape her]. After that they some- times got engaged, but sometimes not. Those groups were from different places and different villages, and the kidnapping was always against the other village."[127] We asked her if the women ever fought back or ran away. "*Manam*," she lamented, "What can she do if she's being carried away by several guys? They'd carry her away in a premeditated effort."[128]

Huaychaino men interpreted these actions as direct affronts to com- munal integrity and did their best to avenge sexually assaulted women. *Mama* Juana still remembered the altercations that ensued whenever a young man discovered that his sister had been sequestered by a man from another village. During these disputes, men would turn the talcum powder, streamers, and other festival items into weapons, hurling them at one another to instigate fights.[129] At other times, brawls would break out between groups of men from each village. According to *mama* Juana, this happened a number of times between men from Huaychao and neighboring Huaynacancha. As soon as they saw their neighbors com- ing up the mountain, Huaychainos prepared themselves for the worst. "Here come the people from Huaynacancha *rumi makis* [stone-in-hand]. Surely they will hit us all," they alerted one another. "Hit them with rocks from above!" the Huaychainos resolved. But the Huaynacanchinos were prepared, taunting their neighbors: "If you want it, come and get it. I'm going to hit you so hard!"[130] *Tayta* Ciprián recalled that during these battles, the neighbors would challenge one another to fight "like men." "Let's fight without slings, without whips, without rocks. Let's fight fist to fist [*pulso a pulso*]!"[131] *Mama* Juana made a similar observation, claiming that the feuding neighbors would call each other "yutu caldo" and "wallpa leche."[132] Translated as "partridge soup," *yutu caldo* denoted a person who reported his opponents to local authorities immediately following the altercation; it was a sort of Quechua "tattletale."[133] The insult was meant to suggest that one's opponent would not simply "let the best man win." Meaning "chicken's milk," *wallpa leche* referred to men who would sooner drink away their problems than resolve the dispute through physical confrontation. Such emasculating insults were sure to escalate the quarrel and after retorting, "Ah, *carajo* [dammit], don't call me *yutu caldo* and don't call me *wallpa leche!*" physical fighting typically followed.[134]

The altercations usually ended there, however. As *mama* Juana explained, the fighters made amends following a physical confrontation, and in many cases the rapist married the woman in question.[135] *Tayta* Ciprián also confirmed that such intervillage altercations occurred "only during the fiestas when [people] were drinking and not every day."[136] Unlike in Chuschi, then, intervillage disputes in Huaychao were not long lasting, and they were socially accepted in the setting of the village fiesta.

This attitude is best illustrated in an incident that took place during the 1981 Carnival. At about nine o'clock on Sunday morning, 22 February, roughly half a dozen young Huaychainos poured themselves some aguardiente and wandered toward the top of mount Uchuy Compañía Ccasa, where the yearly *cortamonte*[137] ritual was set to take place. The men were in no rush to get to the ceremony, spending the next couple of hours wandering the hills, downing cane liquor, and playing musical instruments as other male youths joined the group. After a while, the young Huaychainos came across another gang from Tupín, a former annex that had since become an independent village. Emboldened, no doubt, by both the alcohol and their numbers, young men from both sides began sizing each other up, exchanging words and brandishing the *chicotes*, *látigos*, and stones that they had brought with them in anticipation of such an encounter. Before long the men were engaged in an all-out brawl. During the melee that ensued, men from both gangs exchanged blows with fists, feet, whips, and stones. One of these weapons landed squarely on the head of Tupino Marcelino Yaranqa. This was most likely the defining moment that led the combatants to disperse.[138]

The badly injured Yaranqa struggled to walk home. Huaychaina Cecilia Quispe had been grazing her livestock just outside the village when Yaranqa approached and collapsed onto the ground. Quispe immediately called for help, flagging down her neighbors to carry Yaranqa back to his village.[139] Alejandra Ccente was one of the first villagers to attend to Yaranqa once he reached the village. The elder peasant shared her memory of this event with Julián and me. As she recalled, Yaranqa had been hit in the head with a cowbell. *Mama* Alejandra remembered that Yaranqa's head had been covered in so much blood that it was choking him. After recounting the violent episode, *mama* Alejandra shuddered, as if to shake the image from her memory.[140] Marcelino Yaranqa remained bedridden for three days before succumbing to his wounds.[141]

None of the young men involved in the incident suggested that Yaranqa's death had been anything but an unfortunate circumstance of Carnival. No personal vendettas. No intervillage rivalries. When asked what had been the motive behind the killing, Marcelino Quispe, one of the accused, replied simply, "*No hubo* [There wasn't any]." According to Marcelino, "There wasn't any [bad blood] between us that would have led us to commit such a grave act as the one committed." He and Yaranqa had never "at any time been on bad terms." If anything, Marcelino clarified, he and Yaranqa had been on quite friendly terms before the altercation. The two had known each other "since I was a baby" and were in fact related. What had occurred on the Sunday morning in question was simply one of those unfortunate things that sometimes happened during times of festive drinking. Marcelino therefore accepted his twelve-month prison sentence without putting up much of a legal fight.[142] Even *mama* Alejandra accepted Marcelino's general assessment: "The author of the crime won because he said: 'That happened during Carnival, and five or more people always die during Carnival.'" After making this statement *mama* Alejandra sighed and conceded: "Things like that happen in every village during Carnival."[143]

What we have described here is a form of "legitimate" intercommunity violence that was built into Iquichano culture. Peasants in Huaychao and neighboring communities tolerated a degree of intervillage violence as long as it occurred during times of festive drinking. Because the Tupinos interpreted Yaranqa's death as an unfortunate casualty of Carnival, they saw no reason to retaliate with more violence. This also explains the circumstances behind Eulogio Ramos's death, which also occurred during a local festival. Nor were Iquichano communities the only ones to develop a form of legitimate violence. Ritual battles known as *tinkus* have been well documented throughout the Andes, particularly in Bolivia.[144] These battles generally take place between rival communities or kinship groups and always during times of fiesta. Although the confrontations are highly performative, the violence is very real. Bloodshed is not only common for *tinkus* but also expected, seen as a sign of honor for those who endure it. Although women do participate, *tinkus* are typically male affairs, conceived of by participants and observers alike as an opportunity for men to showcase their masculinity.[145] Masculine competitions such as these have also been chronicled in the Peruvian department of Cuzco, where participants can number up to 1,000. As with the Bolivian case, participants in Cuzco view the violence as legitimate because it occurs on specific dates of the ritual calendar and between two consenting social groups.[146]

Huaychao's intercommunal feuds can be seen as a variation of these ritual battles. While not as institutionalized as these other forms, the intervillage battles that took place in this part of the Iquichano highlands occurred during times of fiesta, followed an implicit code of conduct, and were seen by the local peasantry as a legitimate form of violence. This kind of violence served a double purpose. First and foremost, it offered a socially acceptable forum through which the local populace could engage in aggressive acts. Second, it solidified intercommunal solidarity, extending kinship networks beyond the immediate community. Still, although Huaychao's semiritual battles channeled intervillage hostilities into a well-defined temporal and geographic space, it would be a mistake to conclude that they curtailed external disputes altogether. Intercommunal conflict still occurred outside of the fiesta. One common manifestation of this was through the practice of livestock theft.

Tracing the Tracks: Intercommunal Cattle Rustling

Most cases of intervillage cattle rustling in Huaychao also involved the neighboring village of Huaynacancha. Let us return to the 1975 case in which Huaynacanchino Víctor Gamboa organized a search committee to retrieve his nine missing llamas. After five days of fruitless investigation, the Huaynacanchino search committee noticed that Saturnino Cayetano had been storing llama hide, wool, and meat in his home outside the village. Since Cayetano was away at the time, they asked his wife, Catalina Quispe, how the two had acquired the llamas. Quispe informed them that since she and her husband were *mayordomos* (sponsors) of the upcoming Festival of the Crosses, they had purchased the llamas from Cecilio Díaz and Alejandro Huamán on the night of 30 April just for the occasion. Gamboa testified that the investigators brought Quispe to the village *despacho*, where they informed Lieutenant Governor Jesús Llancce of the situation. The Huaychaino authority called Cecilio Díaz in for questioning; Alejandro Huamán had already fled the zone. According to Gamboa, Díaz not only confessed to his and Huamán's role in the robbery but also was so "repentant" that he agreed to repay his victim for his losses through a combination of money and livestock. Gamboa added that after settling the matter of the repayment, the lieutenant governor set the *abigeo* free.[147]

The testimonies of the accused *abigeos* do not appear in the court record; nor do those of the lieutenant governor or Catalina Quispe. Only Huaychaino Saturnino Cayetano gave testimony in his own defense when police brought him before the court in Huanta City on 28 May. The twenty-six-year-old peasant stated that he had nothing to do with the crime for which he stood accused. He said that it was true that he had come into the possession of a llama earlier that month, but he had obtained it legitimately as part of his role as *mayordomo*. Moreover, at the time the alleged robbery took place he was in Huanta City seeking employment and looking to purchase a plot of land. He had remained there until police brought him in for questioning. Cayetano further denounced Gamboa's claim that his wife, Francisca, had confessed to having purchased llamas from Díaz and Huamán. From what his family back in Huaychao told him, Gamboa and his neighbors had violently sacked his wife's home, committing "a series of abuses" and stealing a llama's hide, three cowbells, and upward of 2,300 soles that he and his wife had wrapped in a handkerchief and stashed inside a basket. Cayetano denied Gamboa's claim that he had found llama meat inside the residence.[148] Having no further incriminating evidence, the court ruled in favor of the defendant.[149]

Nearly every Huaychaino elder had a similar story to tell about Huaynacanchino cattle rustlers. Yet, almost without exception, Huaychaino elders emphasized how authorities from Huaychao and Huaynacancha had worked together to investigate and resolve the crime. One of those elders was Santos Huaylla. We paid *tayta* Santos a visit outside of his hilltop hut on an unusually sunny morning. He told us that, particularly in the post-hacienda period, it was not unusual for people from Huaynacancha, Uchuraccay, and other locations to steal cattle from Huaychao. Typically, they would steer the animals into the nearby mountains, kill them, and take the meat back to their homes. He remembered one case in which another Huaynacanchino named Gamboa stole eighteen llamas from a villager of the annex of Ccarasencca. Gesturing toward each of the adjacent mountains, *tayta* Santos spoke of how he organized a search party to retrieve the lost animals: "That guy took them over there and over there, and in the mountain of Pucaccasa we lost the footprints. But we kept looking and discovered that the footprints led to Huaynacancha." When the search party reached Huaynacancha, local authorities investigated the matter. Together, the search party and the Huaynacancha leaders concluded that Gamboa had been assisted by one of the victim's Ccarasencca neighbors. Authorities from Huaynacancha and Huaychao then brought the alleged accomplice to the Huaychao *despacho* and tied his hands together with a rope "so that he couldn't escape." Next, the authorities interrogated him while flogging him with a *chicote*. Between lashes, the interrogators demanded: "Why did you steal?" Finally the alleged accomplice confessed to his role in the crime and revealed that he and Gamboa had already made use of the animals. Before paying a fine in pigs and sheep, he directed them toward a cave where they would find the remains of the stolen llamas.[150]

Like *tayta* Santos, *tayta* Mariano recalled the degree of cooperation between Huaychaino and Huaynacanchino authorities when it came to solving cattle-rustling cases. After losing a couple of cows sometime in the 1970s, *tayta* Mariano organized a ten-man search committee and traced the tracks to Huaynacancha. When they got there, Huaynacancha leaders authorized them to search each home for the stolen cattle. As they approached the home of Simeón Velásquez and his father Víctor, they could see slabs of meat inside. "They were slick," *tayta* Mariano said of the duo, who he believed had previously stolen cattle from two of his neighbors. When the Huaychainos demanded entry, however, the owners objected violently and a fight erupted as men from both sides began beating each other with clubs. "Even their wives hit us in the head with clubs. And they hit us in our bodies, too!" he added incredulously. Eventually, the Huaychainos overpowered the Velásquezes. Working with the Huaynacancha authorities, however, the Huaychainos finally overpowered the thieves and escorted them to Carhuahurán to report the incident.[151]

Clearly, livestock theft was as much a problem in the Iquichano highlands as elsewhere. The major difference between these villages and those in Chuschi District, however, is in the degree of cooperation that indigenous authorities from neighboring communities extended each other when it came to resolving these disputes. With few exceptions, Huaychaino and Huaynacanchino authorities not only allowed each other's search parties to conduct investigations in their villages but also aided in those investigations. And as we have seen, after authorities and investigators from the two communities identified a suspect, they usually handed him over to local and regional authorities. This is a very different scenario than the one that developed in Chuschi and Quispillaccta, where communal authorities were often the ones leading the charge against the rival community.

To Reach the Mountaintop: Intervillage Hierarchy

Although Huaychao technically fell within the jurisdiction of Huanta City, villagers usually reported serious cases to officials in Carhuahurán, which was much closer and more accessible. Huaychainos preferred to settle disputes internally—and they usually did. For cases that required the attention of external officials, they usually turned first to Carhuahurán and then to Huanta City as a final option. Carhuahurán's de facto political jurisdiction over Huaychao was cemented through the *vara visita*, the same ritualized visit of authorities that occurred on a smaller scale in the village of Huaychao.[152] Beyond the village, Huaychao's top officials would make frequent trips to Carhuahurán to meet with its authorities and pay respect to its religious icons. During Christmas time, for example, Huaychao's authorities traveled to Carhuahurán to pay their respects to its nativity scene. *Mama* Juana explained this to Julián and me one night over a bowl of potato soup: "The people from Carhuahurán controlled this whole area. That's why my grandfather always said, 'The *varayoqs* must go there and greet El Niño Jesús. Otherwise, there will be problems.' So, the new *varayoq* would go and greet El Niño, and that's how it was each year."[153] This tradition not only ensured that Huaychao and neighboring communities remained interconnected socially and politically but also reinforced a regional political hierarchy in which Carhuahurán enjoyed relative hegemony. As *tayta* Mariano's above anecdote implies, however, some Huaychainos resented having to defer to Carhuahurán's political authority. Ideally, they would have preferred to have more autonomy over local affairs.

This intercommunity hierarchy did more than cause resentment toward Carhuahurán. After the Agrarian Reform, Iquichano communities and their indigenous authorities found themselves in competition over matters of political jurisdiction. This explains the petition drafted by Huaychainos Zenobio, Juan, and Julia Quispe in March 1975, just three months before the land reform officially reached Huaychao. The Quispes declared that Faustino Aguilar, the lieutenant governor of nearby Pampalca, had "usurped the right of our own lieutenant [governor] of Huaychau [*sic*]" by meddling in a dispute between them and a Pampalca woman named Ana Ramos. According to the plaintiffs, Aguilar had ruled in favor of Ramos, determining that the Quispes' animals had ruined the fields where her tubers grew. The Quispes dismissed the Pampalca leader's ruling as "completely false," reasoning that if it were true, "our lieutenant governor don Jesús Llancce Huamán would have made use of his rights as authority of the location and not of some other location that doesn't pertain to him," as Aguilar had done. Aguilar's actions, they concluded, could only be interpreted as a blatant "abuse of authority and usurpation of [political] functions."[154] This was more than just an attempt by the Huaychainos to clear themselves of the charges brought against them. What they sought was a legal precedent establishing Huaychao's post–Agrarian Reform political autonomy in the Iquichano highlands.

Coming Home

The nature of intervillage relationships in Chuschi contrasted greatly with those in Huaychao. Clearly, Huaychao was not free of intervillage conflict. The defense of local women against external sexual aggression was a primal concern for Huaychainos, to the point that it could foment collective violence. What is interesting, though, is the way that these bouts of paternalistic violence played out in Huaychao. Many of them occurred under the socially accepted space of the local fiesta, where battles were fought in almost ritualistic fashion with implicit rules of engagement. This helped mitigate any long-term antagonisms that might have developed at the intercommunity level. Moreover, the fiestas themselves and the interpersonal relationships that developed during them encouraged the expansion of kinship and social networks across community borders. This networking was also reinforced through the regional political hierarchy, which encouraged intervillage cooperation when it came to resolving crimes such as cattle theft. Still, this intervillage hierarchy and the issue of village political autonomy became a point of contestation after the Agrarian Reform.

Chuschi, on the other hand, had been engaged in an intense conflict with Quispillaccta during the entire period of this study. This was superficially a dispute over land boundaries and communal autonomy. But this only begins to scratch the surface of what lay behind the rivalry. We learned, for example, that Chuschinos and Quispillacctinos saw them-

selves as distinct ethnic groups. Also at stake was the civil-religious autonomy of each community, which became jeopardized symbolically
whenever inhabitants of the rival village destroyed, defaced, or captured
religious icons. Finally, we learned that this was not a generational conflict
but one that parents passed on to their children through oral tradition,
thereby ensuring that the tensions were still on the minds of local peasants
when Shining Path launched its insurgency in 1980.

. . . .

CHAPTER 3

To Walk in Shoes

Race and Class

"**T**ELL US ANOTHER ONE!**"** I insisted as Huaychao native Narciso Huamán poured himself another cup of aguardiente. When he finished his drink, Narciso poured what was left in his cup onto the dirt floor with a swift fling of the wrist and handed me the cup and bottle. "Salud, compadre," he said. I lifted the cup and repeated, "Salud," pouring myself a teaspoon's worth of the warm cane liquor. Most days, Narciso, an Evangelical *comunero* in his thirties, would decline an invitation to drink alcohol since it conflicts with his religious views. This night was special, however, as I had just been brought into his kinship network by cutting his nephew's hair in a *compadrazgo* ceremony. Tonight, abstinence took a back seat to tradition. I turned to Julián, who was sitting next to me in the circle, and repeated the ritual. Satisfied with the level of participation that Julián and I were displaying in the libation ceremony, Narciso decided to amuse us with one more story. "Very well, I'll tell you a story that my father told me when I was little." Narciso went on to tell a couple of tales about honest Andean heroes who had rare encounters with strict yet benevolent kings. Narciso told the stories in Quechua, without a tape recorder, and after a night of heavy drinking, so I had trouble keeping up. After he made several references to a hacendado, I realized that I was completely lost, so I asked for clarification in Spanish: "Where did the hacendado come from?" Narciso appeared as confused by my question as I had been with his tale, so I got more specific: "I mean, I don't get it. Is there a hacendado in the kingdom, too?" Narciso smiled at my ignorance: "The hacendado *is* the king, compadre."[1]

UP TO THIS POINT our story has centered on relationships and conflicts that developed among indigenous peasants. This chapter moves beyond these relationships to explore those that developed across racial and class lines. Once again, Chuschi and Huaychao offer two divergent histories. Indigenous peasants in Huaychao did not perceive their relationships with elite mestizos as threatening to their way of life. Like the kings in Narciso's stories, Huaychainos remembered their erstwhile estate owners as tyrannical but paternalistic, stern but fair. In Chuschi, in contrast, the actions, behaviors, and attitudes of mestizo notables violated the cultural expectations that peasants had of their nonindigenous power holders. As far as Chuschi's indigenous peasantry was concerned, members of the mestizo elite were more preoccupied with consolidating their political and economic power within the community than with fulfilling their inherent paternalistic obligations, creating what many *comuneros* perceived as a local crisis of authority. In order to better understand this divergence in power relations between Chuschi and Huaychao, it will be useful to explore the historical context under which these relations developed.

Race and Class in a Context of Agrarian Reform

The middle decades of the twentieth century were a time of intensive change in rural politics across the globe. During this period the United States, driven by its own commercial and political interests, began to put pressure on nations in the developing world to modernize agricultural production. But North American capitalists were not the only ones who favored breaking up "feudal" land-tenure systems. As I mentioned in chapter 2, peasants throughout the world had mobilized to demand new land rights and reclaim territories from the landed elite. These new claims of the peasantry sometimes converged with radical, anticolonial ideologies to produce leftist political movements and armed insurgencies. Even after previous political orders had been overthrown, the rural poor in postcolonial nations continued to make important claims to citizenship and entitlement.

Agrarian societies responded to these historical developments in a variety of ways, but a common response in many developing nations was comprehensive land reform. In 1949, shortly after retreating to Taiwan, the Chinese Nationalists replaced most of the island's commercial rice estates with small holdings.[2] In North Vietnam, 85 percent of farm units were collectivized between 1958 and 1960.[3] But war-torn states were not the only ones to experiment with agrarian reform. After ousting the Tutsi landowners in 1960, the Hutu did away with Rwanda's manorial land-tenure system.[4] In the mid-1960s, newly independent India promised major changes to the colonial status quo. Top among those promises was a sweeping land reform.[5]

Virtually every Latin American nation experienced some kind of agrarian reform during this period. Guatemalan president Jacobo Arbenz initiated the process in 1952 with Decree 900. Although the Guatemalan reform met stiff opposition from within and without, it was the most sweeping land reform of its time. By 1954, over 1.4 million acres had been redistributed to roughly 100,000 peasant families.[6] Other Latin American countries would soon follow. In an effort to pacify indigenous peasants who had been mobilizing in the countryside, Bolivia's revolutionary government enacted a comprehensive agrarian reform in August 1953. Bolivia's land reform effectively dismantled the hacienda system and the nation's landed oligarchy, redistributing estate lands to indigenous peasant communities and unions.[7] The state-implemented agrarian reforms of 1950s Guatemala and Bolivia initiated a new era of Latin American land tenure. By 1970 most Latin American countries had enacted similar measures. Peru was one of those countries.[8]

The call for land reform was nothing new in Peru. As early as the 1920s, *indigenistas* such as José Carlos Mariátegui had argued that indigenous peasants' social and economic marginalization was directly related to their lack of control over land.[9] Given, the *indigenistas* argued, that Peru's Quechua speakers were descendants of Incan agriculturalists, it was in the best interests of both their race and the country to restore the land to the indigenous peasants who tilled it. This project would entail a complete dismantling of the hegemony of mestizo landlords. Peruvian *indigenistas* were not the only ones to link progress to land reform. In 1952 activist scholars at Cornell University teamed up with the Peruvian government in an effort to integrate the indigenous peasantry into the market economy. As part of the project, Cornell University leased the 43,750-acre Vicos hacienda in the northern Andes, breaking up the existing peonage system and converting the estate into a public beneficiary society. For the next fourteen years, functionaries of the Cornell-Peru Project facilitated the shift in control over the hacienda's operation and resources into the hands of the local indigenous peasantry.[10]

Notwithstanding these efforts, Peru's landed oligarchy preserved its control over the nation's polity and economy well into the middle of the century. By the mid-1960s some 700 landowners controlled nearly one-third of Peru's productive land and over half of the most productive land on the irrigated coast.[11] In addition to their control over land, mestizo landowners held considerable sway over politicians, military officers, credit sources, and even the press.[12] Landowners controlled people as well as resources, doing their best to restrict their indigenous serfs' access to schools, urban centers, and the media. Because only literates could vote, peasants—more than half of whom could not read or write—had very few legal mechanisms through which to contest the establishment. It was therefore not uncommon for a hacendado to compel those who could vote to cast their ballots for the politician of his choice.[13]

By the 1960s changing political, demographic, and economic realities caused this land-tenure system to gradually break down. The emergence of a capitalist class in Lima provided a "new elite" with which the traditional oligarchy had to contend. At the same time, the Peruvian government, driven by an effort to modernize the countryside and stimulate the flow of goods and capital, began constructing new highways and schools in the Sierra. As more and more highlanders began taking advantage of these highways and migrating to the coast, they merged with Lima's popular classes to form a viable voting bloc.[14] This heightened communication between the highlands and the coast facilitated the peasant mobilizations I discussed in chapter 2.[15] Although these mobilizations focused on issues of class, they were not without a racial component. This is illustrated in the reflections that Hugo Blanco provided after a gathering in Cuzco:

> In Cuzco, for centuries, the Indian had slouched along the streets with his poncho and his whispered Quechua; he had never dared, even when drunk, to mount the sidewalk or speak his Quechua out loud with his head held high. He was fearful of the *misti* [nonindigenous outsider] who was the master of the city. . . . The mass meeting put the Indian on top of the master. A concentration of ponchos in the main plaza. . . . Quechua out loud from the throat; Quechua shouted, threatening, tearing away the centuries of oppression.[16]

The mobilizations of the 1950s and 1960s prompted politicians to begin addressing indigenous peasants' demands for land reform. Fernando Belaúnde Terry was among the first national political figures to address peasant grievances, making repeated visits to the countryside after the 1956 elections.[17] For the 1963 elections, Belaúnde was elected to the presidency due in large part to his campaign promise to deliver comprehensive land

reform. Once in office, however, Belaúnde wavered, passing a highly re-
strictive agrarian reform and even sending in the police to quell several
peasant land invasions, killing thousands in the process.[18]

By the late 1960s Peru was faced with what many observers perceived as
an economic and political crisis. The Belaúnde state had failed to placate
the peasantry, and the country was in the midst of a deep economic recession due to an overdependence on foreign markets.[19] In light of this crisis,
the military led a bloodless coup on 3 October 1968, installing General
Juan Velasco Alvarado as president and establishing a new administration,
the Revolutionary Government of the Armed Forces. The GRFA hoped
that by placating the lower classes, it would engender loyalty toward the
military regime.[20] Velasco sought to achieve this by reversing centuries of
control by the Sierra's mestizo hacendados.

In 1969 the Velasco regime initiated an unprecedented Agrarian Reform, seizing the country's most significant haciendas and converting
them into peasant cooperatives made up of former serfs.[21] Cooperative
members, known as *socios*, collectively shared the duties and entitlements
of workers, managers, and shareholders. Each member of the cooperative
was allowed to vote in its General Assembly, thereby gaining a voice in
the major decisions regarding investments, the budget, and production.
Likewise, cooperative members were entitled to vote for their local representatives, who served on the newly created vigilance and administrative
councils. In addition to allowing cooperative members access to local-
level executive decisions, the government required, through Supreme
Decree 240-69-AP, that each cooperative withhold a portion of its profits
for local investment. This measure, the government believed, would help
modernize the peasantry.

The Velasco government created new agencies and institutions designed to address peasant grievances. The National System of Support for
Social Mobilization (SINAMOS), established in April 1972, was designed
to be the state agency through which peasants could filter their agrarian
demands. In addition to SINAMOS, the government created the Agrarian
Tribunal, or Land Court, a court system designed to handle peasants' legal
battles over land. Recognizing that indigenous peasants were often at a
disadvantage when making claims against landowners, the tribunal provided peasants with public defenders who were fluent in Quechua and
Aymara.[22]

With respect to the peasant cooperatives, Velasco established, through

Decree Law 19400, the National Agrarian Confederation (CNA), an institution intended to ensure the development of self-managing peasant cooperatives.[23] Several subagencies fell under the control of the CNA. Among these were the Integral Rural Settlement Projects (PIARs), the Integral Development Projects (PIDs), the Agrarian Production Cooperatives (CAPs), and the Social Interest Groups (SAISs) — the latter being the most common in the south-central highlands.[24] Through these various state-sponsored institutions, Velasco sought cooperative self-management in the Peruvian agricultural sector.

If nothing else, the Velasco reforms altered land tenure in the Peruvian countryside. In 1968, the year of the military's coup, 51 percent of the gross domestic product was controlled by private business, 33 percent remained with foreign interests, and 16 percent was allocated to the public sector. By 1975 the figures had shifted dramatically. Forty percent of the gross national product in 1975 remained in private hands, only 17 percent in foreign interests, 31 percent in the public realm, and 12 percent went to the newly formed agricultural cooperatives.[25] By the end of 1974 some 54,562 peasant families had been successfully incorporated into forty-eight SAISs across the country.[26] By 1977 nearly all of Peru's large haciendas had been dismantled. According to some estimates, the agrarian reform affected, either directly or indirectly, as much as 40 percent of Peru's economically active population.[27]

The land reform was not without its shortcomings, however. Bent on stimulating community-based labor in the cooperatives, the Velasco state failed to recognize that some peasants preferred privatization to cooperativization. The regime also overestimated the control that landowners held over rural estates. A combination of midcentury land invasions and politicians' repeated promises of land reform had already led many landowners to abandon or dismantle their properties by the time the reform took effect.[28] Additionally, the military's top-down authoritarian structure left little room for peasants to achieve grassroots change.[29] Velasco's rural policy also excluded too many people. For example, since cooperative membership was open only to former hacienda serfs, seasonal workers and *comuneros* of nearby communities could not join, much less receive any of the benefits that came with cooperative membership.[30] The Agrarian Reform ignored most peasant communities entirely. By some accounts, 72 percent (860,000) of the 1.2 million peasant families living in Peru received no structural benefits during the Velasco era.[31]

One of the departments most overlooked by the Agrarian Reform was Ayacucho. Of the 22,035 families that had received lands in the south-central Sierra by late 1971, only 414 were from Ayacucho.[32] Nor did Ayacucho rank high on the GRFA's list of potential beneficiaries. That same year, the government had only allocated land grants to 8 percent of the department's highland peasantry—this compared to 50 percent in the coastal department of Lambayaque.[33] Given this unequal distribution of land, it is not surprising that some peasants in Ayacucho felt that the reforms of the Velasco state had neglected them.[34]

If some peasants felt abandoned during the first phase of military rule, they were downright betrayed during the second phase. "Phase Two" of military rule began on 29 August 1975, when General Francisco Morales Bermúdez ousted an ailing Velasco from the presidency. While the new regime kept the GRFA title, it was revolutionary in name only. Almost immediately, Morales Bermúdez began enacting regressive measures designed to restore the precoup socioeconomic order. During the years of Morales Bermúdez's rule, Peru's popular classes suffered from increased unemployment, and the countryside spiraled into economic stagnation.[35] The GRFA's conservative turn only confirmed the suspicions of many peasants that the government did not have their best interests in mind. In Ayacucho, it was around this time that intellectuals and peasants alike began considering more radical solutions to their problems.[36]

But perhaps the GRFA's most significant shortcoming was its conflation of hacendados with *gamonales*, the abusive power holders so often vilified in populist discourse. "Since now the campesinos own their own land," regime supporters argued, "there are no more lords, there are no more *gamonales*, there is no more bourgeoisie, because land ownership is everything."[37] The term *gamonal* derives from the word *gamón*, which refers to an Andean weed that feeds off of weaker plants.[38] Although used by 1920s *indigenistas* to describe abusive hacendados, the term evolved to encompass a whole class of mestizo power holders—priests, lawyers, local office holders—whose dominion derived from their influence over the political and juridical realm, their control over economic resources, and, as a result, their ability to exploit and abuse indigenous highlanders with impunity.[39] The Velasco state mistakenly assumed that dismantling the economic stranglehold of the landed elite would simultaneously eradicate *gamonalismo*. It did not. The main reason for this was that the Velasco administration, in emphasizing issues of class and land tenure, failed to address the *cultural* dynamics of rural power relationships. As we will see below, indigenous peasants in Chuschi experienced *gamonalismo* despite living outside of hacendado control. In Huaychao, in contrast, peasants lived under hacendado control, but they did not see their landlords as *gamonales* per se. Because the Agrarian Reform focused on dismantling large estates, however, Huaychao's "legitimate" power holders were forced to leave, while Chuschi's illegitimate *gamonales* remained in power.

The Men in the Shoes: Chuschi's Qalas

Chuschinos had a specific name for their mestizo power holders: *qalas.* Derived from the Quechua word meaning "the stripped ones," villagers use the term today to refer to Chuschinos who have been racially, socially, and culturally "stripped" of their indigeneity.[40] As more than one villager told me, the most important marker of a *qala* was not his or her language, phenotype, or material possessions; it was, rather, the person's dress. Specifically, *qalas* wore shoes, while indigenous *comuneros* wore sandals. Far from being mutually exclusive, the two groups depended on one another. *Qalas'* local hegemony hinged on indigenous Chuschinos' recognition of their legitimacy. Conversely, indigenous peasants were willing to concede to the *qalas'* local dominion provided that they met their culturally and morally informed standards for nonindigenous power holders. The result was a mutually—although far from equally—beneficial and dependent power pact predicated on indigenous peasants' cultural views regarding race and class.

Dictators of the Consejo: The Village Patriarchs

Before the 1968 Agrarian Reform, Chuschi's town council, known as the Consejo, was almost exclusively the realm of the district's mestizo notables, or *vecinos*. These *vecino* officials were appointed by, and responded directly to, the Cangallo subprefect. These officials also communicated indirectly with the departmental prefect and other branches of the Peruvian state. Heading this system were, in order of lowest to highest rank, the lieutenant governor, governor, lieutenant mayor, and mayor. Together with the local justice of the peace, these officials were responsible for making and enforcing national and district laws. After the military coup that put Velasco in power, local officials were elected democratically by all married villagers, *qala* and indigenous. This resulted in some indigenous peasants breaking the race barrier. However, since final approval for appointments still went through the provincial subprefect, most bureaucratic positions still remained mestizo controlled. Of course, indigenous peasants did have their own authority structure in the *varayoqs*, but in the eyes of the Peruvian state this system was subordinate, not parallel, to that of the Consejo.

Rather than go into detail about the abuses of each of Chuschi's mestizo authorities—for there were many—I would like to highlight the careers of three individuals who embodied a larger crisis of authority that was under way in midcentury Chuschi. As we will see in chapter 4, each of these authorities would become a key figure in the political violence of the 1980s.

The first authority was Felipe Aycha, the local butcher-turned *abigeo* "boss" whose escapades we learned about in chapters 1 and 2. There, I described Aycha as an indigenous *comunero*. Why, then, does he reappear here as a *qala* authority? In order to make sense of this apparent contradiction, one must appreciate the fluidity of racial identity in the mid-twentieth-century Andes. As occurred elsewhere in Peru, indigenous Chuschinos managed to maintain a cultural and racial claim to both indigenous and mestizo identities.[41] In chapter 1, we discovered how Felipe Aycha's monopoly over cattle rustling afforded him a good deal of power in the village. It did not take long for Aycha to fuse his illegitimate dominion with civilian power. Aycha, it turns out, became one of the few *comuneros* to break the racial barrier of the local bureaucracy in the late 1950s. Given his penchant for brute intimidation, it should come as no surprise that few villagers opposed his ascension to local politics. And so it was that the indigenous Felipe Aycha entered the mestizo-dominated bureaucracy. In many ways, villagers already considered Aycha a *qala*, since his unethical social conduct indicated his disregard for *comunero* values. His record as a political authority did little to convince them otherwise. This explains why *tayta* Víctor described Aycha as "medio moreno" (half-black).[42] Maybe this was an accurate phenotypical depiction, but it may also have been *tayta* Víctor's way of emphasizing that, as far as he was concerned, Aycha was neither fully indigenous nor mestizo. Another informant made a similar distinction about a *comunero* who had successfully infiltrated the mestizo-dominated profession of teachers, referring to him with the diminutive *qalacha* (little *qala*) to imply that he was not fully mestizo.[43]

Another trait Aycha was known for was his temper. The archival record supports this characterization. At around noon on 6 October 1959, Aycha's thirty-two-year-old sister Modesta walked into his governor's office and told him that she was having marital problems.[44] Modesta's husband, Máximo, was consuming cane liquor and *chicha* with his relatives when the equally intoxicated governor barged into the home wielding a *verga*, a whip fashioned from a bull's penis. According to Máximo, Aycha kicked him and his family members—his mother included—and beat them with the weapon repeatedly before taking them back to the village holding cell.[45] While the court record does not include the verdict, we do know that Felipe Aycha was still governor as of 1965.

It was at this point that Mateo Alocer penned a letter to the subprefect charging that Aycha had once again abused his authority. Around July of that year, Alocer had made the mistake of purchasing a pair of horses in Governor Aycha's presence. Sometime in August or September, Aycha confiscated the animals without cause and rode them into nearby Chicllarrazo, setting them free after arriving. About a month later, Aycha sold the two horses in a public auction on the pretext that they had not been claimed by an owner. Aycha even bid on one of the horses himself. When Alocer confronted the governor about the scam, Aycha simply denied it. "Now," Alocer wrote the subprefect, "this same governor is walking around like the owner of [my] lost animal." As far as Alocer was concerned, Aycha was "abusing his authority and discrediting his name as governor of the district of Chuschi."[46] Actions such as these persuaded villagers of Aycha's illegitimacy as a local patriarch. Although he had redeemed himself somewhat by leading villagers into battle against the Quispillacctinos during the 1960 March of Death, this alone was not enough to clear his name in the eyes of the Chuschi populace. To most, Aycha was nothing but a *gamonal* and a thug who needed to be brought to justice for his delinquent behavior.

The same went for Felipe Aycha's indigenous friend, Bernardo Chipana. Chipana was the Chuschino migrant who in 1979 teamed up with Aycha to steal livestock from *vecino* Ernesto Jaime. Because Chipana had spent a good deal of time outside of the village and did not participate in *comunero* activities, indigenous villagers sometimes considered him a *qala*. As was the case with Felipe Aycha, then, Bernardo Chipana's standing in the community illustrates the elasticity of racial identity in twentieth-century Chuschi. Also like Aycha, Chipana took advantage of his ambiguous identity to infiltrate the local bureaucracy, taking a position as governor around 1980. His political reign was not without controversy.

In June 1981 the *comuneros* and authorities of the neighborhood of Yaruca Rumichaca accused him and other mestizo officials of stealing ten heads of communal cattle and using the profits for drinking money.[47] As if this were not enough, Chipana and company then began charging the *comuneros* for everything from the land they owned to the right to build homes, vowing to "demolish the homes, or evict" anyone who could not come up with the arbitrary taxes. Then, "for absolutely no reason," Chipana and his colleagues went around Yaruca Rumichaca and other Chuschi neighborhoods stealing upward of twenty-five sheep.[48] Eager to hold the *qala* authorities to account for their actions, the *comuneros* called for the immediate resignation of Chipana and his colleagues. The villagers sent a statement to the lieutenant mayor reminding him that if he did not honor their request, Chipana and company "might commit far worse crimes against the *comuneros* and to the detriment of this community."[49] The lieutenant mayor responded by holding a town hall meeting inside the church. The *qala* leaders defended their actions, but the indigenous *comuneros* demanded their resignations. While his colleagues stepped down without a fight, Chipana held his ground until eighty-one *comuneros*, a majority of the attendees, voted him out of office.[50]

Whether or not they considered him a full-fledged *qala* or *comunero*, Chipana's behavior violated several core *comunero* values. Rather than defend the interests of his indigenous constituents, Chipana used his new political authority as a vehicle through which to extort them. This was to say nothing of his reputation before becoming an authority, a reputation that had been tainted with allegations of cattle rustling and association with the most despised rustler of all, Felipe Aycha. As we will see in chapter 4, Bernardo Chipana would pay for his social misconduct and political illegitimacy during the Shining Path insurgency.

The third *qala* authority worth mentioning here is Vicente Blanco.[51] Clotilde Bedriñana was one of many Chuschinas to press charges against Blanco. Bedriñana was sleeping in her Chuschi home on the night of 25 December 1969 when she felt a ruffle underneath her sheets. One can imagine Bedriñana's pleasant surprise as she surmised that her husband had cut short his stay in Lima to be with his family on Christmas. Given his long absence, Bedriñana did not give it much thought when he crawled on top of her. In fact, it was not until they began making love that she first suspected something was amiss: her husband was not himself, covering her mouth with his hand as he performed the act. Bedriñana leaned over and lit the candle on her nightstand only to discover that the man making love to her was not her husband at all, but her mestizo neighbor Vicente Blanco![52]

By the 1970s, Blanco, a mestizo schoolteacher and political office holder, had developed a reputation as a womanizer. Even his daughter admitted as much. During a trip from Ayacucho City to Chuschi, the now middle-aged *mestiza* showed me the mountain where *comuneros* engaged in *vida michiy*, an act of indiscriminate sexual intercourse reserved exclusively for unmarried *comunero* adolescents.[53] "Ah, my father was all too familiar with that mountain when I was little," she confessed. "It was his nightclub!"[54] The words of Blanco's daughter reveal that the *vecino* Blanco had overstepped his cultural boundaries by repeatedly engaging in a *comunero* activity. Even if the rumors were true, we would be remiss not to speculate that indigenous men and women *allowed* Blanco to participate. Still, none of this dispels two important facts: first, that the rumors existed, and, second, that they were widespread enough to have reached the ears of Blanco's own daughter. What this reveals is a *perception* among some *comuneros* that Blanco had somehow violated cultural boundaries by engaging in *vida michiy*. For, starters, *vida michiy* was supposed to be off limits to Blanco because he was a married adult, and every man and woman whom we interviewed confirmed that it was the exclusive domain of single adolescents, intended to encourage courtship and marriage. Moreover, it was designed to be a festivity for indigenous *comuneros* and not mestizo notables like Blanco. Blanco probably knew this, for he never hesitated to accuse anthropologist Billie Jean Isbell of engaging in the act during one of his many efforts to expel her from the community.[55] Indeed, when we asked Blanco about the practice, he exhibited an awareness of the general rules of engagement: "[*Vida michiy*] is a nocturnal game between adolescents of both sexes and sometimes married men. . . . It involved singing, dancing, and wasn't allowed inside the village . . . but [rather] in a [remote] hut. Boys and girls would go out in pairs, with their drink of course. . . . And during *vida michiy* one man could have relations with two or more women at a time."[56]

The only major difference between Blanco's description and that which the *comuneros* provided was in the *vecino*'s assertion that married men were entitled to participate in the act. The *comuneros* we interviewed unanimously rejected the notion that any married man or woman could ever engage in the ritual. To them, *vida michiy* was an activity reserved exclusively for *comunero* singles. Although Blanco never admitted to having partaken in the ritual, his invention of the "marriage clause" may have served as a rhetorical justification for his own participation. If Blanco did in fact participate, it would have represented a major cultural affront to *comuneros* because he was both married and a mestizo. By accusing Blanco of frequent participation in *vida michiy*, then, *comuneros* were voicing their concern with his disregard for indigenous cultural norms and racial boundaries. He was in effect encroaching on and denigrating a ritual that was intended to be the strict domain of unmarried indigenous adolescents.

Had gossip been the only thing linking Blanco to the violation of interracial cultural boundaries, he might have been able to keep his reputation intact. But it was the documented cases of unsolicited sexual advances on *comuneras* that really did the mayor in. Clotilde Bedriñana was one of the first women to formally denounce Blanco on these charges. As she reported to authorities, Blanco's transgressions against her had only just begun when he broke into her home and raped her in her sleep. After she discovered that it was he who was violating her, Bedriñana managed to push the drunken teacher off of her and call for help. Moments later, her daughter, stepson, and several neighbors came to her defense. According to Bedriñana, Blanco fled at the first sign of trouble, but not before pocketing 15,000 soles in cash that she kept stashed under her pillow.[57] Bedriñana and her thirteen-year-old daughter chased Blanco all the way back to his house at the edge of the village plaza, demanding that he return the money. Instead, he began beating them until his wife finally broke them up.[58]

That was the last time Blanco's wife intervened on her neighbor's behalf. Weeks later, she joined her husband in attacking Bedriñana outside the police station when the latter went to press charges against Blanco. Bedriñana managed to escape inside the station, but not before Blanco had kicked her in the leg and his wife had pulled her hair by the braids.[59] Months later, Bedriñana was walking home from the village plaza when she sensed brisk footsteps behind her. She turned around only to find her nemesis standing there. "*Paya puta* [old whore]," he said. "Look at you, so happy because you pressed charges against me." Before Bedriñana could react, Blanco struck her in the face, wounding her left eye. Blanco followed up with a series of kicks to the legs, side, and pelvis before leaving Bedriñana unconscious in the middle of the street. When she came to, she noticed that one of Blanco's colleagues was trying to calm him down, to which he replied, "I'm going to kill that whore!" Bedriñana claimed to have still been secreting blood from her vagina when she testified about the incident four days later, a wound that she described as "considerably inhumane for a woman."[60]

If Bedriñana thought she had a good case against Blanco, she was sorely mistaken. The court did find Blanco guilty, but not of rape, assault, or robbery. Instead, the judge sentenced Blanco to just one month in prison and a fine of 300 soles for the crime of breaking and entering.[61] We can only imagine how discouraging this verdict must have been to Bedriñana, particularly when considering her insistence that she was not the only Chuschina Blanco had sexually assaulted. As she told the judge in her initial testimony, "This isn't the first time that the accused [Blanco] has committed acts of this nature, for his delinquent activities are numerous, especially when committed against people from the indigenous population, who due to their ignorance or lack of economic means don't press charges." Bedriñana later went on to list specific *comuneras* whom Blanco had violated in a similar manner, insisting that the only reason they had not denounced him earlier was because they feared his reprisals.[62] Bedriñana never mentioned whether she considered herself one of these indigenous peasants. Given her social status as a local merchant and wife of a prominent mestizo, it is possible that her *comunero* neighbors considered her a nonindigenous *vecina*. Still, her statement indicates that she at least identified with her indigenous neighbors when it came to the abuse she suffered at the hands of Vicente Blanco.

What Bedriñana did not know was that some of the women she mentioned had already accused Blanco of similar transgressions. One of them was Asunta Retamozo, a widow in her fifties. Retamozo was all too familiar with Blanco's antics. In August 1960, some nine years before Blanco's alleged encounter with Clotilde Bedriñana, Retamozo complained to the local governor that Blanco had broken into her home at night in what proved to be an unsuccessful attempt to rape her. At the time, Retamozo insisted that this was not an isolated case: "This abusive . . . individual habitually roams around at night harassing women who are married, widowed, and single."[63] When Clotilde Bedriñana brought rape charges against Blanco in 1969, Retamozo thus offered an unapologetic character assassination. Retamozo alleged that Blanco had made numerous sexual advances over the years. One of these incidents took place a year and a half prior to his alleged encounter with Bedriñana. Retamozo was coming home one evening when Blanco appeared outside her door, asking permission to step inside for a moment. She could tell right away that he had been drinking heavily, especially after he started trying to caress her. Retamozo managed to pry herself away and shut the door, but Blanco persisted, lurking outside her doorway and insisting that she let him in. Retamozo reminded him that she was "a woman of advanced age," which did not seem to bother him in the least. Finally, she opened the door and began beating him with a stick until he finally gave up and left. According to Retamozo, Blanco never let her live that incident down, doing everything in his power to make her life miserable. One day, he situated himself across the street and threw rocks at her house, destroying her roof shingles in the process. At another point, he took advantage of his position as mayor to order the transfer of thirteen pepper trees from her yard to his.[64]

Elderly widows were not the only ones to come forward against Blanco. Two years before Clotilde Bedriñana brought rape charges against him, twenty-one-year-old Baseliaña Dueñas informed the governor that Blanco had snuck into her home in the middle of the night and mounted her while she was sleeping with her two daughters. Dueñas was convinced that had she not cried for help, Blanco would have raped her, for he "had a habit of raping defenseless women."[65] Unlike Dueñas, twenty-six-year-old Lorenza Vilca waited until Bedriñana had brought charges against Blanco before testifying against him. Vilca could not recall the date, but she remembered that it had occurred at a time when her parents had been attending to their livestock in the hills surrounding the village. It was around nine or ten o'clock at night when Blanco came to her door. He carried with him a case of beer, but from what Vilca could tell he had already treated himself to a few rounds before making his visit. Vilca claimed that she initially declined Blanco's invitation to drink with him, but the *vecino* would not take no for an answer. She finally agreed to just one glass, allowing him to enter her home. Once inside, Blanco wrestled her to the floor and attempted to have his way with her. Fortunately, Vilca was able to fend him off with a stick that was just within her reach. Rising to her feet, Vilca reproached Blanco for his actions, reminding him that she had a partner who was away in Lima. Defeated, Blanco grabbed his beers and left the house.[66]

Men were also quick to condemn Blanco's sexual misconduct. Two years before Bedriñana brought charges against him, Chuschi's local authorities signed a joint statement denouncing Blanco's behavior: "For as long as he's been living in this, his native District, [Blanco] has gone around raping married women, widows, and minors."[67] The fact that local authorities were willing to rebuke Blanco in writing suggests that his alleged rapes were a matter of public knowledge. While this may have been inevitable in a small village like Chuschi, it is also possible that Blanco *wanted* to keep these rumors in circulation in order to publicly dishonor his victims.[68] Another reason that he may have allowed for these rumors to become a matter of public record was that he desired to establish symbolically his patriarchal power vis-à-vis the indigenous peasantry. By demonstrating that he could rape or seduce just about any *comunera* he pleased regardless of her marital status or age, Blanco was in effect declaring that he was more powerful than *comunero* men because the normal rules of the patriarchal power pact did not apply to him, and because indigenous men were incapable of defending their women against his sexual attacks.

It turns out that Blanco was more than a raping, cheating womanizer. He was also, in the eyes of the Chuschino peasantry at least, a *gamonal*. Unlike Aycha and Chipana, whose racial identities were ambiguous, Blanco was unequivocally mestizo. Despite his claims to an "autochthonous" Chuschino identity, Blanco's white skin, urban dress, and socioeconomic background distinguished him from his indigenous peasant neighbors. Blanco's story also points to another means through which villagers improved their status: becoming a faculty member in the village schools. Educators in Chuschi enjoyed a degree of social prestige that *comuneros* simply could not achieve. Because most indigenous peasants did not have access to higher education, they often deferred to the authority of the community's nonindigenous intelligentsia in political matters. For this reason, it was not uncommon, particularly from the 1960s onward, for Chuschi's nonindigenous political leaders to simultaneously hold teaching positions in the local schools. Blanco was one of the *qalas* who held both.

There were, of course, limits to the amount of exploitation that indigenous peasants were willing to tolerate from *qala* teachers. One thing they did not accept was the notion of educated *vecinos* using their smarts to take advantage of uneducated *comuneros*. Blanco crossed this line on more than one occasion. In 1970 he was still teaching at the local elementary school when *comunero* Isidro Vilca brought criminal charges against him. Vilca alleged that the instructor had employed dirty tricks to dispossess him of his cornfields in the lowlands of the village. Two years earlier, the fields' legal owner, Gregorio Huaycha, had passed away. During his lifetime, however, Huaycha had recognized the plot of Anccara as Vilca's, since Vilca had possessed and worked it "since time immemorial." In fact, Vilca doubted that Huaycha was even aware that Anccara technically belonged to him; Huaycha may not have been, but Blanco was. According to Vilca, Blanco seized the moment of Huaycha's death to fabricate a land transfer that would place the plot in his possession. What Blanco lacked to complete the transaction was the illiterate Huaycha's fingerprint. The only problem was that Huaycha was now dead. But that did not stop Blanco, who snuck into the location where the corpse was being held and pressed Huaycha's lifeless finger to the document! Vilca added that the reason he had taken so long to report the incident was that he had only recently learned of the teacher's antics. It was a bold accusation, to be sure, but Vilca believed Blanco's record in the community more than illustrated his poor character. "In the town of Chuschi," Vilca stated, "the accused has demonstrated his experienced behavior as a usurper [*arranchador*] of the lands of humble *campecinos* [*sic*], supported by false documents and instruments, and he has a heavy criminal record, of which even the provincial authorities are aware."[69]

That he had a criminal record not even Blanco could deny. When the thirty-eight-year-old teacher gave his deposition in 1972, he admitted that two additional court cases were being brought against him at the moment, one for attempted murder and another for rape. He assured the court that these other charges had been brought against him with the explicit purpose of "ruining his teaching career and creating negative priors to go on my service record." As for the attacks on his character—that his criminal record was "heavy" and that he had a habit of falsifying documents in order to take land from the "humble" peasantry—they, like Vilca's accusation, were simply false. The court concurred, exonerating Blanco of all charges.[70]

It would not be long before Vilca took legal action against Blanco a second time. In 1976 Vilca had much more political clout than he did during the previous litigation, occupying the newly created position of communal president. Blanco, for his part, had just completed a six-year term as mayor. Vilca first suspected that something was awry when the former mayor undertook a public works project to construct a post office. The town council had received a grant from the Peruvian state to hire a contractor for the job, but Blanco ordered the *comuneros* to provide the manual labor for the project instead, pocketing the 147,500 soles that had been allocated for the job.[71] This was not the only time Vicente Blanco compromised his mayoral integrity, Vilca asserted. Blanco had also supervised the construction of a medical post in the community for which he received 20,000 soles from the Peruvian government. The problem was that Blanco never filed a single receipt to show where the money had gone. Nor did he report how he had used public funds to pave Chuschi's Mercado de Abastos (Flea Market). Finally, Vilca charged that the teacher-mayor had been charging *comuneros* to use the community's irrigation water, thus stripping villagers of one of their most basic *comunero* rights. Once again, the mayor had neglected to disclose where the money he collected from this project had gone.[72]

Blanco categorically denied the charges, suggesting that the claimant had challenged his integrity out of spite.[73] And just as the Land Court had cleared him of the charges in the Anccara dispute, so did the Public Ministry vindicate Blanco in the present case.[74] While we cannot be sure whether most indigenous Chuschinos shared Vilca's concerns regarding Blanco's abuse of authority, it is likely that they were aware of these allegations. As small town gossip goes, rumors and accusations can be just as powerful in swaying public opinion as concrete facts.

Villagers did all they could to dethrone their mestizo patriarch. In October 1972, state officials entered the community to perform a visual inspection of a local land conflict between the community and the Catholic Church.[75] Tellingly, *comuneros* took advantage of the presence of the state officials to request Blanco's official expulsion from the community. In their words, Blanco was "abusive, domineering, and conniving." Villagers went on to describe his many abuses, requesting the officials' support in permanently expelling Blanco, whom they described as a "threat to the community." The villagers did not care where the state officials sent Blanco, as long as it was somewhere "far away from [Chuschi]."[76] Unfortunately, the efforts of these Chuschinos proved just as fruitless as those of the men and women who denounced Blanco in previous years. For now, Chuschinos would have to put up with Blanco's misconduct whether they liked it or not.

WHAT WE HAVE DESCRIBED HERE is a power relationship equivalent to those that Sinclair Thomson and Sergio Serulnikov have chronicled in late colonial Bolivia. Thomson argues that in eighteenth-century La Paz, "Andean peasants expected their caciques not only to obey a moral code of economic reciprocity ensuring community material reproduction . . .

but also . . . to 'defend' and 'protect' them from external aggression and abuse."[77] Serulnikov makes a similar observation for Chayanta during the same period, stating that indigenous peasants expected their local leaders to adhere to "traditional forms of reciprocity" and to embody the "collective protest" of the community when leading litigations.[78] Serulnikov and Thomson argue that caciques' inability to meet Andean villagers' cultural demands during the second half of the century created a local crisis of authority.[79] The same argument can be extended to twentieth-century Chuschi, where *qalas* like Vicente Blanco, Felipe Aycha, and Bernardo Chipana fell well short of peasants' cultural expectations. To most villagers, these men embodied the local crisis of authority. It was in part due to the cultural nature of their infractions that Peruvian courts did not find these men guilty of many of the infractions for which they stood accused. Even when indigenous villagers did have a strong legal case, these *qala* leaders always seemed to elude justice, ruling with virtual impunity in the village through the 1970s and into the early 1980s. This only further supported the growing belief among *comuneros* that the justice of the Peruvian state, much like that of the traditional *varayoqs*, had failed to uphold public order and moral authority in the community.

Just because a crisis of authority existed in Chuschi does not mean that it existed throughout the department, however. While some Ayacuchan communities experienced similar crises, others, such as Huaychao, did not. An examination of power relations in preinsurgency Huaychao will help us to understand why this was.

Huaychao's Hacendados

> Peru is a semifeudal and semicolonial country. What does this semifeudalism and semicolonialism represent to the immense masses of campesinos? Oppression and servitude.—Osmán Morote Barrionuevo[80]

The man who wrote these words later become recognized as Shining Path's second-in-command, subordinate only to party leader Abimael Guzmán Reynoso. The citation comes from Morote's 1970 thesis at the National University of San Cristóbal de Huamanga. Morote's thesis focused on San José de Santillana, a highland district not far from Huaychao. When I began my research for this book, I expected to find evidence supporting Morote's observations about class conflict in preinsurgency Huaychao, albeit without the Marxist overtones. I was surprised to find not a single document recording conflict between indigenous Huaychainos and their hacienda lords during the entire forty years leading up to the insurgency. Remembering the historian's mantra that when it comes to archival research, absence of evidence is not evidence of absence, I expected my ethnographic research and interviews to fill the gaps in the written record. Much to my surprise, I found that most Huaychainos who were old enough to remember the days when Huaychao was a hacienda spoke of their former lords with a sense of general respect.

Kings of the Hacienda: Huaychao's Hacendados

The first hacienda baron whom Huaychainos remembered was Rafael Chávez. Chávez's parents, Pedro Chávez and Dolores Cárdenas, had possessed the neighboring haciendas of Huaychao and Macabamba since about the 1920s. When they died, they left Huaychao to Rafael and Macabamba to his brother, Maximiliano.[81]

Although the hacienda was in Huaychao, Chávez often had his laborers rotate week-long shifts, known as *semaneros*, in the valley of Huanta City, where he lived. Around six men would leave Huaychao on Sunday, spending the remainder of the week in the city planting Chávez's corn, plucking the spines from his *tuna*, tending to his fields, and performing domestic chores. The following Sunday, the laborers would return from the city to be replaced by half a dozen new workers. Typically, *semanero* workers received between five and seven soles per week, a sum that was usually enough for them to purchase about a kilogram of sugar and salt and perhaps some bread or even a T-shirt—items hard to come by in the Iquichano highlands.[82]

On the surface, Huaychainos' collective memory regarding Chávez's treatment of his indigenous tenants seems to confirm Osmán Morote's observations. "I knew Rafael Chávez when I was little," said Mariano Quispe, who grew up on the hacienda in the 1940s. Gesturing toward the children running around his yard, *tayta* Mariano added, "Just like my little grandchildren you see there, I was about that size." The first thing *tayta* Mariano recollected about *don* Rafael was how different he was from his indigenous serfs: "He was sort of deaf [*opa*], he hardly understood our language, and his nickname was '*Opa* Rafael.'"[83] *Tayta* Mariano went on to describe Chávez as tall and chubby, two physical traits that few native Huaychainos shared.[84] Chávez was always quick to point out these racial distinctions when dealing with his indigenous field hands. *Tayta* Mariano evoked the manner in which the mestizo landowner talked down to them: "Get to work you midget men! To work, *carajo*!"[85] When we pressed Esteban Huamán on the subject, he confirmed that Chávez sometimes used racial slurs, referring to his indigenous tenants by the derogatory terms *chutos* and *cholos*. But *tayta* Esteban remembered him most for his foul mouth: "Uff! He cursed all the time! '*Mierda*' [shit] this, '*carajo*' that. . . . He'd say, 'Work hard you slackers, or I'll expel you [from my hacienda]!'"[86]

Racial slurs aside, former *semanero* workers criticized the poor conditions under which they worked in Huanta City. "He was very mean to us," *tayta* Mariano said of Chávez. When asked to expand on this point, he explained,

> He was a man who didn't feed us well; he gives [*sic*] us food that one would give to a dog in four [cattle] hides and only one tiny blanket for all six [*semanero* workers to share] on the cement floor in Huanta. . . . He'd only give us two [ears] of corn per person, and he'd give us very few things to cook ourselves. . . . And after working in the fields [all week] we'd return all the way from Huanta fatigued, having not eaten well [or] slept well; just totally fatigued we'd return.[87]

Tayta Mariano remembered one accident in which a fellow serf was nearly crushed to death while attempting to carry two large poles that the hacendado had tied to the man's shoulders. Rather than attend to the fallen worker, the hacendado shouted, "Stand up straight, *carajo*! Stand up, you midget! Get to work!" *Tayta* Mariano said that the serf fell ill and eventually perished as a result of the fall.[88] Sometimes, he recalled, the landlord would spy on his field hands from the nearby woods and catch them lying down in the grass to catch a breather. Whenever this occurred, he would sneak up on them and strike them with his walking stick.[89]

Chávez ran the hacienda in Huaychao with similar tyranny. Rather than pay his serfs for the work they provided him on the estate, Chávez gave each household a share of coca leaves and a plot of land on the hacienda to farm. During a typical harvest, one peasant household kept roughly ten sacks of potatoes for subsistence and stored the remaining fifty or so for the hacienda lord. Chávez would oversee this process during his brief trips to the hacienda.[90] The sight of the mestizo lord ascending on horseback from the fog-laden graveyard must have been a chilling one. After arriving, Chávez would patrol the perimeters of the hacienda wielding a *verga*, threatening to strike anyone who delivered him anything but the best *yucca* tubers.[91] The peasants packed Chávez's share onto horses, llamas, and other beasts of burden and herded them toward Chávez's Huanta City residence. "If you get [to Huanta] and it's less than the quota," *tayta* Mariano told us while chewing on a handful of coca leaves, "well then he takes [sic] away your portion of the harvest or your *costal*."[92] *Tayta* Mariano recalled one particular peasant who always seemed to suffer this fate: "They [sic] would take Geronimo Quispe's *costales*, and sometimes they would take his llamas as compensation for his poor harvests."[93]

While the above discussion certainly seems to corroborate the general observations made by Osmán Morote during his field research in the Huanta highlands, what follows does not. Even while acknowledging that Chávez ran his hacienda with a firm hand, most of the Huaychainos we interviewed described him as a decent hacendado. For instance, when we asked Inocencio Urbano, a man more than 100 years old who had spent most of his adult life in Huaychao, to recount his saddest memory from his days on Chávez's hacienda, he simply lifted his head and murmured, "*Manam*," indicating that he had none. His wife, *mama* Ernestina, who earlier in the conversation had described Chávez as "allinmi runakuna [good people]," agreed: "No, only once the [political] violence began [did we have sad memories], for that was when people started disappearing, some of whom have returned and others not. That was it, before there was no sadness. In those [hacienda] days we were happy just being in the mountains with our livestock."[94] Such nostalgic references to "the good old days" must be treated with some skepticism. Nonetheless, the elderly couple's affirmation that things were good during the days of the hacienda suggests that they did not view the mestizo landowner's behavior and actions as unjust or even excessive. Even peasants who did not explicitly say that Chávez was a good landlord were reticent to denounce him outright. When we asked Isidro Huamán if Chávez had been a good or bad hacendado, he had trouble giving us a straight answer: "Rafael was, well. . . . He hit people with a *verga* and took away their *costal*, so he was bad *in that sense*. . . . That's how things were back then."[95] As *tayta* Isidro spoke I grew frustrated with his refusal to cast the former landlord in a negative light, as he elected instead to qualify his characterization with references to Chávez's specific actions. Why, I wondered, did Huaychainos insist on portraying Chávez as a decent hacendado and human being if they acknowledged that he was oppressive?

The first answer to this question is that they believed there was little they could do about it. President Fortunato and *tayta* Esteban grew up on Chávez's hacienda in the 1950s and 1960s. When we asked them how Chávez's authoritarian reign over the hacienda had made them and their parents feel at the time, President Fortunato responded that they were "already used to it," and *tayta* Esteban added that they obeyed the hacendado out of "obligation."[96] These attitudes explain the lack of archival documentation regarding patron-client conflicts on the Huaychao hacienda. It was not that Chávez had a perfect record when it came to the treatment of his field hands. Rather, the indigenous tenants felt that such exploitation by a mestizo power holder was to be expected. They also feared retaliation should they protest. When asked if Chávez's serfs ever resisted his whippings, *mama* Ernestina refuted, "*Manam*, not at all, they only hunched over and cried. Who knows what he would have done to them had they resisted."[97] President Fortunato made a similar observation: "If you went [to report him], you lost your plot."[98] This psychological intimidation was therefore crucial to the mestizo lord's local hegemony. Finally, indigenous Huaychainos believed, with good reason, that the law was on Chávez's side. "Back then the law protected the hacendados," *tayta* Mariano explained. "In those days we couldn't talk back to the hacendado."[99] Huaychainos were simply not prepared to put their bodies and homes on the line to challenge what they perceived to be a perfectly appropriate power relationship.

Another reason why Huaychainos did not resent Chávez for his abuses is that they expected nothing better from a mestizo landlord. The following conversation with President Fortunato and *tayta* Esteban illustrates this point:

QUESTION: Did [Chávez] get mad a lot?
ESTEBAN: He'd get mad, because he's an aggressive person.
  He's the *patrón*.
FORTUNATO: Everyone was scared of him.
ESTEBAN: People were always looking over their shoulders.
QUESTION: How's that?
ESTEBAN: If he was in a bad mood, people were scared.
QUESTION: What would people say?
ESTEBAN: They respected him.
FORTUNATO: They [respected him] out of fear.[100]

Rather than question Chávez's belligerence, President Fortunato and *tayta* Esteban dismissed it as typical landlord behavior ("He's the *patrón*"). Nor did they hold it against him. Instead, they claimed to have *respected* the mestizo power holder. Yet as I understood here and in several other conversations in which the concept emerged, the word "rispito," the Quechua pronunciation of the Spanish *respecto*, had a slightly different meaning to Huaychainos than it did to me. Whereas I took the term to signify deference, admiration, and esteem, Huaychainos conflated it with fear, submission, and above all, power. This power, moreover, was not negotiable. Thus, when we asked *mama* Ernestina and *tayta* Inocencio if Chávez ever assisted his serfs in the fields, the former scoffed, "They [*sic*] didn't help. How could *they* possibly have helped *us*?" Nodding in agreement, *tayta* Inocencio repeated, "How could they have helped us?"[101] Although the question referred specifically to Rafael Chávez, the elderly couple used the third person, "they," referring to *all* nonindigenous landlords. In other words, indigenous peasants never expected their mestizo lords to labor alongside them.

They did expect landlords to respect peasants' cultural practices, however. According to *tayta* Esteban, Chávez donated various items to help facilitate his tenants' festivities, but he never participated in them.[102] Similarly, when *tayta* Mariano described all the harvest and religious festivals that peasants celebrated throughout the year, he focused on the presence of the customary *varayoqs* in the rituals, saying, "The landlord didn't meddle. 'Just do what you need to do,' he'd tell us." When asked if the estate owner ever showed up during these events, *tayta* Mariano shook his head. "He didn't participate. . . . [He'd just say,] 'Just go and enjoy the fiesta.'"[103] Rafael Chávez thus understood his boundaries as a nonindigenous power holder. On the one hand, he adhered to cultural expectations of reciprocity by supplying certain goods for the festivities. On the other hand, he never attempted to insert himself into the indigenous rituals, keeping his physical and social distance.

Huaychainos also expected Chávez to maintain public order on his hacienda. Nearly every Huaychaino we interviewed commented on the efficient manner in which Chávez administered justice. While the indigenous tenants settled most disputes internally, Chávez personally handled the more serious cases. He was known for carrying around his weapon of choice, the *verga* known around Huaychao as La Comisaría (The Police Station), for its ability to enforce the law on the hacienda. "*Toro su pirichu*

[It was a bull's penis], lined with good spikes, and the tip was like horse's leather," *tayta* Mariano vividly detailed.[104] President Fortunato described Chávez's weapon with comparable precision: "So, the *verga* of the bull was crooked and [Chávez] would hit people with it."[105] Elders Ernestina and Inocencio also remembered the *verga*. "He would lash a *chicote* as if [acting on the authority of] the Bible," *mama* Ernestina recalled. "Comisaría," her husband interjected, adding, "It was a bull's penis." Remembering her manners, *mama* Ernestina set the record straight: "I—I never touched it; I only saw it." The elder woman then raised her arm and made broad strokes in the air: "He would take it out and whip it like this." Intrigued, Julián asked, "How many lashes would he give?" "Two or three times," *mama* Ernestina replied. She then looked at Julián and me and explained, "For example, if you two were in a rage and nobody minded you then you could say, either verbally or by way of the *chicote*, 'Listen up and do as we say!'"[106] I must admit that I took offense when *mama* Ernestina used Julián and me in her example of people who might readily castigate a Huaychaino. She could have just as easily gotten her point across by portraying herself and her husband as the hypothetical "bad guys." It was only after some reflection that I realized why her example made perfect sense. After all, Julián and I were urban dressed, Spanish-speaking outsiders. For all intents and purposes, we were, as the Chuschinos say, *qalas*. As such, we fit the profile of power holders who during the days of the hacienda not only would have been willing to submit indigenous peasants to such brutal treatment but also had the authority to do so.

This was not the only instance in which an Ayacuchan power holder resorted to the *verga* as a correctional instrument.[107] Although it was undoubtedly effective in inflicting physical pain, the bulk of the whip's power was symbolic. By possessing the whip, the hacendado became the man with the biggest copulatory organ, and he could use it to emasculate other men by cracking it on their backs. But the whip was more than just a Freudian tool. Its nickname, La Comisaría, discursively reinforced the notion that it somehow had the capacity to uphold public security on the hacienda.[108]

The fact that the *verga* was fashioned from a bull and not some other animal had powerful cultural significance for the indigenous peasantry. The bull remains the animal most closely associated with masculinity among Andeans, known for its brute strength and virility. During ritual battles, it is not uncommon for indigenous men to wear bull-hide helmets or mimic the beast's bodily movements while shouting, "¡Soy toro, carajo [I'm a bull, dammit]!" Aside from being strong, the bull is seen as unpredictable and difficult to tame.[109] For this reason, a major way for men to assert their bravery is to engage a bull in physical combat. This occurs throughout the Andes in the form of the *corrida de toros*, the annual bullfight, for which male bullfighters take great pride in their ability to endure a bloody bout with the horned beast.[110] Another way for men to demonstrate their bravado is to tame the animal, which in some instances involves physical castration.[111] Thus, by wielding a whip fashioned from a bull's penis, mestizo power holders such as Rafael Chávez demonstrated to their indigenous serfs that that they had literally and symbolically castrated the beast, leaving no doubt as to whom was the alpha male.

For most Huaychainos, receiving two or three lashes of the *verga* paled in comparison to the alternative punishment: eviction from the hacienda.[112] *Mama* Ernestina explained that Chávez personally expelled peasants who "did not follow his orders." She recalled that the hacendado evicted one unfortunate peasant who lost one of the landlord's sheep.[113] Likewise, President Fortunato and *tayta* Esteban claimed that when beating his laborers did not work, Chávez expelled thieves, rapists, and witches from his hacienda. "He evicted them but not before [trying to correct their behavior by] hitting them with the *verga*," *tayta* Esteban explained. "First he'd take away their plot and then he'd expel them, saying, 'There shouldn't be people like this inside [my hacienda].'" According to President Fortunato, Chávez felt that such social outcasts were "dirtying up" his hacienda with their misconduct.[114] President Fortunato remembered one peasant whom Chávez banished "to a place where nobody works." When asked why, the communal president explained, "Because he was a lazy person, and . . . because he was a thief who stole everyone else's finest things. He was lazy and he reaped everyone else's harvests. He was also lazy and the hacendado kicked him out because he didn't want to put up with all that; he kicked him out with the crack of a whip."[115]

While perhaps over the top, Chávez's system of justice did not strike Huaychainos as unreasonable. *Mama* Ernestina assured us that Chávez only resorted to the *verga* "for serious offenses."[116] President Fortunato and *tayta* Esteban agreed. "[Chávez] ruled the hacienda," said the former. "He was respected because on his hacienda there were no thieves, rapists, or witches, because if there were he would punish people with his whip [made] of a bull's penis."[117] Later in the conversation, we asked the two men if they ever reported incidents of robbery to the justice of the peace in nearby Carhuahurán. "Only after the hacienda [days]," President Fortunato replied. During the hacienda period, *tayta* Esteban added, "the landlord would flog [the thieves] and [the robbing] ended right then and there."[118] When we asked President Fortunato and *tayta* Esteban if they felt that Chávez was a "good hacendado," the former replied, "He was good for the good people, bad for the bad people." "In other words," *tayta* Esteban clarified, "he gave good land to obedient people, but he expelled the disobedient ones with a *chicote* and gave their plot to someone else." President Fortunato reiterated, "He only hit disobedient people with his *chicote* and he loved the obedient ones like a father." "Patrón, patrón," *tayta* Esteban affirmed with a nod of the head. President Fortunato continued, "Also, his tenants obeyed him as if they were his child [*sic*]."[119]

It is hard to tell whether or not the hacendado's actions actually curtailed the kinds of social problems Huaychainos described. While I found no comparable petitions from Chávez, a letter penned to the departmental prefect by Mario Cavalcanti Gamboa, owner of the adjacent Huaynacancha hacienda, indicated that cattle rustling was a serious problem in the zone in 1967. Cavalcanti would become a prominent agitator for peasant political mobilizations at the time, his subsequent arrest sparking the Huanta uprising of 1969. This, of course, further supports the thesis about the political and social pacts between regional hacendados and peasants.[120] At the time he petitioned the prefect, however, Cavalcanti seemed more concerned with cattle theft on his estate. While he did not explicitly mention Huaychao, he did complain that *abigeato* had become a problem in Macabamba, Huaynacancha, and several other neighboring estates. Such activity, he wrote, "has made it impossible for the inhabitants of the neighboring estates as well as my own." Included in the petition was a request for the creation of the position of lieutenant governor on the Huaynacancha hacienda "to protect all the inhabitants from the flagrance of cattle rustling."[121] Why did the hacendado not include Huaychao in his list of affected haciendas? Was it because Huaychao, with its lieutenant governor and authoritarian hacendado, had successfully eradicated *abigeato*? Or did the problem exist in Huaychao, and the Huaynacancha baron had simply elected not to mention the neighboring estate? In the end, it is irrelevant whether or not cattle rustling was a problem on the Huaychao hacienda before the Agrarian Reform. What matters is the *belief* held by most Huaychainos that their mestizo proprietor had mitigated the problem with his intimidating and brutal administration of justice.

In addition to administering justice effectively, Chávez understood the implicit code of reciprocity that underlay Andean power relations. President Fortunato and *tayta* Esteban described this exchange. After extracting what they needed for their household subsistence, the serfs would deposit the remaining potato harvest in a storage house at the edge of the village square. Periodically, they emptied the storage and delivered the tubers to the hacendado's Huanta City residence "so that the landlord could eat."[122] As children, President Fortunato and *tayta* Esteban watched as *don* Rafael's overseer delivered *molle*, *chicha*, and cane liquor to the adult workers on the hacienda. President Fortunato recollected, "Back then we children didn't drink, but the adults did drink. The kids just watched." Children did receive food from the hacendado, however. Gesturing toward *tayta* Esteban and then touching his own chest, President Fortunato explained, "The two of us got our share [of food], because in those days our parents worked on the hacienda and we had our own plot."[123] *Tayta* Esteban specified that, children aside, "only those who worked, and not those who didn't work" received these meals and refreshments—this was not charity but the fulfillment of an informal pact. Chávez's brother, who owned the neighboring Macabamba hacienda, also reciprocated his workers. Sometimes, peasants from Huaychao would labor on the Macabamba hacienda just for the corn beer. "Yeah, I used to go Macabamba to drink *chicha*," *tayta* Mariano remembered. "[The hacendado] would treat thirteen of us from Huaychao, Purus, Huaynacancha, etc., to *chicha*. We'd all go and work for *chicha*, not money."[124]

Finally, the landlord respected, and even reinforced, traditional gender roles. When we asked *mama* Ernestina and *tayta* Inocencio to describe their former employer, the former assured us, "Ah, he was a good man," while the latter nodded in agreement. Pressed to expand her answer, *mama* Ernestina discussed the gendered division of labor under Chávez: "[He was good when it came to] our *semanero*; in allowing the widows to [travel to Huanta City to] weave, dry potatoes, and other things. We are better off now for it. The widows would go to Huanta. The married women were *semaneras* to prepare the corn and firewood."[125] Under this system, then, widows had a valued social function. Huaychaino men did not seem to mind that the hacendado put married women to work in traditional roles: cooking, grazing cattle, and weaving. Nor did it bother them that the widows went to Huanta City to carry water and wash clothes for the hacendado.[126] More important, men boasted about the ways that Chávez rewarded displays of masculinity from his male workers. President Fortunato and *tayta* Esteban recalled that Chávez would organize work competitions between ten or twenty male workers from Huaychao, Macabamba, and neighboring Iquichano communities to see who could best work the hacendado's fallow lands. "That's where the best man wins [*ahí tira el que tira*]," President Fortunato asserted with a boyish grin. "The winner walked away an overseer [*capitán*], and he who couldn't hack it was left behind," *tayta* Esteban snickered.[127] The former field hands could not contain their pride when thinking back on the friendly male competition of their youth.

Women in Huaychao assured us that the patriarch never laid a hand on his female tenants. But did he speak to them as disparagingly as he did his male workers? "*Manam*," *mama* Ernestina rebuffed. "He didn't chew out [*resondrar*] the women, only the widows who didn't mind his orders. And he expelled anyone who didn't mind his orders."[128] *Mama* Ernestina therefore accepted that a mestizo lord would verbally abuse widows, provided, first, that he did not physically harm them and, second, that they had "deserved" his haranguing by failing to carry out his orders.

Sitting at the edge of a cliff overlooking the cattle that grazed in the valley below, Brígida Cayetano confirmed that Rafael Chávez did not physically abuse Huaychaina women; he left that task to his wife. *Mama* Brígida was born and raised on the Huaychao hacienda, which made her a teenager during the 1940s when the landlady first whipped her with a *chicote*: "In those days we used to cook pig in a big pot and we couldn't carry the pig, so she'd hit us." While *mama* Brígida certainly did not appreciate the abuse, she did not condemn it, explaining that it served a correctional and developmental purpose: "I was probably . . . thirteen years old, and that's why she hit me, because when you're a little girl you can't do things as well. But no one's going to hit me now, because now I can cook well with vegetables."[129] *Mama* Brígida would probably not have been as understanding had Rafael Chávez been the one hitting Huaychaina women. Not even the men faulted Mrs. Chávez for hitting her female tenants. Their main complaint was that the landlady refused to reciprocate their work. According to *tayta* Mariano, Mrs. Chávez would sometimes visit the hacienda with her husband and eat full meals in front of the workers, ordering them to fetch her water, prepare the firewood, and cook the food. "People would grumble[,] . . . 'Why doesn't Rafael Chávez's señora offer us some, seeing as how we are here watching [her eat] and we're starving to death?' . . . That's how she'd make us suffer."[130]

The only person we interviewed who had nothing positive to say of the Chávezes was Alejandra Ccente. Sitting on a stump outside of her hilltop hut, *mama* Alejandra gave us a cynic's perspective of Rafael Chávez. For her, the hacendado had violated the structural principles of Andean patron-client relationships. "The landlord was bossy," she complained. "Every three months he would come [to Huaychao] and identify the piglets that were on his plot and say, 'The piglets are destroying my plot,' and once they grew he would take them with him." Aside from taking what was not rightfully his, the landowner made unreasonable demands of his male workers. "There was suffering. That Rafael Chávez was repressive because he made the men work like slaves and he hit them and treated them like slaves." *Mama* Alejandra also felt that Chávez was unfair to his female tenants. "He would say of the young widows who could not keep up with the men: 'Get rid of her, *carajo*! Force her to marry a widower on the condition that they both work, *carajo*! Otherwise, she can take a hike, *carajo*!' Oh, how he didn't care for the widows and single mothers!" *Mama* Alejandra went on to say that the punishments Chávez meted out were unfair. Rather than punishing social outcasts and deviants, as her neighbors described, Chávez as she remembers him would reprimand and expel anyone who could not keep up with the demanding workload: "He'd chew us out: 'Work faster, *carajo*, or get off [my hacienda]!' And he'd banish them just like that. . . . He'd kick them, [hit them] with a *verga*, and if they protested he'd kick them out. . . . He'd banish people who were already dying." She invoked one instance in which Chávez evicted a tenant's entire family "because he didn't do things well." As far as *mama* Alejandra was concerned, the hacendado was also unfit to resolve any of Huaychao's internal conflicts. "Only the lieutenant governor resolved those problems," she said. "The hacendado didn't know how to. . . . And besides, there were lieutenant governors and *varayoqs* [resolving those problems] long before [Chávez's tenure]." Rocking her body back and forth with her arms folded to keep warm under the dense fog, *mama* Alejandra declared: "He was far too bad, that *patrón*."[131]

For *mama* Alejandra, then, Rafael Chávez had broken the power pact. First, he exploited the power relationship, treating his serfs like virtual slaves. Second, he had failed in his paternalistic obligation to provide for, protect, and respect the most socially and economically vulnerable tenants, namely, the widows, single mothers, and elders (people who were "already dying"). Finally, his administration of justice was unreasonable and ineffective in upholding public order. However, while *mama* Alejandra's opinion illustrates the heterogeneity of villagers' perceptions regarding their former hacendado, hers was also a minority opinion in Huaychao. Most men and women felt that in spite of his mean streak, Rafael Chávez had respected the power pact and upheld internal order on the hacienda.[132]

In late 1962 Rafael Chávez sold the hacienda to Enrique Juscamaita, a mestizo proprietor from Huamanga who already owned a hacienda in Montehuasi (La Mar Province), for 75,000 soles.[133] If Huaychainos spoke of Chávez with respect, their collective memory of Juscamaita was more flattering. *Tayta* Inocencio described Juscamaita as "good people."[134] Of course, this praise was coming from an indigenous elder who had painted the previous hacendado in a similar light. Yet even Rafael Chávez's most vocal critics spoke affectionately of Juscamaita. For instance, *tayta* Isidro, who had described Chávez as bad "in a sense," said, "Juscamaita was good, but we only were with him for a short time, maybe three or four years."[135] *Tayta* Mariano, who had previously detailed Chávez's harsh treatment of his serfs, said of Juscamaita, "He was a good man. . . . Folks around here have nothing but kind words to say about him."[136] Not even *mama* Alejandra criticized the new landowner, saying only that Huaychainos "entered a period of peace" when Chávez sold the hacienda to Juscamaita.[137]

Huaychainos held Juscamaita in such high esteem because he not only met their cultural expectations for a mestizo overlord but also exceeded them by keeping his distance and refraining from physical, verbal, or psychological violence. For starters, he did not meddle in peasant affairs, as some of Chuschi's power holders had done. *Mama* Alejandra reported, "Mr. Juscamaita never even came here. . . . He only came once to reap his potato crops when we got the news from Lima that there was a law saying that the hacienda had been terminated."[138] "He only came over here once," *tayta* Mariano concurred. "After he came that one time we never saw Enrique [in Huaychao] again."[139] Thus, unlike Chávez, who seemed to get his kicks sneaking up on unsuspecting tenants, Juscamaita did not feel the need to supervise their every move. This gave peasants more liberty to work at their own pace and engage in Andean cultural practices.

Like his predecessor, Juscamaita appreciated Andean codes of reciprocity. *Tayta* Inocencio said that Juscamaita "was a good person, and he used to treat us to aguardiente in Montehuasi."[140] President Fortunato also recalled traveling in groups of two or three tenants at a time to Juscamaita's Montehuasi hacienda to pick up a helping of coca leaves and aguardiente from their mestizo lord.[141] Chewing on a handful of coca leaves, *tayta* Mariano later elucidated this last point: "We would just take [our] potato [harvests] to Tambo, but when we got there, Enrique would wait for us and give us bottles of *trago*." After making this statement, the former field hand leaned back and murmured with a crooked smile, "He sure was good, that *patrón*."[142]

If Huaychainos viewed Rafael Chávez as strict, they saw Enrique Juscamaita as compassionate. Both were acceptable characteristics for a mestizo patriarch, but the latter was preferable. *Tayta* Mariano told us that Juscamaita "was a good man, and he didn't use a *verga*," while *tayta* Inocencio underscored the lord's paternalistic affection for his indigenous tenants: "He would come up to us and embrace us, saying, 'Are you well, Huaychainos?'"[143] *Tayta* Isidro also appreciated Juscamaita's genuine concern for his serfs. When *tayta* Isidro was a young man, he and a group of four or five Huaychainos would labor for a day at a time on Juscamaita's Montehuasi hacienda. With a shy grin, *tayta* Isidro shared his memories of those days: "He would let us work, then pay us and ask us: 'Are you all well in Huaychao?' and we would say, 'We are well, señor.'"[144]

Given that so few Huaychainos objected to the hacienda system, and even fewer to their new landlord Enrique Juscamaita, they initially had mixed feelings about the Agrarian Reform, which reached Huaychao in 1975 and was completed there a year later.[145] It is true that at least some Huaychainos were catalysts of a larger regional movement that had been challenging the hacienda system throughout the 1960s.[146] Identifying those protagonists has been difficult, however, for in addition to an absence of historical documentation regarding Huaychaino participation in the regional movement, villagers themselves came up with few specifics regarding who fought for the reform and how.[147] Instead, villagers with whom we spoke made sweeping statements such as "It was hard" and "We *all* fought for the change." Such generic statements may tell us less about the historical facts than about the manner in which post–Agrarian Reform Huaychainos' constructed the historical narrative about land reform. Still, most villagers embraced the notion of owning their own land. Thinking back on the significance of the land reform for Huaychainos, *tayta* Esteban boasted, "The hacendado left this [hacienda] and the *grupo campesino* was created. The [hacienda] work also ended and the people were happy that they were no longer obligated to work. . . . Now we only worked for ourselves, we no longer had to serve the hacendado at all." The former serf leaned back and sighed, "Ah, we said, '[Thank] Jesus . . . for the rest!'"[148]

Perhaps sensing that his neighbor was getting too melodramatic, President Fortunato interrupted: "But there were people who were close to the hacendado. . . . There were many . . . maybe half." Intrigued, we asked the communal president why this was. "Because," he replied, "they [and the hacendado] were close. [The hacendado] gave them food and that's why they were on [his] side. . . . They said, 'We were just fine [on the hacienda].'" Hearing this, *tayta* Esteban leaned forward and added, "The *patrón* was like their father and they hated those of us who opposed [him], and [they said,] 'Now we won't be happy anymore,' and we would all fight over it."[149] *Tayta* Isidro later confirmed this story: "Some people took the [hacendado's] side. For example, those in [the annex] Ccochaccocha kept defending [the hacienda system] and the hacendado left them some things [after he left]."[150]

Women also had their reservations about the change in land tenure. *Mama* Brígida spoke candidly of her uneasiness when she learned that Huaychao would become a peasant collectivity. It was not that she was opposed to the idea of owning her own land. On the contrary, she felt that it was good to have land for the sake of the peasant household, "because our children eat from it. When someone dies like me, since I'm already an elder, then my grandchildren will be able to eat by [tilling] the land." At the time, however, *mama* Brígida and her neighbors worried that dismantling the hacienda would also bring down the sense of internal order and security that they associated with it: "People said, 'What will happen now? What will become of us?' 'Surely we'll fight among ourselves and take [each other's] land'—that's what I thought." When we asked her if she felt that closing the hacienda had been a good thing, she rebuffed, "*Manam*, because it created confusion."[151] Even *mama* Alejandra, the most vocal critic of the hacienda and the one Huaychaina who had characterized the mode of production on Chávez's hacienda as "slavery," described her ambivalence at the time: "The people [of Huaychao] said, 'That's nice,' and we were happy. But at the same time we worried: 'Now what's going to happen?'"[152]

Thus, far from being united in their support of the Agrarian Reform, men and women in Huaychao were conflicted over the change. On the one hand, they now had the liberty to work their own land without the constraints of a naturally exploitative land-tenure system. On the other hand, they feared surrendering some of the security that the system had offered them, including the paternalistic authority of the mestizo patriarch and the public order that they associated with it.

OUR EVIDENCE FROM HUAYCHAO complicates conventional narratives that emphasize class and racial conflict. While understanding these power-laden conflicts is essential for explaining historical processes, this only tells us part of the story. Equally important are the manifold instances of cooperation that develop across racial and class hierarchies. Emphasizing the cultural logic behind indigenous peasants' affinities with mestizo land barons, this study challenges historians to look beyond landowner-peasant, mestizo-indigenous conflict and to consider how political and cultural "pacts" between the two groups also conditioned historical processes.

If the Shoe Fits

It is true that where there is power there is resistance.[153] Yet it is also true that where there is power there is submission, acceptance, and approval. The challenge for historians, then, is to explain the divergent responses that people from similar socioeconomic, racial, and geographic backgrounds have had to these power relationships at various historical junctures. I have found localized cultural analysis to be an effective explanatory model, but it does not have to be the only one. In the end, scholars would do well to consider the ways power pacts such as the ones described here have shaped power relationships and conditioned historical processes. This chapter has achieved this by complicating conventional narratives that cast indigenous-mestizo relationships as naturally and universally antagonistic, underscoring instead the localized nuances of these relationships. To be sure, race relations in preinsurgency Chuschi and Huaychao were power-laden. How these relationships played out and shaped indigenous peasant consciousness over time contrasted greatly between the two locales, however. Hacendado-peasant relations in Huaychao did not generate widespread hostility because villagers there believed that their mestizo land barons had generally respected the power pact. In Chuschi, by contrast, mestizos' violations of the power pact remained on villagers' minds as 1980 approached. For some Chuschinos, the Shining Path insurgency offered the perfect opportunity to right these wrongs.

CHAPTER FOUR

To Cross the River

Initial Peasant Support for Shining Path

T HE MOMENT HAD FINALLY COME. After twelve years of rule, the Revolutionary Government of the Armed Forces was finally going to relinquish executive power and allow Peruvian citizens to participate in national democratic elections. Florencio Conde was the lone registrar on duty in Chuschi late Saturday night, 17 May 1980—the eve of the election—when a bellowing voice caught his attention from the other side of the door: "¡Abre, carajo, somos militares [Open up, dammit, it's the military]!" Conde had scarcely enough time to react before the door flung open with a loud bang. The five strangers who stormed in were not soldiers at all but armed youths wearing ponchos and ski masks. "Go ahead and yell if you want to die, otherwise keep your mouth shut!" one of them barked. Pressing a gun to Conde's chest, one of the assailants tied him to a bench while the other four ransacked the office. The masked youths then took the ballot boxes out to the village square and lit them on fire before hoisting the communist flag. Conde managed to escape just in time to watch the offices of the registry and Consejo go up in flames.[1]

THE BURNING OF THE BALLOT BOXES and administrative center in Chuschi on 17 May 1980 marked the first episode of the Shining Path guerrilla insurgency in Peru, the famed Inicio de la Lucha Armada (ILA, Initiation of the Armed Struggle). For the next twenty years, Senderistas such as the ones who stormed the Chuschi registry would engage the state in a brutal civil war that would claim the lives of 69,000 Peruvians, most of them indigenous peasants.

This chapter makes sense of the political violence by framing it within the greater cultural and historical framework that I have outlined thus far. The first section provides a brief overview of the historical and political

Administrative center destroyed by Shining Path rebels. Photograph
by Oscar Medrano, *Caretas*; reprinted with permission.

milieu in which Shining Path emerged. From there, I describe the different ways that indigenous peasants in Chuschi supported to the insurgents.
Finally, I analyze this early peasant support for the rebellion by emphasizing the ideological disconnect between the leaders of the insurgency
and the indigenous peasantry who supported the movement. As we will
see, Quechua-speaking peasants' local experiences and collective understanding regarding culture, power, and justice were just as critical to their
initial support of Shining Path as political ideology or fear.

The Peruvian Communist Party–Shining Path in Historical Context

The midcentury agrarian reforms I described in chapter 3 did much to
transform land-tenure patterns, but they did little to improve peasants'
socioeconomic and political plight. Increasingly, leftist political organizations began arguing that more extreme measures were needed in order

to bring about meaningful systemic change. The key, some argued, lay in armed guerrilla revolution. The Chinese Communist Party adopted this philosophy, employing Mao Zedong's strategy of "encircling the cities from the villages." Heavily dependent on the participation of peasants, the Chinese Revolution's lasting legacy lay not in its transformation of China's social and economic structure but in its implications for guerrilla warfare around the world.[2] After 1950 guerrilla groups throughout the world grew increasingly dependent on the recruitment and support of a rural proletariat. This was the strategy adopted by the Viet Cong during the Vietnam War of the 1950s, 1960s, and early 1970s.[3] But this new strategy was not limited to East Asian conflicts. Around the time of Indian independence, the Naxalites took advantage of the peasant land movement in Bengal to lead an armed communist movement that depended heavily on peasant participation. Naxalite leader Charu Mazumdar took on a Maoist ideology, emulating the tactic of encircling the cities from the countryside.[4]

Although guerrilla groups in Latin America and the Caribbean were not as quick to apply a hard-line Maoist strategy, they recognized the importance of winning the support of the rural poor. The first successful revolutionary guerrilla movement in the region was the one led by Fidel Castro and Che Guevara in 1950s Cuba. It is difficult to assess the level of peasant participation in Castro's 26th of July Movement (M-26-7); estimates range from 10 to 75 percent, depending on the source.[5] Nevertheless, Castro's decision to wage a rural guerrilla war in the Sierra Maestra was pivotal. In addition to helping secure a rebel victory in 1959, it established a precedent for the way Latin American guerrilla groups would wage war for the next thirty years.[6] The following decade, the Revolutionary Armed Forces of Colombia (FARC) gained overwhelming peasant support after the Colombian government dismantled the south-central peasant republics.[7] Around the time the FARC was getting started, Guatemala's Revolutionary Armed Forces (FAR) initiated a guerrilla struggle with upward of 90 percent peasant involvement. By the end of the 1960s, virtually every Latin American country had its own rural guerrilla movement.[8]

Peasants—particularly those from indigenous backgrounds—came to take on an even more central role in the second wave of guerrilla activity that swept the region in the 1970s and 1980s. The most successful of these movements was the Sandinista National Liberation Front (FSLN) of Nicaragua. As with the previous movements, the Sandinistas had strong peasant support. Movement leaders went as far as to dub the north-central mountains the "crucible of the revolution." The Sandinista victory in 1979 reinforced the notion that rural guerrilla movements could succeed in toppling Latin American states. The following year marked the formation of Farabundo Martí National Liberation Front (FMLN), an umbrella guerrilla organization bent on toppling El Salvador's newly formed civil-military junta. According to some estimates, the FMLN had as many as 10,000 peasant combatants—many of them indigenous—in the early 1980s, a testament to the group's claim that "our mountains are our people." During the same period, remnants of Guatemala's previous guerrilla insurgency formed the Guerrilla Army of the Poor (EGP). Unlike the 1960s movement, which was heavily concentrated in Ladino (mestizo) centers, the EGP focused on obtaining the support of indigenous peasants. By some counts, the concentration of indigenous peasant combatants in the EGP was as high as 99 percent.[9]

It was during this second wave of guerrilla activity that Peru's Shining Path was born. The group emerged around 1970 as a militant faction of the Peruvian Communist Party (PCP) in Ayacucho. Originally known as "By Way of the Shining Path of Mariátegui," Shining Path traced its ideological roots to the PCP's philosophical forefather, José Carlos Mariátegui.[10] As I mentioned in chapter 3, Mariátegui believed that the highland peasantry had the potential to lift the country from economic ruin, but that campesinos were inhibited by the economic stranglehold of the landed oligarchy, the *gamonales*. In order for Peru to progress as a country, Mariátegui argued, this semicolonial, semifeudal system needed to be dismantled.[11] Mariátegui helped found the Socialist Party, serving as its secretary general until his death in 1930, at which point members formed the Peruvian Communist Party.[12]

For the next three decades, the PCP struggled to gain a foothold in Peruvian civil society. In 1963 political infighting precipitated an internal split, with some members forming the National Liberation Front (FLN). The following year, the PCP split into two factions. One, the PCP-Unidad (Unity, PCP-U), favored a Soviet-style pursuit of socialism through legal political channels, while the other, the PCP–Bandera Roja (Red Flag, PCP-BR), adopted a Maoist emphasis on armed revolution. Much of the activity by the PCP-BR took place in the countryside, with rural youths and teachers espousing Mariátegui's assessment of Peru as a semifeudal, semicolonial society. The only way to overcome this, they believed, was through armed revolution.[13]

The PCP-BR had a strong presence in Ayacucho during the 1960s, particularly on the campus of UNSCH in Ayacucho City. In 1965, at the Fifth Party Conference, members accused party leader Saturnino Paredes of embezzlement and foot-dragging with respect to the party's proposed armed struggle. This led to more internal splintering, with members of the Communist Youth forming the militant PCP–Patria Roja (Red Nation, PCP-PR). The PCP-PR asked UNSCH philosophy professor Abimael Guzmán Reynoso to head the splinter group, but Guzmán declined, electing instead to head up military affairs in Bandera Roja's Special Work Commission. In 1970, however, Guzmán formed his own faction, the PCP–Sendero Luminoso (Shining Path, PCP-SL), a militant party dedicated to immediate, Maoist-style insurrection.[14]

Born a year after Mariátegui's death, the mestizo Guzmán grew up in the cities of Mollendo and Arequipa, located in the southern Peruvian Andes. In 1953 Guzmán enrolled in Arequipa's San Agustín University, where he would earn degrees in philosophy and law. Two senior professors at San Agustín University greatly impacted Guzman's political and philosophical outlook. One, Miguel Angel Rodríguez Rivas, was a philosophy professor who specialized in Kantian theory. Under Rodríguez Rivas's tutelage, Guzmán wrote his thesis on Kant's theory of space. The other instructor to impact Guzman's ideological development was Stalinist painter Carlos de la Riva.[15] After Khrushchev's de-Stalinization campaign challenged conventional communism in Moscow, de la Riva embraced the Maoist doctrine of communism. By the time Guzmán took a faculty position at Ayacucho's UNSCH in 1962, he had followed suit.[16]

To Guzmán, Mao Zedong and the Chinese Revolution offered an appropriate model for combating peasant marginalization in Peru. While Marx and Lenin envisioned a primarily urban, proletarian social movement, Mao saw the agricultural base as the wellspring of revolutionary change. More important, Mao placed armed struggle at the forefront of his political vision. At a time when the Soviet Union and the PCP sided with legal political revisionism, Mao represented the "true" socialist path of an armed agrarian struggle. Guzmán traveled to the People's Republic during the Cultural Revolution of the 1960s, where he received training in everything from Marxist philosophy to guerrilla combat.[17]

On returning from China, Guzmán began to interpret Mariátegui according to his own convictions. He later stated, "I returned to study Mariátegui and understood that we had a first-class Marxist-Leninist who had analyzed our society in depth." Guzmán believed that the *indigenista* would have approved of his penchant for violence. This assumption, Guzmán asserted, was "not speculation but simply a product of understanding the life and work of José Carlos Mariátegui." It was in this context that in 1970 Abimael Guzmán proclaimed Shining Path Mariátegui's inevitable political heir.[18]

Over the next decade, Guzmán began recruiting a modest cohort of UNSCH faculty, students, and regional schoolteachers into his vanguard party and honing its political ideology.[19] Shining Path's Central Committee, which became known as "The Sacred Family," consisted of Guzmán and a select group of his most trusted colleagues. Tired of what they viewed as centuries of corrupt politics, Senderista leaders criticized the "political revisionism" of the Peruvian Left. While other leftist groups continued to pursue their agendas through legal channels, Guzmán drove Shining Path underground and out of the public sphere. Even when the GRFA announced its decision to hold democratic elections in 1980, the PCP-SL chose not to join the other twenty-eight leftist parties at the Constituent Assembly or participate in the general elections.[20]

Guzmán saw himself and his party as protagonists in a broader historical drama. He drove home this point during the second plenary session of the PCP-SL Central Committee, held in March 1980. "The Party," read the minutes of Shining Path's second national conference, "is a vigorous force that moves the whole country."[21] As the self-appointed leader of the party, Guzmán expected due reverence. By this point, he had already assumed the nom de guerre "Presidente Gonzalo" and anointed himself the "fourth sword" of global communism, after Marx, Lenin, and Mao. He had also dedicated much time and effort to crafting party ideology, known as "Gonzalo Thought," which emphasized uncompromising loyalty to the party and a cult of personality to himself.[22] As the Central Committee made clear during this plenary session, only the strictest compliance with Gonzalo Thought would be tolerated. "[We must] learn from Comrade Gonzalo," the committee concluded, "for he is firm in his principles and applies them with flexibility, he stays the course and always comes through."[23]

Primary among Guzmán's beliefs was that armed struggle was both necessary and urgent. He articulated this vision during his famous "We Are the Initiators" speech at the close of the PCP-SL's first Military School on 19 April 1980:

At last, the Party provides the masses of the world with their long-desired liberator. . . . Never before have men had such a heroic destiny, so it is written. . . . It is the most luminous and glorious mission ever entrusted to any generation. . . . The imperialist superpowers of the United States, the Soviet Union, and other powers invade, penetrate, undermine, destroy, and seek to bury their fear. . . . We are entering the strategic offensive of the World Revolution. The next fifty to a hundred years will bring about the sweeping away of imperialism and all oppressors. . . . From darkness will come light, and there will be a new world. . . . We will not proceed by slow and delaying mediations, or in quiet rooms or hallways. We will enter the breach through the din of armed action. This is the way to proceed. The appropriate and correct way. The only way. . . . The future lies in guns and cannons. . . . Let us initiate the armed struggle![24]

The party chose the eve of Peru's national elections as the date for the ILA. Although many Peruvians embraced the democratic transition as a step in the right direction, the Central Committee warned its followers not to be fooled. "People of Peru," read a postelection party pamphlet, "today, after twelve years of false revolution . . . a new government is in charge . . . a so-called 'representative democracy': [but it is a] false democracy, with false rights and liberties, with false concern for the basic needs of the people and of real oppression and exploitation at the hands of the exploiting classes and an imperialist master."[25] The burning of the ballot boxes in Chuschi on 17 May thus represented the PCP-SL's rejection of the notion that the transition to civilian rule would liberate the Peruvian masses.

The Chuschi event was the first of 200 guerrilla acts carried out in 1980. Most of these attacks involved the use of explosives, as the insurgents confiscated dynamite and detonated specific targets.[26] The day after the Chuschi incident, Senderistas destroyed the air control tower in Ayacucho City. A month later, they attacked the departmental capital's police station, a tourist hotel, and the headquarters of a rival political party.[27] Nor were these attacks limited to Ayacucho. On 16 June as many as 200 rebels surrounded the municipal building in Lima's San Martín de Porras district. After crying, "People's War—From the Country to the City!" the rebels hurled Molotov cocktails at the building and watched it burn to the ground.[28] Much of the guerrilla activity during these months was designed to raise awareness about the insurgency. In Ayacucho and elsewhere, rebels painted party slogans on public buildings and circulated communist pamphlets announcing the birth of the insurgency and exalting Presidente Gonzalo. In Lima, party militants hung the corpses of dead dogs from lamp posts with signs attached to their necks that read, "Deng Xiaoping, Son of a Bitch!" a reference to the PCP-SL's rejection of the Chinese leader's move away from hard-line Maoism.[29]

It was not until Christmas Eve that the guerrillas claimed their first victim. At around 5:00 A.M. as many as thirty Senderistas led 200 peasants from the community of Pujas (Cangallo Province)[30] onto the neighboring hacienda San Agustín de Ayzurca. Armed with assault weapons and sticks of dynamite, the invaders detained landlord Domingo Medina, his family, and several aides. After killing Medina and his foreman, the invaders raised the communist flag and claimed the hacienda for themselves.[31] The assassination of Domingo Medina by party militants was only the first in a wave of targeted killings that took place throughout the region and country over the next two years.

That the rebel leadership endorsed this degree of bloodshed should come as no surprise; revolutions are inherently violent phenomena. However, as Peruvian journalist Gustavo Gorriti notes, few political parties in history embraced violence to the degree that the PCP-SL did.[32] For example, the party might ask a guerrilla to kill his or her own parents, siblings, children—even pets. At the same time, the guerrilla had to be prepared to carry this out not by way of a firearm, but in a slow, agonizing manner, using rustic instruments. This was to say nothing of the party's unwavering demand for self-sacrifice. Guzmán constantly reminded cadres about the "quota": "He who speaks of war speaks of sacrifice, he who speaks of sacrifice speaks of the quota."[33] Guzman understood the "quota" as a requirement that party militants lay down their lives in order to build a new and better Peru.[34] This millenarian expectation of martyrdom is by no means unique to twentieth-century Peru.[35] However, physical death was only the beginning. Senderistas also expected to endure excruciating physical torture at the hands of the enemy before sacrificing their lives for the cause. More important, in joining ranks with Shining Path, one was effectively sealing the fates of one's closest family and friends, whose guilt-by-association would lead them down the same tortuous path. Shining

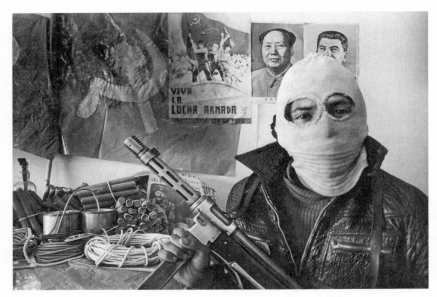

Shining Path guerrilla. Photograph by Oscar Medrano, *Caretas*; reprinted with permission.

Path leaders insisted that all of this violence was essential if the party was to succeed in building an equal and just Peru. In short, Senderistas would only reach socialist-communist utopia by crossing a "river of blood."[36]

Ayacuchans of all walks of life crossed this metaphorical river by aiding, abetting, and even joining the rebels. Most party militants were educated and semieducated youths. They came from places like Mariscal Cáceres High School in Ayacucho City, where, one morning in late 1982, the teenaged students lined up to sing the national anthem suddenly broke out in a synchronized guerrilla anthem. Outraged, the principal grabbed a microphone and demanded that they stop immediately. One of the students calmly walked up to the principal and said, "Don't worry, Mr. Principal, nothing will happen to you as long as you join ranks with Shining Path."[37] Shining Path guerrillas counted on high school and university youths not only to provide the military backbone of the revolution but also, and more important, to serve as intermediaries between the cities and the countryside, where most students' families were from.[38] It was through these networks that the PCP-SL hoped to amass peasant support. The guerrillas achieved this support with varying degrees of success, but by late 1982 state authorities were already complaining about the ease with which the rebels were able to recruit and train peasants—"even elderly women"—in the absence of a strong rural police force.[39]

Chuschi was among the first indigenous peasant communities to support the insurgency. Between 1980 and 1983, Chuschinos and Quispillacctinos symbolically crossed Shining Path's "river of blood" by helping insurgents carry out a series of summary *juicios popularares* (popular trials) of local enemies of the insurgency. After claiming the life of one of these victims in Chuschi's main square around September 1983, the Senderistas announced: "This is how the supporters of [Peruvian president Fernando] Belaúnde die, and that is how you all will die if you don't support us."[40] Taken at face value, this statement suggests that indigenous peasants supported Shining Path either because they subscribed to its political ideology about overthrowing the Belaúnde state and eliminating its supporters or because they were simply too afraid to resist. Yet to the Chuschino and Quispillacctino peasantry, the victim of this popular trial was killed not because he supported the Peruvian state but because he was a moral deviant who had long escaped justice and disrupted public order. He was Amancio Rejas Pacotaipe, the indigenous Quispillacctino whom neighbors had earlier denounced as an *abigeo*, a drunkard, a womanizer, and a bully; the same Amancio Rejas who for years had eluded both customary and state justice.

Shining Path in Chuschi

In a dimly lit Ayacucho City hotel room, native Chuschino Fulgencio Makta[41] recounted to Alberto and me his experiences as a Senderista. Shining Path first entered Chuschi District around 1978. The first party members were faculty connected with the local high school, Ramón Castilla, along with university students from UNSCH. The first Senderistas in Chuschi were not from the district, but they had been stationed there to teach classes. Back then, Fulgencio was only eleven, but he had already proved to be a bright kid. He was also strong-willed and had a short temper, which frustrated both his parents and his teachers. One day, Fulgencio got into a fistfight with another student over a lost textbook. When Fulgencio's father complained to his teacher, the latter confessed that he could not control the boy and suggested that Fulgencio change classrooms. The concerned father heeded the advice, and Fulgencio's new teacher immediately took a liking to him. For the first time, Fulgencio felt that he had a teacher who believed in him. The instructor encouraged the boy in everything from his studies to his love of music.

Before long, Fulgencio's teacher began slipping him political pamphlets and literature about revolution. "What's revolution?" the adolescent would wonder as he flipped through the pages. Finally, the day came when Fulgencio's teacher invited him and a select group of students to learn more about this and other concepts. The curious adolescents followed the professor to a rundown house in the hills outside the main village. The house belonged to Felipe Aycha, the local butcher many believed was running his own cattle-rustling enterprise in the village. But as Fulgencio assured Alberto and me, Felipe was none the wiser. He had no idea that his son, Ignacio, had volunteered his home for the occasion. Ignacio, a UNSCH student and local troublemaker, was now a Shining Path militant. From that point forward, Ignacio, the schoolteacher, and a handful of other Senderistas hosted clandestine meetings of the PCP-SL's local chapter every day after school in the butcher's home. With that, Chuschi's *escuela popular* (popular school) was born.[42]

Much has been made of the ideological training that took place at Shining Path's popular schools.[43] Indeed, Fulgencio emphasized that most of the PCP-SL's clandestine meetings in Chuschi were dedicated to ideological training rather than to military strategy: "It was mostly for learning to read and write leftist literature.... They would teach [the writings of Mao, Lenin, Marx, and Mariátegui] to us every day: 'We're going to make war and do this and that.'" But studies of Shining Path have tended to overemphasize the extent to which these political messages resonated with Andean boys and girls who had relatively little comparative experience. Fulgencio, for one, did not necessarily interpret the PCP-SL's message in the dogmatic fashion in which it was drawn up:

> I would wonder, you know, as a little guy[,] . . . 'What will that be like? Are we going to have planes or something?' . . . I didn't really think that I was going to join a revolution just like that. . . . I just repeated what they told me, mostly [out of gratitude for the] care and respect that they rendered me. That was all. That was all, that was all, that was all. . . . [My participation] had nothing to do [with revolution] or carrying guns, not at all. It was just a matter of doing what [the teacher] told me to do, because I thought that it would please him if I did those things.[44]

As Fulgencio described Chuschi's popular school to Alberto and me, he matter-of-factly remarked: "Oh, and one day [Abimael] Guzmán came [to meet the recruits]. He just came up and started talking to us: 'Hello,' just like that." I could hardly contain my astonishment: "No way, I don't believe you!" Fulgencio nodded, affirming that the Shining Path leader had made a brief visit to Chuschi shortly before the ILA: "They [Guzmán and other PCP-SL leaders] came to the *escuela* and showed us . . . the first weapon [that would be used in the armed struggle]. It was a revolver. It was the party's first weapon, and they put it right there on the table." At the time, however, young Fulgencio did not know who Abimael Guzmán was. "He came [to Chuschi], and I remember it well because years later I saw a photograph of him. And it was only when that picture came out of Comrade Gonzalo that I recognized him: 'Oh, that's the guy [we met at the popular school]!'" Fulgencio chuckled at his own ignorance as he recounted this episode. "It was only then that I realized who he was. I had no idea that he was the *máximo dirigente* [supreme commander]. No, no, no, I had no idea that he was Presidente."[45] It is quite possible that Fulgencio's memory deceived him—that this is a case of a *comunero* thinking that all *qalas* look alike, or that Fulgencio imagined this meeting with Guzmán in order to assign himself a significant place in history. There is also good reason to believe Fulgencio's account, given the significance of the occasion. After all, Chuschi had been selected—probably by Guzmán himself—as the location of the ILA, and the Shining Path leader may very well have insisted on meeting some of the local youths who would participate in that historic event.

Fulgencio was not among the youths chosen to participate in the ILA. In fact, he had no idea that it had taken place. He was about thirteen years old at the time: "I was playing soccer in the village square and I didn't even notice that the office of the registrar was on fire." I chuckled, "You mean you were there?" Fulgencio nodded. "There I was just playing soccer and the next thing I know—*pam!*—they hoisted the [communist] flag. But listen, they had taken that flag from the popular school. And I thought: 'Hey, that's the flag [from the popular school]!'"[46] Shortly after the burning of the ballot boxes on 17 May 1980, however, Fulgencio was invited to take a more active role in the local insurgency:

> I had been playing soccer in a field up in the distance, and afterward
> I went to take a bath [in the river]. Then, [the Senderistas] came

looking for me, saying that they were organizing a committee in the village square, but that they had been looking for me first. I wondered why. Why were they looking for me specifically? . . . When I got [to the village square], they informed me that I had been chosen to lead [the local] *comité popular* [popular committee], and they had me stand before all the villagers like an authority—of the *comité popular!*[47]

Joining the popular school was just one way for *comuneros* to support the guerrillas. Another was to join the ranks of the party's Popular Guerrilla Army (EGP). EGP militants received military training and were mostly drawn from the pool of teachers and university students. Most of the EGP militants were not from Chuschi, although a few, such as Ignacio Aycha, were. Whereas the EGP militants were responsible for military operations and could be dispatched to other areas, members of Chuschi's popular committee dealt mostly with local matters. Their principal function was to select individuals to be tried in Shining Path's popular trials and to come up with appropriate punishments for them. As Fulgencio reiterated, the actual punishments were usually carried out by the Senderista militants of the EGP. All told, only a handful of Chuschinos and Quispillacctinos— maybe fifteen in all—became Senderistas.

There were, of course, ways for local peasants to support the insurgency without joining the popular committee or EGP. These included cooking for the rebels; lodging them in local homes; carrying the communist flag; serving as messengers; serving as *vígias* (lookouts), who alerted the rebels of incoming raids from the Peruvian security forces; informing; suggesting names to be placed on Shining Path's "black list" for future sanctions; aiding in the physical punishment of Shining Path targets; and simply participating in Shining Path rallies, expeditions, incursions, and popular trials. It is in this sense that we can speak of indigenous peasant support for the Shining Path insurgency. For the purposes of this study, I take into account the broad spectrum of support that *comuneros* rendered to Shining Path, from direct participation as Senderistas to passive endorsement. What I would like to emphasize is that, at least in the initial phase of the insurgency, each of these forms of support was voluntary. And were it not for the indigenous peasants who voluntarily rendered varying degrees of support to the insurgency, Shining Path would certainly not have been as successful as it was early on.

Why Support Shining Path?

Why did the PCP-SL enjoy this type of success in Chuschi and Quispi-llaccta during the initial years of the insurgency? The following analysis, while not discrediting intimidation or political ideology as motivating factors, demonstrates that *comuneros'* local experiences and cultural un-derstandings regarding power and justice were crucial to their decision to support the guerrillas. As we will see, indigenous peasants in Chuschi hoped that Shining Path's radical justice would redress many of the local crises that I have discussed in the preceding chapters, thus reestablishing moral authority and public order in their communities.

"Let Them Die!": Local Deviants

In mid-1982, Shining Path guerrillas brought two prisoners before a crowd of *comuneros* in the Quispillaccta neighborhood of Catalinayoq. The reb-els denounced the two men as *abigeos* and requested the villagers' per-mission to make public examples of them. When the villagers agreed, the Senderistas submitted their captives to some 200 whiplashes before kill-ing them. While we do not know the identity of the first victim, we know that the second was local *comunero* Teobaldo Achallma.[48]

Achallma certainly had a history of livestock theft. As we learned in chapter 1, Achallma's neighbors had accused him of cattle rustling on numerous occasions since 1975. As far as his neighbors were concerned, though, theft was only the beginning of a long list of moral infractions Achallma had committed in the community. This was also a man respon-sible for a series of gendered infractions over the previous twenty years. Achallma, one recalls, had been married at least three times and had been accused of everything from infidelity to abandoning his paternal obliga-tions. Fellow villagers also blamed local crop failures on his alleged incest with his mother. But Achallma's neighbors saw him as more than just a cat-tle rustler who violated gender norms. They had also previously accused him of free-riding, arguing that he had neglected his communal work du-ties, failed to pay his share of communal taxes, and illicitly appropriated lands belonging to his neighbors and the collectivity. More important, he had never been punished for any of these social breaches. To the rebels, Teobaldo Achallma may have been just another *abigeo*. To his neighbors, he represented everything that was morally contagious and publicly dis-ruptive: a habitual, unrepentant livestock rustler who stole from his neighbors; a sexual degenerate who had committed adultery and incest; a father who had abandoned his children; and a free-rider who placed individual advancement above that of the collective. He was, in a word, a deviant, and one who continued to scoff at customary authority and communal mores. Achallma's neighbors had weighed the costs of his actions against the extreme justice of the PCP-SL, and Shining Path's justice had prevailed.

Achallma was not the only one whose social conduct came back to haunt him during the early years of the insurgency. Around September of the following year, Amancio Rejas and his son, Jesús, were resting in their Quispillaccta home when a band of about fifteen or twenty armed militants woke them up and escorted them back to the plaza in Chuschi. The band was joined in the plaza by eighty sling-clutching militants and scores of unarmed Chuschino and Quispillacctino men, women, and children. The crowd held an ad hoc popular trial, accusing Amancio of supporting the government and cattle rustling. Young Jesús stood accused as well. His crime: being the son of a cattle-rustling government supporter. The participants later reasoned, "What the father does, later the son will do the same as or worse than his progenitor!" When the militants asked the crowd if the two Quispillacctinos should be killed, the crowd shouted back, "Yes, let them die!" Asked again, the *comuneros* responded with a resounding: "Yes!" The Senderistas happily complied, shooting father and son. Amancio, we are told, died immediately. Jesús did not go so easily, attempting to get up several times before finally succumbing to his wounds.[49]

As was the case with Teobaldo Achallma, Amancio Rejas's neighbors felt that he had earned this extreme punishment. Once again, it was not that Rejas had stolen cattle that got him into trouble with his neighbors during the Shining Path years. Rather, it was the perception that he was a moral deviant who refused to change his ways. Rejas, one recalls, had been linked to theft since he was nineteen. For the next twenty years, his name weaved in and out of the archival record on charges of cattle rustling. But Rejas was more than just an *abigeo* in the eyes of his neighbors. Recall the 1975 meeting in which authorities and *comuneros* accused Rejas of free-riding when they decried his unwillingness to "fulfill his duties as a *comunero*." During that same meeting, one of Rejas's neighbors denounced his brazen womanizing. Many years later, his neighbor Víctor Núñez would recall with candor that Rejas raped some of the women he stole from. To top it all off, Rejas was a known drunkard, a man once accused of stealing 900 soles from a neighbor and blowing it on booze. More important, Rejas was never brought to justice for his long list of moral infractions. This was not because no one tried. His fellow villagers had at one point pleaded with a judge to "punish [Rejas] in the most exemplary manner." There is no record, however, that Peruvian courts ever found Amancio Rejas guilty for any of the crimes for which he stood accused within village borders.

Amancio Rejas's standing as a thief and government supporter may have been enough for the Senderistas to condemn him to death. For his indigenous neighbors, however, it was much more complicated than that. To them, Rejas was another misfit who had never been brought to justice for a long list of moral violations that jeopardized internal public order. Given his long and difficult history with Quispillacctino villagers and authorities, it comes as no surprise that, when given the opportunity, villagers condemned both Rejas and his son to a brutal death at the hands of Shining Path rebels.

Of course, not all *abigeos* were Quispillacctinos. The most notorious *abigeo*—the one locals accused of running his own cattle-rustling enterprise—was the Chuschino butcher Felipe Aycha. Many Chuschinos held Aycha solely responsible for the wave of organized livestock rustling that had been plaguing the village for more than a decade. Although Aycha described himself as a man who had made the necessary sacrifices to put his children through school, his fellow Chuschinos saw him as a shameful patriarch whose own brothers-in-law had disavowed him for beating his wife. Even the members of his gang had complained of his apathy toward traditional codes of reciprocity, citing cases in which he had failed to treat them to helpings of the meat that he had contracted them to steal. Most of all, Aycha had always managed to get away with his misconduct, threatening and mocking anyone—even the customary *varayoqs*—who attempted to bring him to justice.

Yet Aycha was also the father of a Shining Path militant, not to mention the owner of the house where the party's local chapter had held its clandestine meetings. And yet *comuneros* still urged PCP-SL militants to blacklist him. The rebels finally succumbed to this popular pressure around 1983. According to Fulgencio, Aycha learned of the rebels' intentions—his Senderista son most likely tipped him off—and fled the zone before they could detain him. "Who knows what became of him?" Fulgencio pondered. "[The Senderistas] never even punished him, they didn't punish him, but they sure did search for him. They searched for him and when they couldn't find him they killed his wife. They killed his wife, just killed her."[50] On the surface, this measure appears out of sync with *comuneros'* paternalistic ethos. However, when we consider the archival data, this punishment is actually consistent with this cultural framework. Let us revisit the language of the 1977 petition in which Chuschino authorities denounced Aycha's entire peasant household: "As far as we are concerned, every member of that family, starting with the father *don* Felipe Aycha, and [including] *mother* and children, is dedicated exclusively to this aforementioned poor conduct [of *abigeato*.]"[51] To these authorities, the entire Aycha household was engaged in this detestable profession. They believed that Felipe Aycha's shameful patriarchal example had infected his family, and because his wife was not above this criminal behavior, she had in a sense relinquished her implicit right to the community's physical protection. In the end, though, not even Aycha could escape Shining Path justice, for the rebels eventually caught up with and assassinated him as well.[52]

But what of Felipe's son, Ignacio? We know from the above petition that local authorities considered Ignacio Aycha to be part of the family of criminals. We also learned in chapter 1 that Ignacio was one of the local youths who had scoffed at customary values and authority. On the surface, then, Ignacio would have made a logical Shining Path target. Yet Ignacio not only escaped rebel justice but also became a guerrilla. Why the double standard? Consider the following: The rebels had little choice but to bring Ignacio's father to justice, for *comuneros* saw him as one of the village's vilest deviants and biggest threats to public order. Had the guerrillas not bowed to public pressure and brought Felipe Aycha to justice, they would have risked losing legitimacy within the community. Ignacio's case was different. Due to Ignacio's readiness to join the insurgency, the PCP-SL was willing to forgive his previous transgressions provided that he did not revert to his old ways. This was in fact a major strategy the party used to maintain its legitimacy in peasant communities, for this offered one-time deviants an opportunity for forgiveness if they joined the insurgency as armed combatants and refrained from moral backsliding. It was in every sense a moral "rebirth."[53]

This practice of forgiveness represented the first power pact between the guerrillas and the indigenous peasantry. For peasants, this system enabled erstwhile deviants to do the dirty work of bringing other backsliders to justice. At the same time, peasants could rest assured that these one-time delinquents would be held to the same ethical standard as everyone else, and that the guerrillas would not hesitate to punish their own kind for any moral slippage. For the Senderistas, this unwritten pact with the peasantry provided them with a pool of potential cadres who had already demonstrated their penchant for violence and delinquency—only now this delinquent predisposition could be channeled into the revolution. This legitimized the guerrillas in the eyes of the peasantry, for it established that they had at least some moral capacity for forgiveness. In the final analysis, this may have been just as important to peasants as the guerrillas' capacity to punish.

Although the guerrillas insisted that this practice of revolutionary rebirth was purely secular, it appealed to Andean peasants' religious sensibilities. The insurgency took place at a time when Chuschinos were beginning to question the legitimacy of the Catholic Church, whose local practitioners had been riddled with corruption and scandal.[54] Fed up with the religious status quo, some had already found a spiritual alternative in Evangelical Protestantism; others were still searching. For those who had not yet found a viable alternative to Catholicism, the PCP-SL offered precisely the kind of moral and spiritual salvation for which they were looking. More important, Shining Path's practice of accepting repentant deviants into its ranks was consistent with Andean Christianity, reincorporating those who repented their sins into the community of the faithful.

The deviants mentioned above were not the only Chuschinos and Quispillacctinos submitted to Shining Path justice; they were simply among the first and most extreme cases.[55] During the opening three years of the insurgency, numerous villagers were punished for the same types of social infringements as the ones for which Achallma, Rejas, and Aycha paid with their lives. However, *comuneros* rarely advocated death as a punishment, instead encouraging the Senderistas to make public spectacles of moral backsliders. The reason is that, unlike the figures mentioned above, villagers did not see these other targets as people whose conduct was socially and morally hazardous. These people only required a punishment that would discourage them and others from spiraling into moral deficiency. This sentiment is exemplified in a statement made by a *comunero* from Quispillaccta to Peruvian anthropologist Marté Sánchez Villagómez regarding cattle rustlers: "In these parts there used to be people who would steal for the sake of stealing, they'd even take our animals that were tied up, but when the terrorists came, they submitted them to fifty lashes.

They didn't kill them, but if they kept on [stealing], *then* they would kill them!"[56] It is in this sense that Shining Path's system of justice, replete with 'warnings' about more drastic measures, corrected perceived crises in public order and justice.

As these examples have shown, the reasons given by the Senderistas for targeting individuals during the opening phase of the rebellion did not necessarily reflect those of the local peasantry. While the Senderista outsiders put people like Teobaldo Achallma, Amancio Rejas, and Felipe Aycha on their blacklists for offenses against the party, *comuneros* living in the district were more concerned with addressing historically and culturally rooted crises of justice and public order. Villagers turned to the summary popular trials to accomplish what both customary and state justice had failed to do: to correct the behavior of the villagers they considered morally corrupt and corrupting. In most cases, villagers saw PCP-SL justice as a warning against unethical behavior, endorsing the death penalty only for individuals who had relentlessly undermined local mores for years—even decades—on end. Nor were these moral deviants the only ones the peasantry brought to justice during this period. Another group was the illegitimate *qala* authorities, to whom we now turn.

Out with the Old: Race and Class

On the first day of June 1982, ten hooded Senderistas armed with machine guns brought Chuschi governor Bernardino Chipana before a crowd of *comuneros* in the village square. Denouncing Chipana as a police informer, the rebels stripped the *qala* authority naked and paraded him around the village square as the crowd jeered. But when the Senderistas proposed to publicly execute Chipana, the *comuneros* responded with an emphatic "No!"[57]

Chipana's story speaks to *comuneros'* expectations of Shining Path justice. In chapter 1, we introduced Chipana as a Chuschino migrant accused of rustling livestock from his *qala* neighbor, Ernesto Jaime. In chapter 3, we reintroduced Chipana as the *qala* governor whom *comuneros* had voted out of public office for imposing arbitrary taxes on the peasantry and appropriating their livestock. The timing of his run-in with the Senderistas suggests that Chipana either refused to give up his post after being popularly dethroned or simply reassumed it within a year of his removal. Either way, it appears that the indigenous peasantry was unable to keep him out of office. *Comuneros'* perception of Chipana as an illegitimate authority probably weighed more heavily on their decision to submit him to Shining Path justice than his status as an alleged police informer. What the villagers who participated in Chipana's popular trial had intended to do was publicly humiliate a fellow *comunero* whose reputation as a migrant and authority had earned him the status of *qala*. Having accomplished this, they saw no reason to end his life.

Six months after Chipana's brush with Shining Path justice, villagers held popular trials for two additional *qala* authorities before expelling them from the district. One of the accused authorities was Mayor Vicente Blanco.[58] Before running Blanco out of town, the guerrillas stripped him naked, made him walk around the perimeter of the village square, and flogged him with a *chicote*.[59] Blanco, one recalls, had been accused of using his education and his political authority to appropriate the community's economic and natural resources. This was to say nothing of his gendered misconduct, which included numerous charges of raping *comunera* women. Blanco continued to govern in 1982, which explains why *comuneros* submitted him to Shining Path's extralegal tribunal. Yet, as with Chipana before him, the *comuneros* did not ask for Blanco's head. Thinking back on how his Senderista comrades had treated Blanco, Fulgencio recalled: "They whipped [*castigar*] him. They whipped him, but that was it. . . . It was just so that he would stop misbehaving. It was just a warning, that's all."[60]

Bernardo Chipana and Vicente Blanco were just two of several *qala* authorities submitted to this treatment. By the year's end, most *qala* authorities had been displaced from the village. In fact, this power struggle was one of the main reasons why *comuneros* supported the rebels in the first place. Even though he was an adolescent at the time, Fulgencio understood the stranglehold in which the *qala* authorities had kept the villagers. "They were *qalas*. We *had* to obey them," he explained. "The *qalas* were the lettered people. They could do anything to you. They could throw you in jail if you didn't obey them. [They] bossed people around like it was nothing. . . . [They] had other people who took care [of their fields and animals], like: 'Take care of my livestock,' you know, and [their workers] would go and get their livestock. That's who the [*qalas*] were. . . . [The *qalas*] could make or break the village."[61] Fulgencio offered a binary distinction between this group of villagers and the *comuneros*, whom he classified as "the people." If the *qalas* were privileged mestizos who lived in the village, the *comuneros* were indigenous peasants who held modest amounts of land and livestock in the surrounding hills. As far as Fulgencio was concerned, *comuneros* during his youth had no choice but to accept this unequal power relationship: "For example, if a *qala*'s plot needed work, [he could tell any *comunero*:] 'Today you need to water so many *yugadas* of my field.' And [he] could just gather as many people as needed[,] . . . claiming that it would be 'for the good of the community.' . . . I used to live with my grandfather and he would tell me, 'It's always been this way.'"[62]

Clearly, Fulgencio appreciated the long history of conflict between the *vecinos* and *comuneros*. He also recognized that in recent years, *qalas* such as Vicente Blanco had overstepped their authority, disregarding their end of the power pact by neglecting to fulfill *comuneros*' cultural expectations of reciprocity and paternalism. Young Fulgencio joined the guerrilla insurgency in large part to right these wrongs. To him, Chuschi's popular committee, which he had commanded, represented a sort of *comunero* coup. "The first popular committee seized power from the *qalas* and the *qalas* returned to their homes to sleep," he boasted. "From that moment forward all the [local] complaints that used to come to the *qalas* started coming to us. . . . [We were] like the new authority. . . . Like the *varayoq*, the governor, everything, everything." Villagers certainly had reason to be suspicious of the new authority structure that the PCP-SL had thrust on them. For one, the idea of bestowing political authority on unmarried teenagers was completely foreign to *comuneros*. Additionally, the popular committee was appointed by party militants, not the villagers. Yet considering the alternative—the rule of abusive *qalas*—the PCP-SL's local authority was a marked improvement. "It was a novelty to be able to castigate those who misbehaved," Fulgencio admitted. "It was great, and everyone in the community applauded it. Gone were the thieves. Gone were the womanizers."[63] But as Fulgencio attested, the youths who headed up Chuschi's popular committee did not act alone when deciding whom to punish and how. He and the other local Senderistas relied heavily on the wisdom and advice of their *comunero* neighbors, particularly elders and customary authorities: "We would have meetings with the most notable [*comuneros*] and say, 'This is what's happening. What should we do?' . . . The elders alone made the decisions, along with other people who were invited [to the meetings]: the notable elders of the village and the past authorities, too. It was only after consulting them that we would act, the popular committee didn't act alone."[64] Fulgencio's statement allows us to appreciate the divergence between what Shining Path leadership hoped to accomplish and what actually took place on the ground. While the party endeavored to replace all rival authority structures with its own, local cadres preferred to fuse customary and PCP-SL authority.

To indigenous Chuschinos, then, the Shining Path insurgency was as much about race and power as it was about ideology and class. Whereas Shining Path leaders emphasized class conflict, *comuneros* saw the insurgency as an opportunity to turn the racial hierarchy on its head. By stripping nonindigenous authorities naked in front of all the villagers, the rebels were stripping them of their principal status marker—their urban dress—thereby rendering them symbolically equal to the indigenous poor. By flogging the *vecinos*, the oppressed became the oppressor. This act also illustrated that the *qalas'* fair skin could crack and bleed just like that of indigenous peasants. The public expulsion of the mestizo power holders from the community represented the final act of *comuneros* recapturing their political autonomy. Because this was the principal objective of these tribunals for indigenous Chuschinos, they did not insist on killing the *qalas* during the initial phase of violence—the objective was not genocide but the re-equilibration of a broken power pact. This is why indigenous peasants focused on the individual *qalas* they believed had violated the power pact. Those who had generally respected this pact were not targeted. This was one reason why Chuschinos did not castigate or expel mestizo Ernesto Jaime. Among other things, Chuschinos rewarded Jaime for his paternalistic loyalty to the community, remembering his leadership in the March of Death against rival Quispillaccta.[65] At the same time, Chuschinos remembered the Quispillacctinos who had fought against them during that clash.

River of Blood: Intercommunity Conflict

Eucalyptus, cedar, *molle*, and alder trees grow throughout its countryside, and in the center of its valley you will find Chuschi and Quispillaqta [*sic*], villages divided by a stream and united by a bridge; villages inhabited by two rival, antagonistic, native, and agricultural *comuneros*. The rivalry is very old and it has its origins in the ownership of communal lands in the *punas*. Both communities say that the little hill that divides their pastures belongs to them. What is certain is that they will never be able to determine its real boundaries. In the year 1960, there was an armed clash between the two bands and some *comuneros* died.—Antonio Díaz Martínez[66]

The man who wrote these words was known as Shining Path's "third-in-command" during the 1980s, behind Abimael Guzmán and Osmán Morote. He recorded this observation in a piece of ethnography that he wrote in 1969, which means that at the time of the ILA on 17 May 1980, Shining Path leaders were well aware of the historic rivalry between Chuschi and Quispillaccta. It would therefore not be out of the question to consider the possibility that Senderista leaders chose Chuschi for the ILA not because they felt it was a community of politicized rural proletarians but because they hoped to channel intervillage hostilities into the violence of armed struggle. The reverse was also true, that is, that indigenous Chuschinos and Quispillacctinos manipulated the political violence to revisit the historic intervillage feud.

Others have speculated that intervillage hostilities conditioned peasant responses to Shining Path in Chuschi.[67] In order to prove this, however, one must look well beyond the immediate civil war years to understand the nature of these historically rooted conflicts and demonstrate the degree to which they shaped collective consciousness at the time of the insurgency. Having done this in chapter 2, we may now draw direct connections between the intercommunity conflict and the violence of the Shining Path insurgency, thus providing concrete historical evidence for what has until now been a matter of academic speculation.

One woman who was intimately familiar with the Chuschi-Quispillaccta feud was Amancio Rejas's wife, Dámasa Machaca. Dámasa was washing wool in a ravine in the Quispillaccta neighborhood of Tuco in September 1983 when she heard her daughter, Emilia, calling from the distance. When Dámasa got to her daughter's house, she noticed that the young woman was dressed for mourning. Dámasa paid this no mind and asked where they were headed. "Into town," was Emilia's only response as they made their way to the center of Quispillaccta. As she headed toward the village center, Dámasa's suspicions immediately fell on Rejas. She knew her husband well. He was, as she put it, a "strong character" who commonly got into arguments and fights when he drank—and he drank a lot: "I thought that my husband had gotten into a fight with someone, like he always did when he drank." On the way there, Dámasa and her daughter caught up with her son-in-law, amid stares and whispers of local onlookers. "There goes the family of the deceased," villagers commented as the three walked by. Dámasa scarcely had time to register these comments when her son-in-law turned and prepared her for the worst: "*Mama*, you're not going to cry, you're not going to blame anyone, we will only cry in silence." It was at that moment that Dámasa conceded the possibility that her husband was dead. But it was only after talking with the *varayoqs* in the Quispillaccta plaza that Dámasa learned the worst of it: her son had been killed, too. Dámasa immediately suspected that the Chuschinos had put the Shining Path militants up to killing her husband and son. After the popular trial, Dámasa even heard rumors that the Senderistas were looking to kill her, her daughter, and son-in-law. "We have to kill that dog's entire family," she often overheard them say.[68]

Amancio Rejas was one of several Quispillacctinos killed with the support of the Chuschinos during the initial phase of violence. The first public executions in Chuschi took place in the village's main square in August 1981 when eight hooded Senderistas, acting with the full support of the Chuschino villagers, serenely executed two alleged cattle rustlers, both of them from Quispillaccta.[69] Assassinations of Quispillacctinos in Chuschi would be the norm over the next two years. Chuschina Balbina Conde told the Peruvian Truth and Reconciliation Commission (CVR) that the early targets of Shining Path violence in Chuschi were "generally from the neighboring village." She witnessed one of these executions firsthand: "I've seen how they covered one [Quispillacctino] with a newspaper like he was a dog, they took him from the village of Quispillaccta and they killed him in Chuschi, on the paper they wrote his [first and last] names, his family with much fear had to come get them [*sic*]."[70]

Collective memory about this intercommunity conflict certainly reached young Senderistas like Fulgencio. When asked if he had been aware of the previous conflicts with Quispillaccta at the time he joined Shining Path, the Chuschino affirmed: "Of course. . . . Not just my parents, but your [*sic*] grandpa, your uncle, everyone, everyone told you the history [of the conflict]. . . . Everyone knew about it. Everyone. Everyone knew the whole history: how it happened; who attacked whom; who led; who was who; [who was] on horseback; who had slings; who had guns. . . . Even the little kids [knew]. . . . It was like playing an instrument; everyone had to learn it." Nor did local youths perceive this as some distant tension from their parents' generation. On the contrary, their own identity hinged on their perpetuation of the struggle. Fulgencio could hardly keep from smiling as he reminisced about the confrontations between Chuschino and Quispillacctino youths during his adolescence: "For example, look, if there was a party and a Chuschino and Quispillacctino were there, they'd break out in a fight, *carajo*! . . . Or when playing soccer [Chuschino versus Quispillacctino youths] it was a battle to the death, you know, *pan, pan, pan*! And the teachers couldn't do a thing about it."[71] Fulgencio chuckled as he prepared his next anecdote:

> Look, there was this river where a group of us [Chuschino boys would go swim]. Chuschi River. And since I was always the leader I had a lot of friends from school and so we would go . . . just beyond the Chuschi River . . . where there's this lagoon . . . and we'd go swimming there . . . and if we came across a Quispillacctino, we'd beat the shit out of him. We wouldn't let him swim there. . . . Or we'd make the Quispillacctinos pay [money] to be able to swim there, you know? . . . And we would go fishing there, too. . . . We owned [that lagoon]. [The Quispillacctinos] didn't see the light of day there. Sure, they'd make their little pools in it, but we'd go over and destroy them really fast. We'd destroy them because we didn't want them making their own pools. *They* had to [ask permission to swim] with *us*. *They* had to obey *us*.[72]

As Fulgencio's account illustrates, young, future Senderistas not only were aware of the historical rivalry between Chuschi and Quispillaccta but also deliberately and proactively exacerbated it.

Given the lasting impression that the intercommunity feud had on local youths, it should come as no surprise that Chuschinos used the Shining Path insurgency as a pretext for revisiting this conflict. A look at the early targets of Shining Path violence certainly seems to confirm this hypothesis. We recall from chapter 2 that in addition to all his problems in his own village, Quispillacctino Teobaldo Achallma had gotten into trouble with the neighboring village in 1975 when he and a friend were arrested for stealing five bulls from the hills above Chuschi. We know what fate awaited Achallma, but he was not alone. In chapter 2, I introduced Asunción Llalli, the Quispillacctino who in 1981 teamed up with the Mendieta brothers to rustle livestock from Chuschi. The incident, one recalls, was in retaliation for the slaying of the Mendieta brothers' father, Martín, by Chuschinos during the March of Death twenty years earlier. Unfortunately for Llalli, the Chuschinos did not soon forget this act of intervillage theft. Two years later, Shining Path guerrillas executed Asunción Llalli on cattle-rustling charges.[73] To be fair, Llalli did have a local reputation as an unrepentant cattle rustler, and this probably contributed to his denunciation by fellow

Quispillacctinos.[74] Nevertheless, the circumstances and timing of Llalli's death suggest that Chuschinos had a stake in it as well. In other words, the executions of Teobaldo Achallma and Asunción Llalli had different meanings for different historical actors. Whereas Quispillacctinos saw the elimination of these two men as a means through which to purge the village of its moral degenerates, Chuschinos viewed it as an opportunity to settle scores that still lingered from previous episodes in the long intervillage conflict.

The Quispillacctinos also used the insurgency to revisit the intervillage conflict. Gregorio Cayllahua's father, Mariano, was an elder from Quispillaccta who had dared to propose a resolution to end the decades-long struggle between his village and Chuschi. Mariano had a vested interest in this outcome: his wife was a Chuschina. As Gregorio later testified to the Truth Commission, Mariano's staunch defense of the Chuschinos came back to haunt him during the insurgency: "You know that . . . Quispillaccta and Chuschi had a problem over land, and [my father] was the guy who would always talk in favor of Chuschi . . . [so] that there would be respect between those [from] Quispillaccta [and Chuschi]. That's why some were envious of him." One day, a group of Quispillacctinos, accompanied by a column of Senderistas, went into Chuschi looking for Gregorio's father: "That's when my uncle . . . came over [from Quispillaccta] saying, 'Come forward Mariano Cayllahua[,]' . . . hoping to compromise him since he was a leader who spoke in favor of Chuschi. My dad is from Quispillaccta. That's why they said, 'Mariano Cayllahua is talking about [resolving] land [disputes] again.' That's why they wanted to compromise him." Mariano and his son were tending to their fields when they learned that the Quispillacctinos and the guerrillas had entered Chuschi looking for him. According to Gregorio, the Chuschinos came to their defense, chasing out the invaders. Young Gregorio, who was only thirteen at the time, gave chase as well, more "out of curiosity" than anything else, until the guerrillas started firing on their pursuers: "They started after us with bullets and that's when I escaped." Even with their weapons, however, the Senderistas were no match for the Chuschino horde, which this time managed to dispel the intruders.[75]

Other Quispillacctinos commented how they used the insurgency against the Chuschinos. A *comunero* from Quispillaccta remarked, "One time there was a meeting in the neighborhood of Llactahuran and [the Senderistas] told us, '*Compañeros* [Comrades], tonight we will settle scores with the Chuschinos, we will enter where the Chuschinos are, because the Chuschinos are bad!' And the people responded, 'Alright then, let's go!' How could we say, 'No, *compañeros*'? The *cumpas* [comrades] would have killed us."[76] This last statement suggests that villagers obliged only out of fear. However, it is important to note that many of these incidents took place in the midst of or immediately following the 1981 litigation between the two communities. Given the long, bloody history of intercommunity conflict described in chapter 2, we should question such exculpatory testimonies. While some may indeed have been fearful of Senderista reprisals, it would not be incongruous with the preinsurgency record to conclude that some villagers gave the militants genuine support in the initial years of the insurgency. Claiming that they had done so against their will may have served more as a therapeutic strategy to help clear consciences and achieve reconciliation in the wake of a civil war.[77]

Let us now return to the first episode of the Peruvian insurgency—the burning of ballot boxes in Chuschi on 17 May 1980. As it turns out, none of the guerrillas involved in the assault were from Chuschi. At least two of them, however, were from Quispillaccta.[78] "In all honesty I'm not going to lie," Chuschi's evangelical pastor told reporters. "That was [a job done] by the people of Quispillaccta. This is something of which the [police] posts in Cangallo and the police station in Ayacucho are well aware. That night of the burning of the ballot boxes . . . there was a man [in charge] who came from another place, and that man acted with men from Quispillaccta; it was them."[79] This was not just a case of a Chuschino attempting to place the blame for the incident on the neighboring community. Quispillaccta authorities corroborated their rivals' story: "The community wasn't [involved], that is, the Chuschinos. There were also two people from Quispillaccta who also participated, but they were led by a teacher from I'm not sure where."[80] These Quispillacctinos were youths who would have been familiar with—and possibly have experienced firsthand—the mistreatment and racial slurs directed toward them by Chuschinos at the local high school. They would also have been aware of the historical struggle between the two villages. This gives us reason to speculate that even the very first episode of the Shining Path insurgency in Peru, which we have taken to signify the Initiation of the Armed Struggle against the Peruvian state, may have been fueled as much by young Quispillacctinos' desire to burn down their rivals' administrative center as it was by their desire to ignite the flames of communist revolution. Gregorio Cayllahua indicated

as much in his Truth Commission testimony: "There were more terrorists in the zone of Quispillaccta, they were united with them. That's why
they entered Chuschi, they wanted to burn down the . . . Consejo."[81] The
significance of this act would not have been lost on local *comuneros*, serving as a political parallel to the burning of Chuschino religious centers in
years past. All this leads us to the conclusion that in Chuschi the "river of
blood" did not just lead to a classless society. It also led, quite literally, to
Quispillaccta.

Beyond Chuschi: Explaining the Spread of
Guerrilla Violence in Peru

By 1983 the insurgency had spread throughout Peru and was posing a serious threat to the stability of the nation-state. Although the number of
PCP-SL militants never exceeded the low thousands, one reason why the
group was so successful during these initial years was that it could count
on the indigenous peasantry's support. After all, most guerrilla activity
took place in the countryside, and without having indigenous peasants to
aid them, the rebels might not have been able to maintain the insurrection.
Why, then, did some indigenous peasants initially throw their support
behind the PCP-SL? Conventional theories range from economic depri-
vation,[82] to political ideology,[83] to intimidation and fear.[84] While each of
these factors was undoubtedly in play to some extent, we know far less
about the degree to which long-term local conflicts impacted peasants'
decisions to support Shining Path. We have seen how important these locally and historically rooted conflicts were in Chuschi. But was Chuschi
the exception or the rule?

Several scholars have suggested that the desire to punish cattle rustlers,
abusive officials, and the local elite was enough to persuade peasants across
the country to support Shining Path both actively and tacitly.[85] Others
have noted the popularity of Shining Path's promise to bring abusive and
cheating husbands to justice.[86] However, these explanations only get us so
far, focusing on *groups*—cattle rustlers, womanizers, elite peasants, and
mestizos—rather than *individuals*. Take Teobaldo Achallma and Amancio
Rejas. Although denounced by their guerrilla undertakers as *abigeos*, this
label does not begin to explain the role they occupied within their community. To their neighbors, these were individuals who had violated communal mores through a host of deviant acts. Moreover, they had commit-

ted these acts unabashedly, with impunity, and, in most cases, for decades on end. For the villagers who submitted Achallma and Rejas to Shining Path's popular trials, then, the reputation of the individual victim was far more important than his social label. I have found that the best way to establish the reputation of the targeted individual is to first comprehend his relationship with his neighbors in the years leading up to the guerrilla insurgency. Such a task requires greater attention to the historical record.

Available evidence suggests that these historically rooted conflicts were powerful determinants in other Ayacuchan communities as well. In Carhuanca (Vilcashuamán Province), a community that initially sided with Shining Path, conflicts between illiterate peasants and *tinterillos*—men who used their literacy to their economic and political advantage—had been on the rise since the middle of the century.[87] In Uchuraccay, an Iquichano community near Huaychao, an interhousehold feud led one family to solicit Shining Path support to exact vengeance against the other.[88] In Sarhua (Víctor Fajardo Province), a dispute between a land-grabbing *comunero* and his fellow villagers ended with the latter turning the former over to the rebels.[89] Even if we examine the details surrounding the death of the first victim of the civil war—landlord Medina of the Ayzarca hacienda—we find clues that these long-term, personalized antagonisms were in play. As Abimael Guzmán's second-in-command Osmán Morote later testified from prison, landlord Medina had it coming: "[Medina] had a long history not only of humiliating but also of torturing [and] oppressing the people. . . . I think that generally—and in 100 percent of the cases in which [the guerrillas killed someone]—they targeted specific people. Beforehand [the guerrillas] held a meeting with the [peasant] masses in which it was the local populace itself—or at least the great majority of them—that made the decision [to kill]."[90] Even if we strip Osmán's testimony of its political rhetoric, it is entirely plausible that Medina's list of confrontations with the local peasantry went back several years, if not decades.

All this leads us to the conclusion that historically rooted conflicts at the local level played a crucial role in conditioning peasant support for Shining Path. As evidenced from the Chuschi case, however, local conflict alone did not determine this. Equally important was how that conflict was perceived and settled (or not) and the impact that it left on the cultural imagination of the indigenous peasantry. As we have seen, while internal conflicts undoubtedly conditioned local responses to Shining Path, the cultural meanings that indigenous peasants derived from those conflicts played an equally pivotal role.

At the Water's Edge

This analysis of Shining Path has highlighted the ideological disconnect between Shining Path leaders and followers. Whereas PCP-SL leaders demanded justice against a semifeudal social structure, a reactionary nation-state, and capitalist imperialism, Ayacuchan peasants seemed much more concerned with administering justice against moral deviants, illegitimate power holders, and longtime adversaries who had disrupted public order at the local level. Indeed, it was Shining Path's unwillingness to adjust its universalizing, inflexible dogma to local realities that ultimately led to the guerrilla group's downfall. Initially, however, Chuschinos and Quispilla-cctinos concluded that the potential benefits of Shining Path's external authority and justice system outweighed the potential costs. They were willing to experiment with this new system as long as it redressed these local grievances.

This is not to say that *comuneros* were *only* conditioned by local experiences, or that they shared *none* of the political concerns of PCP-SL leaders. One indicator that they may have embraced party ideology is that a handful of local insurgents operated outside Chuschi District. Quispillacctino José Rejas told the Truth Commission that in early 1983 his seventeen-year-old son and six other local adolescents joined a larger Senderista battalion on its way to an expedition in another province. Rejas said that he only learned of what took place next because five of the youths managed to escape the incursion and report what had happened. The teenagers told Rejas that they had been hiding out in a large house, "possibly the hacienda house," when a military helicopter approached overhead. Several soldiers descended from the chopper, engaging the Quispillacctino insurgents. Two of the boys, Rejas's son included, did not make it out alive.[91]

Little did Rejas know that the soldiers had been getting assistance from the local *comuneros*. One of those *comuneros*, an indigenous teenager named Narciso, later told the Truth Commission his side of the story. He said that there were three helicopters in all, representing police and navy forces, and that the male villagers had joined them in the hunt for the Senderistas. Together, the counterinsurgency forces and the villagers surrounded the house where the rebels were hiding. One of the soldiers approached the door and began firing inside to stir the rebels. Rather than surrender, the rebels shouted back in Quechua, "Qatimuwachkankikuray qamuya! Yawarnikipi tusuyta munaspaykiqa [You missed us! Come and get it if you want to dance in your own blood]!" The soldiers fired on the house again, but the Senderistas did not budge. Finally, one of the soldiers tossed a grenade inside the house. After it exploded, the rebels yelled back: "Sikiki toqyaychkaq kaqllat mamchachikamuchkanki, kanachallanmi tuylluykiwampas estatakakakusaqku, qapiylla qapirusaykikuqa [Your explosion couldn't scare us less if it came from your butt. Now we're going to clobber your bones—here we come]!" By Narciso's estimate, roughly twenty Senderista men and women then came running out of the house with guns blazing. A firefight ensued, and the attackers managed to capture and kill at least one of the rebels. Narciso later learned that the fallen Senderista was from Chuschi District, which means that there is good chance that it was José Rejas's son.[92]

This episode becomes even more complicated when we consider another important factor: it took place in Huaychao. The militiamen who had killed José Rejas's Quispillacctino son were Huaychainos. The testimony came from Narciso Huamán, the same Huaychaino whose tales of "hacendado-kings" we learned of in chapter 3. In chapter 5, we will explore the reasons why indigenous peasants in Huaychao and elsewhere felt compelled to align themselves with state security forces and take up arms against Shining Path.

CHAPTER FIVE

To Defend the Mountaintop

Initial Peasant Resistance to Shining Path

O N 22 JANUARY 1983 a group of Huaychainos walked into the Civil Guard station in Huanta City. They had made the long trek from their high Andes village through a tortuous landscape of ravines, crags, and plains. It had been two and a half years since Shining Path launched its revolution in Chuschi, and by now Huanta police had received their share of complaints from peasants regarding missing and murdered persons. But the Huaychainos had not come to report another murder *by* guerrillas; they were there to report the killing *of* seven Senderistas, by the villagers themselves.[1]

THE COUNTERREBELLION in Huaychao altered the historical trajectory of the community, region, and country. Just as the ILA would forever earn Chuschi a spot in Peruvian history as the symbolic birthplace of the Shining Path insurgency, the Huaychao event symbolized peasants' violent rejection of the guerrillas, ushering in a new phase in which civilians would become protagonists in the counterinsurgency.[2] Before long, it seemed as if every prominent journalist, politician, military commander, scholar, and human rights advocate was weighing in on what became known as the Huaychao *linchamiento* (lynching).[3] President Fernando Belaúnde Terry praised the event as an act of heroic patriotism that would forever alter the course of the civil war.[4] Others speculated that Peruvian security forces had compelled the peasants to betray the insurgents.[5] Still others interpreted the counterrebellion as self-defense, a last resort by villagers to protect themselves against Shining Path atrocities.[6]

This chapter complicates the conventional narrative by highlighting the effect that local histories and indigenous cultural understandings had on Andean peasants' decision to support the counterinsurgency. I begin with a brief overview of the national and international context in which Peru's counterinsurgency militias developed. Next, I take an in-depth look at the counterrebellion in Huaychao. From there, I discuss how Huaychainos' decision to mobilize against Shining Path fit within the local history discussed in previous chapters. The chapter concludes on a comparative note, examining the extent to which Huaychao's civil war trajectory reflected that of other communities that resisted Shining Path early on.

The Peasant Counterrebellion in Context

Peru's counterinsurgency militias reflected a broader historical trend. In 1965 the Colombian government authorized the formation of armed self-defense units to combat the significant gains that the guerrillas were making in the countryside.[7] At the end of the following decade, El Salvador's first "death squads" emerged under the auspices of the Salvadoran security forces in the fight against the armed Left.[8] A similar development took place in Guatemala during the early 1980s, where peasant-dominated civil patrols operated in tandem with the Guatemalan military to comb the countryside for guerrillas.[9] Nor were paramilitary groups a purely Latin American phenomenon. In the early 1970s as many as 20 percent of Africa's nation-states reported the existence of civilian militias.[10] As was the case in many of these countries, the roots of Peru's counterinsurgency patrols can be traced to the state's inability to maintain public security in the countryside. As I discussed in chapter 1, some Andean communities had already begun experimenting with forms of extralegal justice before the civil war began. The counterinsurgency militias can thus be seen as a wartime extension of this broader social movement. Peru's counterinsurgency militias even appropriated the name of the original vigilante patrols: *rondas campesinas*.[11]

The peasant counterrebellion coincided with a new counterinsurgency strategy by the Peruvian state. The Armed Forces took control over the state's counterinsurgency effort in December 1982. The Naval Infantry quickly established military bases throughout Ayacucho, prompting many an astute observer to ask what business the navy had in the highlands to begin with. In any event, the infantry had already assumed control over Huanta by the time the Huaychainos reported the *linchamiento* to the police. Naval forces established a base in Carhuahurán in August 1983, placing the 600 families living in the town and its 8 annexes under the control of 36 infantrymen. The navy remained in charge of the counterinsurgency before handing over its responsibilities to the Peruvian Army in 1985. At times, two of the three branches, such as the police and the navy, operated simultaneously in the emergency zone. In many cases, these security forces operated directly with the *rondas campesinas*.[12]

It did not take long for these peasant militias to coalesce. Within days of the Huaychao *linchamiento*, reports came out that peasants from several other Iquichano communities had also killed Senderistas—as many as twenty-five, by some accounts.[13] Then, on 1 February 1983 between 1,500 and 2,000 Huanta highlanders invaded properties surrounding Tambo, in the neighboring province of La Mar. The group was joined by a delegation of anywhere between 40 and 200 *comuneros*. The peasants waved white flags as they paraded around five tightly bound, half-naked alleged Senderistas whose heads had been wrapped in their own clothes.[14]

One of the towns involved in this counterinsurgency alliance was Uchuraccay, a small village located within an hour's walk of Huaychao. Some of Uchuraccay's villagers initially supported the insurgents, a decision that fomented a good deal of controversy within the community. On the morning of 26 January 1983, village leaders confronted a *comunero* they believed had colluded with the insurgents. The young man had spent some time in Huanta City, spoke Spanish, and even dressed differently than most *comuneros*. As a penalty for his alleged collaboration, communal leaders compelled the young man to pay a penalty in the form of aguardiente.[15]

Later that afternoon, village authorities were sipping on the young man's alcohol when they heard a shout from outside: "The terrorists are coming!" The authorities-turned *ronderos* stepped outside just in time to see a group of eight *forasteros* approaching the community. The authorities, joined by other *comuneros*, surrounded the strangers while another group of villagers, armed with sticks, stones, hatchets, and lassos, tracked down a ninth man, a peasant who appeared to have been serving as the group's guide. The foreigners carried not weapons but cameras, and a few of them insisted in Quechua that they were journalists, en route to Huaychao to investigate the *linchamiento* that had taken place there days earlier. The Uchuraccaínos were not convinced, having been instructed by the counterinsurgency police, the *sinchis*, to greet any nonuniformed strangers with utmost suspicion.[16] One of the *forasteros*, sensing the hostility coming from the *comuneros*, spotted a young man dressed in urban clothing and called him over. "Hey, young man, do you speak Spanish?

We're not *terrucos* [terrorists], we're journalists," he said, hoping that this "urbanized" villager would come to their defense. And he did. But fortune was not with the *forasteros*, for the young man in whose hands they had so desperately placed their fate was the same youngster whom local authorities had accused of working with the Senderistas earlier that morning. The young man's willingness to aid these strangers only further cemented *comuneros*' convictions that the outsiders were indeed subversives.[17] The vigilantes quickly roughed up the strangers and hauled them into the village center, where some forty *comunero* men, women, and children brutally executed the eight strangers, their peasant guide, and a local peasant who had defended them.[18]

Only later would the Uchuraccaínos realize that they had killed eight of the country's most respected journalists.[19] The incident at Uchuraccay quickly escalated into a national scandal, completely overshadowing the Huaychao *linchamiento*. The "Uchuraccay Massacre," as the event became known, would go down as one of the darkest, most controversial moments of the civil war—and indeed, in Peruvian history. It sparked three government-sponsored investigations.[20] Each of these investigations has received heavy criticism and has been the subject of intense academic and political debate.[21] For the purposes of this discussion, however, the Uchuraccay massacre represents the extreme point of indigenous Iquichanos' commitment to keeping Shining Path rebels from infiltrating their communities.

Within weeks of the Iquichano uprisings, *comuneros* from Sacsamarca, in present-day Huancasancos Province, learned that Senderista militants had already blacklisted some of them. Villagers met under cover of darkness in the hills surrounding the village to contemplate their response. During these secret meetings, peasants decided to rise up against the Maoists. Success, these men stressed, would depend on their ability to keep the plans for the assault a secret. As one peasant who attended these secret gatherings told the Truth Commission, "No one could know, it was a matter of life and death; we were prohibited from even telling our wives, because people said they were gossips."[22] Taking full advantage of the religious calendar, the clandestine militiamen insisted that local Senderistas allow them to celebrate Carnival. This was, of course, a direct violation of revolutionary protocol, but the rebels, perhaps succumbing to the temptation to enjoy a night of partying and drinking, finally granted this seemingly harmless request. The plan worked, and on the night of the festivities—between 15 and 18 February—the *ronderos* plied the rebels with alcohol. One of the conspirators remembered that as a musician, his job was to play his *cortamonte* and make sure the rebels got drunk: "So when they served me [my drink], I pretended [to drink] and, when no one was looking, I poured it out."[23] At around ten o'clock, the Senderistas, having filled their bellies with alcoholic beverages, called an end to the festivities. Later that night, a group of *ronderos* snuck in through the roof of the house of one of the rebel leaders. The *ronderos* quietly approached the Senderista, who had passed out after a night of heavy drinking, and drove a crowbar into his gut before stoning him to death. *Ronderos* detained the remaining guerrillas and locked them in the local holding cell before dispatching a runner to request military backup.[24]

Peasants across the department soon began taking action. Within less than two years, Ayacucho's *rondas campesinas* had developed into a major social movement throughout the department, with organizations and functions varying from region to region. On 28 June 1984, for example, inhabitants of the Apurímac River Valley, deep in the heart of the Ayacuchan jungle, formed the first regional defense system, the Antisubversive Civil Defense (DECAS).[25] This effort paid enormous dividends. By 1991, 280 communities involved in the regional DECAS had reclaimed control of roughly 95 percent of the former guerrilla stronghold.[26]

Nor was this popular rejection of Shining Path limited to Ayacucho. In early March 1990, peasants from a village near Cochas delivered a package to the provincial army commander of Concepción, twelve miles northwest of Huancayo (Junín Department). In it were the severed heads of nine Senderistas. According to local police, 200 peasants from the newly formed civil defense, armed with machetes, sickles, lances, and makeshift shotguns, had attacked and killed 13 guerrillas. The *ronderos* decapitated all but 5 of the guerrillas and put their heads in bags—along with the communist propaganda and weapons the guerrillas had been carrying—to be delivered to the Concepción army post.[27] This was just one example of peasants' violent rejection of Shining Path. By 1992 more than 3,500 villages across the departments of Ayacucho, Apurímac, Huancavelica, and Junín boasted civil defenses.[28]

The rapid proliferation of the *rondas campesinas* dramatically altered the course of the civil war. Together with the state's security forces, the counterinsurgency militias had displaced Shining Path from most of Ayacucho, Huancavelica, Junín, Pasco, and Huánuco.[29] In the Huanta highlands alone the number of deaths caused by political violence dropped from 935 in 1984 to eighty-six in 1992.[30] By 1995, with most key Shining Path leaders behind bars, the rebellion had been all but defeated due in large part to the efforts of peasant *ronderos*.

Why did so many indigenous peasants take up arms against a guerrilla group that was ostensibly fighting on their behalf? In paying attention to lived experiences and understandings on the ground, I support in this chapter Kimberly Theidon's argument that the PCP-SL presented a *cultural* threat within peasant communities.[31] When and where resistance solidified varied from community to community, depending on how long it took for the guerrillas to present this cultural threat locally. While nationalism, self-defense, and coercion were also important factors, the guerrillas experienced the stiffest resistance once their local behavior and propositions began to challenge indigenous peasants' preconceived notions regarding class, race, gender, authority, and justice. This cultural threat was real enough for some peasants to defend the status quo to the death. Nowhere was this more evident than in Huaychao.

Shining Path in Huaychao

Although the rebels had not entered Huaychao before 1983, they had already breached the surrounding Iquichano highlands by late 1982. The image that Huaychainos had of the guerrillas was therefore incomplete, ephemeral, and inaccurate. Nevertheless, these images shaped villagers' collective consciousness to the effect that when the rebels entered the community in January 1983 many villagers had already made up their minds about Shining Path.

Beware the Strangers with Jagged Fangs: First Encounters

Before 1983 Huaychainos had relied on local and regional trade networks for news regarding the insurgents. *Tayta* Isidro, who served as community scribe at the time, recalled: "As we know, Shining Path didn't appear [first] in this town, but rather from the cities, the fairs.... But in this town people were already talking. Also, the name 'Shining Path' was something else: 'guerrilla.' We didn't know what that was, but people said that they would come around and talk bad about the government."[32] *Tayta* Isidro's comment illustrates villagers' lack of clarity regarding the guerrillas and their agenda. *Mama* Juana recalled being just as confused when she learned of the rebels through a conversation with three traveling salt merchants from Cachi. *Mama* Juana traded with the merchants, providing them with *chuño*, a freeze-dried potato, in exchange for some salt and seeds. The merchants informed her of the strangers who were making their way through the region. "Your town is calm," they said, "but in other areas things aren't so good, because these strangers are coming and if we accept them it's bad for us, and if we reject them it's bad for us." They told her that these strangers carried knives and had jagged fangs. *Mama* Juana sat chewing her coca leaf, wondering whether these so-called Senderistas were people, beasts, or both. The merchants, no doubt sensing her discomfort, tried to reassure her: "It's probably [the Senderistas'] last visit [to these parts], and we may never see them again."[33]

But the Senderistas did come around. By late 1982 the PCP-SL had made its presence known throughout the Iquichano highlands. By then, Huaychainos had heard that Shining Path had been recruiting adolescents and children into its military ranks. They had also heard rumors that the Senderistas were compelling peasants to supply them with food and domestic animals, valued commodities in the zone.[34] *Tayta* Ciprián, a *varayoq* at the time, remembered hearing about Shining Path at the regional market in Pachanga: "People would say: 'The guerrillas attacked this and that'... or, 'The guerrillas burned a tractor.'... We heard people say, 'The *terrucos* are coming and [the poor] will be equal to the rich.'"[35]

Narciso Huamán was an adolescent in late 1982. The future *rondero* had several chance encounters with groups of guerrillas while attending the weekly market in Upiaccpampa. On one occasion, the rebels explained to peasants in attendance that they were comrades who had come to rescue the area's impoverished masses: "We are going to fight against Belaúnde's government, we want the best for the poor people, for we are poor [too] and we will fight for the poor, that's why we need to unite and fight to take power." On another occasion, the guerrillas proclaimed: "The rich men, the villagers who are in favor of the government, the authorities such as lieutenant governor, *varayoq*, we will remove and finish them all off." The rebels then asked the locals if they had come across any *qarachakis* (military soldiers), to which nobody responded. Determined to make their point, the insurgents told the peasants "that if at any moment the soldiers appeared, the villagers would all have to defend themselves, with rocks and slings and that the Senderistas would come from the other side and begin to defend them with their guns."[36]

Before long, PCP-SL cadres began putting their words into action. One day, guerrillas attending the Upiaccpampa fair dragged a man out and stood him in front of the crowd. They claimed that he had "talked bad about the party." Since this was his first offense, he was only whipped. On a later occasion, however, the guerrillas brought the same man before the crowd, alleging that he had once again spoken ill of the party. While we do not know the details or method of his punishment, we do know that he did not survive it.[37]

Rumors also circulated that the rebels had threatened and even attacked local power holders. In late 1982, for example, rebels killed two *varayoqs* in nearby Culluchaca.[38] It did not take long for news of these events to reach Huaychao. *Mama* Alejandra explained: "We had heard that the terrorists were walking around at night and killing authorities and rich folks. . . . A while later, people started talking about how they had appeared in [the Iquichano communities of] Iquicha, Carhuahurán, and Uchuraccay. People told us: 'They walk around with knives and guns, they say they will kill us,' and we wondered, 'Do they have horns and tails or something?' We decided that they must be [real] people and that if we all prayed we could probably figure it out."[39]

Equipped with these inchoate sketches of Shining Path, Huaychainos began talking among themselves and with peasants from other Iquichano hamlets about how best to deal with the rebels. Sometime between November 1982 and January 1983, peasants from Culluchaca met with Iquichanos from Huaychao and nearby villages and informed them that the guerrillas had assassinated their *varayoqs*.[40] Santos Quispe, an influential elder and authority whom one neighbor referred to as "the owner of the village," gathered the Huaychainos to discuss their options. Referring to the new system of justice and authority that the insurgents had been rumored to propose in the region, Quispe told villagers, "There is a new law coming [to town]; it doesn't suit us; I don't think it will suit us." Of course, Quispe and the other elder authorities had a particular interest in defending existing village structures, for they were the people who most profited from them. One villager explained, "The elders didn't want [to let Shining Path take over]. Santos Quispe was not even literate; he was just a guy who was a hot shot [*se creía el más*]. . . . In those days [the elders] decided who would be the local authority, and if there was nobody else, they assumed the role, because whenever they didn't want someone [in power] they would say: 'He's just a *yerno* [in-law] and those guys always mislead the village.'"[41] The emphasis on the term *yerno* was intended to distinguish between native, autochthonous Huaychainos and those who only came into the village through intermarriage. In this case, the term was used to question the loyalty of exogenous kin while cementing that of older villagers who had spent their entire lives in the hamlet. But elders were not the only ones with a vested interest in preserving this cultural value of seniority. Younger authorities and *comuneros* also deferred to the authority of village elders. *Tayta* Isidro recollected, "There were men from [the annex of] Macabamba who were even older than us, and they were certainly talking about not accepting [Shining Path]." Heeding the advice of elderly men, peasants from Huaychao-Macabamba determined to resist Shining Path.[42] Apparently, authorities from nearby Uchuraccay had reached the same conclusion, and they invited representatives from Huaychao and other Iquichano communities to discuss how they would go about resisting the guerrillas.[43]

El Linchamiento: *The Huaychao Counterrebellion*

On 21 January 1983, the rebels provided Huaychainos with an opportunity to solidify their position. That morning, eight armed guerrillas—seven men and one woman—descended on the community and its annex of Macabamba, chanting revolutionary slogans and waving the red communist flag. Village authorities and *comuneros* came out to greet the militants with loud cheers of support, repeating the insurgent mantra: "Long live the armed struggle and Gonzalo!" The Maoists announced: "We are looking [to punish] the rich and the hacendados." Villagers escorted the visitors into their homes for some refreshments before inviting them into their *despacho*.[44]

Roughly forty men, women, and children gathered in the dirt-floored assembly room, at which point the authorities gave the guerrillas the floor. The rebels addressed the locals as "compañeros" and told them all about their socialist-communist revolution. Claiming to be as infinite in number as the sand in the river, the rebels asserted: "We [the masses] are many, we will fight with our might, there will be arms, young and old will fight against the government." The insurgents promised not to stop fighting until they had done away with the rich and the hacendados: "We will be equal with the rich; we will redistribute all their possessions, including livestock." They also claimed to be against the state. As President Fortunato recalled, "They told us: 'We are going to fight against the military, against the government, police, hacendados, and there will be no more thieves, witches, or fathers who leave their children, and we will begin to fight.'"[45]

The rebels then urged the villagers to pledge their allegiance to the communist revolution. A few villagers objected, asking the Maoists to leave and insisting that Huaychao would never support them. Village authorities began arguing with the rebels, informing them that *they* were the government and therefore would not support any revolution that sought to topple it. One of the insurgents turned to the lieutenant governor and retorted, "You must be the one in charge here [*tú eres el que mucho habla*]; when we return next time you will not escape." Neither the authorities nor the *comuneros* seemed intimidated by this threat, and they continued to refute whatever the Senderistas proposed. Villagers reminded the rebels that they "were in *their* [the Huaychainos'] community and therefore had no right to offend them." Others told the militants, "You're just a damn thief [*sic*]; you're not the real law [*no eres una buena ley*]!" At this point, the Senderistas asked one last time: "Are you with us or not?" When nobody responded in the affirmative, the rebels huddled together to contemplate their next move.[46]

Villagers took advantage of this break in the debate to strategize their own course of action. After a hurried discussion, the Huaychainos reached a whispered agreement: "Let's call them over here and take advantage of them before they try to kill us." The peasants beckoned the guerrillas, indicating that they were willing to talk. As the insurgents approached, the villagers calmly surrounded them. Then, without warning, the Huaychainos pounced on the Senderistas. The villagers snatched the guerrillas' weapons and hit them with their bare fists and some stones they had been hiding under their ponchos. One of the rebels, the young woman, managed to pull a stick of dynamite from under her poncho. Just as she was about to light the fuse, Marcelino Quispe grabbed her by the back of the neck and forced her into submission.[47]

Amid the clamor, one of the rebels managed to free himself and fled into the nearby hills. *Mama* Juana was still in her house on the mountaintop of Uchuy Macabamba when she noticed a commotion:

> At first I thought they were chasing a fox. In the morning we were eating soup when suddenly we noticed that someone was being chased . . . below, by the river. . . . We knew that the foxes were always

The original *ronderos* of Huaychao surrounding grave of Senderistas killed during *linchamiento*. Photograph by Oscar Medrano, *Caretas*; reprinted with permission.

trying to eat the sheep, and we were always having to chase them away. That was kind of how they chased him . . . all the way down to Ccarasencca. . . . He escaped down below and a bunch of folks . . . from Macabamba—I can't remember who, they're all dead now—chased him.[48]

Despite the Macabambinos' efforts, the Senderista eluded capture, escaping into the hills toward Carhuahurán.

The Huaychainos dragged the remaining seven guerrillas out to the village square and tied them to the *juez rumi*. After flogging their defenseless captives, the *comuneros* contemplated strangling them to death with ropes. A handful of villagers objected. Women, we are told, were the most vocal opponents of the proposition. *Mama* Juana recalled, "We [women] cried, and we got together and said, 'Killing isn't easy, people die hard, we're better off killing our livestock,' to which some men responded, 'We men know best, even if we pay with our lives.'"[49] Some of the men spoke out against the idea, no doubt hoping to add "rational," masculine validity to the women's "emotionally charged" pleas. "As you know," *tayta* Isidro later clarified, "it was not normal to kill in this community, so I asked them [*comunero* men] not to kill the Senderistas. Likewise, old man Santos said, 'Don't kill them.' But to no avail, the people had already made up their minds." Without further delay, villagers from Huaychao and Macabamba beat, tortured, and strangled to death each of their seven captives.[50]

Alternate Ending: The Macabamba Affair

The above account is based on interviews, Truth Commission testimonies, and journalistic reports conducted shortly after the *linchamiento*. It is worth mentioning, however, that an alternative version of the events now circulates in Huaychao, which credits peasants from the annex of Macabamba for having spearheaded the attack. In this version, between three and six Senderistas entered Macabamba while only two to four stayed behind in the village center of Huaychao. Senderistas had entered Macabamba with the intention of executing one or more communal authorities who had appeared on their blacklist. The list, it seems, came from *comuneros* from Macabamba. President Fortunato explained: "The Macabambinos were aggressive people. They complained to the Senderistas just for spite. So here come these armed people and it's hard not to take advantage of that, so they complained [to the Senderistas about their authorities] and put them on the list." Presuming to have the support of the entire neighborhood, the Senderistas spread the word: "We will gather everyone together and kill the authorities." Apparently, the authorities had more allies than enemies, for the *comuneros* managed to kill all but one of the Senderistas in a manner similar to that described in the story's other version. It is unclear from this alternate account if the villagers attacked the Senderistas in a preemptive strike or in retaliation for the execution of some of the authorities on the list, but the result was the same.[51]

Having bludgeoned and murdered the remaining rebels, an unknown number of Macabambinos, reeking of liquor and carrying clubs in their hands, marched over the hill to the town center in Huaychao, their dogs running closely alongside them. The remaining two or three Senderistas were still debating with the villagers in the *despacho* when the Macabambinos arrived. According to *mama* Alejandra, the Macabambinos proudly explained to the peasants standing outside the *despacho* what they had just done, pressuring their neighbors to do the same: "These [Senderistas] are against the government and against the hacendados." Noticing that some had given food to the rebels, they added, "Ah, maybe you all are in favor of these assassins. . . . We see you are still cooking for these people who have killed our own, now we are going to report you to the police." It was around this time when the Huaychainos attacked, captured, and killed the remaining Senderistas.[52]

In emphasizing the Macabambinos' protagonism in the attack, this version makes some important revelations about village power relations. As the alternate account illustrates, this was not a harmonious relationship. Customary authorities had their share of enemies in the village, and these enemies were willing to submit some of the leaders to guerrilla justice. Yet contempt for local authorities was not a *collective* sentiment, for when the time came to turn their authorities over to the rebels, enough villagers came to the defense of their *varayoqs* to overturn the will of the minority. Indeed, the Macabambinos involved in the counterrebellion were prepared to preserve the local cargo system at all costs, even if it meant killing the guerrillas.

"Surely They Will Kill Us All": The Formation of the Huaychao Militia

There was no going back now. Whether they had intended to or not, the Huaychainos had taken sides in the civil war. *Tayta* Ciprián recounted the gravity of the situation: "It was like we were all disoriented that day. . . . I was not myself." The former *varayoq* later added, "It was a very sad day, the children cried, the dogs howled, the women cried as if they had been related to the deceased [rebels], even the sun shined a low yellow. We were afraid, saying, 'Surely they will kill us all.'" *Tayta* Ciprián and his neighbors knew exactly what they had to do: "From that point forward, the villagers knew they were against the Senderistas and that at any given moment they could come and kill [us], which is why everyone agreed to ready their slings, rocks and knives, so that they could defend themselves against the comrades." Peasants from Macabamba and other annexes joined with those of central Huaychao to form a civil defense, convinced that the guerrillas would exact vengeance on the community that had murdered their comrades.[53]

They were right. The following day, members of the community's ad hoc militia spotted a band of rebels descending on the community from the hills near Carhuahurán. The patrollers quickly alerted their neighbors, who assembled in the village center. The villagers agreed to send a few able-bodied men to the provincial police station to report the events of the previous day and request backup. The remaining militiamen, armed with their slings and the weapons they had confiscated from the murdered Senderistas, went out to intercept the raid. Just then, in a zone known as Badopampa, the guerrillas let off an explosion that, in the words of one witness, "trembled all of [Huaychao]." The battle had begun.[54]

One of the patrollers was an ex-soldier who knew how to handle a weapon. He led the counterattack, manning the weapons of the slain Senderistas, while the remaining militiamen followed closely behind with stones and slings. As the militiamen searched the perimeter of the community, rebels hiding in Mount Uchuy Compañía began firing on them. Between rounds, the Senderistas taunted the Huaychainos: "Miserable [Huaychainos], plate-lickers of Belaúnde, now you will be pulverized, miserable 'black heads.'" The patrollers fired back: "[If we are 'black heads,'] what color are your heads, red?"[55] At around three o'clock in the afternoon, some four to five hours after the initial altercation, the ex-soldier shot and wounded the female leader of the squadron, forcing the rebels to retreat.[56]

One can imagine the surprise of the *sinchi* lieutenant in Huanta that Saturday morning as Huaychao's own Isidro Huamán and Alberto Aguilar, accompanied by Lucas Ccente of Macabamba, attempted to communicate to him through broken Spanish that they had not only killed Senderistas but also retained their corpses as proof. The lieutenant immediately cobbled together a group of twenty civil guards and ushered the Huaychainos into a police helicopter. When they touched down, *tayta* Isidro set foot outside the chopper, took one look around, turned toward the commanding officer, and confessed that this was not his village. After a few moments of confusion, the *sinchis* realized that in their haste they had neglected to ask the Huaychainos which Huaychao they belonged to, Huaychao Grande (Big) or Huaychao Chico (Little), and had flown directly to the larger community in nearby Huamanga Province. By this point, weather conditions had gotten too foggy to fly into the Iquichano highlands. Determined to arrive one way or another in the absence of paved roads, the troops made the long hike to Huaychao. Leading the way, *tayta* Isidro and his fellow villagers carried the tired guards' weapons. When they reached the mountains of Huayllay, the team set up camp for the night.[57]

Comuneros and authorities in Huaychao had already been busy plotting their next move when the expedition arrived the following morning. Peasants from Huaychao and its annexes had gathered together with *comuneros* and authorities from surrounding Iquichano villages—Uchuraccay,

Ccarasencca, and others—on the mountain of Pacopata Uana Lucapa Pu-
cllanan to discuss what had taken place there over the previous forty-eight
hours. These communities agreed to form their own civil defenses and to
aid one another against Senderista incursions. The meeting was still under
way when the highlanders noticed a helicopter circling overhead. Weather
conditions had cleared, so a military chopper was sent in to aid the police
expedition that was arriving on foot. Locals watched as a handful of *linces*
(infantrymen) in green fatigues parachuted from the helicopter. One of
the few bilingual peasants came out to meet the soldiers, bringing them
up to speed on the events of the past two days. The locals escorted the
visitors to the locale where the confiscated guns were being held. One of
the infantrymen studied the weapons and fired off a few test rounds from
one of the guns. The troops in the helicopter, still circulating overhead,
mistook this for enemy fire, unleashed a smoke bomb and began to fire
on the crowd. The troops on the ground emerged from the smoke yelling
at their colleagues: "It's us!" imploring them to cease fire. Fortunately, the
infantrymen in the helicopter realized their mistake before inflicting any
injuries.[58]

Meanwhile, the police team that had made the journey on foot had
reached the outskirts of the village. About 150 Iquichano men, women,
and children came out to meet the party, offering potatoes and broad
beans and joining the march waving white flags. When the group finally
arrived at Huaychao at roughly ten in the morning, some twenty hours
after they had first set out from Huanta City, they were greeted by both
the local *varayoqs* and the infantrymen who had arrived by helicopter earlier that morning. These local authorities walked the security forces over
to the seven corpses, which had been laid out along with the confiscated
weapons in the center of the plaza. The authorities then narrated in Quechua what had transpired on the morning of 21 January 1983. "Well done,"
the *sinchis* commended the peasants. "That's the way you ought to defend
yourselves." But the praise came with a solemn warning of things to come:
"We're hearing talk that in Huaychao young and old will be wiped out [by
the rebels] for having killed the terrorists. As you know, [the Senderistas]
have people all over. That's why you must organize and assemble. And we
will make a defense. There should also be a president, a commando." With
that, the grassroots militias were converted into formal Civil Defense Patrols (CDCs) or, as they would become known more commonly, *rondas
campesinas.*[59]

Why Resist Shining Path?

Although the conventional explanations of nationalism, self-defense, and state coercion were certainly in play, the counterinsurgency in Huaychao was much more complicated than that. In what follows, I discuss the vital role that local history and culture played on Huaychainos' decision to support the counterinsurgency. As we will see, Huaychainos resorted to counterinsurgency violence in an effort to defend locally, historically, and culturally rooted conceptions of power, justice, and community. One way Huaychainos conceived of these first two notions was through the local authority structure, to which we now turn.

Defending the Rock: Authority and Justice

In perhaps the most comprehensive study of Huanta Province's *rondas campesinas*, Peruvian anthropologist José Coronel hypothesizes that the defense of traditional authorities was central to Iquichano highlanders' decision to resist Shining Path.[60] Although Coronel's Uchuraccay informants mistakenly informed him that the rebels had assassinated two Huaychaino authorities prior to the *linchamiento*, his main point—that the villagers of Huaychao-Macabamba would have interpreted such an action as "an attack against 'our father'"—is well taken.[61] As we have seen in previous chapters, Huaychainos often conceived of local power relationships through a paternalistic lens. This is not to say, however, that the counterrebellion was a simple case of childlike peasants blindly protecting their leaders. For most Huaychainos, the decision to join the counterinsurgency was far more complex. What villagers seemed to be defending was not so much the people who headed the local cargo system as the *system* itself, with all of its cultural significance and practical uses.

Narciso Huamán, the former *rondero* I mentioned above, expressed this sentiment after a night of heavy drinking, coca-leaf chewing, and laughter. At one point in the conversation, Narciso looked me square in the eye and confessed: "You know, Shining Path's overall message wasn't really that bad, about punishing wife abusers and cattle rustlers and all. But we couldn't imagine wiping out our *varayoqs*. What for? They were so vital to our community." Narciso looked down into his full cup for a brief moment. As he lifted it to his lips, he added in a near whisper, "Who knows, if it wasn't for all that nonsense about liquidating local leaders, I'd probably be out there right now, fighting alongside [the guerrillas]." As soon as the words left his lips, the one-time *rondero* guzzled down the rest of his alcohol, as if swallowing his own words.[62]

This local power structure was predicated on a collective respect for village elders. It is therefore not surprising that some of the most vocal advocates of village resistance were elders. Shining Path's proposed administrative system posed a clear threat to their traditional hegemony. Illiterate elders feared relinquishing their influence over political decision making to the party's young, college-educated cadres. Fortunately for these elderly men, many peasants also valued age and experience over youth and education.

More than the elder authorities themselves, what villagers were defending was the local system of justice over which they presided. Before January 1983 Huaychainos heard stories of—and some even witnessed first-hand—Shining Path's mechanisms for punishing its enemies. This system had no place in a community like Huaychao, where villagers believed that customary law—throwing deviants in the holding cell, the threat of the *juez rumi*, or, if need be, whipping them—had successfully curbed many social conflicts. Moreover, these forms of punishment typically represented the limits of peasant justice. Death was only seen as an acceptable penalty in extreme cases in which the accused was held by the collective to be consciously and impenitently undermining public order. Thus, when Shining Path cadres proposed submitting local power holders and moral deviants to their radical popular trials—which by this point in the guerrilla insurgency included long, drawn-out executions—Huaychainos adamantly objected. Instead, peasants from Huaychao elected to submit the guerrillas to their own justice as a *preventative measure* in order to defend a local system that they viewed as superior.

As we saw in chapter 1, most villagers recognized local authorities' vital role in preserving the community's social, political, and cultural fabric. To many Huaychainos, the civil-religious hierarchy itself was a symbol of public order, security, and justice during times of intense structural change and in the absence of a strong state. For this reason, when *comuneros* and authorities told the insurgents that they would not support any movement that sought to overthrow "the government," they were referring not to the Peruvian state per se but to this local authority structure. They could not—or, better yet, would not—imagine a world in which this patriarchy did not exist. Nor did they share the guerrillas' critiques of another patriarchal figure: the hacendado.

All the King's Men: Race and Class

As we saw in chapter 4, hacendado-peasant relationships did not generate widespread contempt among Huaychainos in the years leading up to the insurgency. Villagers believed that their former estate owners had generally stayed within the parameters of the power pact. With few exceptions, Huaychainos respected Rafael Chávez's ability to maintain order on the hacienda through his arbitrary administration of justice. Later, they admired Enrique Juscamaita's paternalistic affection for his tenants. On the whole, the two hacendados had respected indigenous autonomy when it came to customary institutions and practices. They also observed reciprocity, supplying their serfs with ample food, alcoholic beverages, and coca leaves in addition to unfixed wages.

Given this background, it stands to reason that Huaychainos rejected the guerrillas' proposition to extinguish the region's remaining landlords. One of the first things the rebels said when they got to Huaychao was: "We are looking [to punish] the rich and the hacendados." Later, they reiterated their intentions: "We will be equal with the rich; we will redistribute all their possessions, including livestock." The Senderista program failed to account for an indigenous moral economy that clearly established the parameters of acceptable behavior vis-à-vis race and class. The Senderistas failed to comprehend that Huaychainos harbored no ill will toward their erstwhile landowners. To most villagers, the behavior of Chávez and Juscamaita was acceptable given their relative power. As long as the mestizo elite abided by the power pact, Huaychainos saw no need to wage class warfare against them.

Up until now, our discussion of Huaychainos' response to Shining Path has focused on *intra*village relationships and conflicts. Our analysis will not be complete, however, until we understand the role that *inter*community relations and conflicts played in peasants' decision to resist the insurgency. We have already seen how notions of communal integrity conditioned the political violence in Chuschi. But did these notions have any effect on the political violence in Huaychao, a community without such a contentious past?

"We Can't Just Live Like Animals": Intervillage Relations

In chapter 2 I argued that the defense of local women against external sexual threats was essential to Huaychaino culture and identity. We saw how men and women in Huaychao upheld this collective value in both theory and practice. Given this close association between gender and community, it should come as no surprise that the impetus to defend local women against external sexual threats was also a major factor in Huaychainos' decision to resist Shining Path. The following excerpt from our conversation with President Fortunato and *tayta* Esteban illustrates men's anxieties about male Senderistas:

> QUESTION: Why do you two think that [resistance to Shining Path] occurred in Huaychao and not in other towns?
> ESTEBAN: People started commenting, "They're going to take our women and we won't be able to do a thing about it," so people started objecting even more.
> QUESTION: How's that?
> FORTUNATO: It's just that the Senderistas said: "If it's all right with you guys, we can make love to your women and run off with them."
> ESTEBAN: There would be "communism."
> FORTUNATO: So [our men] said: "You can't just sleep with our women!"
> ESTEBAN: That was "socialism," and it was definitely why people objected, because it was against the government, and because [our men] said: "They'll steal our women and we can't just live like animals."[63]

How should we interpret this testimony? We can approach it literally, taking the villagers at their word. After all, this would not have been the first time that Huaychainos advocated violence as a means of defending local women against external sexual threats. But while it is plausible that male Senderistas openly coveted Huaychaina women, it is highly unlikely. Most of the recorded cases of rape of indigenous women during the civil war involved members of the Peruvian security forces and not Senderistas.[64] Of course, we can also dismiss this testimony as historical revisionism. Such a postconflict invention would have served an important purpose, offering villagers a cultural justification for the counterrebellion. Under this scenario, *comunero* men would have us believe that they had no choice but to violently overpower the Senderistas, burdened as the villagers were by a paternalistic responsibility to defend communal integrity. Still, this theory does little to explain why our informants felt compelled to mention the guerrillas' ideological terminology. They could just as easily have conveyed their paternalistic motives without mentioning communism or socialism. So, why mention the insurgents' use of these terms unless they had actually used them?

There is a third explanation: that both factors were in play—that is, that parts of the narrative were ex post facto reconstructions and others were not. In all likelihood, the Senderistas in question did discuss socialism and communism, just as rebel columns before them had done throughout the Peruvian countryside. However, they probably never announced their intentions to sleep with the Huaychainas, considering that this particular column was commanded by a woman. This is not to say that villagers did not conclude that the rebels wanted to do so. In chapter 2, we saw how *comuneros* in the past resorted to, advocated, and excused violence as a means of defending village women against external sexual threats. For these Huaychainos, the defense of local women was a primary, ubiquitous anxiety. It follows that villagers would have greeted the Senderista visitors with a good deal of skepticism, on the lookout for any evidence that the guerrillas coveted local women. In all likelihood, the rebels unwittingly provided villagers with that evidence the moment they began espousing their ideology. While some villagers were undoubtedly familiar with leftist rhetoric, others interpreted Shining Path's political discourse through a gendered lens. Unfortunately for the guerrillas, the very terms that they used to describe their ideal society—*socialism, communism*—were terms that, when taken out of context, could easily be misconstrued as having a sexual connotation. Of course, this concern with communist men sharing *everything*—including women—was a common Cold War trope that extended beyond the Andes. Nevertheless, the manner in which Huaychainos dealt with this perceived threat—by tying the insurgents to the rock of justice—was unique to the village. Moreover, it was probably only after the villagers had executed the rebels in this way that they began filling in the official narrative with exculpatory anecdotes about the rebels explicitly yearning for Huaychainas.

Whichever version of the event is to be believed, a common thread runs through both: Huaychainos' anxieties about sexual aggression by nonvillagers. This paternalistic impetus for attacking the insurgents was, in the end, entirely consistent with the complex preconflict history that I discussed in chapter 2. Nor is this the only correlation between preinsurgency notions of community and the political violence in Huaychao.

As I mentioned in chapter 2, Huaychainos did not have a strong history of conflict with another community. While conflicts did emerge between Huaychao and other villages, these altercations usually took place within the "legitimate" realm of the local fiesta. In other cases, indigenous authorities in Huaychao and neighboring communities seemed generally willing to cooperate with one another in the name of justice. Still, this did not keep Iquichano villages from competing for regional power in the wake of the Agrarian Reform. How, then, did this history of intervillage relations and conflict affect the political violence in Huaychao? A closer look at Huaychao's civil war trajectory will help us answer this question.

On 27 January 1983 a Twin Bell 212 military helicopter fought its way through the heavy fog that hovered over Huaychao. The helicopter was one of several that the Peruvian security forces had dispatched to the Iquichano highlands since the *linchamiento*. Down below, the newly formed *ronderos*—not yet recognized as such—from Huaychao and nearby villages approached the aircraft waving white flags. After landing in the village square, military and medical personnel, accompanied by journalist Gustavo Gorriti and photographer Oscar Medrano, of the Peruvian weekly *Caretas*, disembarked from the chopper. "Before the propellers [had] even finish[ed] spinning," reported Gorriti, the *comuneros* were recounting the events of the past week to the Quechua-speaking Medrano. The villagers escorted the team to the village holding cell, where five Shining Path collaborators were being held. Each of the five prisoners was from Carhuahurán. *Coincidence?* wondered Gorriti, asking villagers if there were any pending court cases or boundary disputes between the two communities. Villagers assured him that there were not.[65]

Twenty-three years later, in a holding cell in Ayacucho City's Yanamilla Maximum Security Prison, Mardonio,[66] one of the five Carhuahurano captives referred to in Gorriti's report, told us his side of the story. The crime for which Mardonio was serving his sentence in 2006 had nothing to do with his alleged collaboration with Shining Path nearly a quarter century earlier. After the Huaychainos accused him of colluding with the guerrillas back in 1983, the military detained him in Ayacucho City, but he was released when no evidence was brought against him. He was presently serving a multiyear sentence for having orchestrated the extralegal execution of some narcotraffickers in Carhuahurán a few years earlier. After the Shining Path insurgency, Peruvian officials and NGOs made the defense of human rights a major part of their political campaigns; no longer would the type of vigilante justice that prevailed during the counterinsurgency be tolerated. A top communal authority at the time of the assault of the drug smugglers, Mardonio experienced this zero-tolerance policy firsthand.

When we had arrived at the prison that morning, Mardonio was in the courtyard, taking part in a game of soccer. Mardonio recognized his friend Julián immediately and came over to the gate to greet us. Before telling us that we would have to wait for him inside the courtyard until he finished his game, Mardonio—a killer, but a gentleman—tried his best to squeeze his hand through the opening in the chain links to shake my hand. I did the same, noticing immediately that my fingers were only touching one finger, three nubs, and a thumb. Prison rules required male visitors to remain locked down with the detainee until the gates were reopened at 3:00 P.M. Having not known this ahead of time, we arrived at nine o'clock in the morning, which means that between watching Mardonio play soccer and sitting with him in his cell for six hours, we had plenty of time to ask him how he had lost his fingers, but for now we wanted to know about his version of the events of January 1983.[67]

Mardonio was a teenager at the time of the *linchamiento*. Driven, he claimed, by nothing more than adolescent curiosity, he and six of his friends set out toward Huaychao to investigate: "I went up the mountain. . . . We climbed it from Carhuahurán, and the next thing we knew there were a bunch of people from Huaychao in the mountain throwing rocks at us. They must have thought that we were Shining Path." The Huaychaino captors, who were most likely the newly mobilized militiamen, detained the Carhuahuranos and led them to the *juez rumi* in the center of the village square. There, villagers gathered around and accused the Carhuahuranos of guerrilla activity before tying them to the stone: "As they were grabbing me, some people came to my defense, but more were [in favor of punishing us]," Mardonio explained. In a desperate attempt to pacify the angry mob, Mardonio broke free, climbed on top of the justice rock and addressed his accusers: "If I were with Shining Path, why would I have even come to Huaychao?" Mardonio's effort to reason with the Huaychainos did not produce the desired result. "They had all been drinking, and that's why they decided to throw us in the cell. . . . It was because of the liquor." According to Mardonio, he and his friends remained in the community holding cell for four days before the arrival of Gorriti and the military personnel.[68]

Neither Julián nor I ever mustered the courage to ask Mardonio how he had lost his fingers, and we left the prison with a sneaking suspicion that the *ronderos* had pried Mardonio's fingers off his hand one-by-one during their interrogation.[69] Perhaps other Huaychainos who were present that day would confirm our theory. We later asked *tayta* Ciprián to revisit the events of Mardonio's capture and interrogation. The former *rondero* first reassured us of the Carhuahuranos' guilt:

> QUESTION: Can you talk about that day in detail?
> ANSWER: That's when they said [Mardonio] was a terrorist and they interrogated him.
> QUESTION: What did he say?
> ANSWER: "Yeah, we've been running around with so and so."
> QUESTION: They were only [running around] with Senderistas?
> ANSWER: That's right.[70]

Tayta Ciprián went on to assert that his fellow villagers released the Carhuahuranos because they admitted their involvement with the rebels: "What happened was they said, '[The guerrillas] tricked us. . . . We were recruited.' After that [Mardonio] was recognized by everyone as someone who was now on the right path and nobody gave him any more trouble."[71] Mardonio was even allowed to confirm his new loyalties by joining the regional counterinsurgency, *tayta* Ciprián said. In fact, it was during one of his incursions as a *rondero*—not as a tortured Senderista—that Mardonio lost his fingers: "[Mardonio] was fighting alongside us [*ronderos* from Huaychao], and he was confidently implanting a flag in the hills of Yurac Qasa when [an explosive] from his pocket got hot and exploded in his hands. . . . That's why [Mardonio] doesn't have any fingers."[72] What remains a mystery, however, is whether Mardonio was ever a Senderista militant or sympathizer.

If Mardonio and his friends were "running around" with Shining Path guerrillas, as *tayta* Ciprián so adamantly insisted, they were most likely helping the guerrillas avenge the deaths of the seven fallen Senderistas. If Mardonio and his mates were not involved with the rebels, this means that the Huaychainos captured and mistreated innocent Carhuahuranos. No matter which side we believe, both scenarios lead to the conclusion that the armed conflict served peasants as a pretext for gaining the upper hand in the intervillage power struggle outlined in chapter 2.

This became more evident as the civil war waged on. Whether or not Huaychainos agreed with *mama* Juana's claim that "in Carhuahurán people ate from the same pot as the Senderistas," they certainly treated them as if they had.[73] Over the course of the counterrebellion, *rondero* Ciprián witnessed three separate cases in which suspected guerrillas were tied to the justice rock of Huaychao before being released; all three were from Carhuahurán.[74] Other Carhuahuranos were not so fortunate. From his prison cell, Mardonio recalled that on Christmas morning 1983, *ronderos* from Huaychao stormed Carhuahurán and killed seven alleged Senderistas. Less than two months later, the Huaychao militia claimed the lives of seven authorities from Mardonio's hometown.[75] Even Huaychainos admitted that these things happened during the political violence. President Fortunato and *tayta* Esteban remembered an incident in which *ronderos* from Huaychao dragged two young Carhuahuranos into the village, tied them down, and kicked them to death.[76] *Tayta* Isidro recalled that *ronderos* from his community often captured and tortured villagers from Carhuahurán.[77]

Altercations also erupted between *ronderos* from Huaychao and villagers from Huaynacancha. *Tayta* Esteban told Julián and me about his participation in a feud with villagers from Huaynacancha after the *linchamiento*: "The [*sinchis*] came down [by helicopter] from all over, some over here, others over there, and then they killed Senderistas. . . . But our people helped them to kill. I even fought with two guys in Huaynacancha." As *tayta* Esteban said this, President Fortunato chuckled, reminding him, "That was later." "I know it was later, it was in May," an irritated *tayta* Esteban retorted. "You were off dancing *fiesta* in Yanahuaqra." Laughing at his cousin's claim of having fought two Senderistas was President Fortunato's way of downplaying the altercation. I got the impression that President Fortunato was teasing his cousin for trying to turn a basic intercommunity clash into an act of counterinsurgent heroism. This may also explain why *tayta* Esteban barked back with an equally disparaging remark about partying that questioned President Fortunato's commitment to the counterinsurgency.[78]

Tayta Mariano talked of another curious episode involving Simeón and Víctor Velásquez. As I mentioned in chapter 2, the Velásquezes were the *abigeos* from Huaynacancha who had stolen two of Mariano's cows. The Huaychaino scoffed, "Well, there is a God above who sees everything. 'He will bring justice,' I always say, but the *terrucos* killed [one of the Velásquez brothers]. So there you have it, I'm still alive, but he [*sic*] and all his family were killed and they even took all his animals."[79] *Tayta* Mariano's tone implied that there was more to his story than he was willing to divulge. Did Senderistas really kill the Velásquez brothers, or did a *rondero* from Huaychao pay the *abigeo* a visit during a nightly watch?

Huaychainos boasted that their leadership in the region's counterinsurgency effort gave them a kind of regional respect and authority that they had never enjoyed before. "From that point on," President Fortunato bragged, "we were like a [political] center. . . . After the *linchamiento*, we had power and the other towns were scared of us, because they thought that we would kill them just like we killed the terrorists, that's why [the journalists] wanted to report about us."[80] Through their display of military valor, the *ronderos* of Huaychao believed they had usurped regional hegemony from the municipal center of Carhuahurán.

As these examples demonstrate, the intercommunity power struggle that resulted from the Agrarian Reform took a new trajectory during the counterinsurgency. Nevertheless, these rivalries did not cause the kind of ruptures that they created in Chuschi. This was due in large part to the strong familial and socioeconomic networks that linked Iquichano communities. More important, these were the very intercommunity networks the guerrillas sought to extinguish. Merchants such as the salt traders who informed *mama* Juana of Shining Path's early presence in the region could also inform patrollers of imminent guerrilla forays. Moreover, a peasant's interpersonal contacts in communities near and far—established through trade, fictive kinship, and intermarriage—proved vital in a guerrilla warfare scenario in which it was difficult to distinguish friend from foe.

This was the case for Mardonio. One witness remembered that he and his fellow Carhuahuranos had tried to evoke compassion from their captors by reminding them: "We are mere *yernos*."[81] Mardonio's use of the word *yerno* here differs from previous uses that we have seen. Whereas in other cases villagers used the term "in-law" to emphasize exogamy, the Carhuahuranos used it here to link themselves to the Huaychainos. In effect, the Carhuahuranos were reminding their accusers that, while technically not autochthonous to the community, they were still tangentially connected to the villagers through extended kinship and therefore should be given the benefit of the doubt. And this strategy worked. Mardonio's godfather, Fortunato Huamán, not yet communal president but still a well-respected Huaychaino, came to the young man's defense. While Fortunato's reassurances failed to persuade the hostile mob of the teenager's innocence, they may have saved his life, for villagers elected not to kill any of the Carhuahuranos they captured that day—a courtesy they did not extend to the seven Senderistas they had captured days earlier.[82]

Iquichanos continued to make use of these intervillage networks during the regional defense effort. *Ronderos* alerted patrollers in nearby communities of Senderista advancements by blowing whistles and small horns called *trompetillas*.[83] In other cases, *ronderos* dispatched runners to surrounding villages to request backup, as one *rondero* from Huaychao detailed: "If [Shining Path] attacked Carhuahurán, and [*ronderos* from Carhuahurán] called on us, then we went. We also went to Chuqui, Pampalca, and they all helped us since sometimes our community was attacked. . . . We were also helped by Ccarasencca and Chuqui, also Llaulli and Tupín, and we've always remained united, even now."[84] Gorriti alluded to this intercommunity solidarity network in his report on Huaychao. Just as Gorriti and Medrano were inquiring about the captives from Carhuahurán, village authorities received word that eight Shining Path guerrillas were making their way toward Uchuraccay. Communal authorities quickly dispatched fifty peasant militiamen to lend their neighbors a hand. Major Jorge Barboza considered sending air support to Uchuraccay, but the heavy fog made flight in the Twin Bell 212 helicopter impossible. At that moment, a terrifying thought struck Gorriti: "It is possible, painfully possible, that at this moment, the eight journalists who had left Huamanga one day earlier, with direction toward Uchurajay and Huaychau [*sic*] [to investigate the *linchamiento*], are being attacked and killed by the throng of *comuneros* who—in an almost frantic state of fear—have mistaken them for a group from Shining Path."[85] Unfortunately, Gorriti was right.[86] Nevertheless, the passage highlights the solidarity displayed by Iquichanos when it came to the regional defense.

Like many communities, Iquichano villages had experienced their share of intercommunity conflict in the past. And like other communities, those of the Huanta highlands searched for ways to assert their political autonomy in the wake of an ambitious agrarian reform. There were also some individuals and households who initially aligned with the PCP-SL; some villages were more split over their loyalties than others. Considering the political climate, however, the Iquichanos exhibited tremendous resolve and solidarity, using against the Senderistas the very socioeconomic networks that the guerrillas sought to destroy. When it came to defending their way of life against Shining Path's cultural threats, most Iquichanos agreed: "We will be as one."[87]

THE ABOVE ANALYSIS complicates our understanding of why Huaychainos chose to take up arms against Shining Path. Our evidence suggests that villagers took up arms not just in self-defense. Apparently, the Senderistas had not even entered Huaychao before January 1983, much less inflicted the type of physical injury that would provoke an armed retaliation. Nor did the villagers seem compelled by a heightened sense of nationalism. While it is true that they had recently benefited from a state-initiated agrarian reform, the notion of defending *la patria*, the fatherland, never came up in either the written or oral record. Similarly, these sources do little to support the claim that the Peruvian security forces obligated the villagers to fight the guerrillas. This is not to say that these factors were not in play. If they were, however, they appear to have been secondary concerns, overshadowed by villagers' locally, historically, and culturally rooted anxieties regarding power, justice, and community. But were these factors unique to Huaychao?

Beyond Huaychao:
Explaining the Peasant Counterinsurgency

Available evidence from across the Peruvian countryside suggests that several of the factors that led Huaychainos to resist Shining Path were in play in other communities as well. As with the Huaychainos, these peasants saw the PCP-SL as a threat to their local experiences and cultural understanding of power, justice, and local networks.

We begin with power. While village leaders certainly had their share of enemies at the local level, most peasants rejected Shining Path's proposal to decapitate all forms of customary authority. In response to the nascent civilian opposition, the PCP-SL began indiscriminately killing communal authorities in 1983. The Shining Path leadership hoped that this new strategy would halt all forms of nonguerrilla mobilization. The strategy backfired, fomenting even stiffer resistance to the insurrection. This occurred in Chuschi as well. While many Chuschinos supported the idea of publicly ridiculing and casting out illegitimate *qala* officials, they saw no reason to target authorities they viewed as legitimate, men such as indigenous leaders Francisco Vilca and Juan Cayllahua, whom many peasants revered for breaking the race barrier of the district-level bureaucracy. Even Fulgencio thought these executions crossed a line. The former Senderista said of Cayllahua:

> That guy was a *comunero*. . . . He was a *varayoq* first when I was still in school. Then he helped out in church. . . . He was always going to church, and that was when he started to climb up [the political ladder]. He was a guy who always had the community's best interest in mind, and he made it to be president of the community . . . because he was a really good leader who knew how to organize things and make good decisions. I don't even think he was literate, but he even made it to be mayor!

Chuschinos like Fulgencio, who had held indigenous leaders such as Cayllahua and Vilca in high regard, could not support the non-Chuschino insurgents' decision to assassinate them. Shortly after the rebels murdered these local leaders, the Chuschinos formed their own counterinsurgency militia.[88]

This logic applied not just to indigenous authorities. Senderista outsiders also submitted Ernesto Jaime, the *qala* leader who had led Chuschinos into battle against the Quispillacctinos during the March of Death, to public flogging. The guerrillas claimed that Jaime was a *gamonal*. Had they done their homework, they would have realized that Jaime was one of the few mestizo leaders whom *comuneros* saw as legitimate.[89] Once the PCP-SL began targeting these "legitimate" authorities, many villagers—Fulgencio included—cut all ties with the guerrillas. Fulgencio and the other Chuschino guerrillas held secret meetings with "legitimate" authorities and village elders sometime around 1983 to decide their next course of action. There it was decided that the Chuschino combatants would desert the guerrilla army. Fulgencio was one of several local youths to do so, seeking out a new civilian life in Ayacucho City, where he remains today.[90]

Of course, it is impossible to talk of power without mentioning gender. As was the case in Huaychao, the defense of local women against external sexual threats was a major factor in other peasants' decision to join the counterinsurgency. Miguel, a peasant Senderista from the Apurímac

River Valley, eventually became fed up with his comrades' mistreatment of peasant women: "When [Senderistas] see pretty girls they say, 'I'll protect you,' and they take them away. Once they are bored with them, they say, 'You don't work well with me,' and they ditch her." Driven in large part by his moral imperative to defend peasant women, Miguel defected from the rebel ranks and joined the peasant counterinsurgency.[91]

Just as the guerrillas' gendered behavior threatened peasants' patriarchal logic, their popular trials eventually exceeded the limits of acceptable behavior regarding the administration of justice.[92] It was one thing to punish—and even kill—unrepentant deviants; it was quite another to kill people simply because they did not share the party's political ideology. Shining Path quickly lost support as it radicalized its tactics in guerrilla justice. As the war continued, the PCP-SL ran out of easy scapegoats and began killing peasants whose only infraction was that they did not unconditionally support the party. This occurred in April 1984 when the Maoists entered the hamlet of Pampacancca and demanded that villagers join the revolution. When the villagers refused, the guerrillas held a popular trial for thirty-two random *comuneros* and shot, stabbed, or strangled each one to death.[93] Dozens of incidents such as this one convinced Andeans that Shining Path justice violated peasants' moral code.

The PCP-SL's unwillingness to compromise with peasant customs extended to local networks as well. Insisting on a strictly communitarian socioeconomic model, the guerrillas sought to sever all forms of peasant market participation.[94] In early 1983, for example, armed comrades shut down the Lirio market and detonated explosives along the major highway connecting the town to Huanta, thus cutting off a major Iquichano trade network.[95] But such scare tactics still could not keep highlanders away from the marketplace. In June 1983 *New York Times* reporter Edward Schumacher confirmed indigenous peasants' commitment to trade when he encountered two Huanta Province highlanders on their way to a supply town to trade their surplus for some cooking oil. This encounter occurred just months after Shining Path closed the market at Lirio.[96] In closing down markets, the rebels were not only cutting off peasants' livelihood but also shutting down the very social and familiar networks on which Andean communities were founded. Not only were the *rondas campesinas*, in contrast, open to this type of intercommunity communication, but their success depended on it. For many future *ronderos*, choosing sides in the civil war was a matter of preserving the status quo.

Kings of the Hill

Regardless of whether *rondas campesinas* were imposed on them by Peruvian security forces or mobilized through grassroots efforts, indigenous
peasants hoped that the patrols would defend their communities' core
structures, values, and practices. Most agreed that the customary power
structure served a practical purpose, preserving order and upholding collective values at the local level. At the same time, villagers saw no need
to replace the long-established rule and wisdom of elderly men with the
ideology of a few college-educated teenagers. Most peasants agreed that
literacy and youth were no substitute for life experience in a rural society.
And if the thought of youths calling the shots made traditional patriarchs
quiver, the notion of them sleeping with local women was enough to turn
some villagers violent. Moreover, Shining Path's idea of justice was no easy
substitute for customary law, which peasants in some communities saw as
necessary and just. Peasants in Huaychao, for example, saw no reason to
kill their former landowners who had not violated their power pact with
the peasantry. Finally, the decision to resist Shining Path provided villagers in some communities with an opportunity to reassert their regional
hegemony vis-à-vis neighboring villages while simultaneously preserving
traditional social and economic networks. In sum, Shining Path represented what Quechua speakers refer to as *chaqwa*, a complete and total
disorder in their communities.[97]

. . . .

CHAPTER SIX

To Turn the Corner
After Shining Path

In revolutions, as well as counterrevolutions and civil wars, there comes a crucial
point when people suddenly realize that they have irrevocably broken with the
world they have known and accepted all their lives.—Barrington Moore[1]

ALEJANDRA CCENTE sat on a small wooden stump from
a hilltop overlooking the village square. Sucking on her
lemon-flavored candy, the Huaychaina became distracted
by the photograph in Julián's hands: an image of the village's original *ronderos*, taken by *Caretas* photographer Oscar Medrano during his 1983 visit
to Huaychao. Most of the *ronderos* in the photograph had died defending their community during the civil war. The gregarious widow let out
a nervous giggle and asked, "How is it that you have that picture?" She
snatched the image from Julián's hands and examined it. "Maybe now we'll
interview each other," she teased. "How did you guys get this picture?"
We explained that the archive director at *Caretas* magazine had graciously
donated this and other images to the community since many people from
Huaychao had never seen them. As she looked over the black and white
photograph, *mama* Alejandra's mood suddenly turned somber: "How do
you expect me to look at all this without crying?"[2]

UP TO THIS POINT, I have focused on the causes and manifestations of the
political violence in Ayacucho. This chapter takes the narrative in a new
direction, examining the effect that the armed conflict had on the region's
indigenous peasantry.[3] Regardless of which side they supported, peasant
men and women had to deal with the ramifications of their decisions.
Those who originally sided with the rebels faced a daily threat of attacks
by state counterinsurgency forces. In Chuschi and Quispillaccta, these se-

curity forces carried out mass kidnappings and executions of indigenous peasants. In Huaychao, it was the guerrillas who massacred men, women, and children in retaliation for the community's counterinsurgency efforts. Huaychainos claimed that the guerrillas attacked their hamlet nine times in as many years, killing between sixty and eighty villagers.[4] In both communities, villagers joined the thousands of Andean peasants who fled the emergency zone, seeking refuge in the jungle or in urban centers such as Lima. This mass displacement completely restructured sending and receiving communities alike.[5]

The Peruvian insurrection did more than alter Ayacucho's demographic landscape, however. It also impacted local beliefs, values, and practices. As we have seen, peasants supported or resisted the Shining Path insurgency for a variety of reasons, but one constant for highlanders on both sides of the conflict was an effort to preserve, or return to, the local status quo. In many cases, however, civil war conditions dictated that indigenous peasants set aside previous practices and priorities. As a result, many of the values and structures that peasants had begun fighting for in the first place were altered—some of them permanently. While the political violence affected peasants' lives in a number of ways, this chapter will explore its impact on indigenous Ayacuchans' practices and attitudes regarding (1) authority and justice, (2) gender, and (3) the state and civil society. We begin with authority and justice.

Not for the Faint of Heart: Authority and Justice

Shining Path, and later the *rondas campesinas*, introduced a militarized administration of justice in peasant communities.[6] After receiving initial support, Shining Path militants in Chuschi eventually exceeded the limits of what peasants considered "appropriate" administration of justice. Having weeded out villagers' local enemies, PCP-SL guerrillas continued to execute *comunero* men, women, and children in their popular trials. The arrival of the state's security forces in Chuschi and other guerrilla strongholds introduced peasants to an equally brutal and indiscriminate form of violence that they had never before experienced.

As with Shining Path, the *rondas campesinas* militarized Ayacuchan communities in unintended ways.[7] Since firearms were illegal in Peru, peasants originally relied on knives, rocks, slings, spears, and other makeshift weapons to defend themselves against rebel incursions. As the war

Lacking formal arms, many *ronderos* went into battle with improvised weapons such as the wooden gun displayed here. Photograph by Oscar Medrano, *Caretas*; reprinted with permission.

dragged on, however, *comandos* (militia leaders) began demanding firearms. Hugo Huillca, the controversial *comando* of the jungle DECAS, contended: "[It's] one thing to talk about dialogue, to talk about making laws, to talk about peace . . . and it's another thing to be there in the thick of the action. For us [who live along] the Apurímac River it's impossible to dialogue with Shining Path. Trying to convince the state to pass good laws [is useless]. . . . For us the only way is: 'If they're armed, we need to be armed.'"[8] These demands did not go unnoticed. In 1985 President Alan García provided *ronderos* from the DECAS of Rinconada, in the heart of the Apurímac River valley, with rifles for the counterinsurgency. In 1991 and 1992 President Alberto Fujimori issued Legislative Decrees 740 and 741, which accomplished two things. First, the decrees recognized the counterinsurgency militias as part of the state's official counterinsurgency campaign, redubbing them Self-Defense Committees (CADS) and recognizing them as "the semi-institutionalized fourth branch of the armed forces." Second, the decrees extended to *ronderos* the legal right to bear arms. The military immediately began issuing low-end assault weapons to indigenous militiamen. According to the Ministry of Defense, the Armed Forces had handed out 15,179 Winchesters, Mossbergs, and MGP-43s by the war's end, not counting the thousands more that *ronderos* secured illegally through accords with drug traffickers. Although *ronderos* have since been asked to return their weapons, many continued to hold on to them after the political violence.[9]

Armed with these weapons, *ronderos* were empowered to escalate violence against their own neighbors. A villager from Chaca, a community near Huaychao, explained: "Well, back then there was no good way of solving problems, because back then everything was a punishable offense. Back then there was no judge, only the *comandos* enforced the law, there was also a lieutenant, only those guys castigated people who behaved improperly in the community, they would hit them with the butt of their gun."[10] On rare occasions, *ronderos* went as far as to kill fellow villagers suspected of collaborating with the rebels.[11] In most instances, however, peasants offered "repentant" collaborators readmission into the community after being flogged.[12] This practice of punishment, forgiveness, and readmission was consistent with the customary practices outlined in previous chapters.

In Huaychao, the creation of counterinsurgency militias meant a fusion of the new and old systems. On the one hand, villagers valued *ronderos* who could fire a weapon. *Mama* Juana illustrated this point:

> Some of the guys had done some military service. . . . When the police came they would show everyone how to fire a bullet at a rock, and then they would give the gun to the *licenciado* [former enlisted soldier], who could also hit the rock with the bullet, but the others couldn't. So the one [who could hit the rock] would be called "strong of heart [*corazón fuerte*]" and the others would be called "faint of heart [*corazón débil*]."[13]

On the other hand, Huaychainos frequently employed more traditional measures as part of their local counterinsurgency effort. Turning myth into reality, villagers frequently turned to the *juez rumi* to punish alleged guerrillas. This castigation typically consisted of tying the suspect to the rock and whipping him into submission. Instead of the lieutenant governor and his *varayoqs*, it was the commander of the counterinsurgency militia who oversaw this spectacle. *Tayta* Ciprián, himself a former *ron-dero*, boasted about the efficiency of this system: "Now people accused of being a terrorist could be brought [to Huaychao] by [villagers from] Ma-cabamba, or from Ccarasencca, Uchuraccay, Carhuahurán. They handed [the suspected guerrillas] over to our authorities, who would interrogate them, and [the suspects would] say, 'So and so tricked me [into joining Shining Path].'"[14]

In some communities, *ronderos* and Senderistas replaced customary au-thorities as the principal arbiters of communal justice. After infiltrating a community, the PCP-SL replaced local authorities with guerrilla cadres. At the very least, the rebels cast out the *varayoqs* and replaced them with their own popular committees. In other cases, rebels assassinated communal leaders. Those fortunate enough to avoid these sanctions had no choice but to flee their communities altogether; many of them never returned.[15] After driving out these communal authorities, Shining Path insurgents became the sole arbiters of justice, presiding over their notorious popular trials. A similar development took place in communities with strong coun-terinsurgency militias. In the La Mar community of Huayao, for example, a conflict emerged when a woman accepted her suitor's wedding proposal despite being married in a nearby town. When it appeared that the two men would settle the problem violently, villagers called on the *ronderos* to intervene.[16] Nor was this activity limited to the community level. In 2002 *ronderos* from an organization known as the General Committee for Civil Self-Defense and Development of Huanta Province (CACIDH) decided that they, much like the *rondas campesinas* of northern Peru, would focus on curbing cattle rustling and petty delinquency.[17]

This process realigned village authority structures according to age. Both the PCP-SL and the *rondas campesinas* placed a premium on youth leadership. Fulgencio was barely an adolescent when he joined Shining Path in Chuschi. For the first time ever, single youths like Fulgencio took leadership roles in their communities. Even when Chuschinos decided to break ranks with the rebels, local authorities invited Fulgencio and his young comrades to participate in their clandestine meetings and decision-making processes.[18] Although Fulgencio eventually fled the community, his active participation in village leadership forced *comuneros* to recon-sider former restrictions based on age and marital status. The counterin-surgency had a similar effect on communal authority structures. Referring to the civil defenses, *tayta* Isidro admitted, "The adults couldn't make it far, but the teenagers could and they would come back [to Huaychao] after several days [of patrolling]."[19] As *tayta* Ciprián explained, the fate of the entire community was—for the first time—in the hands of young men and teenage boys: "Young and old [had] put their trust in the watchmen."[20] This phenomenon was not limited to Huaychao. By 1991 an estimated 3,000 minors participated in the militias throughout the emergency zones.[21]

The rapid dissemination of *rondas campesinas* coincided with a palpable crisis of customary authority. Shining Path targeted communal authorities in towns that had organized counterinsurgency militias. Within months of the *linchamiento* in Huaychao, insurgents retaliated by assassinating local leaders Pedro Huamán, Lucas Ccente, and Jacinto Ccente.[22] Shining Path continued to target Huaychaino authorities throughout the armed conflict, forcing many to flee the zone permanently.[23] These conditions required traditional leaders either to share their power with, or relinquish it to, local *comandos*. What is remarkable is that despite these changes, Huaychainos continued to elect traditional leaders throughout the political conflict.[24] These leaders apparently shared political decision-making duties with the *comandos*. *Tayta* Ciprián said that both the *comandos* and the *varayoqs* had the authority to make major tactical decisions, such as the coordination of patrol shifts. The reason traditional authorities in Huaychao never relinquished their power completely had to do with the tremendous respect *ronderos* had for the institution: "Before [the violence] we respected the [traditional] authorities the most . . . because they were strict and well-spoken [and] because they still remembered the advice and wisdom of their grandparents."[25]

Other communities were not so fortunate. Further down the Huanta highlands, in communities such as Chaca and Culluchaca, militia leaders replaced the *varayoqs* altogether as the principal political authority during the civil war.[26] In dire need of military protection, few villagers—not even the remaining communal authorities themselves—resisted the change. After the war, however, Culluchaca's civil-religious leaders tried to resume their traditional posts. Rather than simply relinquish their newly acquired power, *rondero* leaders negotiated joint political control with the traditional authorities: customary leaders would set policies while *comandos* enforced them.[27] Around 1991 young *ronderos* from the Huanta village of Ocana assumed de facto political control because the community's traditional authorities had either fled or been assassinated. After the political violence subsided, some of the traditional authorities returned to the village, but they lacked legitimacy, having broken their power pact to defend the village. While some traditional leaders regained their abandoned positions, young *ronderos* continued to occupy the authority posts for years to come.[28]

The political power of a few *comandos* even extended beyond the community. In June 1984 *ronderos* Antonio Cárdenas and Pompeyo Javier Rivera Terres consolidated local *rondas* into regional DECAS, which controlled almost the entire Apurímac River valley. Cárdenas was only nineteen years old when he emerged as the cocommander of the regional DECAS. Rivera, who operated under the nom de guerre "Comandante Huayuaco," positioned himself as the poster child of the counterinsurgency, boldly declaring: "Give me 500 rifles and I will liberate Ayacucho in one year."[29] With the help of the media, *rondero* authorities such as Comandante Huayhuaco became larger-than-life figures. "They were like gods," a peasant from the Apurímac River valley reported. "They acted like kings, and with the positions they held, they practically were kings."[30] While scandal ended any hopes that Comandante Huayuaco had of seeking public office, other *rondero* leaders were able to make the transition into civilian politics after the civil war's end.[31]

The political empowerment of young, militant men and boys in indigenous communities during the armed conflict was intended to be temporary. The political and cultural impacts, however, were permanent. Today, Huaychainos complain of the lack of respect that younger villagers display toward the elderly. Now considered an elder himself, *tayta* Ciprián explained: "Now the young are bossy. . . . They no longer mind their elders. They argue and act like they know everything. . . . They say, '[The elders] are still living in our grandparents' era because now there's a new law in town.'"[32]

The elderly were not the only ones losing their local prestige in postwar Huaychao. Customary authorities also experienced this loss. The Tiyarikuy festivity I observed is a case in point. After snapping a picture of the *varayoqs* with their authority staffs, I returned to my seat alongside the wall, at which point Leandro leaned in and whispered, "Did you notice how they had their *varas* tucked away in a corner of the room [before you took the picture]? In the old days, they would not have let those staffs out of their sight—they would have been placed front and center for everyone to see." I asked Leandro when this tradition began to change, and he said that it all changed with the violence. Leandro was only twenty-seven, which would have made him almost too young to remember, but his father, *tayta* Isidro, dictated this history to his sons so that they would learn the values and respect that would make them good leaders when they became *varayoqs*. Echoing his father's concern, Leandro lamented that villagers no longer respected or feared the *varayoqs*. Today, he said, their authority was largely symbolic.[33] The wife of Huaychao's lieutenant governor, who had sung that year's Qarawiy, later seconded Leandro's assessment. "We used to put flowers out for the authorities," she remarked. Now, the song was the only remaining symbol of deference offered to the leaders during the Tiyarikuy.[34]

Even the face of the *varayoqs* had changed. *Tayta* Elías, one of the *varayoqs* honored that day, bore virtually no resemblance to the civil-religious leaders of yesteryear. Like the other *varayoqs* honored at the festival, he appeared to be in his late twenties or early thirties, a far cry from the elders who held office before the violence. We later learned that *tayta* Elías was not even from Huaychao. In the past only men from Huaychao could govern the community. Because the civil war claimed the lives of so many authorities and displaced so many more, villagers were forced to reevaluate the viability of this restriction. After all, the violence had ended, but the threat of violence always lingered. What Huaychainos needed were young, athletic men who could lead a civil defense at a moment's notice.[35]

Men, however, were not the only ones called on to lead their communities during the civil war. Women also contributed to the counterinsurgency effort in a variety of ways. Given their participation on both sides of the armed conflict, it comes as no surprise that women demanded a more active role within their communities after the violence subsided.

From the Kitchen to the Battlefield: Women and Gender

Alejandra Vilma hobbled up the slanted road away from the Chuschi plaza. "I hope we catch her," I said. Pointing out the obvious, Julián said, "Miguel, I don't think that's going to be a problem." *Mama* Alejandra's left leg had been warped by the polio she had suffered since childhood. After we caught up to her, she scolded us for not having interviewed her husband, *qala* Ernesto Jaime, a year earlier while he was still alive. Nonetheless, she said she would be happy to talk to us later that evening. She asked where we were headed, and we replied that we were going to have dinner with one of her male neighbors, a former *varayoq*. "Bah!" she scoffed. Later that evening, we found *mama* Alejandra sitting inside a corner store across the street from her house. "What are you up to?" Alberto asked. "Just getting ready to drink my *tragito* [shot of liquor]," she said. "Really?" I asked, excited. I could have used a hard drink myself. "What are you drinking? My treat." She pointed with her walking stick to a bottle of orange juice. "*This* is my *trago*," she said and burst out laughing. *Mama* Alejandra sprung up and headed toward the door. "Just kidding. I'm not drinking anything. Come on, let's go."[36]

Mama Alejandra was a remarkable woman. She wore her disability as a badge of honor. The fact that she could make it up the hill at all, with no assistance other than her wobbly walking stick, was a testament to her determination and independence. Despite her short stature and physical ailment, *mama* Alejandra commanded the respect of her peers. When she talked, people listened. These traits enabled her to become a local leader. But this ascension to communal leadership would not have been possible thirty years earlier. It was only after the political violence hit Chuschi that the patriarchal status quo began to change. While Andean men preferred to relegate women to roles deemed "appropriate" for their gender during the conflict, the exigencies of civil war demanded otherwise. In the end, women on both sides of the conflict came to occupy a more prominent, public role within their communities, subverting conventional notions of gender and power.

Shining Path counted on the support of women for its armed struggle. By some accounts, they made up as much as 50 percent of PCP-SL combatants.[37] Women frequently headed up guerrilla columns and commanded excursions. Once inside a community, women Senderistas typically set up special women's committees for the female peasantry. Men often objected to these gatherings, at times violently.[38] Nevertheless, the very idea of an all-female political gathering may have been both enticing and empowering to women who had never had a voice in local decision-making processes. For others, particularly younger women, the idea of holding a leadership position at the local level—even if this was achieved through PCP-SL mandate—was quite liberating.[39]

Women in Chuschi supported the rebels in a variety of ways. At least one young Chuschina joined the insurgency, taking a leadership position in the district's popular committee.[40] Because the party demanded total submission to its local commanders, Chuschinos had no choice but to follow the young woman's orders. Another young Chuschina did her part by bringing charges of rape against a schoolteacher who refused to toe the party line.[41] In addition to these collaborations, women young and old supported the rebels by denouncing abusive husbands, lovers, and fathers. This is to say nothing of the scores of Chuschinas who actively participated in PCP-SL rallies and popular trials, demanding justice against troublesome neighbors.

Women exhibited similar commitment when it came to the counterinsurgency. In some communities, women joined forces with the *rondas campesinas*, forming their own female units.[42] On occasion, these *ronderas* fought the rebels with makeshift weapons. This occurred in Pampalca in 1983, when twenty women, armed with kitchen utensils and rocks, routed a band of rebel invaders while the men were off on patrol.[43] In 1993 thirty *ronderas* from Ticllas, armed with three shotguns, went out on patrol alongside the community's male *ronderos*.[44] To be sure, these were exceptional cases. Most *ronderas* never saw any combat, raised a weapon, or even ventured beyond community borders. Nevertheless, *ronderas* helped the community defense effort in other important ways. In most cases, *ronderas* would keep a low profile, keeping an eye out for strangers while grazing their animals at strategic lookout points. Immediately after identifying an outsider, these *ronderas* would sing a coded Qarawiy to alert their neighbors of the potential danger.[45]

In Huaychao, *ronderas* organized with the help of the military. "From now on men and women have to be alert [*deben estar moscas*] and they cannot sleep," military commanders instructed villagers.[46] During their drills, male and female *ronderos* assembled in separate formations. Women lined up according to civil status, with married women in one formation and single women and widows in another. Some, such as *mama* Juana, even became *comandas*. "They [the military commanders] picked the [women] who were the best speakers," *mama* Juana explained. "One time they put us into formation and ordered: 'Stand up! Up! Attention! At ease!' Some women couldn't do it because they would fall asleep [referring to women who collapsed or passed out from exhaustion]. Then they'd select the most vocal woman [to be *comanda*]." On this day, the officers selected *mama* Juana, who reluctantly accepted the position, sighing, "Only God knows my fate."[47] As *comanda*, *mama* Juana was in charge of organizing the women's defense. "We [*comandas*] would order [the *ronderas*] be punctual, to line up in formation whenever the whistle blew," she recollected.[48] *Mama* Juana even recalled at one point hearing an inspirational announcement from a Huanta-based radio station: "Stay alive Huaychao, even if it's only one woman! You have our support and we want to return."[49] Thus, even though women occupied a marginal position in the peasant militias, the mere idea of women playing a public role in the physical and symbolic defense of their communities was unprecedented in most areas.

Women who supported the insurgency or counterinsurgency were not the only ones who became politically active at this time. Throughout Ayacucho, peasant women whose husbands, siblings, and children had disappeared mobilized to demand answers as to the whereabouts of their loved ones. Others organized to address the economic crises that ravaged their communities. Alejandra Vilma was one of those women. Her activism began in 1983, when the military kidnapped her mestizo husband, Ernesto Jaime. After learning that Jaime had been relocated to Ayacucho City, *mama* Alejandra moved to the departmental capital. What began as an effort to secure her husband's release from military custody turned into something much bigger. That year, she learned about the Club de Madres (Mother's Club), an organization dedicated to alleviating the stress of Ayacuchan communities affected by the political violence. Her decision to join the club changed her life. "During my time in the Mother's Club," she recollected, "I learned how to organize women."[50] The following year, *mama* Alejandra secured her husband's release from prison and returned to Chuschi. There, she immediately organized a local Mother's Club. At the first meeting, which took place in the village clinic, only ten women showed up. The women set out cleaning the streets of Chuschi. Later, they donated jerky to the local church. In time, more and more villagers took notice of the women's actions, and before long the organization was fifty women strong. At this point *mama* Alejandra and some of the other *comuneras* formed a Vaso de Leche (Glass of Milk) league, dedicated to feeding families affected by the political violence. These organizations expanded with the passing of time, and before long each annex in the district had its own Mother's Club and Glass of Milk organization.[51]

Many women remained active in their communities after the worst of the political violence ended. Having already organized two successful social welfare organizations in the district, *mama* Alejandra became an advocate for peasant women's rights. In the 1990s she helped form the district's Federation of Peasant Women, serving as president for six years.[52] By the early twenty-first century, *mama* Alejandra had set her sights beyond Chuschi, serving as vice president of the federation for the province of Cangallo. Although some Chuschino men objected to and even obstructed the women's solidarity movement, they could do little to thwart it. Some Chuschinas have even broken the gender barriers of the village authority hierarchy, albeit at the lower rungs. *Mama* Alejandra, however, remained optimistic: "I know that we will come to occupy the good positions, like [communal] president, governor. . . . I will continue to fight come what may for women's rights and for my community."[53]

Women who participated in the counterinsurgency effort remained politically active after the civil war. *Mama* Juana's experience as *comanda* landed her the presidency of Huaychao's Asociación de Padres de Familia (Parents' Association). Under her leadership, the association organized sporting events to raise funds for the community school. By the time her term ended, *mama* Juana had earned the respect of her peers as an able community leader. To demonstrate this, *comuneros* elected her vice president of the association in 2002. As vice president, *mama* Juana, a single mother, made the long trip to Huanta, where she petitioned the Unidad Sectoral de Educación (Education Board) for more teachers for the Huaychao school. After that, she became treasurer of the local Glass of Milk league. With *mama* Juana as treasurer, members of the all-women league traveled throughout the Huanta highlands raising funds and providing much needed foodstuffs for orphaned children and widowed wives.[54] In 2006 she was elected president of Huaychao's new Proyecto Mujer (Women's Project). *Mama* Juana explained her vision to us: "Before [the violence] I couldn't speak out, but now I can. Only when I die will my voice finally give out. By means of the Women's Project I want to make cheese, and we will take this cheese to the jungle in accordance with our contract with the families of Quimbiri, Sivia, and Huanta. . . . Through the Women's Project we [women] will be able to harvest fields."[55] When asked why fellow villagers entrusted her with these responsibilities, *mama* Juana answered, "It's because I always go as far as Ayacucho [City] to negotiate things. We've gone with the teachers to Huanta [City], and they always comment, 'She talks with everyone,' and the men say the same."[56]

Former *ronderas* are not the only ones who benefited from the changing political environment. As a respected community leader, *mama* Juana reminded her female neighbors of their right and duty to participate in the community's decision-making processes. "I tell them: 'Ladies, we are people just like these engineers and doctors [who deal with Huaychao]. All we have to do is ask for some guidance.'"[57] Today, married and single women in Huaychao speak out candidly in town assemblies to make their voices heard regarding important community projects and just arbitration over civil disputes. "We get together and tell [the male authorities] we should do this or that, or that so and so is acting up. And they say, 'Very well. We have to abide by the new laws [of the central state and of international human rights].'"[58]

Before the political violence, women never occupied positions of political authority in Chuschi or Huaychao. To be sure, the experiences of Alejandra Vilma and Juana Cabezas are exceptional. Patriarchy is still alive and well in Ayacucho. In most communities, married women still cannot participate in public life. Nevertheless, the active presence of even some women in village life suggests that the politics of gender are changing in these communities, albeit at a slow pace. There is even some hope that the marriage clause of village politics will bend for the right candidate. When asked if she would have taken up political office had her husband still been around, *mama* Juana boasted, "Of course," adding that some married men were already suggesting that their wives should be authorities.[59] But as the cases of *mama* Juana and *mama* Alejandra demonstrate, these changing politics extend beyond the community. Some villagers, both men and women, have oriented their demands toward institutions and organizations at the regional and national levels.

Ayacuchans Speak: Community, State, and Civil Society

I was flipping through TV channels in my Lima residence one afternoon in 2005 when a commercial caught my eye. It featured indigenous women dressed in traditional garb happily entering a health clinic in a remote highland village to receive what appeared to be the best Peru had to offer in prenatal care. As traditional Andean pipes played in the background, the commercial then showed the Peruvian president, Alejandro Toledo, interacting with the villagers, leaving the impression that he was the one responsible for "modernizing" this tiny hamlet. Not leaving anything up to chance, the name of the village popped up on the screen: Chuschi.[60]

Five years later, I was reading the Peruvian weekly *Caretas* online and

was surprised to see Huaychao's own Mariano Quispe—*tayta* Mariano—
on the front page. Intrigued, I clicked on the article and learned that the
Huaychainos were being featured in a new photography exhibit in Lima's
upscale Miraflores district. Financed by a Spanish NGO, the exhibit,
Pakasqa Suyu (The Forgotten Country), was a photographic tribute to
the communities affected by the political violence and featured 100 photographs taken by the Ayacuchan photographer Oscar Medrano. It was
intended to accompany Juntos (Together), an initiative undertaken by
the Peruvian government to give communities such as Huaychao material
reparations for their suffering during the civil war.[61]

One of the most significant ways Peru's armed conflict impacted the
nation was the manner in which it altered the relationship among Ayacuchan communities, the state, and civil society. To be sure, indigenous
Ayacuchans have sought a political dialogue with the Peruvian state since
its inception.[62] What was different this time around, however, was the apparent willingness of both the state and civil society to listen to these peasant voices. As the symbolic birthplace of the Shining Path rebellion, Chuschi now received unprecedented attention from the government, NGOs,
journalists, and scholars. Chuschinos took advantage of this heightened
attention to demand improvements to their community. In doing so, they
downplayed their historical agency as conscious actors in the guerrilla
movement, emphasizing instead their victimization and manipulation by
Shining Path and state forces. In Huaychao, in contrast, indigenous peasants emphasized not only their victimization but also their "patriotic"
defense of the nation against the threat of communism. These accounts
reflect not so much an accurate record of events on the ground as a postconflict narrative constructed by indigenous peasants on both sides of the
armed conflict to gain a foothold in Peruvian civil society.[63]

This strategy has paid off. On 8 April 2001 the government of interim
president Valentín Paniagua declared Chuschi a national symbol of "political unity."[64] Chuschi was also the first community to benefit from the
program Juntos, an initiative of the Toledo administration designed to
distribute monetary reparations to communities affected by the political
violence.[65] But these were not simple acts of state charity. Chuschinos
had been soliciting an increased dialogue with the state from the very
moment they renounced their support of Shining Path. As early as 1983
villagers requested and received a local police station, forever cementing the state's presence in the community.[66] This relationship continued

long after the political violence dissipated. In 2007 the national police presided over the village's Independence Day festivities. *Comunero* men and women watched in silence as the police raised the national flag and sang the Peruvian anthem. Afterward, the officers directed a parade in which villagers in traditional garb marched alongside preschool children dressed as nineteenth-century republican guardsmen and modern-day navy infantrymen.[67]

This is to say nothing of the donations in money, clothing, food, livestock, and other resources that the community has received from Peruvian and international NGOs. One of my most humbling moments in Chuschi occurred in July 2007 when Julián, Alberto, and I began distributing clothing and school supplies donated to Chuschino children by the fifth graders of San Diego's La Jolla Elementary School as part of a Roots and Shoots outreach program. As we began distributing the items, a quarrel broke out among some women who were waiting in line. When we asked what all the fuss was about, the Chuschina mothers explained to us that some of the women standing in the line were from the neighboring village of Canchacancha. Were these gifts not intended for Chuschino children, they asked? Some of the Canchacanchinas were in tears when they pleaded with us: "Please don't kick us out, señores! The Chuschinos always get donations. We Canchacanchinos have suffered, too, so why don't the donations ever reach us?" Although I never verbalized it, I knew the answer: because the Initiation of the Armed Struggle did not occur in Canchacancha.[68]

Nor have these changes only occurred in communities that initially supported Shining Path. Huaychainos' new relationship with the state began the moment they took up arms against the rebels. Villagers welcomed the presence of state counterinsurgency forces in their community. As Narciso Huamán explained, the establishment of a military base in nearby Carhuahurán "relaxed the inhabitants of Huaychao because they felt protected."[69] Peasants' readiness to work with state counterinsurgency forces extended well beyond the Iquichano highlands. In June 1984 some 3,000 peasants from five Ayacuchan communities that had recently formed civil defenses petitioned General Adrian Huamán for military support. In the petition, they requested financial support for community development.[70] While security forces did not grant these *ronderos'* request for money to cultivate their lands, communication between the militias and the state steadily improved. In September 1993 *ronderos* from across the department convened with army officials at the First Congress of the Committees of Antisubversive Self-Defense of Ayacucho, in the interest of forming a meaningful discourse between Ayacuchan communities and the Peruvian military.[71]

Encouraged by the success of their dealings with the military during the civil war, postconflict communities have demanded a sustained conversation with the Peruvian state and civil society. In Huaychao, villagers have sought to bring scholars, NGOs, and government emissaries to their community. Each time they receive a visitor, Huaychainos request a service in return. During my stay, authorities handed me a petition addressed to the director of the archive at *Caretas* in Lima. On their behalf, I was to request the original photographs taken by Oscar Medrano during his 1983 visit. Because my stay fell in the middle of the presidential election campaign, villagers also requested that I use my "academic connections"—which were very limited at the time—to publish an article addressing their demands of the future president-elect.[72] Huaychainos have also been in direct communication with major Peruvian and international NGOs, through which they hope to acquire better livestock and funding for orphaned children.[73] In addition to these efforts, Huaychaino men and women, by way of numerous grassroots organizations such as the Mother's Club, Women's Association, and Glass of Milk, have worked closely with politicians and academics in the provincial and departmental capitals.

Chuschi and Huaychao are just two examples of postconflict communities that have vigorously engaged the state and civil society in order to demand a more participatory role in Peruvian society and politics. Through a variety of strategies—legal petitions, social mobilizations, manipulation of media sources, and alliances with NGOs and scholars—indigenous peasants across the country have begun to demand expanded citizenship rights.[74]

Turning the Corner

For better or worse, the Ayacuchan peasantry is not what it was before the Peruvian civil war. Before 1980 none of these communities was militarized. Communal authorities were almost exclusively elder men, and the relationship between indigenous peasants and the state was tenuous at best. The Shining Path insurrection changed all that. Some indigenous peasants took sides in the conflict, hoping that doing so would either defend or re-store the status quo. Some of these peasants got more than they bargained for. Today, the Ayacuchan peasantry is more militarized than ever. Local authorities, like the rebel and *rondero* leaders of the 1980s and 1990s, tend to be younger and more experienced in armed combat. Although patriar-chy remains the cornerstone of Andean communities, women have made some important inroads. Many women have participated in some form of grassroots organizing, and a few have even entered local and regional poli-tics. Finally, Ayacuchan peasants have turned the Peruvian tragedy into a teachable moment, using the institutions at their disposal—the state, NGOs, and the academy—to educate the country and the world about their plight and demand improvements to their lives as citizens of Peru and the world. Whether these demands will be met remains to be seen.[75]

Conclusion

O N 26 APRIL 2004 indigenous villagers from the Peruvian town of Ilave, in the high Andes department of Puno, rose up and killed their mayor. During the weeks leading up to the event, the villagers of Ilave had been demanding the removal of the mayor, who they believed was abusive and corrupt.[1] Six years later, in October 2010, Andeans from the nearby town of Juliaca attempted to lynch an alleged delinquent who had never been brought to justice for his local crimes.[2] Puno was not the only Andean locality to experience this form of vigilante justice in the early twenty-first century. Between 2000 and 2005 the number of extralegal *linchamientos* of suspected thieves in the Bolivian city of Cochabamba reached the hundreds.[3]

THE FACTORS IN PLAY in the Puno and Cochabamba *linchamientos* were the same ones in play in 1980s Chuschi. It is in this sense that the theoretical and methodological implications of this study extend beyond Ayacucho. More than anything, the preceding pages seek to complicate our understanding of race and class, political violence, and the twentieth century.

While studies of "peasants" and "indigenous peoples" abound, these sweeping sociological categories often obscure the variation *within* these groups. This is not to say that we should altogether abandon race and class as categories of analysis. To do so would be to ignore the exploitation and prejudice that has always existed in any given society. The trick, however, is to maintain a sense of identity formation and structure while remaining sensitive to variation and individuality. As we have seen, Ayacucho's indigenous peasantry was as diverse as Peru itself.[4] These Andeans created internal hierarchies based on more than just wealth and material possessions. Equally important were language, ethnic heritage, geography, skin tone, dress, age, gender, authority, education, and the ability to administer or evade justice. Given these internal divisions, it should come as no surprise that indigenous peasants from the same region had such divergent responses to the political violence of the 1980s. Even those who responded to Shining Path in similar ways often had very different reasons for doing so. Because of this profound diversity at the regional and local levels, it seems a bit inadequate to focus solely on overarching structures and identities. Models that make sweeping generalizations about "indigenous peoples" and "the peasantry" fail to account for the all-important context of local experiences, attitudes, and traditions.

We should be equally cautious when it comes to applying aggrandizing social theories of collective action and political violence. While we cannot deny the explanatory contributions of these theses, our granular evidence shows that they do not tell the whole story. How, for example, do Marxian or Andersonian models explain why people of the same race, social class, nationality, and regional background can have such starkly contrasting reactions to a communist insurgency as did the indigenous peasants living in late twentieth-century Ayacucho? Historical actors—even poor, second-class citizens—do not always act in their best economic or political interests. Nor do they always act in any predetermined or unified way. On the contrary, Ayacuchans had *many* reasons for supporting or resisting Shining Path. It would therefore be a mistake to apply simple explanatory models to complicated historical actors and situations. Instead, one must pay close attention to the particularities of local history and cultural understanding in order to truly make sense of collective behavior.

This approach can help us to understand political violence across time and place. For example, were the Ixil Indians of 1980s Guatemala really caught "between two armies," or did local experiences there have the same type of cultural implications that they did in Ayacucho?[5] We might ask the same question of the rural insurgencies in Cuba, Nicaragua, El Salvador, and Colombia. Even looking beyond Latin America, we can envision local power relationships and cultural understandings shaping the political violence in 1990s Rwanda or twenty-first-century Iraq and Afghanistan— countries whose armed conflicts have been characterized as ideologically and ethnically motivated. Of course, the only way to know this for sure would be to identify the early targets of political violence during these conflicts and then turn back the historical clock to deconstruct these events and players. If the Ayacuchan case is any indicator, such a methodological approach would likely reveal a striking correlation between preinsurgency conflict and insurgency-era violence.

Examining political violence through this localized, cultural, and historical lens can offer useful lessons for policy making. Take the U.S. War on Terror. American policymakers, military commanders, and political pundits often operate on the assumption that Middle Eastern insurgents and counterinsurgents are motivated by deep-seated sentiments of ideology, religion, and anti-American nationalism. That may be the case, but such a narrow view fails to account for the dynamics of power, culture, and justice on the ground. In order to truly comprehend the resurgence of the Taliban in Afghanistan, we must pay attention to the role that the group has played in correcting perceived injustices and providing a sense of public security in local Pashtun communities. Instead of focusing solely on the brutality of Taliban's administration of justice, we should be taking a closer look at who these victims of Taliban justice were before the insurgency. We might find that these targets of "Islamic law" had a record of breaking with local mores and cultural values long before the Taliban took control of these communities. Such an approach in no way excuses Taliban justice, but it can at least help explain why some local actors have found the group so appealing. This argument can be extended to the counterinsurgency in Iraq as well. The conventional U.S. focus on winning the "hearts and minds" of the Iraqi people and rooting out transnational jihadism only gets us so far. While these are certainly factors in the armed violence, they must be understood within a localized historical context of power, culture, and justice.

The deeper we dig into the histories of communities that served as the wellsprings of collective action and violence, the more evidence we will likely find of (1) a disjuncture between the leaders and followers of large-scale movements, and (2) the historical agency of those subaltern actors. We will find, as this book argues, that the human and symbolic targets of collective violence are not just political targets. Nor are they the random victims of immoral, irrational, or irresponsible insurgents. Particularly during the early phase of political violence, these targets are often the embodiment of illegitimate dominion at the micro level, and their victimization is an attempt by subaltern actors to restore a sense of justice, order and security in their communities. This is not to say that local experiences and cultural understandings are the only precursors to political violence, or even that they are the most important ones. Nevertheless, if this book has shown anything, it is that such factors should not be ignored.

Nor should we overlook the significance of late twentieth-century Andean history. As we have seen, many of the historical developments that took place in highland Peru during the second half of the twentieth century also occurred elsewhere in the Third World. Nevertheless, there remains a tendency among nonspecialists to think of the Andes as a timeless geographical bubble that stubbornly resists changes in the broader world. Yet global phenomena did impact the region's history. More important, the region left its mark on the history of the twentieth century. The Shining Path civil war completely broke with previous models of guerrilla warfare. Unlike earlier guerrilla insurgencies, the one carried out by the PCP-SL placed a premium on civilian casualties, making it increasingly difficult for even the most sympathetic observer to defend its tactics on moral grounds. Similarly, Peru's *rondas campesinas* represented one of the first grassroots counterinsurgency efforts in the hemisphere. And this was just Peru. It was the Colombian insurgents who introduced narcoterrorism as a viable model of guerrilla insurgency. Indigenous groups in Bolivia and Ecuador experimented with entirely new forms of protest, employing a combination of legal and extralegal measures to effect systemic political change in the closing years of the century.[6] Despite their important role in global developments, however, the Andes remain on the fringes of historiographical conversations about the twentieth century.

This book represents a first step toward reversing that trend. There remains, of course, a good deal to be mined. Although scholars have done well to fill in the gaps of our historical knowledge about nineteenth-century Andeans, they have not done the same for indigenous peasants living in the twentieth century.[7] While Andeanists in the social sciences have been writing about twentieth-century Andeans with noteworthy care and detail,[8] the amount of historical scholarship on the twentieth-century Andes—and indigenous peoples specifically—is lacking.[9] I have attempted to do my part by examining the latter twentieth century. I hope others will do the same.

This new attention to the Andean twentieth century becomes increasingly critical as the twenty-first century gets under way. If we are to fully comprehend the problems and challenges that face the region in the current century, we must first understand the century that preceded it. Today, the Andes are just as poor as ever. The condition of the region's poorest sectors has not improved. Andean countries and people are still afflicted with the same problems of poverty, oppression, and violence that affected them in the last century. In order to understand why this is, we must have a better understanding of the successes and failures of previous historical developments. Many twentieth-century intellectuals, activists, reformers, and revolutionaries felt that these problems could be remedied through economic measures such as land reform, nationalization, and the redistribution of wealth. Others believed that increased political participation and full citizenship rights would alleviate these problems. Yet many of these measures have been taken and Andean people are still faced with economic depredation, racial marginalization, and an uncertain political future. Why is this the case?

Perhaps we have been looking for solutions in the wrong places. While economic and political reforms are important—even necessary—steps, they do not go far enough in addressing the kinds of problems that have been afflicting the indigenous inhabitants of Puno and Cochabamba. More attention must be paid to the complexities of life, culture, and power in these localities. As the recent wave of vigilante violence in the Andes suggests, the greatest tragedy of the Peruvian civil war is neither the high number of civilian casualties nor the devastating blow it inflicted to the country's economic progress and democratic process. Rather, it is that far too little has been done to address the local injustices and grievances that led ordinary people to resort to violence in the first place.

NOTES

Abbreviations

ACSJA	Archivo de la Corte Superior de Justicia de Ayacucho, Ayacucho City
ADP	Archivo de la Defensoría del Pueblo, Lima
AGN	Archivo General de la Nación, Lima
AMAA	Archivo del Ministerio de Agricultura de Ayacucho, Ayacucho City
APETT	Archivo del Proyecto Especial de Titulación de Tierras, Ayacucho City
ARA	Archivo Regional de Ayacucho, Ayacucho City
ASH	Archivo de la Subprefectura de Huanta, Huanta City
CC	Causas Criminales
CSJ	Corte Superior de Justicia
CVR	Comisión de la Verdad y Reconciliación
exp.	expediente
FPA	Fuero Privativo Agrario
GGC	Gustavo Gorriti Collection on the Peruvian Insurrection, Princeton University Library, Princeton, N.J.
IIP	Instituto Indigenista Peruano, Lima
ILA	Inicio de la Lucha Armada
JP	Juzgado Penal
JT	Juzgado de Tierras
LAQ	Libros de Actas de Quispillaccta
leg.	legajo
MI	Ministerio del Interior
of.	oficios
PA	Prefectura de Ayacucho
SC	Subprefectura de Cangallo
sin leg.	sin legajo
UNSCH	Universidad Nacional San Cristóbal de Huamanga, Ayacucho City

Introduction

1. See Ansión, *Desde el rincón*.
2. IIP, "Estudio de la vivienda," 14.
3. Murra, "El control vertical."
4. IIP, "Informe."

5. Ibid.; IIP, "Tres estudios"; IIP, "Mercados y ferias."

6. IIP, "Informe"; IIP, "Mercados y ferias."

7. Ibid.

8. IIP, "Informe."

9. Ibid.

10. For an excellent study of the historical and social construction of the "Iquichano" identity, see Méndez, "The Power of Naming."

11. ACSJA, JT-FPA, leg. 36, exp. 143, "Expropiación de Huaychao"; AMAA, exp. Huaychao; APETT, exp. Huaychao.

12. ACSJA, JT-FPA, leg. 36, exp. 143, "Expropiación de Huaychao"; AMAA, exp. Huaychao; APETT, exp. Huaychao.

13. Ibid.

14. Isbell, *To Defend Ourselves*; Palmer, "Revolution from Above"; Zuidema, "Algunos problemas"; IIP, "Estudio de la vivienda," IIP, "Informe"; IIP, "Tres estudios"; IIP, "Mercados y ferias."

15. Gorriti, *The Shining Path*, 18.

16. Starn, "Missing the Revolution."

17. Comisión Investigadora, *Informe*, 39.

18. Ibid., 34–36.

19. Ibid., 39.

20. Ibid., 21, 25.

21. For a sampling of this attitude, see the articles reprinted in Cristóbal, *Uchuraccay*.

22. See Degregori, *Las rondas campesinas*; and Fumerton, *From Victims to Heroes*.

23. Van Young, "The New Cultural History."

24. De la Cadena, *Indigenous Mestizos*.

25. See García, "Introduction." For a discussion of the complexities of race and ethnicity in Latin America, see Wade, *Race and Ethnicity*.

26. Fox and Stern, introduction to *Between Resistance and Revolution*, 3.

27. See, for example, Amnesty International, *Peru*; and Americas Watch, *Peru under Fire*.

28. See Kirk, The *Decade of Chaqwa*; and Michael L. Smith, *Entre dos fuegos*.

29. Others have also made this observation. See, for example, Theidon, *Entre prójimos*, 20.

30. Kalyvas, *The Logic of Violence*, 14.

31. Recent publications include Stern, *Shining and Other Paths*; Manrique, *El tiempo del miedo*; Theidon, *Entre prójimos*; Burt, *Political Violence*; and Taylor, *Shining Path*.

32. See Méndez, *The Plebeian Republic*; Heilman, *Before the Shining Path*; and Del Pino, "Looking to the Government."

33. Tilly, *The Politics of Collective Violence*, 23.

34. Kalyvas, *The Logic of Violence*, 22, 6.

35. Van Young, *The Other Rebellion*, 138.

36. See Hunt, *The New Cultural History*; and Bonnell and Hunt, *Beyond the Cultural Turn*.

37. Historical anthropology, of course, is nothing new. See, for example, Axel, *From the Margins*.

38. Dirks, "Annals of the Archive," 47.

39. Ibid., 48.

40. For more on Humberto Ascarza and his conflicts with the Chuschino peasantry, see La Serna, "*Murió comiendo rata.*"

41. This is a pseudonym.

42. Field notes, Chuschi (26 July 2007).

43. For examples, see essays in Axel, *From the Margins*. A notable exception is Mallon, *Courage Tastes of Blood*.

44. Abercrombie, *Pathways of Memory*, 117.

45. Rappaport, *The Politics of Memory*, 12, 16.

46. Mallon, *Courage Tastes of Blood*, 232.

47. Thompson, "The Moral Economy of the English Crowd"; Scott, *The Moral Economy of the Peasant*. For more on the concept of the power pact and its place within a moral economy analysis, see La Serna, "*Murió comiendo rata.*"

Chapter One

1. I borrow this notion of "free-riding" from Popkin, *The Rational Peasant*, 25.

2. A third avenue for justice was through the local church. See La Serna, "'Thank God for the Violence.'"

3. Hammergren, *The Politics of Justice*, 213.

4. Ibid., 232–34; Roldán, *Blood and Fire*.

5. De Souza Martins, "Lynchings"; Benavides and Fischer Ferreira, "Popular Responses."

6. Calleros, *The Unfinished Transition*.

7. Poole, "Between Threat and Guarantee," 42; Pásara, *Derecho y sociedad*, 83, 219–31; Drewieniecki, "Indigenous People."

8. Pásara, *Derecho y sociedad*, 98–104.

9. Ibid.

10. Poole, "Between Threat and Guarantee," 42.

11. For a breakdown of this bureaucratic authority structure, see Isbell, *To Defend Ourselves*, chap. 4.

12. Starn, *Nightwatch*, 49.

13. Orlove, "La posición de los abigeos," 298–99.

14. Starn, *Nightwatch*, 49–50.

15. Pásara, *Derecho y sociedad*, 80.

16. See Aguirre and Walker, *Bandoleros*; and Poole, "Landscapes of Power."

17. Pásara, *Derecho y sociedad*, 252, 254.

18. For a riveting ethnography of the *rondas campesinas*, see Starn, *Nightwatch*.

19. Ibid.

20. Peña Jumpa, *Justicia comunal*.

21. Much has been written on Andean indigenous authorities. See, for example, Isbell, *To Defend Ourselves*, chap. 4. For an in-depth analysis of indigenous authority structures in Bolivia, see Rasnake, *Domination and Cultural Resistance*.

22. Del Pino, "Looking to the Government," 143–50.

23. Montoya, *Lucha por la tierra*, 101.

24. ACSJA, JP Cangallo, leg. 138, exp. 37, "Instrucción contra Teobaldo Achallma por el delito de contra el patrimonio." Instructiva del inculpado Teobaldo Achallma (6 May 1976). The "certificate of conduct" was an official declaration for which local authorities offered moral assessments of an individual's public and private behavior. Used during criminal trials, they served a purpose similar to that of character witnesses.

25. Ibid. The punctuation in many of the textual citations used in this book has been altered for clarity and fluidity.

26. ACSJA, JP Cangallo, leg. 138, exp. 37, Sentencia en la instrucción contra Teobaldo Achallma (25 August 1977).

27. ARA, SC, caja 17, of. Chuschi, 1961, Queja de Teobaldo Achallma ante el Subprefecto (20 June 1961).

28. Ibid.

29. ARA, SC, caja 17, of. Chuschi, 1961, Informe del gobernador de Chuschi al Subprefecto (29 June 1961).

30. ARA, SC, Queja de Teresa Ccallocunto ante el Subprefecto (24 March 1965).

31. ARA, SC, Petición de Teobaldo Achallma ante el Subprefecto (10 October 1966).

32. ARA, SC, caja 30, of. Chuschi, 1967, Solicitud de garantías de Teobaldo Achallma ante el Subprefecto (29 May 1967).

33. ARA, SC, caja 30, of. Chuschi, 1967, Manifestación de Martina Núñez y Felipe Cisneros ante el Subprefecto (31 July 1967).

34. ARA, SC, caja 35, of. Chuschi, 1975, Denuncia contra Teobaldo Achallma (24 August 1975).

35. Mendoza Machaca, "Quispillaccta," 96.

36. Rejas Pacotaipe's physical features are described in several Cangallo court records of the Archivo Regional de Ayacucho. He is described as a "light-skinned" mestizo in ARA, CC Cangallo, leg. 1200, exp. 12, "Instrucción contra Amancio Rejas Pacotaipe por el delito contra el patrimonio," Instructiva de Amancio Rejas Pacotaipe (25 April 1959). In later cases, he is described as an *indígena*. See, for example, ARA, CSJ-JP Cangallo, leg. 125, exp. 7, "Instrucción contra Amancio Rejas Pacotaipe y Fe-

lipe Aycha [pseud.] por el delito de robo de ganado," Instructiva de Amancio Rejas Pacotaipe (3 April 1976); and ARA, CSJ-JP Cangallo leg. 132, exp. 70, "Instrucción contra Amancio Rejas Pacotaipe y otros por el delito de contra el patrimonio," Instructiva de Amancio Rejas Pacotaipe (11 November 1975).

37. ARA, CC Cangallo, leg. 1200, exp. 12, Denuncia de Antonio Galindo Núñez ante el Juez Instructor (13 April 1959).

38. Ibid., Instructiva de Amancio Rejas Pacotaipe (21 April 1959); Sentencia del Juez Instructor en el caso seguido contra Amancio Rejas Pacotaipe (10 May 1962).

39. Aside from the cases mentioned here, see, for example, ARA, CSJ-JP Cangallo, leg. 102, exp. 44, Instructiva contra Santos Pacotaipe, Fernando (Bernabé) Núñez y Amancio Rejas Pacotaype por el delito de calumnia, difamación y injuria (1973); and ARA, CSJ-JP Cangallo, leg. 105, exp. 75, Instructiva contra Amancio Rejas Pacotaipe por el delito de calumnia y difamación (1973).

40. ACSJA, JP Cangallo, leg. 132, exp. 70, "Instrucción contra Amancio Rejas y otros por el delito de contra el patrimonio," Denuncia ante el Juez Instructor contra Amancio Rejas y Antonio Gamboa (30 October 1975).

41. Ibid.

42. ACSJA, JP Cangallo, leg. 132, exp. 70, Instructiva de Cayetana Casavilca y Antonio Ccallocunto (19 December 1975).

43. ACSJA, JP Cangallo, leg. 132, exp. 70, Sentencia en el juzgado seguida contra Amancio Rejas Pacotaipe y otros (3 August 1976).

44. ACSJA, JP Cangallo, leg. 132, exp. 70, Copia del LAQ (24 May 1975).

45. Ibid.

46. Interview with Víctor Núñez, Chuschi (27 July 2007).

47. I have withheld this information out of respect for the alleged victims.

48. ARA, CSJ-JP Cangallo, leg. 102, exp. 44, Instructiva Contra Santos Pacotaipe, Fernando (Bernabé) Núñez, y Amancio Rejas Pacotaype por el delito de calumnia, difamación e injuria, Denuncia de Tomás Núñez ante el Juez Instructor (circa 15 June 1973).

49. Interview with Víctor Núñez, Chuschi (27 July 2007).

50. ACSJA, JP Cangallo, leg. 125, exp. 7, Denuncia contra Amancio Rejas y Felipe Aycha [pseud.] por el delito de abigeato; Sentencia en la instrucción contra Amancio Rejas Pacotaipe y Felipe Aycha [pseud.] (3 September 1976).

51. This is a pseudonym. I have withheld Felipe Aycha's true identity in order to maintain the anonymity of his son, who later became a Senderista.

52. ACSJA, JP Cangallo, leg. 125, exp. 7, Instructiva del inculpado Felipe Aycha [pseud.] (18 July 1975).

53. ARA, CSJ-JP Cangallo, leg. 64, Instructiva contra Felipe Aycha [pseud.] y otros por el delito de abigeato, Instructiva del inculpado Vidal Chuchón (circa November 1968).

54. ARA, CSJ-JP Cangallo, leg. 62, "Instrucción contra Ernesto Jaime y otros por el delito de abigeato y tentativa de homicidio," Denuncia de Ernesto Jaime Miranda ante el Juez Instructor (circa December 1968).

55. ARA, CSJ-JP Cangallo, leg. 62, Instructiva del inculpado Marino Ochoa (circa December 1968).

56. ARA, CSJ-JP Cangallo, leg. 62, Instructiva del inculpado Felipe Aycha [pseud.] (circa December 1968).

57. ARA, CSJ-JP Cangallo, leg. 62, Sentencia en la instrucción contra Felipe Aycha [pseud.] y otros (27 July 1970).

58. ACSJA, JP Cangallo, leg. 166, "Instrucción contra Felipe Aycha [pseud.], Bernardo Chipana y otros por el delito de contra el patrimonio."

59. ACSJA, JP Cangallo, leg. 166, Manifestación de Ernesto Jaime Miranda (18 April 1979); emphasis in the original.

60. ACSJA, JP Cangallo, leg. 166, Documento de Reposición de dos caballos, por Felipe Aycha [pseud.] (2 May 1979); Documento de Reposición de un cerdo, por Bernardo Chipana (2 May 1979).

61. Interview with Víctor Núñez, Chuschi (27 July 2008).

62. Ibid.

63. Ibid.

64. Ibid.

65. This is a pseudonym.

66. Ignacio Aycha's case is particularly illustrative, but there are others not mentioned here. See, for example, ACSJA, JP Cangallo, leg. 127, exp. 24. "Instrucción contra Delfín Tomaylla y otros por el delito de contra la autoridad pública" (1975); and ACSJA, JP Cangallo, leg. 138, exp. 22, "Instrucción contra Esteban de la Cruz y otros por el delito de contra el patrimonio" (1976).

67. Isbell, *To Defend Ourselves*, 85.

68. ACSJA, JP Cangallo, leg. 152, exp. 83. "Instrucción contra Fernando Tapahuasco e Ignacio Aycha [pseud.] por el delito de contra el patrimonio," Manifestación de Teófilo Achallma (27 October 1977); Informe del Instructor (3 November 1977).

69. ACSJA, JP Cangallo, leg. 152, exp. 83, Referencia del menor Ignacio Aycha [pseud.] (28 October 1977); Ampliación de la referencia del menor Ignacio Aycha [pseud.] (circa 28 October 1977); emphasis added. I discuss Felipe Aycha's tenure as village authority in chapter 3.

70. ACSJA, JP Cangallo, leg. 152, exp. 83, Denuncia de Teófilo Achallma y otros ante el Juez Instructor (18 November 1977).

71. ACSJA, JP Cangallo, leg. 152, exp. 83, Denuncia de Daniel Mendoza ante el Juez Instructor (15 December 1977).

72. ACSJA, JP Cangallo, leg. 152, exp. 83. "Instrucción contra Fernando Tapahuasco e Ignacio Aycha [pseud.] por el delito de contra el patrimonio," Manifestación de Teófilo Achallma (27 October 1977); Informe del Instructor (3 November 1977).

73. ACSJA, JP Cangallo, leg. 152, exp. 83, Certificado de las autoridades de Chuschi sobre la conducta de Ignacio Aycha [pseud.] (12 November 1977).

74. Ibid.

75. ACSJA, JP Cangallo, leg. 152, exp. 83, Denuncia de Teófilo Achallma y otros ante el Juez Instructor (18 November 1977).

76. ACSJA, JP Cangallo, leg. 152, exp. 83, Sentencia en la instrucción contra Fernando Tapahuasco e Ignacio Aycha [pseud.] (16 April 1979).

77. For a detailed description of Chuschi's indigenous prestige hierarchy, see Isbell, *To Defend Ourselves*, chap. 4.

78. Ibid., 85.

79. Ibid.

80. Ibid., 75–83, 86.

81. Quoted in ibid., 85.

82. Ibid., 95.

83. Merick, "Population Pressures"; Sabot, introduction to *Migration and the Labor Market*.

84. Contreras and Cueto, *Historia del Perú contemporáneo*, 285.

85. Eric Mayer, "State Policy and Community Conflict," 321, 330–31; Mitchell, *Peasants on the Edge*, 23.

86. Lobo, *A House of My Own*, 6.

87. Matos Mar, *Las barriadas de Lima*, 25, 145.

88. See Degregori, *Ayacucho*.

89. Interview with Fortunato Huamán and Esteban Huamán, Huaychao (5 February 2006).

90. ASH, exp. 1968, Informe del Subprefecto al Teniente Gobernador de Huaychao sobre queja interpuesta por Zenobio Quispe contra Julián Bautista sobre robo de 3 llamas (29 May 1968).

91. ARA, CSJ-JP Huanta, leg. 7, exp. 218, "Instrucción contra Víctor Guillén y Víctor Quispe por el delito de abigeato," Manifestación del inculado Víctor Guillén (14 Feburary 1967); Instructiva del inculpado Víctor Guillén (18 February 1967); Preventiva de Francisco Cayetano (21 February 1967).

92. ACSJA, JP Huanta, leg. 109, exp. 799, "Instrucción contra Lucas Ccente por el delito de tentativa de homicidio," Manifestación de Lucas Ccente (13 June 1979).

93. Ibid.

94. ACSJA, JP Huanta, leg. 109, exp. 799, Carta del Teniente Gobernador de Huaychao al Juez Instructor sobre la conducta del denunciado Lucas Ccente (21 May 1979).

95. ACSJA, JP Huanta, leg. 109, exp. 799, Sentencia en la instrucción seguida contra Lucas Ccente (9 July 1979).

96. Field notes, Huaychao (5 February 2006). In previous years, villagers consumed *chicha* and aguardiente during this ritual. The transition to nonalcoholic bev-

erages is a reflection of villagers' recent conversion from Catholicism to evangelical Protestantism.

97. Ibid.

98. Ibid.

99. Interview with Ciprián Quispe, Huaychao (5 February 2006).

100. Ibid.

101. Ibid.

102. Interview with Alejandra Ccente, Huaychao (6 February 2006).

103. Interview with Isidro Huamán, Huaychao (21 May 2006).

104. Interview with Fortunato Huamán and Esteban Huamán, Huaychao (5 February 2006).

105. Interview with Ciprián Quispe, Huaychao (5 February 2006).

106. Interview with Brigida Cayetano, Huaychao (6 February 2006).

107. Interview with Alejandra Ccente, Huaychao (6 February 2006).

108. Interview with Brigida Cayetano, Huaychao (6 February 2006).

109. Ibid.

110. Interview with Ciprián Quispe, Huaychao (5 February 2006).

111. For a discussion of the gendered aspect of this notion in the Iquichano highlands, see Del Pino, "Los campesinos en la guerra."

112. Interview with Isidro Huamán, Huaychao (21 May 2006).

113. Interview with Ciprián Quispe, Huaychao (5 February 2006).

114. Ibid.

115. Interview with Isidro Huamán, Huaychao (21 May 2006).

116. See Hobsbawm and Ranger, *The Invention of Tradition.*

117. Interview with Ciprián Quispe, Huaychao (5 February 2006).

118. Interview with Alejandra Ccente, Huaychao (6 Feburary 2006).

119. Interview with Mariano Quispe, Huaychao (7 February 2006); interview with Ciprián Quispe, Huaychao (5 February 2006).

120. All appointments had to be approved by the Huanta Province subprefect, however.

121. ASH, exp. 1963, Mandato del Subprefecto al Gobernador (30 November 1963); Informe del Subprefecto al Prefecto (3 December 1963).

122. Interview with Fortunato Huamán and Esteban Huamán, Huaychao (5 February 2006). For more on the regional land struggle, see Del Pino, "Looking to the Government."

123. ASH, exp. 1972, Informe del Empadronador al Jefe de Sección (21 September 1972).

124. ASH, exp. 1972, Informe del Teniente Gobernador al Ingeniero Provincial del Censo Nacional (circa 22 September 1972).

125. ASH, exp. 1972, Solicitud de vecinos de Huaychao sobre renovación de Teniente Gobernador (26 September 1972).

126. ASH, exp. 1975, Solicitud de garantías de Ana Ramos (7 March 1975).

127. See chapter 3 for a discussion of why some Huaychainos favored the hacienda system and allied with the hacendado.

128. ACSJA, JP Huanta, sin leg. (1980, 20 expedientes), exp. 139, "Instrucción contra Vicente Quispe y otros por el delito de contra la administración de justicia y otros," Nombramiento de Teniente Gobernador de Huacyhao (11 January 1980); Denuncia de Anselmo Quispe ante el Juez Instructor (14 July 1980).

129. ASH, exp. 1982, Nombramiento de Teniente Gobernador de Huaychao (12 January 1982).

130. Interview with Fortunato and Esteban Huamán, Huaychao (5 February 2006).

131. Interview with Alejandra Ccente, Huaychao (6 February 2006).

132. Ibid.

133. Interview with Santos Huaylla, Huaychao (21 May 2006).

134. Interview with Ciprián Quispe, Huaychao (5 February 2006).

135. Typically, Huaychainos would submit a list of three popularly elected candidates to the subprefect and the provincial bureaucrat would make his appointment based on that recommendation.

136. Tupín became an annex of Huaychao after the Agrarian Reform.

137. A *yugada* is a measurement of land, typically the amount workable in one day with two oxen.

138. ARA, CSJ-JP Huanta, sin leg. (1954–59, 20 expedientes), exp. 99. "Instrucción contra Julio Ruiz Pozo por el delito de robo de especies," Denuncia de Luis Huamán ante el Prefecto (20 February 1956).

139. ARA, CSJ-JP Huanta, sin leg. (1957, 33 expedientes), exp. 11, Carta del Teniente Gobernador de Huaychao al propietario de la hacienda Tupín (6 March 1955).

140. ARA, CSJ-JP Huanta, sin leg. (1954–59, 20 expedientes), exp. 99, Copia de la carta de Julio Ruiz a Román Bautista (circa 17 February 1957).

141. ARA, CSJ-JP Huanta, sin leg. (1957, 33 expedientes), exp. 11, Informe del Teniente Gobernador de Huaychao ante el Subprefecto (18 February 1956); ARA, CSJ-JP Huanta, sin leg. (1954–59, 20 expedientes), exp. 99, Denuncia de Luis Huamán ante el Prefecto (20 February 1956).

142. ARA, CSJ-JP Huanta, sin leg. (1957, 33 expedientes), exp. 11, Denuncia de Luis Huamán ante el Prefecto (6 February 1957).

143. ARA, CSJ-JP Huanta, sin leg. (1954–59, 20 expedientes), exp. 99, Manifestación policial de Ramón Bautista (13 March 1957).

144. ARA, CSJ-JP Huanta, sin leg. (1957, 33 expedientes), exp. 11, Manifestación de Julio Ruiz Pozo (13 March 1957).

145. ARA, CSJ-JP Huanta, Sin Leg (1957, 23 expedientes), exp. 153, "Instrucción contra Luis Huamán por el delito de lesiones," Preventiva de Ramón Bautista (9 February 1957); Instructiva de Luis Huamán (9 February 1957).

146. ARA, CSJ-JP Huanta, sin leg. (1957, 33 expedientes), exp. 11, Instructiva de

Julio Ruiz Pozo ante el Juez Instructor (20 October 1957); Sentencia en el caso sobre Ramon Bautista (9 April 1958).

147. Interview with Fortunato Huamán and Esteban Huamán, Huaychao (5 February 2006); interview with Mariano Quispe, Huaychao (7 February 2006).

148. Interview with Inocencio Urbano and Ernestina Ccente, Huaychao (6 February 2006).

149. Interview with Alejandra Ccente, Huaychao (6 February 2006).

150. Ibid.

151. Interview with Mariano Quispe, Huaychao (7 February 2006).

152. Interview with Inocencio Urbano and Ernestina Ccente, Huaychao (6 February 2006).

153. ASH, 1979, Nombramiento de Teniente Gobernador de Huaychao (12 January 1979); interview with Isidro Huamán, Huaychao (21 May 2006).

154. For more on these nineteenth-century forms of Iquichano authority and justice, see Méndez, *The Plebeian Republic*, chap. 6.

155. Mallon, *Peasant and Nation*; Del Pino, personal correspondence to author (15 February 2008).

Chapter Two

1. Field notes, Ayacucho City (26 July 2007).

2. The literature on these midcentury peasant movements is too vast to list here. For a systematic analysis of these works, see La Serna, "The Corner of the Living," introduction.

3. Rivera Cusicanqui, *Oppressed but Not Defeated*, 56–57.

4. Klein, *Bolivia*, 234.

5. Hobsbawm, "Peasant Land Occupations."

6. Ibid., 129–30.

7. Mallon, *Courage Tastes of Blood*, esp. chap. 4.

8. Paige, *Agrarian Revolution*, 82.

9. Gupta, *Understanding Terrorism*, 117–18.

10. Handelman, *Struggle in the Andes*, 62.

11. Ibid., 70–74, 82; Heilman, "Leader and Led."

12. Cotler, "Traditional Haciendas," 544–45.

13. Handelman, *Struggle in the Andes*, 99–110.

14. Ibid., 86.

15. Hobsbawm, "Peasant Land Occupations," 141.

16. Some notable exceptions for the Mexican case are Dennis, *Intervillage Conflict*; and Van Young, "Conflict and Solidarity." For the Peruvian case, see Bonilla, "La defensa del espacio comunal."

17. ARA, JT-FPA, leg. 36, exp. 64, Informe de Emilio Núñez Conde ante el Juez de Tierras (12 October 1981).

18. For more on the history of the Indigenous Affairs body and its policies toward indigenous communities, see Davies, *Indian Integration*.

19. APETT, exp. Chuschi (27 September 1940).

20. APETT, exp. Chuschi (15 August 1940); emphasis added.

21. Ibid.

22. APETT, exp. Chuschi (19 May 1941).

23. APETT, exp. Chuschi (1 August 1941).

24. APETT, exp. Chuschi (21 October 1941); ARA, CSJ-JP Cangallo, sin leg. (1960, 25 exp.), exp. 39.

25. APETT, exp. Chuschi (17 November 1941).

26. Ibid.

27. AGN, MI, PA 1953, Solicitud del pueblo de Quispillaccta sobre autonomía económica y administrativa municipal (15 April 1985).

28. Bonilla, "La defensa del espacio comunal."

29. Zuidema, "Algunos problemas," 74–75; Isbell, "Andean Structures," 37–43; Earls and Silverblatt, "Ayllus y etnías."

30. ARA, SC, caja 17, of. Chuschi 1960 (29 November 1959).

31. By "invasion," the plaintiffs in this and subsequent cases implied any forceful occupation of the land in question.

32. APETT, exp. Chuschi (6 May 1960).

33. ARA, SC, caja 17, of. Chuschi 1960 (7 December 1959).

34. Ibid.

35. ARA, CSJ-JP Víctor Fajardo, sin leg. (1969, 14 exp.), exp. 685. This allegation was disputed by the Chuschinos, who claimed to have constructed it more than forty years prior to the incident. See ARA, CSJ-JP Cangallo, sin leg. (1960, 25 leg.), exp. 40.

36. APETT, exp. Chuschi, Solicitud de Braulio Pacotaipe al Inspector Regional de Asuntos Indígenas (2 April 1960).

37. Ibid.

38. Ibid.

39. ARA, CSJ-JP Cangallo, sin leg. (1960, 25 exp.), exp. 40, Informe de los peritos sobre el valor de la Virgen de Santa Rosa (23 June 1960).

40. The Chuschino accusers speculated that the Quispillacctinos had turned the icon over to the bishop as proof that they were the rightful owners of the disputed territory, but it is unclear why such a gesture would have constituted such proof. A more reasonable explanation is that the Quispillacctinos simply did not want to risk the Chuschinos' recovering the saint. Regardless, the bishop returned the saint to the Chuschinos, and as of July 2007 it remained on display in their main cathedral, located at the edge of the village square.

41. ARA, CSJ-JP sin leg. (1960, 25 exp.), exp. 40, "Instrucción contra Fidel Conde y otros por el delito de lesiones, incendio y robo" (26 April 1960).

42. ARA, CSJ-JP Cangallo, sin leg. (1960, 25 exp.), exp. 33, "Instrucción contra Fidel Conde y otros por el delito de lesiones y otros en agravio de la Comunidad de Chuschi" (14 May 1960).

43. Ibid.

44. ARA, CSJ-JP Cangallo, sin leg. (1960, 25 exp.), exp. 40, "Instrucción contra Fidel Conde y otros por el delito de lesiones, incendio y robo" (26 April 1960).

45. ARA, CSJ-JP Cangallo, sin leg., exp. 687, Preventiva de Luis Núñez Ccallocunto y Martín Vega en la instrución contra Ernesto Jaime y otros (3 June 1960).

46. Urton, *The Social Life of Numbers*.

47. Field notes, Huaychao (13 January 2006).

48. Libros de Actas de Huaychao (2006).

49. Mallon, *Peasant and Nation*, 194.

50. Field notes, Chuschi (26 July 2007).

51. For more on the relationship between communal solidarity and saint-stealing, see Van Young, "Conflict and Solidarity"; and Van Young, *The Other Rebellion*, 412.

52. Durkheim, *The Elementary Forms*, 124.

53. The episode described here is found in a multivolume criminal proceeding of the Superior Court of Ayacucho, located in the Regional Archive of Ayacucho. The case, expediente 687, "Instructiva contra Ernesto Jaime y otros," consists of at least eleven volumes, seven of which I have been able to recover. Six of the seven volumes can be found in unnumbered legajos of the Corte Superior de Justicia–Penal, Cangallo (hereafter ARA, CSJ-JP Cangallo, sin leg., exp. 687). These are sin leg. (1967–68, 6 exp.); sin leg. (1963, 18 exp.); sin leg. (1960, 11 exp.: 2 vols.); sin leg. (1963, 11 exp.); sin leg. (1964, 16 exp.). The seventh volume is found in Corte Superior de Justicia–Penal, Víctor Fajardo (hereafter ARA, CSJ-JP Víctor Fajardo, sin leg., exp. 687). I thank Freddy Taboada for helping me locate this misplaced volume.

54. ARA, CSJ-JP Cangallo, sin leg., exp. 687, Preventiva de Luis Núñez Ccallocunto y Martín Vega (3 June 1960).

55. ARA, CSJ-JP Cangallo, sin leg., exp. 687, Preventiva de Asunción Ccallocunto Núñez (24 June 1960); ARA, CSJ-JP Cangallo, sin leg., exp. 687, Ampliación preventiva de Asunción Ccallocunto Núñez (13 August 1963). The statement about Ccallocunto's captors calling him a thief (*ladrón*) appears in the eyewitness testimony of Quispillacctino Justiniano Mendoza. See CSJ-JP Cangallo, sin leg., exp. 687, Preventiva de Justiniano Mendoza Conde (11 June 1960).

56. ARA, CSJ-JP Cangallo, sin leg., exp. 687, Preventiva de Luis Núñez Ccallocunto y Martín Vega (3 June 1960).

57. ARA, CSJ-JP Víctor Fajardo, sin leg., exp. 687, Acusación Fiscal (14 September 1966).

58. ARA, CSJ-JP Cangallo, sin leg., exp. 687, Preventiva de Luis Núñez Ccallocunto y Martín Vega (3 June 1960).

59. Ibid.; ARA, CSJ-JP Cangallo, sin leg., exp. 687, Declaración de Daniel Núñez Huamaní (22 March 1961).

60. ARA, CSJ-JP Cangallo, sin leg., exp. 687, Preventiva de Luis Núñez Ccallocunto y Martín Vega (3 June 1960).

61. ARA, CSJ-JP Cangallo, sin leg., exp. 687, Preventiva de Cristina Huamaní Ccallocunto (6 July 1960). The description of the victim's physical state at the time of death appears in the medical autopsy. See ARA, CSJ-JP Cangallo, sin leg., exp. 687, Diligencia de autopsia del cadáver de Martín Mendieta (1 March 1961).

62. ARA, CSJ-JP Cangallo, sin leg., exp. 687, Preventiva de Justiniano Mendoza Conde (11 June 1960).

63. ARA, CSJ-JP Cangallo, sin leg., exp. 687, Declaración de Pascual Conde Huamán (13 June 1960).

64. ARA, CSJ-JP Víctor Fajardo, sin leg., exp. 687, Acusación Fiscal (14 September 1966).

65. ARA, CSJ-JP Cangallo, exp. 687, Preventiva de Luis Núñez Ccallocunto y Martín Vega (3 June 1960).

66. ARA, CSJ-JP Cangallo, sin leg., exp. 687, Informe de los peritos (26 July 1963).

67. ARA, CSJ-JP Cangallo, sin leg., exp. 687, Preventiva de Pascuala Huamaní Mejía (6 July 1960). The description of the victim's physical state and death appears in the medical autopsy report. See ARA, CSJ-JP Cangallo, sin leg., exp. 687, Diligencia de autopsia del cadáver de Sebastián Mendieta (1 March 1961).

68. ARA, CSJ-JP Cangallo, sin leg., exp. 687, Preventiva de Marcela Mejía Huamaní (11 July 1960); ARA, CSJ-JP Cangallo, sin leg., exp. 687, Diligencia de autopsia del cadáver de Antonio Galindo Espinoza (1 March 1961).

69. ARA, CSJ-JP Cangallo, sin leg., exp. 687, Instructiva del inculpado Ernesto Jaime Miranda (27 March 1963); Confrontación del testigo Leonardo Conde Machaca y del inculpado Felipe Aycha [pseud.] (13 August 1963).

70. ARA, CSJ-JP Cangallo, sin leg., exp. 687, Preventiva de Luis Núñez Ccallocunto y Martín Vega (3 June 1960).

71. ARA, CSJ-JP Cangallo, sin leg., exp. 687, Confrontación del testigo Leonardo Conde Machaca y del inculpado Felipe Aycha [pseud.] (13 August 1963).

72. ARA, CSJ-JP Cangallo, sin leg., exp. 687, Confrontación del testigo Daniel Núñez Huamaní y del inculpado Felipe Aycha [pseud.] (13 August 1963); ARA, CSJ-JP Cangallo, sin leg., exp. 687, Confrontación del testigo Bernabé Fernando Núñez Conde y del inculpado Felipe Aycha [pseud.] (13 August 1963).

73. ARA, CSJ-Pen. Cangallo, sin leg., exp. 687, Preventiva de Luis Núñez Ccallocunto y Martín Vega en la instructión contra Ernesto Jaime y otros (3 June 1960).

74. Interview with Ignacio Huaycha, Chuschi (27 July 2007).

75. ARA, CSJ-JP Cangallo, sin leg., exp. 687, Acta de la Comunidad de Chuschi para la defensa de la integridad territorial (16 April 1960).

76. ARA, CSJ-JP Cangallo, sin leg., exp. 687, Acta de Renovación de Casos de la Comunidad de Chuschi (16 April 1960).

77. Badiou, *Being and Event*.

78. ARA, CSJ-JP Víctor Fajardo, sin leg., exp. 68, Acusación Fiscal (14 September 1966).

79. ARA, CSJ-JP Cangallo, sin leg. (1962, 9 expedientes), exp. 187 (5 vols.), Acusación Fiscal de la instrucción contra Manuel Núñez y otros (26 October 1963).

80. This episode is chronicled in a criminal proceeding of the Superior Court of Ayacucho, located in the Archivo Regional de Ayacucho. See ARA, CSJ-JP Cangallo, sin leg. (1962, 9 expedientes), exp. 187, "Instrucción contra Manuel Núñez y otros por el delito de homicidio y lesiones" (5 vols.) (hereafter ARA-JP Cangallo, sin leg., exp. 187). The above description is taken from Manifestación de Dámaso Allcca Chuchón ante el Instructor de la Guardia Civil (17 March 1962).

81. ARA, CSJ-JP Cangallo, sin leg., exp. 187, Solicitud de libertad provisional de Manuel Núñez (4 May 1962).

82. ARA, CSJ-JP Cangallo, sin leg., exp. 187, Testimonial de Seferino Juan Pomahualcca Maldonado ante el Primer Juzgado de Instrucción (2 April 1962); ARA, CSJ-JP Cangallo, sin leg., exp. 187, Informe del Juez Instructor (19 August 1963); ARA, CSJ-JP Cangallo, sin leg., exp. 187, Manifestación de Dámaso Allcca Chuchón ante el Instructor de la Guardia Civil (17 March 1962).

83. ARA, CSJ-JP Cangallo, sin leg., exp. 187, Manifestación de Teófilo Machaca Conde (18 March 1962).

84. ARA, CSJ-JP Cangallo, sin leg., exp. 187, Manifestación de Dámaso Allcca Chuchón ante el Instructor de la Guardia Civil (17 March 1962).

85. ARA, CSJ-JP Cangallo, sin leg., exp. 187, Manifestación de Sabino Ccallocunto Galindo ante el Instructor de la Guardia Civil (17 March 1962).

86. ARA, CSJ-JP Cangallo, sin leg., exp. 187, Ampliación de la denuncia de Agripino Aronés, Dámaso Allcca y Juana Quispe vda. De Pacotaipe (22 March 1962).

87. ARA, CSJ-JP Cangallo, sin leg., exp. 187, Instructiva de Dionisio Núñez Ccallocunto (24 March 1962).

88. ARA, CSJ-JP Cangallo, sin leg., exp. 187, Instructiva de Víctor Conde (circa March 1962); Acusación Fiscal (26 October 1963).

89. ARA, CSJ-JP Cangallo, sin leg., exp. 187, Instructiva de Dionisio Núñez Ccallocunto (24 March 1962).

90. ARA, CSJ-JP Cangallo, sin leg., exp. 187, Manifestación de Nicasio Machaca Vilca (26 March 1962).

91. Ibid.

92. ARA, CSJ-JP Cangallo, sin leg., exp. 187, Manifestación de Dámaso Allcca Chuchón ante el Instructor de la Guardia Civil (17 March 1962).

93. Ibid.; ARA, CSJ-JP Cangallo, sin leg. (1962, 9 expedientes), exp. 187, Preventiva ampliatoria de Dámaso Allcca Chuchón (27 March 1962).

94. Personal correspondence with Vicente Blanco [pseud.], Chuschi (26 July 2007).

95. Zuidema, "Algunos problemas," 71; Isbell, "Andean Structures," 41–42.

96. Earls and Silverblat, "Ayllus y etnías," 162–65.

97. See Muñoz Ruiz and Núñez Espinoza, *Los Kanas de Quispillaccta*. This phenomenon was by no means unique to Quispillaccta. Peasants in the highland community of Huasicancha, in neighboring Junín Department, developed a twentieth-century political consciousness that stemmed from their historical memory of resistance to Inca imperialism during the Spanish conquest. See Gavin Smith, *Livelihood and Resistance*.

98. For a detailed account of these conforntations, see La Serna, "To Cross the River of Blood."

99. ACSJA, JP Cangallo, leg. 132, exp. 77 (2 vols.), "Instrucción contra Teobaldo Achallma Chuchón y Candelario Alarcón Ayala por el delito de contra el patrimonio," Manifestación de Teobaldo Achallma Chuchón ante el Instructor de la Guardia Civil de Pampa Cangallo (12 November 1975).

100. ACSJA, JP Cangallo, leg. 132, exp. 72, Manifestación de Candelario Anastasio Alarcón Ayala ante el Instructor de la Guardia Civil de Pampa Cangallo (12 November 1975).

101. ACSJA, JP Cangallo, leg. 132, exp. 72, Instructiva de Candelario Alarcón Ayala (13 November 1975).

102. ACSJA, JP Cangallo, leg. 132, exp. 72, Instructiva de Teobaldo Achallma Chuchón (13 November 1975).

103. ACSJA, JP Cangallo, leg. 132, exp. 72, Certificado de las Autoridades de Chuschi sobre el carácter del inculpado Teobaldo Achallma (24 November 1975).

104. ACSJA, JP Cangallo leg. 132, exp. 72, Sentencia contra Teobaldo Achallma Chuchón y Candelario Anastasio Alarcón Ayala (20 March 1979).

105. ACSJA, JP Cangallo, leg. 132, exp. 72, Manifestación de Alejandro Allcca Vilca ante el Instructor de la Guardia Civil de Pampa Cangallo (11 November 1975).

106. See ACSJA, JP Cangallo, leg. 180, exp. 61.

107. See La Serna, "To Cross the River of Blood."

108. ACSJA, JP Cangallo, leg. 191, exp. 28, "Instrucción seguida contra Narciso Achallma y otros por los delitos de contra el patrimonio y robo de ganado."

109. ARA, JT-FPA, leg. 36, exp. 64, Informe de Emilio Núñez Conde ante el Juez de Tierras (12 October 1981).

110. Rappaport, *The Politics of Memory*.

111. ACSJ, JP Huanta, leg. 68, exp. 67, "Instrucción Contra Saturnino Cayetano y otros sobre el delito de robo en agravio de Víctor Gamboa," Denuncia ante el Juez Instructor contra Saturnino Cayetano y otros (26 May 1975).

112. Interview with Fortunato Huamán and Esteban Huaman, Huaychao (5 February 2006).

113. Interview with Alejandra Ccente, Huaychao (6 February 2006).

114. Interview with Juana Cabezas, Huaychao (6 February 2006); interview with Inocencio Urbano and Ernestina Ccente, Huaychao (6 February 2006); interview with Alejandra Ccente, Huaychao (6 February 2006).

115. Interview with Mariano Quispe, Huaychao (7 February 2006).

116. Mallon, *Peasant and Nation*, 194.

117. ACSJA, JP Huanta, sin leg. (1975, 7 exp.), exp. 48, "Instrucción contra Alejandro Quispe y otros por el delito de contra la vida," Certificado de nacimiento de Emilia Huaylla (24 November 1959); Manifestación de Emilia Huaylla (5 May 1975); Ampliación de la manifestación de Emilia Huaylla (15 May 1975); Declaración informativa de Emilia Huaylla (25 June 1975).

118. ACSJA, JP Huanta, sin leg. (1975, 7 exp.), exp. 48, Manifestación de Alejandro Quispe (12 May 1975); Declaración instructiva ampliatoria del inculpado Alejandro Quispe (5 August 1975); Sentencia en la instrucción contra Alejandro Quispe y otros (3 February 1976).

119. See Mallon, *Peasant and Nation*, 194.

120. Field notes, Huaychao (13 January 2006).

121. Field notes, Huaychao (21 June 2007).

122. Ibid.

123. Ibid.

124. Ibid.

125. For more on the relationship between metaphor and culture, see Pérez, *Cuba in the American Imagination*, 2–4, 138.

126. Interview with Fortunato Huamán and Esteban Huamán, Huaychao (5 February 2006).

127. Interview with Juana Cabezas, Huaychao (6 February 2006).

128. Ibid.

129. Ibid.

130. Ibid.

131. Interview with Ciprián Quispe, Huaychao (5 February 2006).

132. Interview with Juana Cabezas, Huaychao (6 February 2006).

133. Ibid.

134. Ibid.

135. Interview with Juana Cabezas, Huaychao (6 February 2006).

136. Interview with Ciprián Quispe, Huaychao (5 February 2006).

137. *Cortamonte* is a ritual performed during *carnavales* in which villagers take turns chopping down a tree while the others dance and drink in a circle around it.

138. ACSJA, JP Huanta, sin leg. (1981, 14 exp.), exp. 27, "Instrucción contra Mar-

NOTES TO PAGES 93–103 · 237

celino Quispe y otros por el delito de riña y muerte," Manifestación de Marcelino Quispe (11 March 1981); Manifestación de Simeon Quispe (13 March 1981); Instructiva del inculpado Marcelino Quispe (17 March 1981).

139. ACSJA, JP Huanta, sin leg. (1981, 14 exp.), exp. 27, Declaración informativa de Cecilia Quispe (23 March 1981); Testimonial de cargo de Vicente Bautista (19 May 1981); Declaración informativa de Victoriano Yaranqa (14 April 1981).

140. Interview with Alejandra Ccente, Huaychao (6 February 2006).

141. ACSJA, JP Huanta, sin leg. (1981, 14 exp.), exp. 27, Manifestación del Teniente Gobernador Zenobio Quispe (13 March 1981).

142. ACSJA, JP Huanta, sin leg. (1981, 14 exp.), exp. 27, Manifestación de Marcelino Quispe (11 March 1981); Instructiva del inculpado Marcelino Quispe (17 March 1981); Sentencia en la instrucción contra Marcelino Quispe y otros (16 November 1984).

143. Interview with Alejandra Ccente, Huaychao (6 February 2006).

144. Much has been written on the Andean practice of *tinku*. See, for example, Platt, "The Andean Soldiers of Christ"; Harris, "Condor and Bull"; and Harvey, "Domestic Violence."

145. Harris, "Condor and Bull," 46–47.

146. Harvey, "Domestic Violence," 78–79.

147. ACSJA, JP Huanta, leg. 68, exp. 67, Denuncia ante el Juez Instructor contra Saturnino Cayetano y otros (26 May 1975).

148. ACSJA, JP Huanta, leg. 68, exp. 67, Instructiva de Saturnino Cayetano (28 May 1975).

149. ACSJA, JP Huanta, leg. 68, exp. 67, Sentencia sobre la instrucción contra Saturnino Cayetano y otros (19 March 1976).

150. Interview with Santos Huaylla, Huaychao (21 May 2006).

151. Interview with Mariano Quispe, Huaychao (7 February 2006).

152. See chapter 1 for a more detailed description of the *vara visita* in Huaychao.

153. Interview with Juana Cabezas, Huaychao (6 February 2006).

154. ASH 1975, Queja ante el Subprefecto contra el Teniente Gobernador de Pampalca (10 March 1975).

Chapter Three

1. Field notes, Huaychao (6 February 2006).

2. Paige, *Agrarian Revolution*, 81.

3. Wolf, *Peasant Wars*, 192.

4. Paige, *Agrarian Revolution*, 82.

5. Gupta, *Understanding Terrorism*, 142.

6. Gleijeses, *Shattered Hope*, 150, 155–56.

7. Klein, *Bolivia*, 234–35.

8. See Stavenhagen, *Agrarian Problems*.

9. Larson, *Trials of Nation Making*; Davies, *Indian Integration*; de la Cadena, *Indigenous Mestizos*; Mariátegui, *Seven Interpretive Essays*.

10. Stein, *Deconstructing Development Discourse*; http://courses.cit.cornell.edu/vicosperu/vicos-site/index.htm.

11. McClintock, *Peasant Cooperatives*, 64, 73.

12. Lowenthal, "Peru's Ambiguous Revolution."

13. McClintock, *Peasant Cooperatives*, 75–76, 127.

14. Bourque and Palmer, "Transforming the Rural Sector," 183.

15. Handelman, *Struggle in the Andes*; Heilman, "Leader and Led"; Del Pino, "Looking to the Government," chap. 5.

16. Blanco, *Land or Death*, 47.

17. Bourque and Palmer, "Transforming the Rural Sector," 184–85; Heilman, *Before the Shining Path*, 122–23.

18. McClintock, *Peasant Cooperatives*, 71; Heilman, *Before the Shining Path*, 124.

19. Bourque and Palmer, "Transforming the Rural Sector," 185.

20. Cotler, "Democracy and National Integration," 22.

21. For an excellent account of the Agrarian Reform, see Enrique Mayer, *Ugly Stories*.

22. Ibid., 192.

23. Ibid., 37.

24. For more on the social interest groups, see, for example, Knight, "New Forms"; and Enrique Mayer, *Ugly Stories*.

25. Fitzgerald, "State Capitalism in Peru," 70–71.

26. Knight, "New Forms," 365.

27. Hünefeldt, "The Rural Landscape," 110.

28. Harding, "Land Reform and Social Conflict," 222–23.

29. Cotler, "The New Mode," 76; McClintock, *Peasant Cooperatives*, 35; Cleaves and Pease García, "State Autonomy," 239; Bourque and Palmer, "Transforming the Rural Sector," 215–16. As Enrique Mayer points out, however, peasants did find effective ways of challenging this system to effect change. See Mayer, *Ugly Stories*.

30. McClintock, *Peasant Cooperatives*, 36–37; Knight, "New Forms," 362. Bourque and Palmer, "Transforming the Rural Sector," 189–90.

31. Schydlowsky and Wicht, "The Anatomy of an Economic Failure," 104.

32. Palmer, "Revolution from Above," 188, 192–93.

33. Ibid.

34. Hünefeldt, "The Rural Landscape," 121.

35. Cleaves and Pease García, "State Autonomy," 226; Schydlowsky and Wicht, "The Anatomy of an Economic Failure," 109–10.

36. Hünefeldt, "The Rural Landscape," 112.

37. Quoted in Montoya, *Lucha por la tierra*, 151.

38. Poole, "Landscapes of Power," 372.

39. Ibid., 372–74; de la Cadena, *Indigenous Mestizos,* 78–84; Enrique Mayer, *Ugly Stories,* 88–90; Heilman, *Before the Shining Path,* 28.

40. For more on Chuschi's *qalas,* see Isbell, *To Defend Ourselves,* 68–73.

41. De la Cadena, *Indigenous Mestizos,* 129–30.

42. Interview with Víctor Núñez, Chuschi (26 July 2007).

43. Interview with Fulgencio Makta [pseud.], Ayacucho City (31 July 2007).

44. ARA, SC, caja 33, of. Institutos Armados 1959, Manifestación de Modesta Aycha [pseud.] (9 October 1959).

45. ARA, SC, caja 33, of. Institutos Armados 1959, Manifestación de Máximo Vilca Fernandez (9 October 1959); Manifestación de Demetrio Vilca Fernandez (9 October 1959); Manifestación de Clemente Núñez Mendoza (9 October 1959).

46. ARA, SC, 1965, Queja ante el Subprefecto contra el Gobernador Felipe Aycha [pseud.] (5 November 1965).

47. APETT, exp. Chuschi, Denuncia de los comuneros de Yaruca-Rumichaca ante el Teniente Alcalde del Consejo Municipal (26 June 1981).

48. Ibid.

49. Ibid.

50. APETT, exp. Chuschi, Acta de Asamblea Comunal Extraordinaria (14 June 1981). The record book did not indicate how many constituents voted for Chipana to retain his post, indicating only that the figure of eighty-one represented a majority.

51. This is a pseudonym.

52. ARA, CSJ-JP, leg. 62, exp. 175, "Instrucción contra Vicente Blanco [pseud.] por el delito de violación sexual y otros," Denuncia de Clotilde Bedriñana (27 December 1969); Instructiva de Clotilde Bedriñana (circa 28 diciembre de 1969).

53. For more on this practice, see Isbell, *To Defend Ourselves,* 119.

54. Personal correspondence, Chuschi (26 July 2007).

55. Isbell, *To Defend Ourselves,* 233. For an analysis of why Blanco wanted to expel Isbell, see La Serna, "The Corner of the Living," chap. 2.

56. Personal correspondence with Vicente Blanco [pseud.], Chuschi (27 July 2007).

57. ARA, CSJ-JP Cangallo, leg. 62, exp. 175, Instructiva de Clotilde Bedriñana (circa 28 December 1969).

58. Ibid.

59. ARA, CSJ-JP Cangallo, leg. 62, exp. 175, Instructiva de Clotilde Bedriñana (6 January 1970).

60. ARA, CSJ-JP Cangallo, leg. 71, exp. 54, "Instrucción contra Vicente Blanco [pseud.] por el delito de tentativa de homicidio y lesiones," Denuncia de Clotilde Bedriñana (22 May 1970).

61. ARA, CSJ-JP Cangallo, leg. 62, exp. 175, Sentencia sobre la instrucción seguida contra Vicente Blanco [pseud.] (circa 1970).

62. ARA, CSJ-JP Cangallo, leg. 62, exp. 175, Denuncia de Clotilde Bedriñana (27 December 1969); Instructiva de Clotilde Bedriñana (circa 28 diciembre de 1969).

63. ARA, CSJ-JP Cangallo, leg. 62, exp. 75, Copia de la denuncia de Asunta Retamozo ante el Gobernador de Chuschi (26 August 1960).

64. ARA, CSJ-JP Cangallo, leg. 62, exp. 175, Instructiva de Asunta Retamozo (circa 6 January 1970).

65. ARA, CSJ-JP Cangallo, leg. 62, exp. 175, Copia de la denuncia de Baselia Dueñas ante el Gobernador de Chuschi (21 October 1967).

66. ARA, CSJ-JP Cangallo, leg. 62, exp. 175, Instructiva de Lorenza Vilca (circa 6 January 1970). It is worth noting that Vilca's mother, Felicíta Cayllahua, later attempted to have this testimony stricken from the record. Bedriñana later charged that Blanco had bribed Cayllahua to retract her daughter's statement. See ibid., Testimonio de Clotilde Bedriñana (circa February 1970); Testimonio de Lorenza Vilca (circa February 1970); and Instructiva de Clotilde Bedriñana (circa February 1970).

67. ARA, CSJ-JP Cangallo, leg. 62, exp. 175, Certificado de las autoridades de Chuschi sobre el conducto de Vicente Blanco [pseud.] (21 February 1971).

68. This was a common strategy used by Andean men for centuries. See Hünefeldt, *Liberalism in the Bedroom*, 183.

69. ARA, CSJ-JP Cangallo, leg. 69, exp. 28, Denuncia de Isidro Vilca contra Vicente Blanco [pseud.] por el delito contra la fé pública (12 Janaury 1970).

70. ARA, CSJ-JP Cangallo, leg. 69, exp. 28, Instructiva de Vicente Blanco [pseud.] (8 August 1972). The court's ruling is not included in the file, but Vicente Blanco alluded to the ruling in a subsequent litigation. See ACSJA, JP Cangallo, leg. 142, exp. 101, Instructiva de Vicente Blanco [pseud.] sobre el delito de malversión de fondos (circa 28 October 1976).

71. ACSJA, JP Cangallo, leg. 142, exp. 101, Denuncia de Isidro Vilca ante el Agente Fiscal sobre malversión de fondos (28 October 1976).

72. Ibid.

73. ACSJA, JP Cangallo, leg. 142, exp. 101, Instructiva de Vicente Blanco [pseud.] sobre el delito de malversión de fondos (Circa 28 October 1976).

74. ACSJA, JP Cangallo, leg. 142, exp. 101, Sentencia del Ministerio Público en el juicio contra Vicente Blanco [pseud.] por el delito de malversión de fondos (22 August 1978).

75. For more on this conflict, see La Serna, "'Thank God for the Violence.'"

76. APETT, of. Chuschi, Informe sobre el Inspección Ocular de las tierras de las cofradías de Chuschi (12 October 1971).

77. Thomson, *We Alone Will Rule*, 137. See also 43.

78. Serulnikov, *Subverting Colonial Authority*, 36, 51.

79. Ibid., 21; Thomson, *We Alone Will Rule*, 69–70.

80. Morote Barrionuevo, "Luchas de clases," 87. I thank Ponciano Del Pino for furnishing me with a copy of this thesis.

81. AMAA, exp. Huaychao, Escritura de compraventa (15 November 1962).

82. Interview with Mariano Quispe, Huaychao (7 February 2006).

83. Ibid.

84. Ibid.

85. Ibid.

86. Interview with Fortunato Huamán and Esteban Huamán, Huaychao (5 February 2006).

87. Interview with Mariano Quispe, Huaychao (7 February 2006).

88. Ibid.

89. Ibid.

90. Ibid.

91. Ibid. Apparently, the use of the *verga* in Ayacucho was not as uncommon as one might think. Jaymie Patricia Heilman also records its appearance in twentieth-century Carhuanca. See Heilman, *Before the Shining Path*, 139–40.

92. A *costal* (literally, a sack) is a measurement of harvest.

93. Interview with Mariano Quispe, Huaychao (7 February 2006).

94. Interview with Inocencio Urbano and Ernestina Ccente, Huaychao (6 February 2006).

95. Interview with Isidro Huamán, Huaychao (21 May 2006); emphasis added.

96. Interview with Fortunato Huamán and Esteban Huamán, Huaychao (5 February 2006).

97. Interview with Inocencio Urbano and Ernestina Ccente, Huaychao (6 February 2006).

98. Interview with Fortunato Huamán and Esteban Huamán, Huaychao (5 February 2006).

99. Interview with Mariano Quispe, Huaychao (7 February 2006).

100. Ibid.

101. Interview with Inocencio Urbano and Ernestina Ccente, Huaychao (6 February 2006); emphasis added.

102. Interview with Fortunato Huamán and Esteban Huamán, Huaychao (5 February 2006).

103. Interview with Mariano Quispe, Huaychao (7 February 2006).

104. Ibid.

105. Interview with Fortunato Huamán and Esteban Huamán, Huaychao (5 February 2006).

106. Interview with Inocencio Urbano and Ernestina Ccente, Huaychao (6 February 2006).

107. In addition to the case in Chuschi documented in this study, see Heilman, *Before the Shining Path*, 139–40.

108. I thank Ponciano Del Pino and Jaymie Patricia Heilman for their insights regarding the discursive function of the *verga*.

109. Harris, "Condor and Bull," 46, 50–51.

110. Mitchell, *Voices from the Global Margin*, 27; Poole, "Performance, Domination and Identity," 121.

111. Harris, "Condor and Bull," 56.

112. Interview with Mariano Quispe, Huaychao (7 February 2006).

113. Interview with Inocencio Urbano and Ernestina Ccente, Huaychao (6 February 2006).

114. Interview with Fortunato Huamán and Esteban Huamán, Huaychao (5 February 2006).

115. Ibid.

116. Interview with Inocencio Urbano and Ernestina Ccente, Huaychao (6 February 2006).

117. Interview with Fortunato Huamán and Esteban Huamán, Huaychao (5 February 2006).

118. Ibid.

119. Ibid.

120. I thank Jaymie Patricia Heilman for making this important connection.

121. ASH, 1967, Solicitud del propietario del fundo de Huaynacancha ante el Prefecto (22 May 1967).

122. Interview with Fortunato Huamán and Esteban Huamán, Huaychao (5 February 2006).

123. Ibid.

124. Interview with Mariano Quispe, Huaychao (7 February 2006).

125. Interview with Inocencio Urbano and Ernestina Ccente, Huaychao (6 February 2006).

126. Interview with Fortunato Huamán and Esteban Huamán, Huaychao (5 February 2006); interview with Mariano Quispe, Huaychao (7 February 2006).

127. Interview with Fortunato Huamán and Esteban Huamán, Huaychao (5 February 2006).

128. Interview with Inocencio Urbano and Ernestina Ccente, Huaychao (6 February 2006).

129. Interview with Brígida Cayetano, Huaychao (6 February 2006).

130. Interview with Mirano Quispe, Huaychao (7 February 2006).

131. Interview with Alejandra Ccente, Huaychao (6 February 2006).

132. Ibid.

133. AMAA, exp. Huaychao, Escritura de compraventa (15 November 1962).

134. Interview with Inocencio Urbano and Ernestina Ccente, Huaychao (6 February 2006).

135. Interview with Isidro Huamán, Huaychao (21 May 2006). Juscamaita owned the hacienda about ten years longer than Huamán credited him for.

136. Interview with Mariano Quispe, Huaychao (7 February 2006).

137. Interview with Alejandra Ccente, Huaychao (6 February 2006).

138. Ibid.

139. Interview with Mariano Quispe, Huaychao (7 February 2006).

140. Interview with Inocencio Urbano and Ernestina Ccente, Huaychao (6 February 2006).

141. Interview with Fortunato Huamán and Esteban Huamán, Huaychao (5 February 2006).

142. Interview with Mariano Quispe, Huaychao (7 February 2006).

143. Ibid.; interview with Inocencio Urbano and Ernestina Ccente, Huaychao (6 February 2006).

144. Interview with Isidro Huamán, Huaychao (21 May 2006).

145. AMAA, exp. Huaychao, Resolución Directorial de afectación del predio de Huaychao (5 June 1975); ACSJA, JT-FPA, leg. 36, exp. 143, Expropriación de Huaychao (1976).

146. For a more nuanced discussion of this land movement in highland Huanta, see Del Pino, "Looking to the Government."

147. A noteworthy exception is the figure of Jesús Ccente, who became Huaychao's first postreform authority.

148. Interview with Fortunato Huamán and Esteban Huamán, Huaychao (5 February 2006).

149. Ibid.

150. Interview with Isidro Huamán, Huaychao (21 May 2006).

151. Interview with Brígida Cayetano, Huaychao (6 February 2006).

152. Interview with Alejandra Ccente, Huaychao (6 February 2006).

153. Foucault, *The History of Sexuality*, 95.

Chapter Four

1. Gorriti, *The Shining Path*, 17; Vallejos, "Volver a los 17"; ADP, Testimonio 100883; Sánchez Villagómez, *Pensar los "Senderos,"* 116.

2. For more on the role of the peasantry in the Chinese Revolution, see, for example, Moore, *Social Origins*; and Skocpol, *States and Social Revolutions*.

3. For more on the role of the peasantry in the Vietnam War, see, for example, Wolf, *Peasant Wars*; Migdal, *Peasants*; Scott, *The Moral Economy of the Peasant*; and Popkin, *The Rational Peasant*.

4. Gupta, *Understanding Terrorism*, 142–43.

5. Wickham-Crowley, *Guerrillas and Revolution*, 26.

6. This is not to say that Castro's urban strategy was irrelevant. See Sweig, *Inside the Cuban Revolution*.

7. This initial peasant support for the FARC has since dwindled.

8. Wickham-Crowley, *Guerrillas and Revolution*, 26–28.

9. Ibid., 209–14, 217–18.

10. CVR, *Informe final*, 2:30.

11. Mariátegui, *Seven Interpretive Essays*, 21, 23–24, 43.

12. Núñez, *Pensamiento político peruano*, 51.

13. Poole and Rénique, *Peru: Time of Fear*, 30–31; CVR, *Informe final*, 2:28–30.

14. Degregori, *Ayacucho*, 172–84; Poole and Rénique, *Peru: Time of Fear*, 31.

15. Hinojosa, "On Poor Relations," 66.

16. Poole and Rénique, *Peru: Time of Fear*, 32; Gorriti, "Shining Path's Stalin and Trotsky," 152–53.

17. Poole and Rénique, *Peru: Time of Fear*, 33; Rochlin, *Vanguard Revolutionaries*, 33–34.

18. Poole and Rénique, *Peru: Time of Fear*, 33–34; Rochlin, *Vanguard Revolutionaries*, 34–35.

19. For more on the role of UNSCH in the development of Shining Path, see Degregori, *Ayacucho*.

20. Poole and Rénique, *Peru: Time of Fear*, 46–48; Hinojosa, "On Poor Relations," 72–73; Gorriti, "Shining Path's Stalin and Trotsky," 173, 177.

21. GGC, box 2, folder 2, PCP-SL, Notas de la segunda conferencia nacional del Partido Comunista Peruano–SL (May 1980). This collection is also available at Geisel Library, University of California, San Diego, under the title "Documenting the Peruvian Insurrection." Although I conducted research in both locations, I will refer to the collection by its original title.

22. Degregori, *Ayacucho*, 183–212.

23. GGC, box 2, folder 2, PCP-SL, Notas de la segunda conferencia nacional del Partido Comunista Peruano–SL (May 1980). For more on the proceedings of the PCP-SL's second plenary session, see Gorriti, *The Shining Path*, chap. 3.

24. Guzmán Reynoso, "We Are the Initiators," 311–14.

25. GGC, box 2, folder 2, PCP-SL pamphlet, "¡A nuestro heroico pueblo combatiente!" (1 January 1981).

26. Centro de Estudios y Promoción del Desarrollo, *Violencia política en el Perú*, 65–66.

27. Poole and Rénique, *Peru: Time of Fear*, 58.

28. Ibid.

29. Degregori, "Return to the Past," 51–52.

30. Today, this region corresponds to the province of Vilcashuamán, which until 1985 was part of Cangallo Province.

31. GGC, Group A, box 3, folder 1, "Estadísticas de ataques al 12/80"; CVR, *Informe final*, 5:46.

32. Gorriti, *The Shining Path*.

33. GGC, box 2, folder 2, PCP-SL, Notas de la tercera conferencia nacional del PCP-SL (July 1983).

34. Gorriti, *The Shining Path*, 98–106.

35. See, for example, Vanderwood, *The Power of God*; and Pérez, *To Die in Cuba*.

36. Gorriti, *The Shining Path*, 104.

37. GGC, box 3, folder 2, Informe del Ministerio Público de Ayacucho a G. Ortiz de Zevallo sobre la situación subversiva (19 November 1982).

38. Degregori, "Harvesting Storms," 128–31.

39. GGC, box 3, folder 2, Informe del Ministerio Público de Ayacucho a G. Ortiz de Zevallo sobre la situación subversiva (19 November 1982).

40. ADP, Testimonio 200806.

41. This is a pseudonym.

42. Interview with Fulgencio Makta [pseud.], Ayacucho City (31 July 2007); for more on the PCP-SL's *escuelas populares*, see CVR, *Informe final*, 5:37–38.

43. See, for example, Tarazona-Sevillano, "The Organization of Shining Path," 196–98; Gorriti, *The Shining Path*, 29–36; and Sánchez Villagómez, *Pensar los "Senderos,"* 99–101.

44. Interview with Fulgencio Makta [pseud.], Ayacucho City (31 July 2007).

45. Ibid.

46. Ibid.

47. Ibid. For more on the function of the *comités populares*, see CVR, *Informe final*, 5:36.

48. Sánchez Villagómez, *Pensar los "Senderos,"* 176.

49. Ibid., 176, 256–61; ADP, Testimonio 200158.

50. Interview with Fulgencio Makta [pseud.], Ayacucho City (31 July 2007).

51. ACSJA, JP Cangallo, leg. 152, exp. 83, Certificado de las autoridades de Chuschi sobre la conducta de Ignacio Aycha [pseud.] (12 November 1977); emphasis added.

52. This is according to information collected in Sánchez Villagómez, *Pensar los "Senderos,"* although I have withheld the page number here in order not to reveal the family's surname.

53. I borrow this notion from ibid., 177–78.

54. La Serna, "'Thank God for the Violence.'"

55. For more examples of Chuschinos who were brought to justice during this period, see La Serna, "The Corner of the Living."

56. Quoted in Sánchez Villagómez, *Pensar los "Senderos,"* 170; emphasis added.

57. Centro de Estudios y Promoción del Desarrollo, *Violencia política*, 83.

58. Isbell, "Shining Path and Peasant Responses," 86.

59. Interview with Fulgencio Makta [pseud.], Ayacucho City (31 July 2007).

60. Ibid.

61. Ibid.

62. Ibid.

63. Ibid.

64. Ibid.

65. For more on why peasants chose not to submit Ernesto to Shining Path justice, see La Serna, "*Murió comiendo rata.*"

66. Díaz Martínez, *Ayacucho*, 100.

67. Isbell, *To Defend Ourselves*, viii.

68. ADP, Testimonio 200158.

69. Isbell, "Shining Path and Peasant Responses," 83.

70. ADP, Testimonio 100883.

71. Interview with Fulgencio Makta [pseud.], Ayacucho City (31 July 2007).

72. Ibid.

73. Llalli's assassination is recorded in Sánchez Villagómez, *Pensar los "Senderos,"* 256–57n.

74. See La Serna, "The Corner of the Living," chap. 1.

75. ADP, Testimonio 200801.

76. Quoted in Sánchez Villagómez, *Pensar los "Senderos,"* 137.

77. Theidon, "Traumatic States," 212–14.

78. Gorriti, *The Shining Path*, 17.

79. GGC, box 5, folder 4, "Testimonios en Cangallo (1985–1986)," Entrevista de Elba Carrasco [pseud.] al pastor evangélico de Chuschi (1985).

80. GGC, box 5, folder 4, "Testimonios en Cangallo (1985–1986)," Entrevista de Elba Carrasco [pseud.] a autoridades de Quispillaccta (1985).

81. ADP, Testimonio 200801. Cayllahua went on to say that the burning of the ballot boxes took place during the elections that led to the inauguration of Alan García, which would have placed it in 1985 and not on 17 May 1980. However, the reference to the burning of the Consejo is a direct reference to the ILA, suggesting that Cayllahua simply confused his dates.

82. McClintock, "Why Peasants Rebel."

83. That Peru's indigenous peasantry was ripe for communist revolution was an idea expressed in the preinsurgency scholarship of future Shining Path leaders. See, for example, Díaz Martínez, *Ayacucho*; and Morote Barrionuevo, "Luchas de clases."

84. Amnesty International, *Peru*; Americas Watch, *Peru under Fire*.

85. See, for example, Favre, "Perú"; Taylor, *Shining Path*, 127–29; Manrique, "La década de la violencia"; Isbell, "Shining Path and Peasant Responses"; and Berg, "Peasant Responses."

86. See, for example, Coral Cordero, "Women in War"; and Stern, "Introduction to Part Four," 342.

87. Heilman, *Before the Shining Path*, 97–114.

88. Del Pino, "Looking to the Government," chap. 3.

89. Gonzalez, *Unveiling Secrets*, 103–13, 145–53.

90. Quoted in CVR, *Informe final*, 5:46–47.

91. ADP, Testimonio 200818.

92. ADP, Testimonio 201700.

Chapter Five

1. Gorriti, "Trágicos linchamientos."

2. For more on how events can take on a history of their own, see Badiou, *Being and Event*.

3. The term "linchamiento" here refers more to collective, vigilante violence than a hanging per se.

4. "Días antes del linchamiento."

5. See, for example, Montoya, "Uchuraccay"; and Montoya, "Otra pista."

6. See, for example, Fumerton, *From Victims to Heroes*.

7. Mazzei, *Death Squads*, 80.

8. Ibid., 167.

9. Stoll, *Between Two Armies*, chap. 4.

10. Bates, "Probing the Sources," 20–22.

11. Starn, *Hablan los ronderos*.

12. CVR, *Informe final*, 2:430–31, 436.

13. Comisión Investigadora, *Informe*, 13.

14. "Temor y muerte en las alturas."

15. Hosoya, *La memoria post-colonial*, 24.

16. CVR, *Informe final*, 5:134–36.

17. Hosoya, *La memoria post-colonial*, 24–25.

18. CVR, *Informe final*, 5:136–37.

19. The journalists in question were Eduardo de la Piniella, Pedro Sánchez, and Félix Gavilán of *El Diario de Marka*; Jorge Luis Mendívil and Willy Retto of *El Observador*; Jorge Sedano of *La República*; Amador García of *Oiga*; and Octavio Infante of *Noticias*.

20. The first investigation was carried out in February 1983 by the Comisión Investigadora de los Sucessos de Uchuraccay, headed by famed novelist Mario Vargas Llosa. A subsequent investigation was carried out by the Poder Judicial and issued on 9 March 1987. This investigation brought criminal charges against the alleged perpetrators of the assault. The final investigation was carried out by the Peruvian Truth and Reconciliation Commission (CVR) and summarized in its 2003 *Informe final*.

21. Enrique Mayer, "Peru in Deep Trouble"; Montoya, *Eulogio de la antropología*, 261–96. For a more historical study of Uchuraccay, see Del Pino, "Looking to the Government."

22. Quoted in CVR, *Informe final*, 5:80.

23. Quoted in ibid.

24. Ibid., 5:80–82.

25. Ibid., 2:433–35.

26. Del Pino, "Tiempos de guerra," 118.

27. "Peruvian Farmers Said to Kill Rebels," A13. This event is also chronicled in Mallon, *Peasant and Nation*, 306.

28. Starn, "Villagers at Arms," 224.

29. CVR 2003, *Informe final*, 2:442.

30. Starn, "La resistencia de Huanta," 35.

31. Theidon, "Terror's Talk."

32. Interview with Isidro Huamán, Huaychao (21 May 2006).

33. Interview with Juana Cabezas, Huanta City (9 June 2006).

34. Gorriti, "Trágicos linchamientos," 23–24.

35. Interview with Ciprián Quispe, Huaychao (5 February 2006).

36. ADP, Testimonio 201700.

37. Ibid.

38. Coronel, "Violencia política," 71.

39. Interview with Alejandra Ccente, Huaychao (6 February 2006).

40. Coronel, "Violencia política," 71.

41. Interview with Isidro Huamán, Huaychao (21 May 2006).

42. Ibid.; interview with Alejandra Ccente, Huaychao (6 February 2006); interview with Juana Cabezas, Huanta City (9 June 2006).

43. CVR, *Informe final*, 5:131.

44. Interview with Juana Cabezas, Huanta City (9 June 2006); Gorriti, "Trágicos linchamientos," 23–24; interview with Ciprián Quispe, Huaychao (5 February 2006).

45. Interview with Fortunato Huamán and Esteban Huamán, Huaychao (5 February 2006); interview with Ciprián Quispe, Huaychao (5 February 2006); interview with Juana Cabezas, Huanta City (9 June 2006); ADP, Testimonio 201700; interview with Isidro Huamán, Huaychao (21 May 2006); interview with Alejandra Ccente, Huaychao (6 February 2006); interview with Santos Huaylla, Huaychao (21 May 2006).

46. Interview with Fortunato Huamán and Esteban Huamán, Huaychao (5 February 2006); interview with Ciprián Quispe, Huaychao (5 February 2006); interview with Juana Cabezas, Huanta City (9 June 2006); ADP Testimonio 201700 (emphasis added); interview with Isidro Huamán, Huaychao (21 May 2006); interview with Santos Huaylla, Huaychao (21 May 2006).

47. ADP, Testimonio 201700; Gorriti, "Trágicos linchamientos," 23–24; interview with Ciprián Quispe, Huaychao (5 February 2006).

48. Interview with Juana Cabezas, Huanta City (9 June 2006).

49. Ibid.

50. ADP, Testimonio 201700; interview with Isidro Huamán, Huaychao (21 May 2006).

51. Interview with Fortunato Huamán and Esteban Huaman, Huaychao (5 February 2006); interview with Alejandra Ccente, Huaychao (6 February 2006).

52. Interview with Alejandra Ccente, Huaychao (6 February 2006).

53. Interview with Ciprián Quispe, Huaychao (5 February 2006); interview with Ciprián Quispe, Huaychao (21 May 2006); ADP, Testimonio 201700.

54. ADP, Testimonio 201700.

55. The colloquial term "black heads [*cabezas negras*]" refers to Peruvian security forces, who often carried out their operations in the countryside while wearing black ski masks. The "red" reference is more obvious, referring to the red communist flag that rebels paraded in and out of highland villages.

56. ADP, Testimonio 201700; emphasis added.

57. ADP, Testimonio 201700; interview with Isidro Huamán, Huaychao (21 May 2006); interview with Fortunato Huamán and Esteban Huamán, Huaychao (5 February 2006).

58. ADP, Testimonio 201700.

59. Gorriti, "Trágicos linchamientos," 23–24; interview with Ciprián Quispe, Huaychao (5 February 2006); interview with Juana Cabezas, Huanta City (9 June 2006).

60. Coronel, "Violencia política," 47–48.

61. Ibid.

62. Field notes, Huaychao (8 February 2006).

63. Interview with Fortunato Huamán and Esteban Huamán, Huaychao (5 February 2006).

64. Kirk, *Untold Terror*.

65. Gorriti, "Trágicos linchamientos," 23–24.

66. "Mardonio" was the subject's name at the time he was captured in Huaychao in 1983. He now goes by another name, which I have withheld for security purposes.

67. Field notes, Ayacucho City (circa 13 March 2006).

68. Personal correspondence, Ayacucho City (circa 13 March 2006).

69. Field notes, Ayacucho City (circa 13 March 2006).

70. Interview with Ciprián Quispe, Huaychao (21 May 2006).

71. Ibid.

72. Interview with Isidro Huamán, Huaychao (21 May 2006).

73. Interview with Juana Cabezas, Huanta City (9 June 2006).

74. Interview with Ciprián Quispe, Huaychao (5 February 2006).

75. Personal correspondence, Ayacucho City (13 March 2006).

76. Interview with Fortunato Huamán and Esteban Huamán, Huaychao (5 February 2006).

77. Interview with Isidro Huamán, Huaychao (21 May 2006).

78. Interview with Fortunato Huamán and Esteban Huamán, Huaychao (5 February 2006).

79. Interview with Mariano Quispe, Huaychao (7 February 2006).

80. Interview with Fortunato Huamán and Esteban Huamán, Huaychao (5 February 2006).

81. Interview with Ciprián Quispe, Huaychao (21 May 2006).

82. Personal correspondence, Ayacucho City (circa 13 March 2006).

83. Interview with Ciprián Quispe, Huaychao (5 February 2006).

84. Interview with Ciprián Quispe, Huaychao (21 May 2006).

85. Gorriti, "Trágicos linchamientos," 23–24.

86. For an overview of this event, see Comisión Investigadora, *Informe*; CVR, *Informe final*, vol. 5; and Del Pino, "Looking to the Government."

87. Interview with Isidro Huamán, Huaychao (21 May 2006).

88. Interview with Fulgencio Makta [pseud.], Ayacucho City (31 July 2007).

89. For more on Ernesto Jaime's exceptionalism as a "legitimate" *qala* authority, see La Serna, "*Murió comiendo rata.*"

90. Interview with Fulgencio Makta [pseud.], Ayacucho City (31 July 2007).

91. Reyes, "Ronderos combaten a Senderistas," 15.

92. Degregori, "Harvesting Storms," 137–40; Del Pino, "Family, Culture, and 'Revolution,'" 167–69.

93. "Maoist Rebels," A9.

94. Degregori, "Harvesting Storms," 133; Fumerton, *From Victims to Heroes*, 78.

95. Vargas Llosa, "Inquest in the Andes," SM33.

96. Schumacher, "Insurgency in Peru," A1.

97. Kirk, *The Decade of Chaqwa.*

Chapter Six

1. Moore, *Social Origins*, 100.

2. Interview with Alejandra Ccente, Huaychao (6 February 2006).

3. For more on the effects of the political violence on various aspects of peasant life, see Theidon, *Entre prójimos*; Yezer, "Anxious Citizenship"; Gamarra, "Exploración"; and Pederson et al., "Violencia política."

4. Interview with Fortunato Huamán and Esteban Huamán, Huaychao (5 February 2006).

5. Kirk, *The Decade of Chaqwa.*

6. Yezer, "Anxious Citizenship," 123, 156–58.

7. For more on this phenomenon, see ibid., chap. 4.

8. Huillca, "El diálogo con Sendero es imposible."

9. CVR, *Informe final*, 2:432, 437, 448n; Kruijt, "Exercises in State Terrorism," 43; U.S. State Department, *Human Rights Report on Peru.*

10. Quoted in CVR, *Informe final*, 2:442.

11. Theidon, "La micropolítica de la reconciliación," 116; Starn, "Missing the Revolution," 241; CVR, *Informe final*, 2:431–32.

12. Theidon, *Entre prójimos*, 200.

13. Interview with Juana Cabezas, Huaychao (6 February 2006).

14. Interview with Ciprián Quispe, Huaychao (5 February 2006).

15. CVR, *Informe final*, 8:311.

16. Fumerton, *From Victims to Heroes*, 191.

17. CVR, *Informe final*, 2:453–54.

18. Interview with Fulgencio Makta [pseud.], Ayacucho City (31 July 2007).

19. Ibid.

20. Interview with Ciprián Quispe, Huaychao (5 February 2006).

21. "Peru: On Child Victims."

22. Interview with Mariano Quispe, Huaychao (7 February 2006).

23. Interview with Isidro Huamán, Huaychao (21 May 2006).

24. Ibid.

25. Interview with Ciprián Quispe, Huaychao (21 May 2006).

26. CVR, *Informe final*, 2:442; Coronel, "Violencia política," 74–75.

27. Coronel, "Violencia política," 74–75.

28. Ibid., 83–86.

29. De Althaus and Morelli Salgado, "Comandante Huayhuaco."

30. Quoted in CVR, *Informe final*, 2:443.

31. Fumerton, *From Victims to Heroes*, 289.

32. Interview with Ciprián Quispe, Huaychao (5 February 2006).

33. Field notes, Huaychao (5 February 2006).

34. Personal correspondence, Huaychao (7 February 2006).

35. Field notes, Huaychao (8 February 2006).

36. Field notes, Chuschi (26 July 2007).

37. Wickham-Crowley, *Guerrillas and Revolution*, 215.

38. CVR, *Informe final*, 5:130.

39. Kirk, *Grabado en piedra*.

40. Interview with Fulgencio Makta [pseud.], Ayacucho City (31 July 2007).

41. ACSJA, JP Cangallo, sin leg. 1980 (case number suppressed).

42. Quoted in CVR, *Informe final*, 2:444.

43. Ibid.

44. Ibid., 445.

45. Ibid., 444.

46. Interview with Juana Cabezas, Huaychao (6 February 2006).

47. Interview with Juana Cabezas, Huanta City (9 June 2006).

48. Interview with Juana Cabezas, Huaychao (6 February 2006).

49. Interview with Juana Cabezas, Huanta City (9 June 2006).

50. Interview with Alejandra Vilma, Chuschi (26 July 2007).

51. Ibid.

52. Ibid.

53. Ibid.

54. Interview with Juana Cabezas, Huaychao (6 February 2006).

55. Interview with Juana Cabezas, Huanta City (9 June 2006).

56. Interview with Juana Cabezas, Huaychao (6 February 2006).

57. Ibid.

58. Ibid.

59. Ibid.

60. Field notes, Lima (circa September 2005).

61. "El país escondido," 57.

62. Méndez, *The Plebeian Republic*; Heilman, *Before the Shining Path*; Del Pino, "Looking to the Government."

63. For more on these ex post facto peasant narratives, see Theidon, *Entre prójimos*, 232; and Yezer, "Anxious Citizenship," 12.

64. Sánchez Villagómez, *Pensar los "Senderos,"* 39.

65. "Estas mamachas son de Mamey," 41–45.

66. Isbell, "Shining Path and Peasant Responses," 87.

67. Ibid.

68. Field notes, Chuschi (27 July 2007).

69. ADP, Testimonio 201700.

70. "Ayacucho Peasants Rebel," V1.

71. Tapia, *Autodefensa armada*, 33–35.

72. See La Serna and Berrocal Flores, "Gritos en el silencio."

73. Interview with Isidro Huamán, Huaychao (20 May 2006); interview with Ciprián Quispe, Huaychao (21 May 2006).

74. García, *Making Indigenous Citizens*; Montoya, "¿Un movimiento político indígena en Perú?"; Naveda Felix, "The Reconstitution of Indigenous Peoples."

75. There is already some evidence that these state-peasant relations are breaking down, as Ayacuchan peasants are increasingly mistrustful and skeptical of state promises. See Yezer, "Who Wants to Know?"

Conclusion

1. "Barbarie, turbas y política en Puno."

2. "Otro intento de linchamiento."

3. Goldstein, *The Spectacular City*, 179.

4. See Degregori, *No hay país más diverso*.

5. Stoll, *Between Two Armies*.

6. See Postero and Zamosc, *The Struggle for Indian Rights*; and Postero, *Now We Are Citizens*.

7. See, for example, Larson, *Trials of Nation Making*; Méndez, *The Plebeian Republic*; Walker, *Smoldering Ashes*; and Thurner, *From Two Republics*.

8. See, for example, de la Cadena, *Indigenous Mestizos*; and García, *Making Indigenous Citizens*.

9. Some notable exceptions are Becker, *Indians and Leftists*; and Heilman, *Before the Shining Path*.

BIBLIOGRAPHY

. . . .

Manuscript Sources

Archivo de la Corte Superior de Justicia de Ayacucho, Ayacucho City
Archivo de la Defensoría del Pueblo, Lima
Archivo de la Subprefectura de Huanta, Huanta City
Archivo del Ministerio de Agricultura de Ayacucho, Ayacucho City
Archivo del Proyecto Especial de Titulación de Tierras, Ayacucho City
Archivo General de la Nación, Lima
Archivo Regional de Ayacucho, Ayacucho City
"Documenting the Peruvian Insurrection," Geisel Library, University of California,
    San Diego
Gustavo Gorriti Collection on the Peruvian Insurrection, Princeton University
    Library, Princeton, N.J.
Instituto Indigenista Peruano, Lima
Pontificia Universidad Católica del Perú, Lima
Universidad Nacional de San Marcos, Lima
Universidad Nacional San Cristóbal de Huamanga, Ayacucho City

Governmental and Nongovernmental Reports

Americas Watch. *Peru under Fire: Human Rights since the Return to Democracy.*
    New Haven, Conn.: Yale University Press, 1992.
Amnesty International. *Peru: Human Rights in a Climate of Terror.* London:
    Amnesty International Publications, 1991.
Centro de Estudios y Promoción del Desarrollo (DESCO). *Violencia política en el
    Perú: 1980–1988.* 2 vols. Lima: DESCO, 1989.
Comisión de la Verdad y Reconciliación del Perú. *Informe final.* 9 vols. Lima, 2003.
Comisión Investigadora de los Sucesos de Uchuraccay. *Informe sobre los sucesos de
    Uchuraccay.* Lima, 1983.
Cornell-Peru Project. http://courses.cit.cornell.edu/vicosperu/vicos-site/index.
    htm.
Instituto Indigenista Peruano. "Estudio de la vivienda en Incaraqay, Chuschi y
    Catalinayoq, Ayacucho." 1968.
———. "Informe sobre la comunidad de Chuschi." 1967.

————. "Mercados y ferias en Chuschi y Cangallo." 1969.

————. "Tres estudios en la zona de Cangallo." 1968.

Kirk, Robin. The *Decade of Chaqwa: Peru's Internal Refugees*. U.S. Committee for Refugees, May 1991.

————. *Untold Terror: Violence against Women in Peru's Armed Conflict*. New York: Human Rights Watch, 1992.

U.S. State Department. *Human Rights Report on Peru*. Washington, D.C., 1992.

Periodical Sources

"Ayacucho Peasants Rebel against Shining Path." *Foreign Broadcast Information Service* (22 June 1984).

"Barbarie, turbas y política en Puno." *La República* (28 April 2004).

de Althaus, Jaime, and Jorge Morelli Salgado. "Comandante Huayhuaco (Ardilla), jefe de los ronderos del río Apurímac." *Expreso* (25 March 1989).

"Días antes del linchamiento Belaúnde alentó orgía de sangre." *El Diario* (1 February 1983).

"El país escondido." *Caretas* 2122 (25 March 2010).

"Estas mamachas son de Mamey." *Caretas* 1962 (8 February 2007).

Gorriti, Gustavo. "Trágicos linchamientos." *Caretas* 733 (31 January 1983).

"Maoist Rebels in Peru Kill Thirty-Two in Andes Village." *New York Times* (27 April 1984).

Montoya, Rodrigo. "¿Un movimiento político indígena en Perú? Desafío cercano." *América Latina en movimiento* (24 May 2008).

————. "Otra pista para entender lo que pasó en Uchuraccay." *La República* (21 January 1984).

————. "Uchuraccay: Dos preguntas esenciales." *La República* (14 February 1983).

"Otro intento de linchamiento en Juliaca." *La República* (14 October 2010).

"Peru: On Child Victims of Political Violence." *NotiSur* (27 November 1991).

"Peruvian Farmers Said to Kill Rebels." *New York Times* (4 March 1990).

Reyes, Francisco. "Ronderos combaten a Senderistas por todo Ayacucho." *La República* (27 June 1992).

Schumacher, Edward. "Insurgency in Peru: The Unarmed Are Dying." *New York Times* (8 June 1983).

"Temor y muerte en las alturas." *Caretas* 734 (7 February 1983).

Vallejos, Rosa. "Volver a los 17: A diecisiete años del inicio de su cruenta 'lucha armada' Sendero Luminoso reaparece con aparatoso atentado." *Caretas* 1466 (May 1997).

Vargas Llosa, Mario. "Inquest in the Andes." *New York Times* (31 July 1983).

Secondary Sources

Abercrombie, Thomas. *Pathways of Memory and Power: Ethnography and History among an Andean People*. Madison: University of Wisconsin Press, 1998.

Aguirre, Carlos, and Charles F. Walker, eds. *Bandoleros, abigeos y montoneros: Criminalidad y violencia en el Perú, siglos XVIII–XX*. Lima: Instituto de Apoyo Agrario, 1990.

Ansión, Juan. *Desde el rincón de los muertos: El pensamiento mítico en Ayacucho*. Lima: Grupo de Estudios para el Desarrollo, 1987.

Axel, Brian Keith, ed. *From the Margins: Historical Anthropology and Its Futures*. Durham, N.C.: Duke University Press, 2003.

Badiou, Alain. *Being and Event*. Translated by Oliver Feltham. London: Continuum, 2005 (1988).

Bates, Robert H. "Probing the Sources of Political Order." In *Order, Conflict, and Violence*, edited by Stathis N. Kalyvas, Ian Shapiro, and Tarek Masoud. Cambridge: Cambridge University Press, 2008, 17–42.

Becker, Marc. *Indians and Leftists in the Making of Ecuador's Modern Indigenous Movements*. Durham, N.C.: Duke University Press, 2008.

Benavides, Maria-Victoria, and Rosa-Maria Fischer Ferreira. "Popular Responses to Urban Violence: Lynchings in Brazil." In *Vigilantism and the State in Modern Latin America: Essays on Extralegal Violence*, edited by Martha K. Huggins. New York: Praeger, 1991, 33–45.

Berg, Ronald H. "Peasant Responses to Shining Path in Andahuaylas." In *Shining Path of Peru*, edited by David Scott Palmer. New York: St. Martin's, 1994, 101–22.

Blanco, Hugo. *Land or Death: The Peasant Struggle in Peru*. Translated by Naomi Allen. New York: Pathfinder, 1972.

Bonilla, Heraclio. "La defensa del espacio comunal como fuente de conflicto: San Juan de Ocros vs. Pampas (Ayacucho), 1940–1970." Documento de Trabajo No. 34. Lima: Instituto de Estudios Peruanos, 1989.

Bonnell, Victoria E., and Lynn Hunt, eds. *Beyond the Cultural Turn: New Directions in the Study of Society and Culture*. Berkeley: University of California Press, 1999.

Bourque, Susan C., and David Scott Palmer. "Transforming the Rural Sector: Government Policy and Peasant Response." In *The Peruvian Experiment*, edited by Abraham F. Lowenthal. Princeton, N.J.: Princeton University Press, 1975, 179–219.

Burt, Jo-Marie. *Political Violence and the Authoritarian State in Peru: Silencing Civil Society*. New York: Palgrave MacMillan, 2007.

Calleros, Juan Carlos. *The Unfinished Transition to Democracy in Latin America*. New York: Routledge, 2009.

Cleaves, Peter S., and Henry Pease García. "State Autonomy and Military Policy Making." In *The Peruvian Experiment Reconsidered,* edited by Cynthia McClintock and Abraham F. Lowenthal. Princeton, N.J.: Princeton University Press, 1983, 209–44.

Contreras, Carlos, and Marcos Cueto. *Historia del Perú contemporáneo.* Lima: Instituto de Estudios Peruanos, 2000.

Cotler, Julio. "Democracy and National Integration in Peru." In *The Peruvian Experiment Reconsidered,* edited by Cynthia McClintock and Abraham F. Lowenthal. Princeton, N.J.: Princeton University Press, 1983, 3–38.

———. "The New Mode of Political Domination in Peru." In *The Peruvian Experiment,* edited by Abraham F. Lowenthal. Princeton, N.J.: Princeton University Press, 1975, 44–78.

———. "Traditional Haciendas and Communities in a Context of Political Mobilization in Peru." In *Agrarian Problems and Peasant Movements in Latin America,* edited by Rodolfo Stavenhagen. Garden City, N.Y.: Anchor, 1970, 533–58.

Coral Cordero, Isabel. "Women in War: Impact and Responses." In *The Shining and Other Paths,* edited by Steve J. Stern. Durham, N.C.: Duke University Press, 1998, 345–74.

Coronel, José. "Violencia política y respuestas campesinas en Huanta." In *Las rondas campesinas y la derrota de Sendero Luminoso,* edited by Carlos Iván Degregori et al. Lima: Instituto de Estudios Peruanos, 1996, 29–116.

Cristóbal, Juan, ed. *Uchuraccay, o el rostro de la barbarie.* Lima: San Marcos, 2003.

Davies, Thomas, Jr. *Indian Integration in Peru: A Half Century of Experience, 1900–1940.* Lincoln: University of Nebraska Press, 1974 (1970).

de la Cadena, Marisol. *Indigenous Mestizos: The Politics of Race and Culture in Cuzco, Peru, 1919–1991.* Durham, N.C.: Duke University Press, 2000.

de Souza Martins, José. "Lynchings—Life by a Thread: Street Justice in Brazil, 1979–1988." In *Vigilantism and the State in Modern Latin America: Essays on Extralegal Violence,* edited by Martha K. Huggins. New York: Praeger, 1991, 21–32.

Degregori, Carlos Iván. *Ayacucho, 1969–1979: El surgimiento de Sendero Luminoso.* Lima: Instituto de Estudios Peruanos, 1990.

———. "Harvesting Storms: Peasant *Rondas* and the Defeat of Sendero Luminoso in Ayacucho." In *Shining and Other Paths: War and Society in Peru, 1980–1995,* edited by Steve J. Stern. Durham, N.C.: Duke University Press, 1998, 128–57.

———. "Return to the Past." In *Shining Path of Peru,* edited by David Scott Palmer. New York: St. Martin's, 1994, 51–62.

———, ed. *Las rondas campesinas y la derrota de Sendero Luminoso.* Lima: Instituto de Estudios Peruanos, 1996.

———. *No hay país más diverso: Compendio de antropología peruana.* Lima: Instituto de Estudios Peruanos, 2000.

Del Pino, Ponciano. "Los campesinos en la guerra, o como la gente comienza a ponerse macho." In *Perú: El problema agrario en debate/SEPIA IV*, edited by Carlos Iván Degregori et al. Lima: SEPIA, 1992, 487–508.

———. "Family, Culture, and Revolution: Everyday Life with Sendero Luminoso." In *Shining and Other Paths: War and Society in Peru, 1980–1995*, edited by Steve J. Stern. Durham, N.C.: Duke University Press, 1998, 158–92.

———. "Looking to the Government: History, Politics, and the Production of Memory and Silences in Twentieth-Century Ayacucho, Peru." Ph.D. diss., University of Wisconsin, Madison, 2008.

———. "Tiempos de guerra y de dioses: Ronderos, evangélicos y Senderistas en el valle del río Apurímac." In *Las rondas campesinas y la derrota de Sendero Luminoso*, edited by Carlos Iván Degregori et al. Lima: Instituto de Estudios Peruanos, 1996, 117–88.

Dennis, Philip A. *Intervillage Conflict in Oaxaca*. New Brunswick, N.J.: Rutgers University Press, 1987.

Díaz Martínez, Antonio. *Ayacucho: Hambre y esperanza*. Lima: Mosca Azul, 1985 (1969).

Dirks, Nicholas B. "Annals of the Archive: Ethnographic Notes on the Sources of History." In *From the Margins: Historical Anthropology and Its Futures*, edited by Brian Keith Axel. Durham, N.C.: Duke University Press, 2003, 47–65.

Drewieniecki, Joanna. "Indigenous People, Law, and Politics in Peru." Paper prepared for the Latin American Studies Association Annual Meeting, Washington, D.C., 28–30 September 1995.

Durkheim, Emile. *The Elementary Forms of Religious Life*. Translated by Karen E. Fields. New York: Free Press, 1995 (1912).

Earls, John, and Irene Silverblatt. "Ayllus y etnías en la región Pampas-Qaracha: El impacto del imperio incaico." In *III Congreso peruano del hombre y la cultura andina*, vol. 1, edited by Ramino Matos M. Lima: Universidad Nacional Mayor de San Marcos, 1977, 157–77.

Favre, Henry. "Perú: Sendero Luminoso y horizontes oscuros." *Quehacer* 31 (1984): 25–34.

Fitzgerald, E. V. K. "State Capitalism in Peru: A Model of Economic Development and Its Limitations." In *The Peruvian Experiment Reconsidered*, edited by Cynthia McClintock and Abraham F. Lowenthal. Princeton, N.J.: Princeton University Press, 1983, 65–93.

Foucault, Michel. *The History of Sexuality*, vol. 1. Translated by Robert Hurley. New York: Vintage, 1990 (1978).

Fox, Richard G., and Orin Starn. "Introduction." In *Between Resistance and Revolution: Cultural Politics and Social Protest*, edited by Richard G. Fox and Orin Starn. New Brunswick, N.J.: Rutgers University Press, 1997, 1–16.

Fumerton, Mario. *From Victims to Heroes: Peasant Counter-rebellion and Civil War in Ayacucho, Peru, 1980–2000.* Amsterdam: Rozenberg, 2002.

Gamarra, Jefrey. "Exploración sobre las economías campesinas en un contexto de posviolencia en los andes peruanos." In *El desplazamiento y la integración de la economía rural al mercado: Los casos de Ayacucho, Perú,* edited by Tatsuya Shimizu, Alfredo Valencia, and Jefrey Gamarra. Ayacucho City: Institute of Developing Economies, 2003, 53–72.

García, María Elena. *Making Indigenous Citizens: Identity, Development, and Multicultural Activism in Peru.* Stanford, Calif.: Stanford University Press, 2005.

———. "Introduction: Indigenous Encounters in Contemporary Peru." *Latin American and Caribbean Ethnic Studies* 3:3 (November 2008): 217–26.

Gleijeses, Piero. *Shattered Hope: The Guatemalan Revolution and the United States, 1944–1954.* Princeton, N.J.: Princeton University Press, 1991.

Goldstein, Daniel M. *The Spectacular City: Violence and Performance in Urban Bolivia.* Durham, N.C.: Duke University Press, 2004.

Gonzalez, Olga M. *Unveiling Secrets of War in the Peruvian Andes.* Chicago: University of Chicago Press, 2011.

Gorriti, Gustavo. *The Shining Path: A History of the Millenarian War in Peru.* Translated by Robin Kirk. Chapel Hill: University of North Carolina Press, 1999 (1990).

———. "Shining Path's Stalin and Trotsky." In *Shining Path of Peru.* Edited by David Scott Palmer. New York: St. Martin's, 1994 (1992), 167–88.

Gupta, Dipak K. *Understanding Terrorism and Political Violence: The Life Cycle of Birth, Growth, Transformation, and Demise.* New York: Routledge, 2008.

Guzmán Reynoso, Abimael. "We Are the Initiators." In *The Peru Reader: History, Culture, Politics,* edited by Orin Starn et al. Durham, N.C.: Duke University Press, 1995, 310–15.

Hammergren, Linn A. *The Politics of Justice and Justice Reform in Latin America.* Boulder, Colo.: Westview, 1998.

Handelman, Howard. *Struggle in the Andes: Peasant Political Mobilization in Peru.* Austin: University of Texas Press, 1975.

Harding, Colin. "Land Reform and Social Conflict in Peru." In *The Peruvian Experiment,* edited by Abraham F. Lowenthal. Princeton, N.J.: Princeton University Press, 1975, 220–53.

Harris, Olivia. "Condor and Bull: The Ambiguities of Masculinity in Northern Potosí." In *Sex and Violence: Issues in Representation and Experience,* edited by Penelope Harvey and Peter Gow. London: Routledge, 1994, 44–65.

Harvey, Penelope. "Domestic Violence in the Peruvian Andes." In *Sex and Violence: Issues in Representation and Experience,* edited by Penelope Harvey and Peter Gow. London: Routledge, 1994, 66–89.

Heilman, Jaymie Patricia. *Before the Shining Path: Politics in Rural Ayacucho, 1895–1980.* Stanford, Calif.: Stanford University Press, 2010.

———. "Leader and Led: Hugo Blanco, La Concepción Peasants, and the Relationships of Revolution." M.A. thesis, University of Wisconsin, Madison, 2000.

Hinojosa, Iván. "On Poor Relations and the Nouveau Riche: Shining Path and the Radical Peruvian Left." In *Shining and Other Paths*, edited by Steve J. Stern. Durham, N.C.: Duke University Press, 1998, 60–83.

Hobsbawm, Eric J. "Peasant Land Occupations." *Past and Present* 62 (February 1974): 120–52.

Hobsbawm, Eric J., and Terence Ranger, eds. *The Invention of Tradition.* Cambridge: Cambridge University Press, 1992.

Hosoya, Hiromi. *La memoria post-colonial: Tiempo, espacio y discursos sobre los sucesos de Uchuraccay.* Documento de Trabajo. Lima: Instituto de Estudios Peruanos, 2003.

Huillca, Hugo. "El diálogo con Sendero es imposible." In *Hablan los ronderos: La búsqueda por la paz en los Andes*, edited by Orin Starn. Lima: Instituto de Estudios Peruanos, 1993, 44–45.

Hünefeldt, Christine. *Liberalism in the Bedroom: Quarreling Spouses in Nineteenth-Century Lima.* University Park: Pennsylvania State University Press, 2000.

———. "The Rural Landscape and Changing Political Awareness: Enterprises, Agrarian Producers, and Peasant Communities, 1969–1994." In *The Peruvian Labyrinth: Polity, Society, Economy*, edited by Maxwell A. Cameron and Philip Mauceri. University Park: Pennsylvania State University Press, 1997, 107–33.

Hunt, Lynn, ed. *The New Cultural History.* Berkeley: University of California Press, 1989.

Isbell, Billie Jean. "Andean Structures and Activities: Towards a Study of Transformations of Traditional Concepts in a Central Highland Peasant Community." Ph.D. diss., University of Illinois, Champaign-Urbana, 1973.

———. *To Defend Ourselves: Ecology and Ritual in an Andean Village.* Prospect Heights, Ill.: Waveland, 1985 (1978).

———. "Shining Path and Peasant Responses in Rural Ayacucho." In *Shining Path of Peru*, edited by David Scott Palmer. New York: St. Martin's, 1994 (1992), 77–99.

Kalyvas, Stathis N. *The Logic of Violence in Civil War.* Cambridge: Cambridge University Press, 2006.

Kirk, Robin. *Grabado en piedra: Las mujeres de Sendero Luminoso.* Lima: Instituto de Estudios Peruanos, 1993.

Klein, Herbert S. *Bolivia: The Evolution of a Multi-ethnic Society.* Oxford: Oxford University Press, 1992 (1982).

Knight, Peter T. "New Forms of Economic Organization in Peru: Toward Workers' Self-Management." In *The Peruvian Experiment*, edited by Abraham F. Lowenthal. Princeton, N.J.: Princeton University Press, 1975, 350–401.

Kruijt, Dirk. "Exercises in State Terrorism: The Counter-insurgency Campaigns in Guatemala and Peru." In *Societies of Fear: The Legacy of Civil War, Violence, and Terror in Latin America*, edited by Kees Koonings and Dirk Kruijt. London: Zed, 1999, 33–62.

La Serna, Miguel. "The Corner of the Living: Local Power Relations and Indigenous Perceptions in Ayacucho, Peru, 1940–1983." Ph.D. diss., University of California, San Diego, 2008.

———. "*Murió comiendo rata*: Power Relations in Pre-Sendero Ayacucho, Peru, 1940–1983." *A Contracorriente* 9:2 (Winter 2012), forthcoming.

———. "'Thank God for the Violence': Church-Peasant Relations on the Eve of the Shining Path Insurgency." Paper presented at the American Historical Association–Conference on Latin American History annual meeting, San Diego, 7–10 January 2010.

———. "To Cross the River of Blood: How an Inter-community Conflict Is Linked to the Peruvian Civil War, 1940–1983." In *Power, Culture, and Violence in the Andes*, edited by Christine Hünefeldt and Milos Kokotovic. Brighton, U.K.: Sussex Academic Press, 2009, 110–44.

La Serna, Miguel, and Julián Berrocal Flores. "Gritos en el silencio: La campaña electoral en Huaychao." *Quehacer* 159 (March–April 2006): 42–47.

Larson, Brooke. *Trials of Nation Making: Liberalism, Race, and Ethnicity in the Andes*. Cambridge: Cambridge University Press, 2004.

Lobo, Susan. *A House of My Own: Social Organization in the Squatter Settlements in Lima, Peru*. Tucson: University of Arizona Press, 1982.

Lowenthal, Abraham F. "Peru's Ambiguous Revolution." In *The Peruvian Experiment*, edited by Abraham F. Lowenthal. Princeton, N.J.: Princeton University Press, 1975, 3–43.

Mallon, Florencia. *Courage Tastes of Blood: The Mapuche Community of Nicolás Ailío and the Chilean State, 1906–2001*. Durham, N.C.: Duke University Press, 2005.

———. *Peasant and Nation: The Making of Postcolonial Mexico and Peru*. Berkeley: University of California Press, 1995.

Manrique, Nelson. "La década de la violencia." *Márgenes* 3:5–6 (1989): 137–82.

———. *El tiempo del miedo: La violencia política en el Perú, 1980–1996*. Lima: Fondo Editorial del Congreso del Perú, 2002.

Matos Mar, José. *Las barriadas de Lima, 1957*. Lima: Instituto de Estudios Peruanos, 1977.

Mariátegui, José Carlos. *Seven Interpretive Essays on Peruvian Reality*. Translated by Marjory Urquidi. Austin: University of Texas Press, 1971 (1928).

Mayer, Enrique. "Peru in Deep Trouble: Mario Vargas Llosa's 'Inquest in the Andes' Reexamined." *Cultural Anthropology* 6:4 (November 1991): 466–504.

———. *Ugly Stories of the Peruvian Agrarian Reform*. Durham, N.C.: Duke University Press, 2000.

Mayer, Eric. "State Policy and Community Conflict in Bolivia and Peru, 1900–1980." Ph.D. diss., University of California, San Diego, 1995.

Mazzei, Julie. *Death Squads or Self-Defense Forces? How Paramilitary Groups Emerge and Challenge Democracy in Latin America*. Chapel Hill: University of North Carolina Press, 2009.

McClintock, Cynthia. *Peasant Cooperatives and Political Change in Peru*. Princeton, N.J.: Princeton University Press, 1981.

———. "Why Peasants Rebel: The Case of Peru's Sendero Luminoso." *World Politics* 37 (1984): 48–84.

Méndez, Cecilia. *The Plebeian Republic: The Huanta Rebellion and the Making of the Peruvian State, 1820–1850*. Durham, N.C.: Duke University Press, 2005.

———. "The Power of Naming, or the Construction of Ethnic and National Identities in Peru: Myth, History, and the Iquichanos." *Past and Present* 171 (May 2001): 125–60.

Mendoza Machaca, Valeriano. "Quispillaccta: Cosmovisión del clima y su importancia en la actividad agropecuaria." Thesis, Universidad Nacional San Cristóbal de Huamanga, 1998.

Merick, Thomas. "Population Pressures in Latin America." *Population Bulletin* 41:3 (July 1986): 1–50.

Migdal, Joel S. *Peasants, Politics, and Revolution: Pressures toward Political and Social Changes in the Third World*. Princeton, N.J.: Princeton University Press, 1974.

Mitchell, William P. *Peasants on the Edge: Crop, Cult, and Crisis in the Andes*. Austin: University of Texas Press, 1991.

———. *Voices from the Global Margin: Confronting Poverty and Inventing New Lives in the Andes*. Austin: University of Texas Press, 2006.

Moore, Barrington, Jr. *Social Origins of Dictatorship and Democracy: Lord and Peasant in the Making of the Modern World*. Boston: Beacon, 1993 (1966).

Montoya, Rodrigo. *Eulogio de la antropología*. Lima: Fondo Editorial de la Facultad de Ciencias Sociales Universidad Nacional Mayor de San Marcos, 2005.

———. *Lucha por la tierra, reformas agrarias y capitalismo en el Perú del siglo XX*. Lima: Mosca Azul, 1989.

———. "¿Un movimiento político indígena en Perú? Desafío cercano." *América Latina en movimiento* (24 May 2008).

Morote Barrionuevo, Osmán. "Luchas de clases en las zonas altas de Huanta (Distrito de Santillana)." Thesis, Universidad Nacional San Cristóbal de Huamanga, 1970.

Muñoz Ruiz, Urbano, and Oseas Núñez Espinoza. *Los Kanas de Quispillaccta: Historia de un pueblo quechua*. Ayacucho City: Territorio Kana, 2006.

Murra, John V. "El control vertical de un máximo de pisos ecológicos en la economía." In *Formaciones económicas y políticas del mundo andino*. Lima: Instituto de Estudios Peruanos, 1975, 59–115.

Naveda Felix, Igidio. "The Reconstitution of Indigenous Peoples in the Peruvian Andes." *Latin American and Caribbean Ethnic Studies* 3:3 (November 2008): 309–17.

Núñez, Germán. *Pensamiento político peruano, siglo XX.* Lima: Universidad de Lima, 1993.

Orlove, Benjamin. "La posición de los abigeos en la sociedad regional: El bandolerismo social en el Cusco en vísperas de la reforma agraria." In *Bandoleros, abigeos y montoneros: Criminalidad y violencia en el Perú, siglos XVIII–XX,* edited by Carlos Aguirre and Charles F. Walker. Lima: Instituto de Apoyo Agrario, 1990, 278–305.

Paige, Jeffery M. *Agrarian Revolution.* New York: Free Press, 1975.

Palmer, David Scott. "Revolution from Above: Military Government and Popular Participation in Peru, 1968–1972." Ph.D. diss. Cornell University, 1973.

Pásara, Luís. *Derecho y sociedad en el Perú.* Lima: Virrey, 1988.

Pederson, Duncan, Jefrey Gamarra, María Elena Planas, and Consuelo Errázuruz. "Violencia política y salud en las comunidades alto-andinas de Ayacucho, Perú." Documento de Trabajo. Ayacucho City: Instituto de Investigación y Promoción del Desarrollo y Paz en Ayacucho (IPAZ), 2001.

Peña Jumpa, Antonio. *Justicia comunal en los Andes del Perú: El caso de Calahuyo.* Lima: Pontificia Universidad Católica del Perú, 1998.

Pérez, Louis, Jr. *Cuba in the American Imagination: Metaphor and the Imperial Ethos.* Chapel Hill: University of North Carolina Press, 2008.

———. *To Die in Cuba: Suicide and Society.* Chapel Hill: University of North Carolina Press, 2005.

Platt, Tristan. "The Andean Soldiers of Christ: Confraternity Organization, the Mass of the Sun and Regenerative Warfare in Rural Potosí (Eighteenth–Twentieth Centuries)." *Journal de la Société des Américanistes* 73 (1987): 139–92.

Poole, Deborah. "Between Threat and Guarantee: Justice and Community in the Margins of the Peruvian State." In *Anthropology in the Margins of the State,* edited by Veena Das and Deborah Poole. Santa Fe, N.M.: School of American Research Press, 2004, 35–66.

———. "Landscapes of Power in a Cattle-Rustling Culture of Southern Andean Peru." *Dialectical Anthropology* 12 (1988): 367–98.

———. "Performance, Domination and Identity in the *Tierras Bravas* of Chumbivilcas (Cusco)." In *Unruly Order: Violence, Power, and Cultural Identity in the High Provinces of Southern Peru,* edited by Deborah Poole. Boulder, Colo.: Westview, 1994, 97–132.

Poole, Deborah, and Gerardo Rénique. *Peru: Time of Fear.* London: Latin America Bureau, 1992.

Popkin, Samuel L. *The Rational Peasant: The Political Economy of Rural Society in Vietnam.* Berkeley: University of California Press, 1979.

Postero, Nancy Grey. *Now We Are Citizens: Indigenous Politics in Postmulticultural Bolivia*. Stanford, Calif.: Stanford University Press, 2007.

Postero, Nancy, and Leon Zamosc, eds. *The Struggle for Indian Rights in Latin America*. London: Sussex Academic Press, 2004.

Rappaport, Joanne. *The Politics of Memory: Native Historical Interpretation in the Colombian Andes*. Durham, N.C.: Duke University Press, 1998.

Rasnake, Roger Neil. *Domination and Cultural Resistance: Authority and Power among an Andean People*. Durham, N.C.: Duke University Press, 1988.

Rivera Cusicanqui, Silvia. *Oppressed but Not Defeated: Peasant Struggles among the Aymara and Qhechwa in Bolivia, 1900–1980*. Geneva: United Nations Research Institute for Social Development, 1987.

Rochlin, James F. *Vanguard Revolutionaries in Latin America: Peru, Colombia, Mexico*. London: Lynne Rienner, 2003.

Roldán, Mary. *Blood and Fire: "La Violencia" in Antioquia, Colombia, 1946–1953*. Durham, N.C.: Duke University Press, 2002.

Sabot, Richard H. "Introduction." In *Migration and the Labor Market in Developing Countries*, edited by Richard H. Sabot. Boulder, Colo.: Westview, 1982, 1–11.

Sánchez Villagómez, Marté. *Pensar los "Senderos" olvidados de historia y memoria: La violencia política en las comunidades de Chuschi y Quispillaccta, 1980–1991*. Lima: Fondo Editorial de la Facultad de Ciencias Sociales Universidad Nacional Mayor San Marcos, 2007.

Schydlowsky, Daniel M., and Juan Wicht. "The Anatomy of an Economic Failure." In *The Peruvian Experiment Reconsidered*, edited by Cynthia McClintock and Abraham F. Lowenthal. Princeton, N.J.: Princeton University Press, 1983, 94–143.

Skocpol, Theda. *States and Social Revolutions: A Comparative Analysis of France, Russia, and China*. Cambridge: Cambridge University Press, 1979.

Scott, James C. *The Moral Economy of the Peasant: Rebellion and Subsistence in Southeast Asia*. New Haven, Conn.: Yale University Press, 1976.

Serulnikov, Sergio. *Subverting Colonial Authority: Challenges to Spanish Rule in Eighteenth-Century Southern Andes*. Durham, N.C.: Duke University Press, 2003.

Smith, Gavin. *Livelihood and Resistance: Peasants and the Politics of Land in Peru*. Berkeley: University of California Press, 1989.

Smith, Michael L. *Entre dos fuegos: ONG, desarrollo rural y violencia política*. Lima: Instituto de Estudios Peruanos, 1992.

Starn, Orin. "Missing the Revolution: Anthropologists and the War in Peru." *Cultural Anthropology* 6:3 (1991): 63–91.

———. *Nightwatch: The Politics of Protest in the Andes*. Durham, N.C.: Duke University Press, 1999.

———. "La resistencia de Huanta." *Quehacer* 84 (1993): 35.

————. "Villagers at Arms: War and Counterrevolution in Peru's Andes." In *Between Resistance and Revolution: Cultural Politics and Social Protest*, edited by Richard G. Fox and Orin Starn. New Brunswick, N.J.: Rutgers University Press, 1997, 223–49.

————, ed. *Hablan los ronderos: La búsqueda por la paz en los Andes*. Lima: Instituto de Estudios Peruanos, 1993.

Stavenhagen, Rodolfo, ed. *Agrarian Problems and Peasant Movements in Latin America*. Garden City, N.Y.: Anchor, 1970.

Stein, William W. *Deconstructing Development Discourse in Peru: A Meta-ethnography of the Modernity Project at Vicos*. Lanham, Md.: University Press of America, 2002.

Stern, Steve J. "Introduction to Part Four." In *Shining and Other Paths*, edited by Steve J. Stern. Durham, N.C.: Duke University Press, 1998, 341–44.

————, ed., *Shining and Other Paths: War and Society in Peru, 1980–1995*. Durham, N.C.: Duke University Press, 1998.

Stoll, David. *Between Two Armies in the Ixil Towns of Guatemala*. New York: Columbia University Press, 1993.

Sweig, Julia. *Inside the Cuban Revolution: Fidel Castro and the Urban Underground*. Cambridge: Harvard University Press, 2002.

Tapia, Carlos. *Autodefensa armada del campesinado*. Lima: Centro de Estudios para el Desarrollo y la Pacificación, 1995.

Tarazona-Sevillano, Gabriela. "The Organization of Shining Path." In *Shining Path of Peru*, edited by David Scott Palmer. New York: St. Martin's, 1994, 189–208.

Taylor, Lewis. *Shining Path: Guerrilla War in Peru's Northern Highlands*. Liverpool: Liverpool University Press, 2006.

Tilly, Charles. *The Politics of Collective Violence*. Cambridge: Cambridge University Press, 2003.

Theidon, Kimberly. *Entre prójimos: El conflicto armado interno y la política de la reconciliación en el Perú*. Lima: Instituto de Estudios Peruanos, 2004.

————. "La micropolítica de la reconciliación: Práctica de la justicia en comunidades rurales ayacuchanas." *Allpanchis* 60 (2002): 113–41.

————. "Terror's Talk: Fieldwork and War." *Dialectical Anthropology* 26 (2001): 19–35.

————. "Traumatic States: Violence and Reconciliation in Peru." Ph.D. diss., University of California, Berkeley, 2002.

Thompson, E. P. "The Moral Economy of the English Crowd in the Eighteenth Century." *Past and Present* 50 (February 1971): 76–136.

Thomson, Sinclair. *We Alone Will Rule: Native Politics in the Age of Insurgency*. Madison: University of Wisconsin Press, 2002.

Thurner, Mark. *From Two Republics to One Divided: Contradictions of Postcolonial Nationmaking in Andean Peru*. Durham, N.C.: Duke University Press, 1997.

Urton, Gary. *The Social Life of Numbers: A Quechua Ontology of Numbers and Philosophy of Arithmetic*. Austin: University of Texas Press, 1997.

Van Young, Eric. "Conflict and Solidarity in Indian Village Life: The Guadalajara Region in the Late Colonial Period," *Hispanic American Historical Review* 64 (February 1984): 55–79.

———. "The New Cultural History Comes to Old Mexico." *Hispanic American Historical Review* 79:2 (May 1999): 211–47.

———. *The Other Rebellion: Popular Violence, Ideology, and the Mexican Struggle for Independence, 1810–1821*. Stanford, Calif.: Stanford University Press, 2001.

Vanderwood, Paul. *The Power of God against the Guns of Government: Religious Upheaval in Mexico at the Turn of the Nineteenth Century*. Stanford, Calif.: Stanford University Press, 1998.

Wade, Peter. *Race and Ethnicity in Latin America*. Chicago: Pluto, 1997.

Walker, Charles. *Smoldering Ashes: Cuzco and the Creation of Republican Peru, 1780–1840*. Durham, N.C.: Duke University Press, 1999.

Wickham-Crowley, Timothy P. *Guerrillas and Revolution in Latin America: A Comparative Study of Insurgencies and Regimes since 1956*. Princeton, N.J.: Princeton University Press, 1992.

Wolf, Eric. *Peasant Wars of the Twentieth Century*. Norman: University of Oklahoma Press, 1999 (1969).

Yezer, Caroline. "Anxious Citizenship: Insecurity, Apocalypse and War Memories in Peru's Andes." Ph.D. diss., Duke University, 2007.

———. "Who Wants to Know? Rumors, Suspicions, and Opposition to Truth-Telling in Ayacucho." *Latin American and Caribbean Ethnic Studies* 3:3 (November 2008): 271–89.

Zuidema, Tom R. "Algunos problemas etnohistóricos del Departamento de Ayacucho." *Wamani* 1:1 (Ayacucho City, 1966): 68–75.

Abercrombie, Thomas, 15

Abigeato (livestock theft): by adolescents, 36–38; Felipe Aycha as *abigeo* "boss," 33–35, 109, 146, 151, 152; in Chuschi, 31–35, 41, 42, 82–84, 109, 110, 146, 151, 154; Civil Guard's response to, 23; court cases on, 25–26, 29–30, 36–37, 95–96; economic sanctions for, 49, 56, 96, 97; and hacendados, 127–28; in Huaychao, 41–43, 54–56, 95–98; indigenous peasants' condemnation of, 19; intervillage theft, 82–84, 85, 95–98, 160–61; justices of the peace on, 21; lieutenant governor's administration of justice for, 54–56; lieutenant governor's coverup of, 54–55; and masculinity, 41, 49; punishment for and violence against perpetrators of, 21, 24, 49–51, 56, 74, 79–81, 83, 96, 97, 149–51, 153–54, 159, 160–61, 163, 190–91, 201; in Quispillaccta, 25–26, 28, 29–31, 41, 149–51, 153–54; by Quispillacctinos against Chuschino families, 69, 70; social stigma of, 41

Achallma, Teobaldo: abandonment of paternal duties by, 27, 28, 149–50; blacklisting of, by Shining Path, 154; court case against, 25–26; execution of, by Shining Path, 149, 153, 161, 163–64; as free-rider, 27, 28, 149–50; incest accusations against, 26, 27, 149–50; landholdings of, 27; livestock theft by, 25–26, 28, 82–84, 149, 160; marital problems of, 26–27, 149–50

Achallma, Teófilo, 36

Administradores (foremen of haciendas), 46

Adolescents: and conflict between Chuschi and Quispillaccta, 84–85, 159–60, 162; crime by, 35–38, 40, 152; education of, 40; in *rondas campesinas*, 201–2; and Shining Path, 85, 141, 144, 145–46, 156, 162, 165–66,

173, 196, 201; troubled youth in Chuschi, 35–38, 40, 152. *See also* National University of San Cristóbal de Huamanga

Adultery, 19, 30, 50, 51, 54, 55, 88, 149–50, 163

Afghanistan, 216, 217

Africa, 168

Agrarian Production Cooperatives (CAPS), 106

Agrarian Reform Law, 6, 45, 54, 98–99, 187. *See also* Land reform

Agrarian Tribunal (Land Court), 105, 118

Agriculture: census of, 54; crops cultivated in Chuschi, 3; and end of land-tenure system, 63, 102–4, 106, 134, 137; in Huaychao, 6; irrigation water for, 118; and livestock, 4; modernization of, in developing countries, 102; and peasant cooperatives, 105–6; price controls in, 39; and Proyecto Mujer, 208; by *semanero* workers, 121–22, 128–29; size of *minifundios* in Chuschi, 4. *See also* Food; Hacendados; Land reform

Aguardiente (cane liquor), 93, 101, 110, 128, 132, 169, 227 (n. 96). *See also* Alcohol use

Aguilar, Alberto, 180

Aguilar, Faustino, 98–99

Aguilar, Luis F., 67

Albacea (apprentice or personal servant to *varayoqs*), 46

Alcántara Cárdenas, Vidal, 53

Alcohol use: aguardiente (cane liquor), 93, 101, 110, 128, 132, 169, 227 (n. 96); *chicha* (beer), 87, 110, 128, 227 (n. 96); *chicha de molle* (peppercorn beer), 86; drunkenness of adult men, 30, 31, 33, 145, 150–51, 158; at festivals and celebrations, 86, 87, 91, 93, 94, 170–71; and reciprocity code, 184; during Tiyarikuy fiesta, 227–28 (n. 96);

tragito (shot of liquor), 205; during *vara* visits, 52; by *varayoqs* at home only, 47

Alejandra, *Mama. See* Ccente, Alejandra; Vilma, Alejandra

Allcca, Alejandro, 84

Allcca, Dámaso, 78–81

Allcca family, 32–33

Alocer, Mateo, 110

Ancash Department, 39

Andean peasants. *See* Chuschi; Counterinsurgency; Huaychao; Indigenous peasants; Shining Path

Animals. See *Abigeato*; Livestock

Antisubversive Civil Defense (DECAS), 171, 199, 203

"Apotheosis of agency," 8–9

Apurímac River Valley, 194–95, 199, 203

Arbenz, Jacobo, 103

Army, Peruvian, 168–69, 181, 187, 192, 200

Aronés, Agripino, 79

Asociación Padres de Familia (Parents' Association), 208

Assembly room (*despacho*), 1, 43–44, 47, 56, 88, 97, 175, 178

Authority. *See* Justice system; Lieutenant governors; Paternalism; Political hierarchy; Power relationships; *Qalas*; *Varayoqs*

Ayacucho City: Teobaldo Achallma's travel to, for legal matter, 83; Ignacio Aycha in, 35, 38; bishop in, 69; cemetery in, 81; hospital in, 75; Ernesto Jaime's military kidnapping and relocation to, 207; Fulgencio Makta in, 145–48, 155–56, 159–60, 194; migration to, 40; road connecting Chuschi with, 4; San Juan Bautista fair in, 78; Shining Path guerrilla activities in, 142, 143; Yanamilla Maximum Security Prison in, 187–89. *See also* National University of San Cristóbal de Huamanga

Ayacucho Department: CEISA in, 62; counterinsurgency in, 168–71; ecological crisis during 1940s in, 39; emigration from, 39, 40; fatalities from civil war in,

1; hierarchization in, 81–82; influences on, during late twentieth century, 9; and land reform, 107; local justice system in, 24; meaning of name of, 1–2; Peruvian Communist Party in, 139–45; *verga* in, 241 (n. 91). *See also* Chuschi District; Chuschi; Huaychao; Shining Path

Aycha, Felipe: as *abigeo* "boss," 33–35, 109, 146, 151, 152; abuse of authority by, 110, 151, 152; alcohol use by, 31, 33; arrest of, 34; blacklisting of, by Shining Path, 151–52, 154; court case against, 32; crimes of, 31–35, 151; execution of, by Shining Path, 152, 153; execution of wife of, by Shining Path, 152; intimidation by, 34–35, 39, 109–10; and March of Death (1960), 75–77, 110; physical appearance of, 31, 34, 39; as *qala*, 109–10, 119; racial identity of, 109; son of, 35–38; spousal abuse by, 33, 151; temper of and violence by, 109–10

Aycha, Ignacio: as delinquent youth, 35–38, 40, 152; and Shining Path, 146, 148, 151, 152; as university student, 35, 38, 40

Aymara peasants and Aymara language, 24, 81–82, 105

Azcarza, Humberto, 13–14

Barboza, Jorge, 192

Barriadas (squatter settlements), 39

Bautista, Ramón, 57–58

Bedriñana, Clotilde, 111–15, 240 (n. 66)

Belaúnde Terry, Fernando, 39, 64, 104–5, 145, 167, 173

Berrocal, Julián (research assistant): on age of oldest resident of Huaychao, 71–72; and Felipe Aycha, 33–34; and distribution of clothing and school supplies in Chuschi, 211; on Pedro Huamán as lieutenant governor, 55; initial visit of, to Chuschi, 13; and *juez rumi*, 88–89; and kinship networks in Huaychao, 86; and libation ceremony, 101; and Mardonio, 188–89; on punishment by *varayoqs*, 49–50; as Quechua speaker, 71; and Rejas, 30, 31;

and *verga* used by Chávez, 125; and women's role in intervillage conflicts, 81

Blanco, Hugo, 64, 104

Blanco, Vicente: abuse of political authority by, 116–18, 155, 156; assault of Clotilde Bedriñana by, 113–14; attempts to expel from Chuschi, 118; complaints and criminal charges against, 14, 111–18, 240 (n. 66); as *gamonal*, 116; interview of, by La Serna, 14; land fraud by, 116–17; as mestizo, 116; as *qala*, 111–19, 155, 156; as schoolteacher, 112, 116–17; sexual misconduct by, 111–17, 155, 240 (n. 66); and Shining Path, 14; Shining Path popular trial of, 155; on women's role in intervillage conflicts, 81

Bolivia, 63, 94–95, 103, 118–19, 215

Brazil, 21

Brígida, *Mama. See* Cayetano, Brígida

Bullfights, 126

Cabezas, Juana: on Christmas visit to Carhuahurán, 98; as *comandas* (militia leader), 206–7, 208; leadership of, 208–9; on male violence, 92–93; on rape and attempted rape, 92–93; on *ronderos*, 200; on Shining Path and counterinsurgency, 172–73, 176–77, 190, 191, 200

Cabezas negras ("black heads" or Peruvian security forces), 180, 249 (n. 55)

CACIDH (General Committee for Civil Self-Defense and Development of Huanta Province), 201

CADs (Self-Defense Committees), 199–200

Calahuyo (Puno Department), 24

Canas, 81

Canchacancha, xvii, 4, 211

Candelario, 82–83

Cane liquor. *See* Aguardiente

Caporales (foremen of haciendas), 46, 56–59

CAPS (Agrarian Production Cooperatives), 106

Cárdenas, Antonio, 203

Cárdenas, Dolores, 120

Caretas, 187, 197, 209–10, 212

Cargo system, 57, 179, 182

Carhuahurán: executions of criminals by local authorities in, 24; military base in, 168, 211; political jurisdiction of, over Huaychao, 98–99, 127; population of, 168; Shining Path and counterinsurgency in, 168, 174, 179, 187–91, 201

Carhuanca (Vilcashuamán Province), 164, 241 (n. 91)

Carnival: alcohol use during, 86, 91, 93, 94; *cortamonte* ritual during, 93, 171, 236 (n. 137); and counterinsurgency in Sacsamarca, 170–71; fights during, 48–49, 91–95; in Huaychao, 47, 86, 91–94; sexual relations and rape during, 47, 91–92

Casavilca, Cayetana, 29

Castro, Fidel, 138

Catholic Church, 118, 153

Cattle. *See Abigeato*; Livestock

Cavalcanti Gamboa, Mario, 127

Cayetano, Brígida, 49, 129–30, 133

Cayetano, Francisco, 41–42

Cayetano, Saturnino, 95–96

Cayllahua, Felicíta, 240 (n. 66)

Cayllahua, Gregorio, 161, 162–63, 246 (n. 81)

Cayllahua, Juan, 194

Cayllahua, Mariano, 161

Ccallocunto, Sabino, 79

Ccallocunto, Teresa, 26–27

Ccallocunto Núñez, Asunción, 74, 75, 78

Ccarasencca, 181, 192, 201

Ccente, Alejandra: on *caporales*, 59; on fights during Carnival, 48–49; on hacendados, 130–31; on injuries and death of Yaranqa, 93–94; on land reform, 133; on lieutenant governor's authority, 55, 130; on Shining Path and counterinsurgency, 174, 178, 197; on Tiyarikuy fiesta, 51; on *varayoqs*, 47, 55, 130

Ccente, Elías, 42

Ccente, Ernestina: on *caporales*, 58, 59; on hacendados, 122, 123, 125, 126, 128, 129

Ccente, Jacinto, 202

Ccente, Jesús, 53

Ccente, Lucas, 42–43, 180, 202

CDCs (Civil Defense Patrols), 181

CEISA (Center for Social Research of Ayacucho), 62

Censo agropecuario (agriculture and livestock census), 54

Center for Social Research of Ayacucho (CEISA), 62

"Certificates of conduct," 25, 28, 224 (n. 24)

Chaca, 200, 202

Chacolla, xvii, 4

Chaqueccocha, 33

Chaqwa (disorder), 196

Chávez, Maximiliano, 120, 128

Chávez, Pedro, 120

Chávez, Rafael, 120–31, 184

Chávez, Mrs. Rafael, 129–30

Chicha (beer), 86, 87, 110, 128, 227 (n. 96). *See also* Alcohol use

Chicotes (whips), 34, 48, 49–50, 56, 59, 93, 97, 125, 127, 129, 155

Chile, 63

Chinchausuri hacienda, 64

Chinese Communist Party, 138, 140, 143

Chinese Nationalists, 102

Chipana, Bernardo: abuse of authority by, 111, 154–55; livestock theft by, 32–33, 110, 111, 154; as *qala*, 110–11, 119, 154–55, 239 (n. 50); Shining Path popular trial of, 154–55

Christmas, 98

Chuchón, Vidal, 31–32

Chuqui, 192

Church. *See* Catholic Church; Evangelical Protestantism

Chuschi District: capital of, 2; political hierarchy in, 22; Shining Path in, 145–63; villages in, 4

Chuschi River, 65, 66, 81

Chuschi: adult misfits in, 32–35, 60–61; agriculture in, 2–3; attacks by Quispillacctinos (1960) on Lachocc chapel and homes of Chuschinos, 69–73; boundary disputes between Quispillaccta

and, 65, 67–70; buildings in, 2; bureaucratic officials in, 52; burning of ballot boxes and administrative center (1980) by Senderistas in, 136, 137, 142, 147, 162–63, 246 (n. 81); Catholic Church in, 118, 153; climate of, 2–3; Club de Madres in, 207; conflict between Quispillaccta and, 13, 62, 65–85, 99–100, 157–63; Consejo (town council) in, 108–18, 136; counterinsurgency in, 193–94; crime in, 31–35, 60–61; description of, 2–4; deviants in, 25–38, 149–54; early altercations between Quispillacctinos and Chuschinos, 68–73; ecology and landscape of, 2–3; emigration from, 198; and *gamonalismo*, 108, 110, 116, 194; improvements in, after Peruvian civil war, 210–11; Independence Day festivities in, 211; ILA in, 1, 7, 136–37, 147, 158, 162–63, 167, 246 (n. 81); irrigation water in, 118; livestock in, 4; livestock theft in, 33–35, 41, 42, 82–84, 109, 110, 146, 151, 154, 160–61; local justice system in, 19–20, 32–35, 60–61, 114; main square in, 2, 3; March of Death (1960) against Quispillaccta by Chuschinos, 70, 73–78, 84, 110, 157, 160, 194; market and merchants in, 4, 118; medical post in, 118; numerical hyperbole by Chuschinos on number of Quispillacctino attackers, 71; origins and ethnic identity of Chuschinos, 81–82, 85, 99–100; peace accord (1941) between Quispillaccta and, 67, 68; petition of, for legal recognition as *comunidad indígena*, 65, 67; police station in, 210–11; population of, 2; post office in, 117; *qalas* in, 102, 108–19, 135, 154–57, 193–94; and rape charges against Chuschinos, 72; reconciliation between Quispillaccta and, 161, 162; religious icons in, 69, 73, 100, 231 (n. 40); road in, 2, 4; scholarly and media attention on, 7, 209; schools and schoolteachers in, 4, 112, 116–17; Shining Path in, 145–63, 193–94, 205–6; size of *minifundios* in, 3–4; theft between

Quispillaccta and, 82–84; theft of patron saint from, 69, 73, 231 (n. 40); theoretical and methodological framework of, 11–18; troubled youth in, 35–38, 40, 152; *varayoqs* in, 34, 36, 38–40, 109, 194; Vaso de Leche league in, 207; violence against Pacotaipe and Allcca by Quispillacctinos, 78–81; women's leadership in, 205, 207–8

Ciprián, *Tayta. See* Quispe, Ciprián

Civil Defense Patrols (CDCs), 181

Civil Guard, 22–23, 82, 83

Class: hacendados in Huaychao, 102, 104, 108, 119–35; land reform and, 102–8; and power relationships, 134–35; *qalas* in Chuschi, 102, 108–19, 135, 154–57; and Shining Path's justice against *qalas*, 154–57. *See also* Indigenous peasants; Mestizos

Club de Madres (Mother's Club), 207, 212

CNA (National Agrarian Confederation), 106

Coca leaves, 31, 79, 121, 122, 132, 173, 182, 184

Cocobolos (metal-tipped whips), 74, 75

Cofradía (religious brotherhood), 74

Colombia, 21, 85, 138, 168, 216, 218

Comandos/as (militia leaders), 199–203, 206–7, 208

Comisión Investigadora de los Sucessos de Uchuraccay, 247 (n. 20)

Communal presidents, 22, 55, 59

Communist Party: Chinese, 138, 140, 143; Peruvian, 139–45

Compadrazgo ceremony, 101

Comuneros. See Chuschi; Huaychao; Indigenous peasants; Quispillaccta

Comunidad indígena (indigenous community), 65

Conde, Balbina, 159

Conde, Florencio, 136

Conde, Leonardo, 76

Conde Huamán, Pascual, 75

Consejo (town council), 108–18, 136

Consejo Nacional de Justicia (National Council of Justice), 23, 30

Cooperatives. *See* Peasant cooperatives

Cornell University, 103

Coronel, José, 182

Corrida de toros, 126

Cortamonte ritual, 93, 171, 236 (n. 137)

Counterinsurgency: and administration of justice by *rondas campesinas*, 1, 23–24, 198–204; capture and interrogation of villagers from Carhuahurán, 187–91; in Chuschi, 193–94, 197–98; and DECAS, 171, 199, 203; and defense of Huaychaino women against external sexual aggression, 184–86, 194–95; and defense of local authority and justice, 182–83, 193–94; and execution of journalists in Uchuraccay, 7, 8, 169–70, 192, 247 (nn. 19–20); and hacendado-peasant relationship, 184; in Huaychao, 1, 7–8, 17, 165–67, 172–93, 200–201, 211–12; impact of, on indigenous peasants, 197–213; and indigenous peasants, 10–11, 17, 165–96; and intervillage relations of Huaychao, 184–93; and Macabamba Affair, 178–79; national and international context of, 168–72; and Peruvian army and navy, 168–69, 181, 187, 192, 200; and power pact, 16–17; in Quispillaccta, 197–98; reasons for peasant support of, 172, 182–96; in Sacsamarca, 170–71; and *sinchis*, 8, 169, 180–81, 190, 197–98; spread of, in Peru, 193–95; statistics on, 169, 170, 171, 211; success of, 171–72; violence by and casualties of, 165–66, 169–72, 175–80, 190, 197, 198, 247 (nn. 19–20); weapons used by, 171, 180, 198–200, 206; and women, 176, 177, 206–7. *See also Rondas campesinas*

Courts. *See* Justice system

Crime: by adolescents, 35–38, 40, 152; by adult misfits, 25–35, 60–61; in Chuschi, 31–38, 41, 42; extralegal execution of drug smugglers, 187–88; in Huaychao, 41–43; in Quispillaccta, 25–32. *See also Abigeato*

Criminal trials. *See* Justice system

Cuba, 138, 216

Culluchaca, 174, 202

Cuzco Department, 64, 95

CVR (Peruvian Truth and Reconciliation Commission), 11, 159, 161, 162–63, 165–66, 178, 247 (n. 20)

DECAS (Antisubversive Civil Defense), 171, 199, 203
De la Piniella, Eduardo, 247 (n. 19)
De la Riva, Carlos, 140
Del Pino, Ponciano, 71–72, 88, 240 (n. 80), 241 (n. 108)
Deng Xiaoping, 143
Despacho (assembly room), 1, 43–44, 47, 56, 88, 97, 175, 178
Deviant behavior. See *Abigeato*; Crime; Domestic impropriety
Díaz, Cecilio, 95–96
Díaz Curo family, 24
Díaz Martínez, Antonio, 157–58
Dirks, Nicholas, 12–13
Domestic impropriety: abandonment of paternal duties, 19, 27, 28, 55, 149–50; adultery, 19, 30, 50, 51, 54, 55, 88, 149–50, 163; drunkenness of adult men, 30, 31, 33, 145, 150–51, 158; incest, 19, 26, 27, 48, 88, 149–50; incidence of, 19–20, 26, 27, 28, 30, 33; punishment of, 48, 149–54; spousal abuse, 19, 30, 33, 48, 151, 163; types of, 19
Domestic violence. See Spousal abuse
Drug trafficking, 187–88, 200, 218
Dueñas, Baseliaña, 115

Ecuador, 218
Education: and challenge to status quo, 40, 104; in Chuschi, 4, 116; cost of, 40; in Huaychao, 208; Shining Path's *escuela popular*, 146–48; status of schoolteachers, 116–17; university education, 35, 36, 38, 40; upward social mobility and prestige via, 40. See also National University of San Cristóbal de Huamanga
EGP (Guerrilla Army of the Poor in Guatemala), 139
EGP (Popular Guerrilla Army of Shining Path), 148

Elías, *Tayta*, 204
El Salvador, 20, 139, 168, 216
Envarados. See *Varayoqs*
Ernestina, *Mama*. See Ccente, Ernestina
Espinosa, Fancisco, 79–80
Esquilas (musical instrument), 48
Esteban, *Tayta*. See Huamán, Esteban
Evangelical Protestantism, 101, 153, 227–28 (n. 96)
Executions: extralegal execution of drug smugglers, 187–88; Huaychao *linchamiento* of Senderistas, 1, 167, 168, 169, 175–79, 202; of journalists in Uchuraccay, 7, 8, 169–70, 192, 247 (nn. 19–20); by local justice systems, 24, 183; for robberies and livestock theft, 24, 159; by Shining Path, 145, 149, 150–53, 158–61, 163–64, 174, 183, 193–95, 198, 201, 202

Faenas (collective public works), 27, 50
Farabundo Martí National Liberation Front (FMLN), 139
FARC (Revolutionary Armed Forces of Colombia), 138
Farming. See Agriculture
FAR (Revolutionary Armed Forces) of Guatemala, 138
Federation of Peasant Women, 207–8
Festival of the Crosses, 95
Fiestas Patrias (Independence Day celebrations), 62
Fifth Party Conference (1965), 140
Fighting. See Violence
FLN (National Liberation Front), 139
Food: *chala* (jerky), 33; *chuño* (freeze-dried potato), 173; for counterinsurgency forces, 181; *mondongo* (soup), 33; *pan chapla* (bread), 86; potatoes for peasant households, 121; potato soup, 98; and reciprocity code, 128, 151, 184; for Senderistas, 148; theft of, 57, 58, 68, 70
Forasteros, 169–70
Fortunato, President. See Huamán, Fortunato

Fox, Richard G., 10
"Free-riding" (neglecting one's duties toward the collective), 19–20, 27, 28, 30, 149–51
FSLN (Sandinista National Liberation Front), 138–39
Fujimori, Alberto, 199–200

Galindo, Basilio, 30
Galindo, Luciano, 80
Galindo, Ramón, 80
Galindo Espinoza, Antonio, 28–29, 75
Gamboa, Víctor, 85, 95–97
Gamonales (abusive power holders), 107–8, 110, 116, 139, 194
García, Alan, 199, 246 (n. 81)
García, Amador, 247 (n. 19)
Gavilán, Félix, 247 (n. 19)
Gender: and abandonment of paternal duties, 19, 27, 28, 55, 149–50; bull as symbol of masculinity, 125–26; and caporales, 58–59; defense of Huaychao women against external sexual threats, 72–73, 86–93, 99, 184–86, 194–95; emasculating insults resulting in violence, 92–93; forastero fictional tale on cultural attitude toward, 89–91; hacendados and gendered division of labor, 128–31; and Huaychao linchamiento of Senderistas, 177–78; Huaychao's attitudes about, 87–93; impact of Shining Path and counterinsurgency on, 204–9; and intervillage disputes, 72–75, 81, 159–60; masculinity and work competitions organized by hacendados, 129; masculinity of "honorable" men versus cattle rustlers, 41, 49; patriarchal authority structure and paternalism, 46, 51–52, 58, 76, 87–93, 130–31, 134, 184–86, 194–95, 205; and Qarawiy, 44–45, 51–52, 204; and Shining Path ideology, 185–86; and tinkus, 95; and varayoqs, 47–49; and women's leadership, 204–9, 213. See also Adultery; Rape and attempted rape; Spousal abuse; Women

General Committee for Civil Self-Defense and Development of Huanta Province (CACIDH), 201
Glass of Milk (Vaso de Leche) league, 207, 208, 212
Gonzalo, Presidente/Comrade. See Guzmán Reynoso, Abimael
Gorriti, Gustavo, 143, 187, 188, 192
GRFA. See Revolutionary Government of the Armed Forces
Grupo campesino (peasant collectivity), 133
Guatemala, 103, 138, 139, 168, 216
Guerrilla Army of the Poor (EGP) in Guatemala, 139
Guerrillas and paramilitaries, 21, 138–39, 168, 179–81. See also Counterinsurgency; Rondas campesinas; Shining Path
Guevara, Che, 138
Guillén, Víctor, 41–42
Guzmán Reynoso, Abimael, 119, 140–43, 147, 158, 164

Hacendados (landlords): Rafael Chávez as hacendado, 120–31; criticisms of, 130–31; eviction of peasants from hacienda by, 126–27, 129, 130; gamonales distinguished from, 107–8; in Huaychao, 102, 104, 108, 119–35, 184; and land reform, 132–33; and livestock theft, 127–28; maintenance of public order by, 124–28, 131; paternalistic obligation of, 130–31, 134; racial slurs by, 121; and reciprocity code, 124, 128, 131–32, 184; relationship between caporales and, 56–58; respect of, for peasants' cultural practices, 124, 131–32; stories of king as hacendado, 101; treatment of women workers by, 128–31; treatment of workers by, 120–24, 128–33; verga used by, 121–22, 124–28, 130; women on, 122, 123, 125, 126, 128–31; work competitions organized by, 129
Health care, 118, 209
Heilman, Jaymie Patricia, 241 (nn. 91, 108), 242 (n. 120)

Helicopters, 165, 180–81, 187, 190, 192

Hinojosa, Nilo, 69

Hondazos (sling shots), 74

Horses. *See* Livestock

Huamán, Adrian, 211

Huamán, Alejandro, 95–96

Huamán, Esteban: on *caporales*, 58; on fights during festivals, 91–92; on hacendados, 123–24, 126–29, 133; on kinship networks, 86; on land reform, 132–33; on livestock thefts, 41; on macho behavior, 41; on racial slurs by hacendados, 121; on reciprocity code, 128; on Shining Path and counterinsurgency, 185, 190

Huamán, Fortunato: on *caporales*, 58; on fights during festivals, 91–92; on hacendados, 123–29, 132, 133; on kinship networks, 86; on land reform, 133; and Mardonio's capture and interrogation, 190–92; on rape, 48; on reciprocity code, 128, 132; and Shining Path and counterinsurgency, 175–76, 178, 185, 190–92; and Tiyarikuy fiesta, 43–44; on *verga* used by Chávez, 125

Huamán, Isidro: on hacendados, 122, 131–33; on Huaychao *linchamiento* of Senderistas, 177–78; on land reform, 133; and Shining Path and counterinsurgency, 172, 175, 177–78, 180, 201–2; on Tiyarikuy fiesta, 204; on *varayoqs*, 48, 49–50; on whippings by *varayoqs*, 49–50

Huamán, Leandro, 44, 88–89, 203–4

Huamán, Luis, 57–58

Huamán, Marcial, 53

Huamán, Narciso, 101, 165–66, 173, 182–83, 211

Huamán, Pedro, 55, 202

Huamán Curo family, 24

Huamaní Ccallocunto, Cristina, 74

Huamaní de Mejía, Pascuala, 75

Huanta City: Santurnino Cayetano in, 96; Rafael Chávez in, 120–22; and counterinsurgency, 167–69, 180, 181; distance of Huaychao from, 4; political jurisdiction of, over Huaychao, 52, 53, 98; widows' work for hacendados in, 128–29

Huanta uprising (1969), 127

Huaracas (slings), 70

Huasicancha, 64, 235 (n. 97)

Huayao, 201

Huaycha, Gregorio, 116–17

Huaycha, Ignacio, 76

Huaychao: age-based authority structure in, 46–47; age of oldest resident of, 71–72; agriculture in, 6; Asociación Padres de Familia in, 208; buildings in, 5; *caporales* in, 46, 56–59; capture and interrogation of villagers from Carhuahurán in, 187–91; Carhuahurán's de facto political jurisdiction over, 98–99; Carnival in, 47, 86, 91–95; and Christmas visit to Carhuahurán, 98; climate of, 6; Club de Madres in, 207; communal presidents of, 55, 59; counterinsurgency in, 1, 7–8, 17, 165–67, 172–93, 200–201, 211–12; description of, 4–6; *despacho* in, 1, 43–44, 47, 56, 88, 97, 175, 178; ecology and landscape of, 6; emigration from, 40, 198; *faenas* in, 50; gender relations and paternalism in, 87–93; geographical isolation of, 6; *grupo campesino* of, 5–6; hacendados in, 102, 104, 108, 119–35, 184; improvements in, after Peruvian civil war, 210, 212; intervillage hierarchy in, 98–99; intervillage relations and conflicts in, 85–99, 184–93; *juez rumi* in, 1, 5, 50–51, 56, 59, 88–89, 177–78, 186, 188, 190, 200–201; justice system of *rondas campesinas* in, 200–201; kinship networks in, 86–93, 99, 191; land reform in, 45, 53, 54, 98–99, 132–34, 187, 191; lieutenant governor in, 43–45, 47–48, 52–56; *linchamiento* of Senderistas in, 1, 167, 168, 169, 175–79, 202; livestock in, 5, 6; and livestock theft, 41–43, 54–55, 85, 95–98; local justice system in, 19–20, 25, 40–60, 88–89, 98, 183; location of, 4; and Macabamba Affair, 178–79; main square in, 5; marriage in, 86; militia in, 179–83, 189–92, 200–201; patriarchal authority structure in, 46; photography exhibit on, 210;

political hierarchy in, 45–46; population of, 6; Proyecto Mujer in, 208; regional authority of, after *linchamiento*, 191; and regional trade networks, 6, 172–73, 191; religious festivities in, 86–87, 124; road to, 4, 6; scholarly and media attention to, 7–9, 209–10; school in, 208; Shining Path in, 198, 202; theoretical and methodological framework of, 11–18; Tiyarikuy fiesta in, 43–45, 51–52, 203–4, 227–28 (n. 96); *vara visita* in, 98; *varayoqs* in, 43–60, 181, 202; Vaso de Leche league in, 208, 212; women's leadership in, 208–9

Huaylla, Basilio, 57

Huaylla, Emilia, 87–88

Huaylla, Santos, 96–97

Huaynacancha, xviii, 85, 86, 91–92, 95–98, 127, 190–91

Huillca, Hugo, 199

Human rights, 187–88

Hutu, 63, 102–3

ILA. *See* Inicio de la Lucha Armada; Shining Path

Ilave (Puno Department), 215

Incas, 81–82, 103, 235 (n. 97)

Incest, 19, 26, 27, 48, 88, 149–50

Independence Day festivities, 211

India, 64, 103, 138

Indigenous Affairs Department, 65, 67

Indigenous community (*Comunidad indígena*), 65

Indigenous peasants: and "apotheosis of agency," 8–9; citizenship rights for, 212; and communist revolution, 246 (n. 83); compared with *qalas*, 108, 155–56; and counterinsurgency against Shining Path, 10–11, 17, 165–96; definition of, 10; as descendants of Incan agriculturalists, 103; diversity among, 215–16; and guerrilla movements in Latin America, 21, 138–39; health care for indigenous women, 209; and historical memory, 15; identity of, in Peru, 10; impact of Peruvian civil war on,

197–213; in India, 64; land movement and mobilization of, 63–65, 102, 104–5, 132; in Latin America, 63; mathematical skills of, 71; numerical hyperbole by, 71–72; and peasant cooperatives, 105–7; and power pact, 16–17, 152–53; power relationship between *qalas* and, 108–19, 155–57; Quechua spoken by, 104; racial and ethnic categories of, 81–82; racial slurs against, 62, 80, 81–82, 121, 162; reasons for support of counterinsurgency by, 172, 182–96; reasons for support of Shining Path by, 10–11, 149–65; and reciprocity code, 124, 128, 131–32, 151, 184; and reparations for communities' suffering during civil war, 210; rights of peasant women, 207–9; sandals worn by, 108; and Shining Path, 10–11, 85, 148, 172–73; state-peasant relations in twenty-first century, 252 (n. 75); stereotypes of, 8; theoretical and methodological framework of, 11–18, 215–16, 218–19. *See also* Chuschi; Huaychao; Shining Path; Women

Infante, Octavio, 247 (n. 19)

Inicio de la Lucha Armada (Initiation of the Armed Struggle—ILA), 1, 7, 136–37, 142–43, 147, 158, 162–63, 167, 246 (n. 81). *See also* Shining Path

Inocencio, *Tayta. See* Urbano, Inocencio

Integral Development Projects (PIDS), 106

Integral Rural Settlement Projects (PIARS), 106

Iquicha, 174

Iquichano highlands: intercommunity relations and conflicts in, 62–63; intervillage networks and cultural practices in, 85–95; land reform in, 54, 98–99; livestock theft in, 41, 95–98; local justice system in, 24; location of Huaychao in, 4; nineteenth-century local justice system in, 60; regional trade networks in, 6, 172–73, 191, 195; and Shining Path, 7–8, 172–74, 192–93. *See also* Huaychao

Iraq, 216, 217

Iruro (Lucanamarca Province): local justice system in, 24
Isbell, Billie Jean, 14, 38, 112
Isidro, *Tayta. See* Huamán, Isidro
Ixil Indians, 216

Jaime, Ernesto: and conflict between Chuschi and Quispillaccta, 75–77; and March of Death (1960), 157, 194; military kidnapping of, and relocation to Ayacucho City, 207; and Shining Path justice system, 157, 194; theft of livestock of, 32–35, 110, 154; wife of, 204, 207
Journalists' execution, 7, 8, 169–70, 192, 247 (nn. 19–20)
Juana, *Mama. See* Cabezas, Juana
Judicial system. *See* Justice system
Juez de paz (justices of the peace), 21, 30, 108
Juez de tierras (land court judges), 65
Juez rumi (rock of justice), 1, 5, 50–51, 56, 59, 88–89, 177–78, 186, 188, 190, 200–201
Juicios popularares (popular trials) of Shining Path, 145, 148–64, 174, 183, 193–95, 198, 201, 202
Juliaca, 215
Junín Department, 64, 235 (n. 97)
Juntos (Together), 210
Juscamaita, Enrique, 52, 131–32, 184
Justices of the peace (*juez de paz*), 21, 30, 108
Justice system: abandonment of cases by courts, 21–22; Agrarian Tribunal (Land Court), 105, 118; Ayachucho local justice system, 24; in Brazil, 21; of Calahuyo assembly in Puno Department, 24; and "certificates of conduct," 25, 28, 224 (n. 24); Chuschi local justice system, 19–20, 25–35, 60–61; in Colombia, 21; Consejo Nacional de Justicia, 23, 30; cost of litigation in Peruvian courts, 21; in El Salvador, 20; and hacendados, 124–28, 131; Huaychao local justice system, 19–20, 25, 40–60, 88–89, 98, 183; Huaychao's intervillage hierarchy for, 98–99; impact of Shining Path and counterinsurgency

on, 198–204; and *juez de paz*, 21, 30, 108; lieutenant governor's role in, 54–56, 130; nineteenth-century local justice system in Uchuraccay hacienda, 60; and *personero* (elected communal representative), 22; Peruvian state institutions of, 19–23, 25, 119; punishments by local justice systems, 24, 48–51, 56, 74, 183; and *qalas*, 109–19; Quispillaccta local justice system, 20; and *rondas campesinas*, 1, 23–24, 198–204; Shining Path's *juicios popularares*, 145, 148–64, 174, 183, 193–95, 198, 201, 202; Supreme Court in Peru, 23; of Taliban, 217. *See also Caporales*; Executions; Lieutenant governors; *Varayoqs*
Juvenile delinquency. *See* Adolescents

Kalyvas, Stathis N., 11, 12
Kant, Immanuel, 140
Khrushchev, Nikita, 140
Kinship: and *compadrazgo* ceremony, 101; in Huaychao, 86–93, 99, 174–75, 191; and *yernos*, 174–75, 191

La Convención (Cuzco Department), 64
Lambayaque Department, 107
Land Court (Agrarian Tribunal), 105, 118
Land court judge (*juez de tierras*), 65
Landlords. *See* Hacendados
Land reform: and Agrarian Reform Law, 6, 45, 54, 98–99, 187; and Belaúnde, 104–5; and end of land-tenure system, 63, 102–4, 106, 134, 137; history of, in Peru, 103–8; in Huaychao, 45, 53, 54, 98–99, 132–34, 187, 191; in India, 64, 103, 138; in Latin America, 63, 103; mixed feelings about, among Huaychainos, 132–34; and peasant cooperatives, 105–6; and peasant mobilization, 63–65, 102, 104–5, 132; race and class in context of, 102–8; by GRFA, 105–8; in Rwanda, 63, 102–3; shortcomings of, 106–8; statistics on, 106–7; women on, 133–34
Látigos (leather whips), 48, 56, 93

Latin America. *See* Indigenous peasants; Land reform; *and specific countries*

Lenin, V. I., 140, 141, 146

Libation ceremonies, 49, 101

Lieutenant governors: administration of justice by, 54–56, 130; Felipe Aycha as lieutenant governor, 36; challenges to political authority of, 53–55; and *despacho*, 56; and disrespect toward *varayoqs*, 55; function of, 47, 48, 52–55; in Huaychao, 43–45, 47–48, 52–56; and *juez rumi*, 56; *látigo* (whip) used for punishment by, 56; and livestock theft, 54–56; loss of moral authority of, 54–55; in political hierarchy, 22, 52–53, 59; selection of, 56–57; Tiyarikuy fiesta for, 43–45, 227–28 (n. 96); *varayoqs'* relationship with, 47–48, 52–56

Lima: migration of Andean peasants to, 39, 40, 104, 198; Shining Path guerrilla activities in, 142–43

Linces (infantrymen), 181

Lirio, 195

Livestock, 4, 5, 6, 54. See also *Abigeato*

Llalli, Asunción, 84, 160–61

Llamas. See *Abigeato*; Livestock

Llanccce Huamán, Jesús, 95–96, 99

Llaulli, 192

Lynching: in Bolivia, 215; in Brazil, 21; Huaychao *linchamiento* of Senderistas, 1, 167, 168, 169, 175–79, 202; in twenty-first century, 215, 219

Macabamba: hacendados in, 120, 127–29; livestock theft in, 42, 127; as part of Huaychao, 6; Shining Path and counterinsurgency in, 175–80, 182, 201

Macabamba Affair, 178–79

Machaca, Dámasa, 158–59

Machaca, Teófilo, 78–79

Makta, Fulgencio, 145–48, 155–56, 159–60, 194, 201

Mallon, Florencia, 15

Mao Zedong and Maoism, 138–41, 143, 146, 170, 175–76, 195

Mapuche Indians, 63

March of Death (1960), 70, 73–78, 84, 110, 157, 160, 194

Mardonio, 187–92, 249 (n. 66)

Mariano, *Tayta. See* Quispe, Mariano

Mariátegui, José Carlos, 103, 139–41, 146

Marriage: in Huaychao, 86; of *varayoqs*, 47, 54; and women's political authority, 209. *See also* Adultery; Kinship

Marx, Karl, 140, 141, 146

Masculinity: bull as symbol of, 125–26; and gendered division of labor on haciendas, 128–31; of "honorable" men versus cattle rustlers, 41, 49; and work competitions organized by hacendados, 129. *See also* Gender; Paternalism

Mayer, Enrique, 238 (n. 29)

Mayordomos (sponsors), 95, 96

Mazumdar, Charu, 138

Medina, Domingo, 143, 164

Medrano, Oscar, 187, 192, 197, 210, 212

Mejía, Teodoro, 78–79

Mejía Huamaní, Marcela, 75

Mendieta, Faustino, 84

Mendieta, Martín (father), 74, 75, 76, 160

Mendieta, Martín (son), 84

Mendieta Tucno, Sebastián, 75

Mendívil, Jorge Luis, 247 (n. 19)

Mendoza Conde, Justiniano, 75, 76

Mestizos: abuse and crimes against local indigenous population by, 13, 14; as bureaucratic officials in Chuschi, 52, 76–77; in Civil Guard, 22–23; clothing of, 108, 116; as hacendados, 57–58, 104, 108, 119–34; as justices of the peace, 21, 22; as landowners, 103–4; and March of Death (1960), 76–77; peasants passing as, 28, 31; physical traits of, 120; in political hierarchy, 22, 104; *qalas* in Chuschi, 102, 108–19, 154–57; as Shining Path leaders, 10; as state security forces, 10

Mexico, 12, 63

Middle East, 216–17

Millones, Luis, 8

Minifundios (small individual plots), 3

Moore, Barrington, 197

Morales Bermúdez, Francisco, 107

Morote Barrionuevo, Osmán, 119–20, 122, 158, 164

Mother's Club (Club de Madres), 207, 212

Mujeriégo (womanizer), 27, 30

Narcoterrorism, 187–88, 218

National Agrarian Confederation (CNA), 106

National Council of Justice (Consejo Nacional de Justicia), 23, 30

National Liberation Front (FLN), 139

National System of Support for Social Mobilization (SINAMOS), 105

National University of San Cristóbal de Huamanga (UNSCH), 35, 36, 38, 119, 140, 141, 145

Navy, Peruvian, 168–69

Naxalites, 138

New York Times, 195

NGOs (nongovernmental organizations), 187–88, 210–13

Nicaragua, 138–39, 216

Nongovernmental organizations (NGOs), 187–88, 210–13

North Vietnam, 102

Núñez, Bernabé, 30, 76

Núñez, Daniel, 76

Núñez, Dionisio, 79–80

Núñez, Martina, 27

Núñez, Melchora, 30

Núñez, Valentín, 79–80

Núñez, Víctor, 30, 31, 33–35, 109

Núñez Ccallocunto, Luis, 70, 73–76

Núñez Conde, Emilio, 65, 84–85

Núñez Conde, Manuel "Ccoriñahui" (Golden Eyes), 78

Núñez Pacotaipe, Gregorio, 84

Ocana, 202–3

Occekuna (darkies), 62

Occes (racial slur), 62, 80, 81–82

Ochoa, Marino and Juvencio, 32

Pacheco, Cesário, 42–43

Pacotaipe, Braulio, 69

Pacotaipe, Miguel, 70, 78–81

Pakasqa Suyu (The Forgotten Country) (photography exhibit), 210

Pampacancca, 195

Pampalca, 192

Pampas River Valley, 2. *See also* Chuschi

Paniagua, Valentín, 210

Paramilitaries. *See* Guerrillas and paramilitaries; Shining Path

Paredes, Saturnino, 140

Parents' Association (Asociación Padres de Familia), 208

Pariona, Mamerto, 68

Pasco communities, 64

Paternalism: abandonment of paternal duties, 19, 27, 28, 55, 149–50; defense of Huaychao women against external sexual threats, 72–73, 86–93, 99, 184–86, 194–95; by hacendados, 130–31, 132, 134; impact of Shining Path and counterinsurgency on, 204–9; by *varayoqs*, 51–52. *See also* Gender

Paucartambo valley haciendas, 64

PCP. *See* Peruvian Communist Party

PCP@–Bandera Roja (Red Flag) (PCP-BR), 139–40

PCP@–Patria Roja (Red Nation) (PCP-PR), 140

PCP@–Sendero Luminoso (Shining Path) (PCP-SL), 140–42, 146–66, 172, 173, 192, 193, 195, 201, 206, 218. *See also* Shining Path

PCP–Unidad (Unity) (PCP-U), 139

Peasant cooperatives, 105–6

Peasants. *See* Chuschi; Huaychao; Indigenous peasants

Peones (laborers, serfs), 33

Personeros (elected communal representatives), 22, 67, 68–69, 79

Peru: army and navy of, 168–69, 181, 187, 192, 200; CVR in, 11, 159, 161, 162–63, 165–66, 178, 247 (n. 20); economy of, in 1960s, 105; impact of Shining Path and counterinsurgency on community, state, and civil society in, 209–13, 252 (n. 75); Indigenous Affairs in, 65, 67; indigenous identity in, 10; judicial system of, 19–23, 25, 119; leftist groups in, 141; migration of Andean peasants to Lima, 39, 40, 104, 198; political hierarchy of, 22; political independence of, from Spain, 60; population of, 39; and reparations for communities' suffering during civil war, 210; semifeudalism and semicolonialism in, 119–20, 139, 165; spread of Shining Path violence in, 163–65; voting in, 104, 136. See also Chuschi; Huaychao; Indigenous peasants; Land reform; Revolutionary Government of the Armed Forces; Shining Path; and other towns and villages

Peru National Archives (AGN), 19

Peruvian Communist Party (PCP), 139–45. See also Shining Path; and PCP headings

Peruvian Socialist Party, 139

PIARS (Integral Rural Settlement Projects), 106

PIDS (Integral Development Projects), 106

Poder Judicial, 247 (n. 20)

Police: Chuschi's police station, 210–11; Peruvian Civil Guard, 22–23, 82, 83; sinchis, 8, 169, 180–81, 190, 197–98; unreliability of, 23

Political hierarchy: in Chuschi, 108–19; in Huaychao, 45–46, 52–56; unreliability of, 22; and varayoqs, 46, 109; vecinos in, 108. See also Lieutenant governors; Varayoqs

Pomahuallcca, Ignacio and Juan, 78

Popular Guerrilla Army (EGP) of Shining Path, 148

Power relationships: definition of, 16; and gamonales, 107–8, 110, 116, 139, 194; in hacendado-peasant relations, 119–35, 184; in qala–comunero relations, 108–19, 155–57; and race and class, 134–35; and reciprocity code, 124, 128, 131–32, 151, 184; and support for or opposition to Shining Path, 16–17. See also Hacendados; Justice system; Paternalism; Qalas; Varayoqs

Presidents of communities. See Communal presidents

Protestantism, 101, 153, 227–28 (n. 96)

Proyecto Mujer (Women's Project), 208

Pueblos jóvenes (young towns), 39

Pujas (Cangallo Province), 143

Punishment. See Justice system; Violence

Qalas (mestizo power holders): abuse of authority by, 110–11, 135, 154–57; characteristics of, 125; in Chuschi, 102, 108–19, 135, 154–57, 193–94; meaning of term, 108; and Shining Path justice, 154–57, 193–94; shoes worn by, 108

Qarawiy (song of reverence for varayoqs), 44–45, 51–52, 204, 206

Quechua language, 104, 105. See also Indigenous peasants

Quichca, Emilio, 32

Quispe, Alejandro, 87–88

Quispe, Anselmo, 54–55

Quispe, Catalina, 95–96

Quispe, Cecilia, 93–94

Quispe, Ciprián: as albacea, 46; on juez rumi, 50; on justice system of counterinsurgency, 201; on lieutenant governor's administration of justice, 56; on Mardonio's capture and interrogation, 189; on marriage, 47; on moral respectability of varayoqs, 47; on punishment by varayoqs, 48, 49, 50; on rondas campesinas, 202, 203; on Shining Path and counterinsurgency, 173, 179, 189, 190, 201–3; on varayoqs and counterinsurgency, 202, 203; on violence to avenge sexually assaulted women, 92

Quispe, Clemencia, 44–45

Quispe, Geronimo, 122

Quispe, Juan, 98–99

Quispe, Julia, 98–99

Quispe, Marcelino, 94, 176

Quispe, Mariano: on caporales, 58, 59; on festivals in Huaychao, 86; on hacendados, 120–24, 131, 132; on juez rumi, 50; on livestock theft, 97, 98, 190–91; photograph of, 210; on reciprocity code, 132; on *verga* used by Chávez, 125

Quispe, Pablo, 87

Quispe, Santos, 43, 59, 174–75

Quispe, Vicente, 54–55

Quispe, Víctor, 41–42

Quispe, Zenobio, 53–54, 98–99

Quispillaccta: adult misfits in, 25–32, 145; attacks by Quispillacctinos (1960) on Lachocc chapel and homes of Chuschinos, 69–73; boundary disputes between Chuschi and, 65, 67–70; and Chuschi's petition for legal recognition as *comunidad indígena*, 65, 67; communal fund of, 27, 28; communal lands in, 27; conflict between Chuschi and, 13, 62, 65–85, 99–100, 157–63; counterinsurgency in, 197–98; crime in, 25–32; description of, 4; early altercations between Chuschi and, 68–73; economic and administrative autonomy of, 67; *faenas* in, 27, 28, 67; history of, 13; livestock theft in, 25–26, 28, 29–31, 41, 149–51, 153–54; local justice system in, 20, 25–32; March of Death (1960) by Chuschinos against, 70, 73–78, 84, 110, 157, 160, 194; numerical hyperbole by Chuschinos on number of attackers from, 71; origins and ethnic identity of, 81–82, 85, 99–100; peace accord (1941) between Chuschi and, 67, 68; population of, 71; racial slur against, 62, 80, 81–82; and rape charges against Chuschinos, 72; reconciliation between Chuschi and, 161, 162; Shining Path in, 145, 148–50, 153–54, 157–63, 165–66; theft between Chuschi and, 82–84, 160–61; and theft of patron saint from Chuschi, 69, 73, 231 (n. 40); violence against Chuschinos Pacotaipe and Allcca by Quispillacctinos, 78–81

Race: of Chuschinos versus Quispillacctinos, 81–82, 85, 99–100; fluidity of racial identity, 109, 110; hacendados in Huaychao, 102, 104, 108, 119–35; land reform and, 102–8; and power relationships, 134–35; *qalas* in Chuschi, 102, 108–19, 135, 154–57; and racial slurs, 62, 80, 81–82, 121, 162; and Shining Path's justice against *qalas*, 154–57. *See also* Indigenous peasants; Mestizos

Ramos, Ana, 99

Ramos, Eulogio, 86–88, 94

Rancas, 64

Rape and attempted rape: during Carnival, 47, 91–92; charges against rapist, 206; by Chuschinos, 72, 111–17, 155, 240 (n. 66); defense of Huaychao women against external sexual threats, 72–73, 86–93, 99, 184–86, 194–95; by Peruvian security forces during civil war, 185; punishment for, 48, 72–73, 150; by Quispillacctinos, 30, 150; and Shining Path, 185

Rappaport, Joanne, 15, 85

Reciprocity code, 124, 128, 131–32, 151, 184

Reconciliation: CVR, 11, 159, 161, 162–63, 165–66, 178, 247 (n. 20); libation ceremony for, 49; and "repentant" collaborators, 200; among villagers following violence, 49, 93

Rejas, Jesús, 150

Rejas, José, 165, 166

Rejas Pacotaipe, Amancio: blacklisting of, by Shining Path, 154; court cases against, 28–30, 151; drunkenness of, 30, 31, 145, 150–51, 158; execution of, by Shining Path, 145, 150–51, 153, 158–59, 163–64; as freerider, 30, 150; livestock theft by, 28–31, 35, 145, 150; mistreatment of women by, 30, 145, 150; physical appearance of, 28, 224 (n. 36)

Retamozo, Asunta, 114–15

Retto, Willy, 247 (n. 19)

Revolutionary Armed Forces of Colombia (FARC), 138

Revolutionary Armed Forces (FAR) of Guatemala, 138

Revolutionary Government of the Armed Forces (GRFA): and agrarian reform, 105–8; census of agriculture and livestock by, 54; end of, and 1980 democratic elections, 136, 141; establishment of, 105; judicial reforms of, 23, 46; and political hierarchy, 22, 108–9

Rimachi, Serafina, 44–45

Rinconada, 199

Rivera Terres, Pompeyo Javier, 203

Robberies. See Abigeato

Rocha Huamaní, Gonzalo, 68

Rock of justice (juez rumi), 1, 5, 50–51, 56, 59, 88–89, 177, 186, 188, 190, 200–201

Rodríguez Rivas, Miguel Angel, 140

Rondas campesinas (peasant patrols): administration of justice by, 1, 23–24, 198–204; and comandos/as, 199–203, 206–7, 208; communication between Peruvian state and, 211–12; death of ronderos, 197; and DECAS, 171, 199, 203; definition of, 1, 168; and Huaychao linchamiento, 177; and Huaychao militia, 179–83, 189–92, 200–201; and intercommunity communication, 195; and licenciado (formerly enlisted soldier), 200; and Peruvian security forces, 169, 187; role of, 23–24, 196, 198–204, 206; as CADs, 199–200; significance of, 218; success of, 171–72; weapons of, 171, 180, 198–200, 206; women in, 206–7, 208; youth leadership of, 201–3. See also Counterinsurgency

Ruiz Pozo, Julio, 57–58

Rwanda, 63, 102–3, 216

Sacsamarca (Huancasancos Province), 170–71

SAISS (Social Interest Groups), 106

San Agustín University, 140

Sánchez, Pedro, 247 (n. 19)

Sánchez Villagómez, Marté, 153–54

Sandinista National Liberation Front (FSLN), 138–39

San Juan de París hacienda, 64

San Pedro de Jajas (Junín Department), 64

Santos, Tayta. See Huaylla, Santos

Sarhua (Víctor Fajardo Province), 164

Schools. See Education

Schumacher, Edward, 195

Sedano, Jorge, 247 (n. 19)

Self-Defense Committees (CADs), 199–200

Semanero (week-long shift) workers, 120–22, 128–29

Senderistas. See Shining Path

Serulnikov, Sergio, 118, 119

Sexual activity: Blanco's sexual misconduct, 111–17, 155, 240 (n. 66); during Carnival, 47, 91–92; of unmarried adolescents in vida michiy, 112–13; of varayoqs, 47, 54. See also Adultery; Incest; Rape and attempted rape

Sexual assaults. See Rape and attempted rape

Shining Path: beginning of guerrilla insurgency of, 85, 100, 136–37, 139, 142–43, 145; blacklisting by, 148, 151–52, 154; burning of ballot boxes and administrative center (1980) by Senderistas in Chuschi, 136, 137, 142, 147, 162–63, 246 (n. 81); in Carhuahurán, 187–90; and Carnival in Sacsamarca, 170–71; and casualties of civil war, 1, 136, 143, 164, 165–66, 169–72, 175–80, 190, 197, 198, 218, 247 (nn. 19–20); Central Committee of, 141; in Chuschi, 145–63, 193–94, 205–6; comité popular of, 148, 156; communist flag carried by rebels, 10, 136, 143, 147, 148, 175, 180, 249 (n. 55); and conflict between Chuschi and Quispillaccta, 157–63; counterinsurgency against, in Huaychao, 1, 7–8, 17, 165–67, 172–93; defeat of, 165, 171–72; defense of Huaychaino women against sexual aggression by, 184–86, 194–95; escuela popular of, 146–48; executions by, 145, 149, 150–53, 158–61, 163–64, 174, 183, 193–95, 198, 201, 202; forgiveness of onetime deviants by, 152–53; and Guzmán, 119, 140–43, 147, 158; historical context of, and Peruvian Communist Party, 137–45;

in Huaychao, 198, 202; and Huaychao *linchamiento*, 1, 167, 168, 169, 175–79, 202; Huaychao militia against, 179–83, 189–92, 200–201; ideological disconnect between leaders and followers of, 165–66; ideology of, as "Gonzalo Thought," 141–42, 173, 175–76, 182, 185–86, 195, 196; and ILA, 1, 7, 136–37, 142–43, 147, 158, 162–63, 167, 246 (n. 81); impact of, on indigenous peasants, 197–213; and indigenous peasants, 10–11, 85, 144–45; and *juicios popularares*, 145, 148–64, 174, 183, 193–95, 198, 201, 202; justice of and punishment by, 148–63, 193–94; leaders of, 10, 119–20, 122, 140–43, 157–59, 164; and Macabamba Affair, 178–79; peasant markets shut down by, 195; Popular Guerrilla Army (EGP) of, 148; preinsurgency scholarship of, 246 (n. 83); and *qalas*, 154–57, 193–94; in Quispillaccta, 145, 148–50, 153–54, 157–63, 165–66; reasons for peasants' resistance to, 16–17, 152–53, 172, 182–96; reasons for peasant support of, 16–17, 149–65, 152–53; rumors about, among peasants, 172–74; spread of, in Peru, 163–65; statistics on militants in, 163; students' and other adolescents' participation in, 85, 141, 144, 145–46, 156, 162, 165–66, 173, 196, 201; support by local peasants for, 10, 148, 205–6; theoretical and methodological framework of, 11–18; violence endorsed by, 140–44, 173, 193–95; weapons of, 147, 173, 174; women in, 145, 180, 205–6. *See also* Counterinsurgency

SINAMOS (National System of Support for Social Mobilization), 105

Sinchis (counterinsurgency police), 8, 169, 180–81, 190, 197–98

Social class. *See* Class

Social Interest Groups (SAISS), 106

Socialist Party in Peru, 139

Socios (cooperative members), 105

Soviet Union, 140

Spousal abuse, 19, 30, 33, 48, 151, 163

Starn, Orin, 7, 10

"Structured forgetting," 15

Taboada, Freddy, 71, 88, 232 (n. 53)

Taiwan, 102

Taliban, 217

Tapahuasco, Fernando, 36, 37

Teniente gobernador. See Lieutenant governors

Terrorism, 217

Theft. *See Abigeato*

Theidon, Kimberly, 172

Thomson, Sinclair, 118–19

Ticllas, 206

Tilly, Charles, 12

Tinkus (ritual battles), 94–95

Tinterillos (literate men taking economic and political advantage), 164

Tiyarikuy (Seating or Enthroning) fiesta, 43–45, 51–52, 203–4, 227–28 (n. 96)

Toledo, Alejandro, 209, 210

Tomaylla, Marcelino, 76

Town council. *See* Consejo

Trade networks, 6, 172–73, 191, 195

Trompetillas (horns), 192

Truth and Reconciliation Commission (CVR) in Peru, 11, 159, 161, 162–63, 165–66, 178, 247 (n. 20)

Tucle hacienda, 64

Tucno, Alberto (research assistant): and Felipe Aycha, 33–34; and distribution of clothing and school supplies in Chuschi, 211; initial visit of, to Chuschi, 13, 14; interview of Fulgencio Makta by, 145–48; and Rejas, 30, 31; and women's role in intervillage conflicts, 81

Tupín, 192

Tutsi, 63, 102–3

Uchuirre, xvii, 4, 30

Uchuraccay: counterinsurgency in, 169–70, 180–81; execution of journalists in, 7, 8, 169–70, 192, 247 (nn. 19–20); local justice system during nineteenth century in, 60;

and religious festivals in Huaychao, 86, 91–92; Shining Path in, 164, 169, 174, 192, 201

Uchuraccay Massacre, 7, 8, 169–70, 247 (nn. 19–20)

United States, 102, 217

UNSCH. *See* National University of San Cristóbal de Huamanga

Upiaccpampa, 174

Urbano, Inocencio, 71–72, 122, 125, 131, 132

Van Young, Eric, 8–9, 12

Vara visita (*vara* visit), 52, 98

Varayoqs (civil-religious indigenous authorities): administration of justice by, 47–51, 130; and adolescents' criminal behavior, 36; and age-based authority structure, 46–47, 204; *albacea* to, 46; alcohol use by, 47; and Felipe Aycha's arrest, 34; use of *chicotes* for punishment by, 34, 48, 49–50, 56, 97; Christmas visit by, from Huaychao to Carhuahurán, 98; in Chuschi, 34, 36, 38–40, 109, 194; conflict resolution by, 47–48; disrespect toward, 55; executions of, by Shining Path, 174, 201; function of, 20, 24, 38, 46, 52; in Huaychao, 43–60, 181, 202; impact of Shining Path and counterinsurgency on, 202–4; and *juez rumi*, 1, 5, 50–51, 59; lieutenant governor's relationship with, 47–48, 52–56; loss of authority of, 38–39; mentoring of, by elders, 46–47; moral conduct and authority of, 47, 54; opposition of, to Lieutenant Governor Quispe, 53–54; paternalism by, 51–52; and patriarchal authority structure, 46; and political hierarchy, 46, 109; in prestige hierarchy, 38–39, 46; punishment by, 48–51; Qarawiy for, 44–45, 51–52, 204; selection of, 56; Tiyarikuy fiesta honoring, 43–45, 51–52, 203–4, 227–28 (n. 96); *varas* (wooden staffs) for, 38, 44, 46, 48, 203; and *vara visita*, 52; violent altercations settled by, 48–49

Vargas Llosa, Mario, 8, 247 (n. 20)

Vargas Llosa Commission, 8

Vaso de Leche (Glass of Milk) league, 207, 208, 212

Vecinos (non-*comunero* residents), 32, 33, 108, 110, 157

Vega Tomaylla, Martín, 70, 73–76

Velasco Alvarado, Juan, 23, 46, 105–8

Velásquez, Simeón, 97, 190–91

Velásquez, Víctor, 97, 190–91

Verga (whips), 110, 121–22, 124–28, 130, 241 (nn. 91, 108)

Vicos hacienda, 103

Víctor, *Tayta. See* Núñez, Víctor

Vida michiy (sexual activities by unmarried adolescents), 112

Vietnam War, 138

Vígias (lookouts), 148

Vilca, Francisco, 194

Vilca, Isidro, 116–18

Vilca, Lorenza, 115, 240 (n. 66)

Vilma, Alejandra, 204–5, 207–9

Violence: attacks by Quispillacctinos (1960) on Lachocc chapel and homes of Chuschinos, 69–73; *caporales'* use of whips, 59; during Carnival, 48–49, 91–95; between Chuschi and Quispillaccta, 13, 62, 65–85, 99–100, 157–63; of counterinsurgency, 165–96; in defense of Huaychao women against external sexual threats, 72–73, 86–93, 99, 184–86, 194–95; emasculating insults resulting in, 92–93; lieutenant governors' use of whips, 56; in March of Death (1960), 70, 73–78, 84, 110, 157, 160, 194; and punishment for livestock theft, 21, 24, 42, 49–51, 56, 74, 79–81, 83, 97, 149–51, 160–61, 190–91; reconciliation among villagers following, 49, 93; scholarship on political violence, 215–19; Shining Path's use of, 140–44, 149–63, 173–74, 179–80, 193–95; and *tinkus*, 94–95; in twenty-first century, 215, 219; *varayoqs'* settlement of violent altercations among villagers, 48–49; *varayoqs'* use of whips, 34, 48, 49–50, 56. *See also* Counterinsur-

gency; Executions; Rape and attempted rape; Shining Path; Spousal abuse
Voting, 104, 136

Weapons: of *rondas campesinas*, 171, 180, 198–200, 206; of Shining Path, 147, 173, 174
Whips. See *Chicotes*; *Cocobolos*; *Látigos*; *Verga*
Womanizer (*mujeriégo*), 27, 30
Women: on *caporales*, 58–59; and Club de Madres, 207, 212; and counterinsurgency, 176, 177, 206–7; defense of Huaychao women against external sexual threats, 72–73, 86–93, 99, 184–86, 194–95; on fights during Carnival and reconciliation following, 48–49; on hacendados, 122, 123, 125, 126, 128–31; health care for indigenous women, 209; and Huaychao *linchamiento* of Senderistas, 177; impact of Shining Path and counterinsurgency on, 204–9; on land reform, 133–34; leadership roles for, 205–9, 213; on lieutenant governors, 55; in March of Death (1960), 74–75; and patriarchal authority structure, 46, 58; and Qarawiy, 44–45, 51–52, 204, 206; rights of peasant women, 207–9; role of, in intervillage disputes, 72–75, 81; in Shining Path, 145, 180, 205–6; spousal abuse of, 19, 30, 33, 48, 151, 163; treatment of, by hacendado's wife, 129–30; on *varayoqs*, 47–49; and Vaso de Leche league, 207, 208, 212. *See also* Adultery; Gender; Indigenous peasants; Rape and attempted rape
Women's Project (Proyecto Mujer), 208

Yanacocha, 64
Yaranqa, Marcelino, 93–94
Yaranqa, Marcelo, 53–54
Yernos (in-laws), 174–75, 191
Youth. *See* Adolescents